HOLLYWOOD SHACK JOB

A volume in the
CounterCulture Series

Also available:

This Is Rebel Music: The Harvey Kubernik InnerViews
    by Harvey Kubernik

New Buffalo: Journals from a Taos Commune
    by Arthur Kopecky

AfterBurn: Reflections on Burning Man
    by Lee Gilmore and Mark Van Proyen, editors

Seema's Show: A Life on the Left
    by Sara Halprin

Leaving New Buffalo Commune
    by Arthur Kopecky

Editors: David Farber, History, Temple University

Beth L. Bailey, American Studies, Temple University

HOLLYWOOD SHACK JOB

Rock Music in Film and on Your Screen

Harvey Kubernik

University of New Mexico Press ⧚ Albuquerque

Library of Congress Cataloging-in-Publication Data

Kubernik, Harvey, 1951–

  Hollywood shack job : rock music in film and on your
screen / Harvey Kubernik.

      p. cm. — (CounterCulture series)

  Includes index.

  ISBN-13: 978-0-8263-3542-5 (pbk. : alk. paper)

  ISBN-10: 0-8263-3542-x (pbk. : alk. paper)

1. Motion pictures and rock music.

2. Motion picture producers and directors—Interviews.

I. Title.

  ML2075.K83 2006

  781.66′1542—dc22

                        2006028612

Design and composition: Melissa Tandysh

For the initial exposures . . .

The Four Star, Beverly Canon Theater, Pantages Theater, The Orpheum,
The Baldwin, The Culver, The Pan Pacific, The Wilshire, The Meralta,
The Paradise, The Sepulveda Drive-In, The La Reina, The NuArt,
The Pix, The Egyptian, The Oriental, The Carthay Circle, The Liemert,
The El Rey, The Ken Theater, The Regent, The Picwood,
The Gilmore Drive-In, The Beverly Theater, The State, The Encore,
The Canon, The Village, The Hawaiian, The Vista, The Rialto,
Fine Arts Theatre, The Van Nuys Drive-In, The Mayan,
The Writer's Guild Theater, The Directors Guild of America, The Bruin,
Grauman's Chinese Theater, The Plaza, Pacific's Cinerama Dome,
The Tiffany, The Music Hall, Toho La Brea, The Royal,
The Sherman Oaks Galleria, The Encino Theater, The Sherman Theater,
The Van Nuys Theater, The Corbin Theater, UCLA Melnitz Hall,
The Aero, The Los Angeles Theater, The Fairfax,
The Silent Movie Theater, The Pacific Theater, The Ritz Theater,
The Vogue Theater, The Crest Theater, The Lido Theater,
The Gordon Theater, The Stanley Warner Theater,
The Granada Theater, The Loyola, The Academy, The Picfax,
The Baronet, The Fox Venice, The Palms, The Million Dollar Theater,
KTLA, KHJ, KTTV, KCOP, KCET, Wallach's Music City, The Frigate,
Norty's, Flash Records, Aron's Records, Dolphin's of Hollywood,
Amoeba Records, Freakbeat Records, Adelphia Cable,
YouTube, Raleigh Studios, and Netflix.

For Bob, Nancy, Ellen, Lesley, Rosemarie, Ken and David:

"Obviously Seven Believers."

CONTENTS

LIST OF ILLUSTRATIONS

PROLOGUE

The Academy of Motion Picture Arts and Sciences celebrated its 75th anniversary in 2003 with a reception at its new home on the former site of the Beverly Hills Water Works, on the corner of Olympic and La Cienega Boulevards. It's just up the street from where my dad Marshall worked for years as a stockbroker; a Frisbee-toss from the Discount Record Center store, where I purchased a sealed copy of the Doors' *The Soft Parade* and my brother Ken bought the Beatles' *Sgt. Pepper's Lonely Hearts Club Band* album—in mono.

I came to the party, and to these memories of musical milestones, at the invitation of poet-actor Harry Northup, who wrote the words "Without a song, I could not live." Harry has his own deep link with film and the rhythm of rock 'n' roll from his work on movies like *Taxi Driver*, *Mean Streets*, and *Over the Edge*.

My first stop was Edith Head's six-sided design table, with lobby posters of *North by Northwest* and the original storyboards for *The Postman Always Rings Twice*; Lana Turner in pencil sketch; Cary Grant and Eva Marie Saint hanging off a cliff in late '50s black-and-white; composer Alex North's sheet music and scorebooks. When I worked at MCA Records in the late '70s as an A&R man at Universal Studios, my parking spot was next to Head's, across the pavement from Alfred Hitchcock's office, and sometimes his limo would divide our slots.

I talked to director Arthur Hiller, who reminded me that we'd met before. I responded with a detailed analysis of his ancient *Route 66* and *The Fugitive* directorial credits. Episodic black-and-white TV shows are my deal. "That's some kind of unique deal," he concluded.

I took it upon myself to introduce producer Richard D. Zanuck to Harry. Zanuck and I talked UCLA basketball for a couple of minutes. I see him at the Pauley Pavilion games. Harry knows that I produced instructional recordings on Basketball Hall of Famers John R. Wooden and Bill Walton, with sound design music provided by the Doors' Ray Manzarek, a UCLA Film School graduate. I've been following UCLA hoop since 1960, when I was in grade school and lived in Culver City, just blocks away from the MGM lot. Zanuck was relieved that I wasn't pitching him a project or asking about his father, studio owner Darryl F. Zanuck, or even talking about his own career running 20th Century Fox and producing films. Richard told us that he was "at the opening of Pauley Pavilion sports arena on campus in 1965 and saw Lew Alcindor (now known as Kareem Abdul-Jabbar) kick the varsity's ass." Lew had fifty-six points that night as a freshman.

Harry and I were sitting with Oscar-winner Martin Landau when a friend of Harry's, actor Robert Forster, of *Jackie Brown*, sat down for another helping of food and the Academy's birthday sing-along. I told Forster that for a season in the mid-'60s my mother, Hilda, had typed scripts for his *Banyon* television series when she was a floating secretary at Gower Gulch at Columbia-Warner. Robert and I discussed the *Jackie Brown* soundtrack as we noshed. When I split, Robert yelled: "Say hello to your mom!" And he later suggested Harry for a TV acting job he got on *Karen Sisco* in 2003. Good guy.

In the food line I fell in next to actor Gene Barry, one of the stars of the classic movie *War of the Worlds*, as well as the *Bat Masterson* and *The Name of the Game* TV shows. We talked briefly about *Burke's Law*, and I told him I just penned the obituary in *Goldmine* magazine for B. J. Baker, who voiced the opening title on the program. Writer-director and author Paul Mazursky then appeared. Very funny, and deserving of a statue just for delivering *I Love You, Alice B. Toklas*.

I was reintroduced to producer Mark Johnson of *Diner* fame, who partnered with Barry Levinson on *The Natural*. I love the way Eddie Cochran's "Somethin' Else" was used in *Diner*. Eddie played drums on the recording.

The highlight of the evening was a ten-minute conversation with producer Saul Zaentz. He was so pleased to talk about his *One Flew Over the Cuckoo's Nest*, and not *The English Patient* or *Amadeus*. Zaentz is a big supporter of jazz as well, and is married to one of Charles Mingus's former wives, Celia. I produced a jazz audio biography on Buddy Collette, the man who suggested to Mingus to get his first bass, and who was his lifelong friend. Zaentz owns the prestigious Fantasy Records, Takoma Records, and Stax Records catalogues. I was also aware of his debut film, *Payday*. When I told him I recorded actor Michael C. Gywnne, of *Hollywood Night Shift* radio fame—who was in *Payday* as a road manager—for a pilot a few years back, Zaentz told me about the *Payday* casting agent who suggested Gwynne. "Here's a black-and-white (photo) on an actor who might work." And Zaentz responded with: "Hey! That's the same guy who does voice-overs, and was a jazz and rock DJ in San Francisco who broke Creedence Clearwater Revival when I first took over the label in 1968. He's hired, and no table reading required!"

Inevitably the name of composer Jack Nitzsche came up. Jack, who following his breakthrough musical score for *Performance*, received an Oscar nomination for *Cuckoo's Nest*, and is the subject of as many tall tales as the movie stars themselves. Saul laughed and shook his head when I reminded him of a story Jack used to tell about why he and the Who's Pete Townshend were seated toward the back of the room in the Shrine Auditorium in downtown Los Angeles at the 1975 Oscars. Pete was nominated for *Tommy* that year. In true and candid Nitzsche fashion, Jack told Pete, "It doesn't matter where they put us. Neither of us is going to win. They always give it to someone who had a family tragedy or recent public drama in their lives." Jack was sometimes insensitive, supportive, mean, inspiring, fascinating, competitive, dreadful, wonderful, but brutally honest. Jack was Hollywood.

At the end of the night, I got to thinking about what I know best about the Hollywood machinery. I told Harry I thought a book needed to be written about the music, especially the rock 'n' roll we hear on the screen and collect as soundtrack albums; the interaction of the music and the cinematography clicking together like a Motown rhythm section; the story of how the music gets inside the films, and how rock 'n' roll in particular has been utilized in television the last six decades. A Hollywood shack job if there ever was one.

So more than a little while later, here it is. This is my Hollywood. "You Can Get It if You Really Want."

Harvey Kubernik,
Hollywood, California

SEE THE LAST SET OF STAPLE SINGERS
PLUS "MANCHURIAN CANDIDATE" FOR $1.50 AFTER 1 A.M.

KALEIDOFLICKS

MANCHURIAN CANDIDATE
SUNDAY SEPTEMBER 1 7 & 9:30 P.M.

TICKETS AT ALL WALLICH'S & MUTUAL AGENCIES

6230 SUNSET BLVD. NEAR VINE   HOLLYWOOD, U.S.A.   464-2

Kaleidoflicks advertisement, Los Angeles Free Press, 1968.
From the Harvey Kubernik collection.

PART ONE
THE PIONEERS WHO MADE IT POSSIBLE

D.A. Pennebaker with Bob Dylan. Photo courtesy of Pennebaker Hegedus Film.

D. A. PENNEBAKER

D. A. (DONN ALAN) PENNEBAKER was born July 15, 1925 in Evanston, Illinois.

His body of work has always had a strong relationship to music, especially rock 'n' roll. Pennebaker made his filmmaking debut with the 1953 short *Daybreak Express*, an abstract five-minute piece about the Third Avenue L Train set to the celebrated Duke Ellington song. In 1959, Pennebaker, along with Richard Leacock and Albert Maysles, joined Drew Associates, a group of filmmakers organized by Robert Drew and Time Inc., which was dedicated to expanding the use of film in journalism.

Drew Associates is where the legendary documentary editor and later producer, Charlotte Zwerin, met David and Albert Maysles. That team later went on to make the highly regarded Rolling Stones' tour documentary, *Gimme Shelter*.

Drew was a pioneer of direct cinema and a style that captured reality on film. Pennebaker and his partners forged the use of the first fully portable 16mm synchronized camera and sound system that developed a new grammar for movie making. The "direct cinema," or "cinema verité," an unobtrusive style of filmmaking, brought viewers right into the action by using hand-held cameras and techniques, where audiences had previously felt isolated from traditional narration documentaries.

Drew, Leacock, Pennebaker, and the team produced such landmark films as 1960's *Primary*, about Hubert Humphrey and John F. Kennedy in Wisconsin, and *Crisis*, a confrontation between Attorney General Robert Kennedy and Governor George Wallace over desegregation of the University of Alabama. The group also filmed *Jane*, which chronicled actress Jane Fonda's Broadway debut.

In 1964, Leacock and Pennebaker formed their own company and in 1965, Albert Grossman, Bob Dylan's manager, approached them about filming Dylan's '65 tour. The film was released in 1967.

D. A. Pennebaker shot twenty hours of film of Bob Dylan in a three-week period on that monumental U.K. '65 tour. "Penne" lensed most of the film himself with a camera and a microphone on his back, in that cinema verité style that he and his peers pioneered. Dylan celebrated his twenty-fourth birthday during that '65 tour, and Pennebaker turned forty during the making of *Don't Look Back*.

Pennebaker's rejection of the earlier established voice-over narration format in favor of recording real people, events, and environments as they happened changed the documentary film category forever. In the process he allowed documentaries to be made with as little direction from the filmmaker as possible. D. A. Pennebaker has always been a director without an ego or an entourage. He even favors the use of a minimal crew on his films.

The title, *Don't Look Back* was not lifted from a Dylan lyric, or even the 1959 British movie *Look Back in Anger*, but was a quote from baseball pitcher Satchel Paige who said: "Don't look back, something might be gaining on you."

Pennebaker's next major film event was *Monterey Pop*, capturing the wonderful West Coast 1967 festival that showcased Jimi Hendrix, the Mamas and the Papas, Otis Redding, the Association, Johnny Rivers, Quicksilver Messenger Service, Laura Nyro, Janis Joplin, the Who, and Jefferson Airplane. A DVD of this epic event was issued in 2003, while in spring 2005, a three-disc, 238-minute Criterion Collection edition of the film included such extra features as interviews and audio commentary tracks, as well as extended concert footage not included in the original version, all in a digitally remastered format.

In 1970, Pennebaker also filmed a documentary about the recording of the original cast album to Stephen Sondheim's *Company*, now available in retail outlets.

In 1972 his *Keep On Rockin'* was released, featuring Bo Diddley, Chuck

Berry, and Jerry Lee Lewis, among others. In 1973, Pennebaker filmed David Bowie's final concert appearance as *Ziggy Stardust and the Spiders from Mars*. In the last couple of decades his links to music and film collaborations have continued.

In 1976 Pennebaker became partners with Chris Hegedus. Over the past quarter of a century they have collaborated on a multitude of films. Their first effort, *The Energy War*, in 1977 was a five-hour "political soap opera" about President Jimmy Carter's battle with Congress to deregulate gas. Recently Pennebaker was the executive producer for wife Hegedus, whom he married in 1982, for *Startup.com*.

The year 1989 saw the release of the 120-minute road movie of Depeche Mode's concert tour, ending at the Southern California Rose Bowl. The documentary, *Depeche Mode 101*, garnered a Platinum Video Award for more than fifty thousand sales.

The following year, *Sweet Toronto*, a document of the 1969 Toronto Rock 'n' Roll Festival, was out as well, with John Lennon and Yoko Ono marking the debut of the Plastic Ono Band.

In the '90s the team of Pennebaker and Hegedus profiled Branford Marsalis and his trio as they toured and jammed with musicians Sting and Jerry Garcia for *The Music Tells You*.

In 1992 Pennebaker and Hegedus presented *Jimi Hendrix at Woodstock*, a complete unreleased performance with Band of Gypsies. And there have been additional projects with Joplin, Little Richard, Chuck Berry, and Jerry Lee Lewis.

In 1993, the telling documentary he made with Hegedus, *The War Room*, focusing on James Carville and George Stephanopoulos, about Bill Clinton's run for the U.S. Presidency, won an Oscar nomination for Best Documentary Feature. *The War Room* also won the D. W. Griffith Award for Best Documentary.

In 2003, Pennebaker Films issued *Only the Strong Survive*, a documentary on R&B soul music, distributed by Miramax Films, with Isaac Hayes, Mary Wilson of the Supremes, Ann Peebles, Carla and Rufus Thomas, Wilson Pickett, Sam Moore, and others. In stores is *Down from the Mountain*, a celebration of Bluegrass musicians as they gathered in Nashville, produced by the Coen brothers, featuring music from their film, *O Brother, Where Art Thou?*

D. A. Pennebaker's filmography and work with Hegedus also includes various music videos and short form features on Soul Asylum, Suzanne Vega, and Victoria Williams. D. A. also documented a Randy Newman live concert from 1980, and forty years ago, made the film *David*, about dope fiends at the Synanon House in Santa Monica, with Joe Pass.

While in Hollywood for his IDA Award, D. A. Pennebaker, based out of Pennebaker Hegedus Films, Inc. in New York, sat down with me at the Sunset Marquis Hotel in West Hollywood to extensively discuss *Don't Look Back*, as well as *Monterey Pop* and *Ziggy Stardust and the Spiders from Mars*, and some of his feelings about the current marriage of music, film, and television.

Q: With the DVD release of *Don't Look Back* it seems more than ever that *Don't Look Back* keeps finding a new audience, and lots of kids are discovering the work.

A: Yes. It kind of makes you feel like you did something right once (*laughs*). It doesn't make me feel bad at all. It interests me that people have the same fascination with Dylan that a lot of people had without being able to quite understand it. I know how I feel about Lord Byron. I think he's an important person in our culture and why everything is derived from what Byron set forth. Dylan I think in a hundred years will have some kind of same quality that people will look back and say, "Oh, that's where that came from." So it interests me now that people see it in the movie, that when it was made it was all a guess.

Q: With *Don't Look Back*, I'm seeing people title bands from words in the film, and a friend of mine, writer Mick Farren, has just published his autobiography, *Give the Anarchist a Cigarette*, a line from the movie.

A: Now there's a magazine in Australia called *Who Threw the Glass?*—I've got a copy of it.

Q: You're kidding! And the *Don't Look Back* title is an ode to baseball player Satchel Paige.

A: I always felt that was right. What he was saying made perfect sense for anybody who was doing something really well—they had to be careful not to look back and see how well they were doing it; they had to keep going, and couldn't become archivists of their own material.

Q: *Don't Look Back* was officially released in 1967, a year when Bob Dylan wasn't touring. In fact, when *Don't Look Back* played underground cinemas and the art house movie circuit between 1967 and 1973, Dylan was really off the road. So the only Dylan that people could see was on the screen in *Don't Look Back*.

A: Right.

Q: But did you anticipate that, as *Don't Look Back* is just now out on

DVD, around for the home video market, and still shown in theaters, it would be available in a twenty year period where Dylan is doing a hundred shows a year?

A: I think that it will take fifty or a hundred years to really digest him. He's like John Brown. He's out there singing a song and he's gonna sing it until he drops. And it's like he doesn't have to understand it completely. That's what he's going to do. The concerts now are like transfigurations, but they're interesting because you can't sit on a talent like that. Whatever you do is going to be interesting.

Q: You've seen *Don't Look Back* on the big screen in a movie theater. You've released it on home video for the small television screen format. Now DVD.

A: When DVDs came along I was really intrigued. I see them as a whole new thing. They're like magazines. And what the people were doing was interviewing the director, which is only mildly interesting at best and usually boring. You could get people of talent, which is what magazines do, to come in and bring it to life, and we kind of wanted to find out first of all how it works. So we didn't want to get into interviews, and I said to Bob Neuwirth, "Why don't you and I just lock ourselves in the studio and we'll talk for a couple of hours?" No production meetings. We each had a microphone. Kim Hendrickson was the person who kind of produced it with us, because she understood that we didn't want to get into any of the jazz of interviewing.

Q: When you were adding the running commentary, did you carry some anecdotes in your head that you wanted to make sure were said during the taping?

A: I don't really worry about those things. If people want to know and do it themselves, they find out, they look it up. I don't feel like explaining everything to everybody.

Q: And your original intent was not to make a concert film. You told writer Thomas White in the magazine *International Documentary*, "I was just going to go along and watch what happened. But that's kind of the way I operated anyway, so that wasn't a new idea for me. I didn't need any plans or concept particularly. Happily, they didn't want to make one, either. I think you could have made that film many different ways. But for me, that was the way the trip was. While I was knocked out by the songs, what I really wanted was the songs intermixed with the guy. That was the feeling I had. I wanted to write a novel, not a collection of songs."

A: Right. Once you start a concert film it's really hard. People say, "I want to hear more songs." But they can hear them on a record. So I didn't want to do that. But there were songs. I love some of the songs and I thought this is a chance to get these songs 'cause Sony (Columbia) is never going to release them. We recorded every concert, so we have fantastic pieces of music. It seemed to me a good time to release them, and we figured that the people who really wanted to hear those songs would buy the DVD just for the songs, y'know? It didn't matter whether they had a video copy of the film.

Q: Do you ever think that the new information provided with DVDs dilutes the original intent of the work, or at least gets in the way of the viewer's sense of discovery?

A: I think that that's a problem. And I think what you have is a new generation of watchers, like my fourteen-year-old, and she works off a keyboard and she plays what she wants to see and the rest can go to hell. She may never look at it her entire life.

So I think we're not talking about people who look at things in a linear way anymore. And if it were that way, I would agree and I would be against it. But I think it introduces a whole new way of getting information and not necessarily information that you'd expect. Because we've done three now, *Moon Over* and *Company* being the other two. And they all are different. DVD is where it's at. That's what's gonna be 'cause they're cheap to make. It's like a 78 record. You stamp 'em out—you don't have to go from front to back on a tape. In the end you're gonna get quality at a low price and everything is going to be DVD. But I think it's more interesting than that. We're not sure what we think totally about it. We're experimenting a little bit. I think what people can do with DVD is in a way what Ira Glass is doing with radio. And really revolutionizing something that everybody thinks is always said. And I don't think it's said at all. Which is what movies are like when you see them at home. They are different than when you go out to see them at the theater. That's only one aspect of it. Seeing a movie all by yourself. I think different people might want to watch it in different ways, but they just don't know it yet.

Q: Like you, I've seen *Don't Look Back* on a big screen, a TV screen, and most recently, a computer screen. You even released a laser disc version. Did you welcome the home video format initially for *Don't Look Back*, knowing there would be a small screen reduction at least in the visual aspects of the presentation?

A: I think it's kind of a Zen thing. How big is the moon? Your mind is able to deal with it on any size. Big is nice, especially if you have bad eyesight, and big is terrific in a theater. And we've made a 35mm blow-up of that, and there's no theatrical release on it. But I love seeing it in 35mm, and we show it at some festivals and it looks great. But the fact is that I think people who are used to video look at a video and see the same movie. The laser disc had good quality 'cause it's not compressed. People don't care that much about that. Only the guys in the studio worry about compression.

Q: Did you have any concerns when you put the DVD together about the pace and the flow of the supplemental commentary?

A: It's a conversation. I don't think about it. It's like when I have to go give a speech, I don't think about it, much less write it out. I don't know how to do that. If I try to do that, it's a disaster. I have to open my head and my mouth and see what comes out.

Q: The *Don't Look Back* DVD revealed to me how much Dylan's friend and road manager Bob Neuwirth was involved in the actual film. You talk a little about it in the new DVD commentary.

A: He made all kinds of shit happen. I didn't have to ask him or talk to him about anything. We never talked about it at all. He understood immediately how the thing worked and made it work better. And Dylan understood a little bit, but he didn't understand how naked he'd appeared. That was the thing that surprised him. Neuwirth knew from the start how it was gonna be. I don't know why. He's an artist, and he shot some films himself. That amazed me. Neuwirth's role in that film was crucial and that's why I wanted him to be the one I talked to.

Q: Dylan is a very photographic personality and artist. But are you amazed, looking back at a film that is a third of a century old, that his songs have such durability?

A: Yeah, I'm amazed. I always thought they were good. I thought he was a fantastic songwriter and even the bad songs stick. They just stick. It's just interesting because later when he was with The Band and Robbie, "down from the east," you knew what was Dylan and the rest were OK. It's an amazing thing he can do that. Where does he know to do that? And he hardly ever misses. It's an amazing thing, so it's like Byron. He's inventing a whole new age of some sort and we're not even there yet.

Q: People are still talking about the scene of manager Albert Grossman and agent Tito Burns captured in a business negotiation. When I was a teenager and first saw *Don't Look Back* and their segment, I decided I didn't want to be a manager or agent.

A: You could never have that scene today. Management wouldn't allow it. One time a groupie came up to a table where I was sitting at The Kettle of Fish in New York with Albert, and this girl said to Albert, "I can't believe I saw you in that movie and you looked like some sort of bandit from the swamps or something." And I said, "Albert, I feel badly if I ruined your reputation in the village." "Don't think about it," he said. "It's exactly what it should be." I thought, that's the way to deal with it. Taking it as if it wasn't going to be his lifetime put-down. Tito Burns and I talked years ago and he liked himself on-screen.

Q: Do you remember the first time you screened *Don't Look Back* for Dylan? On the DVD you mention he brought along a big yellow pad to the viewing.

A: Yeah. I didn't know what was going to happen. But I knew that room was full of people that I hated. I didn't know where they came from or where they went to. Two nights. At the end of the first night he said, "We're gonna do the same thing tomorrow." It was a terrible screening anyway. It was out of synch and I was really depressed. And then we were going to figure out how to change it, or whatever he was going to do. And then the next night, y'know—bang! "It's fine. That's it." He had an empty pad. So I thought, well this guy is an amazing person, and I was really lucky not only to be able to film but to have his mind there contemplating its release.

Q: In *International Documentary,* you also felt, "He's a person who doesn't like to reveal himself very much to people he doesn't know—or even to people he does know. He's a very secretive person, and he was just amazed and surprised that this dumb camera with one person running it could do that. But, when he thought about it for twenty-four hours later, he realized it was something complete; he couldn't touch it or change it or improve it or take things out that were embarrassing. That has always kind of amazed me, and I have always been grateful that it came down like that, because you could have terrible problems when you do these things with people." What about Dylan as a camera subject?

A: Well—he is what he is. He's different in the afternoons than he is in the mornings. So you're never sure whom you are getting. He's the twins. I think he's a person who understood theater very well. Even though he was very naïve about a lot of things. You'd often talk to him about somebody and he wouldn't know who you were talking about—"Jesus, he's gotta know who this person is." Then other people he would know a lot about. It amazed me where he got his kind of primal information, because it was always right on the nose. It didn't seem like he'd been through a lot of education. He seemed to have gotten it from the streets.

Q: Were there any advantages in shooting a film in black-and-white as opposed to color?

A: Well, it's different. You put your mind into that and then it sits there and you don't have to think anymore. What you want to do is to get so that when you're shooting you don't have to think. You don't have to think about "Should I be closer?" As soon as you think in those things, the film disappears. You want your feet to take you where you should be. You want the camera to film what you want it to film. You don't want anything to happen so you won't have to think about it. And then it can happen in some part of your brain that's non-word-oriented, or something. I don't know. But I get in that camera and I don't want to come out.

Q: What did you learn from the process of doing *Don't Look Back* and filming *Eat the Document* that you applied to *Monterey Pop*? I know for *Monterey Pop* you shied away from the use of interview footage in that documentary.

A: I learned to trust myself. Before, I wasn't sure I could make movies, and it wasn't until *Jane* that I knew I could do it. Then I felt like I just shot five fifty-cent pieces. In *Don't Look Back* it was a whole—one thing—and I did it almost totally by myself. I had Jones Alk doing sound and I had Bob Van Dyke doing the concerts, and Bob was doing the sound when I was doing Albert and Tito. He was known for his late nights and some drinking, and he fell asleep on the corner of the desk. I have a picture of him holding the microphone up all the time and I didn't want to wake him up.

It's like the tennis player, Chris Evert Lloyd. I adore her and I want to make a film of her. I love that she's in the zone. She was the first person I ever heard use the term, "in the zone." I understood exactly. When you're in the zone you cannot make a mistake. You can jump out the window and land soft.

I was in the zone for *Don't Look Back*. Maybe Dylan was in the zone. I knew that once I got started I just had to roll and not plan anything.

I didn't try and be smart about anything. I never asked him a question. I didn't want to know anything. I just wanted to get inside that camera and not come out. For me, that's in the zone, and I felt like Chris Evert Lloyd. The feeling that you are God.

Q: Was there a tough feeling of just letting go when *Don't Look Back* began? I mean, you didn't storyboard anything or work from a script.

A: There was, because originally it began in the dressing room where he says, "You start off standing, right?" I said, "That's a cute way to start, and I'll put a little title in and put my name in. That's all I need to do." And the first time I looked at it, I thought, "Shit, it didn't work—maybe because you don't know who the hell this guy is—and he's being cute in the dressing room, but why should you care?" And then we had that thing we shot that was Dylan's idea, to shoot the cue card scene for the opening with "Subterranean Homesick Blues." So I stuck that on the front and that did it. So you just do it and when you're in that zone, whatever you do will probably work. And I had a never-before-seen version of "Subterranean Homesick Blues" that we have on the DVD.

Q: Sound is very important in *Don't Look Back*. Jones Alk, who did your sound in the film, is a thread throughout the movie and she was palming and carrying a microphone. And the movie is dialogue-driven since I know you didn't want to make a concert movie. And no lighting and no boom microphones. Jones Alk wasn't intrusive in the movie.

A: I don't like booms. You look peculiar with a boom. There are many ways of getting the sound. In *Don't Look Back* you never see a mic in Jones Alk's hand and never know she was doing sound. She's just watching what is going on. She was using two Sennheiser microphones and one was a directional ("shot gun mike"). In her lap. I never told her what to do. From the beginning. She was Dylan's friend. She managed to always keep it out of the camera. She'd watch me just enough so I'd know how to contact her and didn't have to think about it. I don't think she had ever done sound before in her life. I have no idea. She was perfect. I've never found a better sound person, ever. That's what I mean by being in the zone. I hadn't met her before I got to London. Dylan brought in Howard Alk, but I didn't want to have another camera. I didn't want to get into "shooting the concerts." I thought, "Gee, if I have a second camera, then we'll have to have a lot of film for the second camera, because he's not going want to stop shooting." And I was ready to shoot little bits of songs, 'cause we recorded every concert. So I knew I had soundboard and it was all mono on a Nagra.

Q: On the new DVD version, as part of your rap you explain how you created "stereo echo" for "Love Minus Zero/No Limit." You added room tone to the song in a live setting—and it works.

A: I did that in a most interesting way. At the time I didn't know how to do an echo. But I had a machine that could slow down, so I made two transfers, one at slightly slower speed, and one I kept at the same speed. It changed the rate of slowdown, and I just ran it to the edit. And it was perfect.

Q: And you edited *Don't Look Back* in three weeks?

A: With a viewer. No Avids then. You move faster and it's closer to what the Avid will do. It's much faster than a Steenbeck (flatbed editing system). A little screen and a light in there, and you take a synchronizer which you draw your tape and your film through, and on the synchronizer we'd put a little head and we built these magnetic pick-ups, which fed into a little squeak box, or into your ear phones. Then, when you pulled it through, if you had a twenty-two-frame pull-up, you heard the sound that went with the picture that was in the actual viewer and you could go very fast. And for me, moving fast through a film I'm editing is really important. I don't know why exactly. I hate to dwell on stuff, because then you start to make it pretty.

Q: What was the biggest change you noticed in Bob Dylan as an artist and songwriter since you filmed the 1966 European tour that has emerged in a cut of *Eat the Document*?

A: Well, I felt that he was really writing music sort of with Robbie (Robertson) and for Robbie. He was trying to show Robbie how to write music. There was something going on that drove him so that he would stay up all night. I filmed him endlessly where he'd write many songs during the night and Robbie would play along. Robbie made him somehow do this. And on the first tour there was nobody doing that. Neuwirth never made him do that. He never felt competitive with Dylan.

In 1965, I would look through my lenses and the words would drop on the music. I was just amazed at how anybody could produce that kind of electricity. To me that was what art was about.

Sondheim, Bowie, and Dylan have a lot of characteristics in common. Stephen, when he was young, I know, was a mathematician, as

I was. At the MET we were looked on as "little boy geniuses," which for me didn't last long. So I knew that his peculiar silences were the silences of somebody trying to figure out the "Tic-Tac-Toe" program. But, for both David and Bob, they went into their heads from time to time and disappeared, and I always assumed it was some sort of music room.

Q: You offer in the DVD narrative that all films have a center. *Don't Look Back* has a center. Does a film arrive and then wind down?

A: Yes! Absolutely. I never know when we are shooting, but in editing I find it out later. Shooting is just summer camp. When I saw *Don't Look Back*, I knew exactly what was the center, and it changed the whole ending of the film. And it's when he says "Don't Think Twice, It's Alright," and you go to the train. That's the end of that part, and from then on it's different in my head. Now, nobody else may see it that way, and I don't want to say this or indicate in any way 'cause that film belongs as much to anybody watching it as it does to me, and that's its strength I think.

Q: I was taken by the tension, the anticipation of the crowds and fans and the hysteria around Dylan that you caught on film.

A: I caught that in the audience.

Q: Haskell Wexler, who in the late '60s directed *Medium Cool*, told me you used modified portable Auricon camera equipment for *Don't Look Back*, and you let him borrow that camera for some of his earlier shoots like the *March on Washington*.

A: Yes, but on *Don't Look Back* the camera I had was the best one I made yet. I used Angenieux lenses. He was a Frenchman and he's dead now. He invented the zoom lens. A marvelous guy. He had this lens for studio cameras where he had this long finder 'cause you had it on a tripod, right, and you had to stand by and look. And I told him, "That's not going to work for me." And he said, "Why not?" And I showed him my camera on my shoulder and my eye was right there at the thing.
And I told him what I wanted, and he said, "Oh boy—that is really hard and I can hardly wait." And he made me one. He made me one.

Q: What about film stock?

A: I think I was using Tri-X and pushing it (increasing film speed). And I did it through Humphries in London 'cause they were a really good lab and they did I think a pretty good job, and we wanted it right away. I had no lights. We used available light. The people I showed it to at United Artists wished I had used more lights. They saw it as a ratty, underexposed film, you see, because they weren't thinking that that was Dylan's film, that's what Dylan should make. They saw it in terms of Katherine Hepburn. So it lacked.

Q: You had a prestigious track record before *Don't Look Back*. I remember that films like *David*, shot at the Synanon House in 1962, won awards at the Boston International Film Festival in 1962, and *Daybreak Express* was honored at the Mannheim Film Festival in 1964. Eventually, in 1968, *Don't Look Back* won Outstanding Film of the Year at the London Film Festival, after release. Yet I'm shocked to know that you couldn't find a distributor for *Don't Look Back,* and actually had to open your movie in San Francisco. The New York art movie circuit and general movie distribution world didn't want to give you any action. You were hawking a movie about a guy who, in 1966 and 1967, had charted and broken top forty AM radio the year before with "Like a Rolling Stone," and had massive critical acclaim for a few years. And you couldn't convince Dylan's label, Columbia Records, to help finance the production.

A: (*laughs*) There's always a delay between the people at the gates and the public. I still have the letter of rejection from a guy at Warner 7 Arts. It's very funny. Finally he took his daughter to see it in San Francisco, and at the end of the letter he said, "The funny thing was my daughter really liked it." It opened at the Presidio in San Francisco. I was desperate, because I showed it to a lot of people and took it out to places like Milwaukee and showed it at civic centers, and the place would be filled with people who afterward would come up with tears in their eyes. And I said to myself, "There's an audience. Why can't I get the local theater to run it?" They wouldn't even look at it. Theater owners don't look at films. Usually they go by their distributors. So I was stuck.

Don't Look Back advertisement, Los Angeles Free Press, 1967. From the Harvey Kubernik collection.

Then this guy walked in one day and said, "I'm told you have this film about this singer." He didn't know who Dylan was. "I represent a bunch of theaters out in the West called Art Theater Guild and we run mostly . . ." I think he meant porno films, and was looking to clean up his act. So I showed it to him and he said, "Y'know, it's exactly what I'm looking for. It looks like a porno film but it's not. I'll open it in the Presidio." I didn't know where the Presidio was at all. Somebody later told me, "That's a wild porno house out in San Francisco!"

Ricky (Leacock) and I came up after Monterey and I was so pleased we had gotten it in a theater finally that I didn't want to tell Ricky what it was. We stayed over in North Beach and the next day with a very heavy heart I said, "Let's go see how our movie is playing." It had played two or three weeks there. So we went to the theater and I said to Ricky, "Watch this." And Ricky was very nervous about money in general. He saw the big long line outside and thought, "We're just making money for the theater and they're never going to pay us." So I said, "Ricky, watch." I went up to the place—this old falling-apart porno house—and I said to the guy, "Would you give me some money?" "How much?" I said, "Five hundred dollars." And he made me sign a note, and Leacock just died. That was a great moment for the two of us. We totally recognized that we could make movies. We didn't have a 35mm print. San Francisco had my answer print. It played in San Francisco for almost a year in 16mm. Then New York came around some four months later when it showed at the 34th Street East. The company didn't even have to run ads.

Q: You still go to Dylan concerts, and he's viewed the *Don't Look Back* DVD.

A: Yeah. We're partners. We deal with Jeff (Rosen) in his office all the time. But Dylan came over and he looked at some footage on the DVD and said at one point, "How did you get that great sound?" I said, "Well, Bob, you're gonna be surprised at this. It's all mono." "Mono— I gotta tell the guys down at Sony about this . . ."

Q: When you shot Dylan singing "Hattie Carroll" in a *Don't Look Back* performance, you had an interesting camera angle.

A: In your face from the underside of the floorboards. I was lying on the floor and the only way to keep it steady was to lie down. I started figuring it out from one concert to another and would shoot a little bit. I never saw anything until I got back to New York. You look through the camera and you kind of know what you got and you think about it: "Where should that go?" I didn't know what to think. Your feet take you there and you go.

Q: After countless viewings and question-and-answer sessions after screenings, and feedback from a few different generations, what have been some of the reactions that have been consistent over the years?

A: They love the science student (Terry Ellis, later cofounder of Chrysalis Records). Somebody just interviewed Ellis last week for a film they are making about me and Chris, and there he was saying it's the funniest thing in the world to have been in a movie when he was just trying to get a free ticket to get in. It was all really just off the wall. People discover things like the High Sheriff's lady introducing her sons with the same names. Things like that. People respond to things where you don't rub it in too hard. And earlier when I was working with Drew Time-Life, Inc., we were always narrating, saying "now look at this," "now listen to this." With *Don't Look Back*, there was a way to make films in the real world and not upset it. With *Don't Look Back*, it was more like a magazine, just to make sure that it was what you did in a magazine. Make sure everybody got it. And I liked the idea of a lot of people not getting it. And the people who did get it knowing there were people around them who didn't get it. I like that whole chemistry of people figuring out where they are in terms of what they get at that time. They may go back and see the film another time and get a whole other thing.

Q: Travel was a big thing in *Don't Look Back*. Taxis, cars, trains. Movement in general.

A: Yes. That's what we did. I had shot transportation and car shots before. I think it's like when people are watching television when they are driving cars, or driving in cars they become more absolute in some ways, They become more real. I like the information they give in those situations. So it's a good place to get people, especially if you want them reflective. They feel in charge of something and they don't mind letting you in.

Q: I love the insert shots and footage of Allen Ginsberg. I like the segment where Dylan is writing a song at the piano with producer Tom Wilson sitting next to him. A couple of months later from that moment Wilson would be producing Dylan on "Like a Rolling Stone," which was birthed on that U.K. tour. And Wilson went on to produce many classic recordings and albums on Simon & Garfunkel, the Animals, and the Mothers of Invention.

A: Right. The interaction with Bob. Tom Wilson made some contributions. I knew Allen when he was a teenager. I did a lot of stuff with Allen on film. I knew him through Jack Kerouac and Barbara Hale, and Lucien Carr, who is still around.

Q: *The Monterey International Pop Festival* has been available for years on home video. It's out since 2002 on DVD—that release coincided with the thirty-fifth anniversary of the festival, which until recently was still available in a four-CD box set of live performances from Rhino

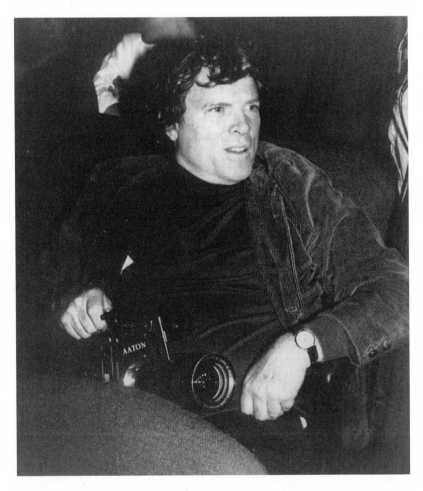

D. A. Pennebaker filming at the Monterey International Pop Festival, 1967.
Photo courtesy of Pennebaker Hegedus Film.

Records. I know when you did that movie you made a conscious decision not to really do interviews for it?

A: Interviews didn't interest me—and I had access to do it. I didn't want to take the time. I wanted everybody to concentrate on music. Well remember, the guys I had filming for me there—except for Ricky [Leacock], he was the only other camera—they were all beginners. And I wanted them as I put them, in pivotal positions 'cause they could be with the music. They served the music and that was the thing. And I didn't want them to think about anything except getting film to match that music.

Q: How did the genesis of the *Monterey Pop* movie begin?

A: Bob Rafelson (*The Monkees* TV show, *Head*) called me up and he said, "Would you like to do a film of a concert in California?" And I thought about it and I had just seen Bruce Brown's *Endless Summer*, which is not about surfing at all, but all about California. Every kid out of high school, the one thing they wanted to do was get to California, and *Endless Summer* didn't hurt.

I saw Rafelson once, maybe, but he was never involved. It was always [Monterey International Pop Festival organizers] Lou Adler and John Phillips that I dealt with. And we flew up with Cass [Elliot] to see the place, and I looked at it and it was this tiny place. I had no idea what was going to happen there. I had never seen a music festival at all. Not even Newport, so I didn't know what to expect. It had a really nice feeling to it and I loved Monterey and it's a lovely place. And I sort of thought, "Well, these guys know what they are doing." John and Lou. John was a total genius. He was part Indian and had a mystical view on everything he did. And he hadn't been playing music for long. The Journeymen a couple of years before the Mamas and the Papas. Everything he was doing was like he'd been touched, and as long as the spell was there it just flowed out of him. I loved John. He was marvelous. Lou knew what he was doing, and I knew he was a real good sound mixer 'cause I had listened to some of the stuff he had done, but I knew they were hatching a real interesting game. Which was from the beginning, "Get rid of the money." That was the big thing. Get rid of the money. And I could see that that was gonna make it work. It was a very Zen thing but . . .

I could see that, and later I saw what happened at Woodstock, and I really didn't want to get involved with that at all. One of the producers of Woodstock saw the film of *Monterey Pop* and wanted to do a festival.

Janis Joplin and James Gurley of Big Brother & the Holding Co. at the Monterey International Pop Festival, 1967. Photo by Henry Diltz.

Q: I dug the *Monterey Pop* outtake performances I've seen from your original shoot. The Association, Paul Butterfield, the Electric Flag, and especially Laura Nyro. The music informs your film.

A: She called me up about a year before she died and wanted me to work with her on a music video.

Q: And the music sounded so good. I'm talking sonically—the official released version and the unreleased footage.

A: Well, we had Brian Wilson's tape recorder, that was one thing that made it possible. Those two eight-tracks made it possible, and Lou and John mixed that thing in John's house while I sat there and listened to it and they did a fantastic mix. They were really good at doing mixes.

Q: You had some limitations imposed on you at Monterey, like when Albert Grossman, who managed Janis Joplin, didn't want you to film her performance. But eventually she's included in the film and she's wearing different pieces of clothing for the set in your concert footage of her.

A: She was the one thing we were told we couldn't shoot. Although I did shoot a little, but Grossman said, "I'll pull her the minute I see a

camera going on her. All the cameras have to be pointed at the ground."
We went through a whole big drill and it got me really intrigued,
y'know, with this going on, and then when I heard her, the first song,
"Combination of the Two," and I said, "Jesus Christ—This is impossible." So I went to Albert and I said, "Whatever it takes. I mean, we've
got to get her." So he disappeared, and the next thing I knew she came
out and she said, "Oooh, I'm gonna do it again and you can film me
this time." So we did.

(Joplin and her band even did a second set the following night at
the festival, at which "Ball and Chain" was filmed.)

Q: Jimi Hendrix really connected with the Monterey audience and you got
him on film. And Otis Redding's performance. In 1986 you released his
complete set at Monterey Pop, *Shake! Otis at Monterey.*

A: We had no idea about Hendrix going in. John had said, "Listen, this
guy will kill you. He sets himself on fire." And he comes out and

Mickey Dolenz at the
Monterey International
Pop Festival, 1967.
Photo by Henry Diltz.

Tommy Smothers at the Monterey International Pop Festival, 1967, where he was one of the onstage hosts. Photo by Henry Diltz.

he's chewing on his flat pick. I thought he was chewing gum, and I thought, "This is blues?" I mean, I didn't know what to expect. We had thought we would save film a little bit and shoot one song for every group. So we had this lamp with a little red light, and Neuwirth, I, and John Cooke were gonna figure out what songs to do; and in the end, Neuwirth kind of mostly figured it out, he was like the music director. And when Hendrix came on, I think the light was on for the first song—I don't know why, but I remember that that light went on very soon and never went off for all the Hendrix thing, and everybody shot everything. They had film for it.

Otis Redding was stunning. It's a great film, almost a perfect film. He had a pretty good band. I was editing, or reediting the section of his for *Monterey Pop* in late '67, and changed the film a little bit when he went into the lake. I remember that's when I got into all that stuff of doing things with the lights, and I know at the time I felt, "Gee. What am I doing? This is crazy." But I left it that way because I felt so bad that he kind of died on us, and that made me sad. So the only thing I could do to mark that was to edit that way. In editing *Monterey Pop* I had my first Steenbeck.

Q: Did it make editing things quicker?

A: No, it was a little slower but I could hear the music really well. And I was making edits in the music sometimes. I've edited chunks out of it that you don't know are missing, but I would've normally never done it on a viewer or in my old editing bay.

I knew when I saw Ravi Shankar we would have to end with that. I remember sitting down at Max's Kansas City, and I wrote out a little thing on the back of a menu of what I thought the order of the music would be, and you know, it was very close to what ended up being. The only things I pulled out were Butter (Butterfield) and the Electric Flag, for very peculiar reasons. But the fact is that I almost knew going in, without even thinking about it, that it had to build from Canned Heat to Simon & Garfunkel to whatever it was. It had to be a history of popular music in some weird way that I didn't ever have to explain to anybody, 'cause I had John's music as a narration for the whole film, and that just covered me.

Brian Jones at the
Monterey International
Pop Festival, 1967.
Photo by Henry Diltz.

Q: In 1973 you filmed David Bowie's *Ziggy Stardust and the Spiders from Mars*. A cinematic dude. I would also imagine you connected with him—who knows, maybe afterward—partially because he nicked the line "spiders from Mars" from Kerouac's *On the Road*, and has acknowledged beat writer William S. Burroughs' cut-up method on his own songwriting.

A: There's an aspect to this kind of filmmaking—*Don't Look Back, Ziggy, Down from the Mountain*—that you don't so much learn it, but it's a rigor that you have to sort of go through. When you first start a film, like when I first met Bowie, the first shot I ever took of him is still the best shot I ever took of him. It's on my wall somewhere. At that moment you want to fix a face so that the audience will remember that face forever. It's really hard in a documentary getting people onstage. They all look alike, no matter how different they are. One is blonde, one has brown hair.

Q: But with David Bowie and his Ziggy character you were walking into a situation where things were pretty colorful and theatrical already, underscoring the music being created.

A: Yes, but the dressing room was where you see him just sitting there, so that in the beginning you use a long lens—that's why I use a zoom—and you can stand far away and the sound person can be close and you can really get onstage physically.

So people know that he looks different from somebody else. If you take these faces right, you have portraits. But then, as the movie goes forward, somewhere down the line there comes a point where you don't need to do that anymore, so you go to wide angle. And usually with wide angle you don't have a finder, 'cause you've got to line up and pull the camera up, and you start getting what is happening, rather than picture to music. From then on everybody is going to recognize who's who and you don't have to worry about it, and that's the way the films go, most of them.

Q: You walked into a cosmic moment in history. Bowie came to the party with the whole package, and you were getting his last "Ziggy" show. Were you a fan before you did the project?

A: No. I didn't know who he was! I thought it was Bolan. I thought I was going to see Bolan, and I loved glitter rock and I didn't know much about it.

At the time before *Ziggy*, I was out on the Mississippi on a raft, and ABC got hold of me and said, "We want you to go do a film of David

Bowie." I thought they said Bolan, Marc Bolan. I thought, "This is great—glitter rock." But I said, "I can't, I'm on this raft." They called back a day later and said, "You gotta go and we'll fly you out . . ." We couldn't get out of New York because there was some sort of strike, so we actually had to take a tour plane, that we snuck onto with our equipment, to Italy, to Rome. There had been a big thing about terrorists at the airport there, so they arrested us. Guys got out with machine guns. We finally got through that and got to London and we got there two days before the concert.

So we saw one concert that night. I saw him once and I shot some stuff 'cause I wanted to see if we needed to lift the lighting or anything. And the lighting, I could see, was really crucial to this. We couldn't fake it. I shot some stuff and we took it down that night to a lab and they processed it and we looked at it and I made a couple of changes, like the blues were too strong, and I went over it with the lighting person. And the next night we did the whole concert and there were only three of us. We had a skeleton crew, and a Brit we hired with a camera way back in the rafters to get a broad shot in case we ever needed it, but we never actually used it.

Q: And the glitter critters in front of the stage really knocked me out in the film. What about Bowie in the dressing room?

A: There was a lot of kinetic energy around Bowie. He was like an orchestra leader. I was a fan of the *Ziggy* album and we used to play it all the time when I was mixing that film. I had it set up actually in real Dolby and we showed it in this little room where the sound was fantastic, and that was the sexiest film you ever saw in your life.

Q: He had the ability to project to both men and women.

A: Yes, absolutely. I mean, I could practically feel myself getting a hard-on watching it (*laughs*). I don't know. He represented sexuality without it even being a man or a woman. It was an element of it for me.

Q: Both Dylan and Bowie, when you worked with them, had an extensive grasp of song and music history.

A: When I first met Dylan, at the Cedar Tavern (in Greenwich Village, New York), we talked and there was a woman sitting in the corner of the bar, and Dylan asked me if I thought it was Lotte Lenya. I was interested that he even knew who she was.

Q: What are some of your feelings about the marriage of music and television?

A: My own sense is that if you use music just as promotion, it's like using words for advertising. They're effective and nobody hates you, but you're not taken seriously—you don't really take what's behind it seriously. And performance is when a guy who probably couldn't do anything else in his life, because he was a loser, got drawn into practicing long hours on a guitar or something, and he got good at it—because if you do anything long enough you get good at it—and pretty soon he got some ideas in his head, I don't know where, and then one day he's up there as an icon, y'know, playing music. That's his thing, that's who he is; and when he performs and he's good, and you're filming him, then you really want to see the performance, you don't want to hype something else. So, when Jim Desmond was shooting Hendrix at Monterey, we left almost all of his shot in. We had other terrific shots—I was right behind him, Nick Doob, we had great shots from every direction—but you don't need to cut necessarily, so I'm not big on cutting to enhance performance. I like to watch the person doing it handle it, kind of move it around and make it grow in front of you. That's what's interesting to me about performance. And I do miss that a lot in what I see on TV. But you know, "what we're doing is old-fashioned. We'd better get with it or we're gonna lose our socks." So I know there are different ways of looking at this, and I'm sure kids raised on this hard, strong cut are gonna say, "Oh shit, that's really boring," when they see something drag out long. Even just a little of that. Longfellow must have run into that.

Q: Now people and fans are really discovering your own body of documentary work.

A: Well, it's history and people. There's a certain kind of history people want to examine over and over again. And I think it's like Hendrix. Nobody expected that he'd be history—in the beginning, you couldn't give him away. When I showed Hendrix to ABC they said "No thanks." And they owned the film, and all they had to do was sign some shit and they would have taken it free, but they let it go because they knew he couldn't play on their network, and then a year later they bought the movie for two hundred and fifty grand.

Q: If you could give one tip to directors or the talent onstage making music videos today, what would it be?

A: Well I think it's who you get to do it. And the videos are done pretty well now, but basically they're choreographed now and it's all dance, dance, dance. So the singing is almost a minor aspect. But the first thing you have to do is be circumspect about your audience. Know who the hell they are, because if they all are teenyboppers and want to see the Back Street Boys close up, then you'd better get wide angle lenses and get their tongues on view.

Q: With the recent release of *Only the Strong Survive* and the 2002 and 2003 *David Bowie: Ziggy Stardust and the Spiders from Mars, Monterey Pop*, and *Don't Look Back* DVDs now out in commercial release, how do you feel about the new DVD medium? On the *Don't Look Back* DVD you serve as a narrator to both original and newly remixed audio and film footage.

A: I think it's added something quite interesting to our films. It's like listening to radio shows. It gives us a place to dump stuff that's essentially valuable, but we don't know how to put it to film. So you feel, "Well, at least it's in a drawer." You can close it and think it's safe. The DVD picture is better than on videotape. We did a lot of work on these DVDs, especially on *Monterey*. We went back to the original sound, and remixed things with the 5.1 Dolby sound for the DVD player.

※

D. A. Pennebaker: Select Filmography

Don't Look Back
The Monterey International Pop Festival
Keep On Rockin'
Ziggy Stardust and the Spiders from Mars
The Energy War
Startup.com
The Music Tells You
Only the Strong Survive
Down from the Mountain
Jimi Hendrix at Woodstock
Depeche Mode 101
Sweet Toronto
The War Room

FRED RAPHAEL AND JUDY RAPHAEL

JUDY RAPHAEL WAS BORN in New York and brought up in the hills above Hollywood Boulevard, across the road from actress Linda Darnell, and near the estates of producer Mark Hellinger and actor Donald Crisp. The family home was built by pioneering producer B. P. Schulberg, father of screenwriter Budd Schulberg, in 1901. Judy attended grammar school with Johnny Mercer's daughter Amanda, Lena Horne's son, and young Ricky Nelson, and she remembers peeking through the banisters to see such dinner guests as Billy Eckstine, Nat King Cole, Tony Martin, Cyd Charisse, Mel Blanc, and Jack Benny.

Judy went to Hamilton High School in West Los Angeles. After receiving a B.A. in Theater Arts at UCLA, she did graduate work in film from 1963 to 1965, studying with director Jean Renoir and documentary filmmaker Alberto Cavalcanti. Now settled in Los Angeles, she has lived in San Francisco and New York.

Since 1979, Judy Raphael has been a freelance writer, specializing in music, lifestyle, and travel for such publications as *L.A. Weekly*, *Los Angeles Times*, *Los Angeles Herald-Examiner*, *Los Angeles Reader*, *Los Angeles Daily News*, as well as *Music Connection* and *New Country Magazine*.

Judy was also a contributor to *HollyWord*, a spoken word album collection I produced in 1990. She has done extensive research on her

Judy and Fred Raphael, Beverlywood, California, 1954.
Photo by Hermione Raphael, courtesy of Judy Raphael.

family and has the papers and archives of her father, the seminal yet overlooked film and music publishing industry pioneer, Fred Raphael, a founding father of the merger between the recorded song and the screen in the post-World War II era. Fred Raphael Music still exists, based in Cathedral City, California, and is administered by MizMo Music in Burbank, California.

Judy provided me an initial biography of her father, who died in 1966, and we jointly curated a text below that I feel underscores the Hollywood music and sound scenes from the late '40s until the mid-'50s, when rock 'n' roll started to be placed on soundtrack products and in movie houses.

We discussed Fred's life as a music publisher and his early work when rock 'n' roll was first integrated into the celluloid playing field.

Fred Raphael opened Disney Music Company in 1949 and guided the scores of its "silver age" animated classics through the 1940s to the mid-1950s.

A self-made man, Fred was born to immigrant parents in Washington Heights, New York, on April 9, 1908. He quit high school to help in his father's parking garage. His show business career began in 1928, when he got a job as an usher at the Capitol Theater, owned by Metro Goldwyn Mayer. By age twenty-two, he was music librarian for *The Major Bowes Original Amateur Hour* and *The Sunday Morning Hour*, broadcast over WHN Radio from New York, and in short order was promoted to program director. Fred's other task—the wellspring of his life's work—was to find classical music and buy synchronization rights for MGM movies.

In the early 1940s he went into music publishing, first for Shapiro-Bernstein Music and then Bourne Music, in a self-created position as a West Coast liaison to the studios.

While in Hollywood during a motion picture strike, Fred had the bright idea to approach Walt Disney about starting his own music company. Disney had been giving its music to such companies as Saintly-Joy and Bourne to handle its publishing.

Wally Gould, a former bandleader on RKO Radio, then working for Howard Hughes, recommended Fred to Walt as "a man you should talk to—very knowledgeable about music."

Fred went to Walt and asked why he would pay companies to publish his music when he could do it himself.

Walt apparently liked the idea.

Fred set up offices at Selma and Argyle, just east of Nickodell's restaurant. Initial publication was to be three songs from *Cinderella* by Tin Pan Alley writers, Al Hoffman and Jerry Livingston, aimed for a holiday release.

However, it was an outside song that opened the company. In fall of 1949, former Disney staff writer Johnny Lange was shopping a demo of a song called "Mule Train." When the publisher down the hall turned it down, he took it to Fred, who recognized it as a hit. On a business trip to Chicago, Fred played the song for Mitch Miller, famed A&R man for Mercury Records, explaining that Vaughn Monroe had first rights on it.

Miller jumped the release date and put it out with artist Frankie Laine, and the song was a #1 hit within a week. Disney Music was in business.

Major hits with Bing Crosby, Tennessee Ernie Ford, and Monroe followed, although Laine's version was the best seller, at two million copies. The song was also featured in the Vaughn Monroe movie *Singing Guns* and a second movie, called *Mule Train*.

According to Fred's widow, Hermione Raphael Greene, Walt gave him an "open book" to do what he wanted. "He told him, 'Find songwriters, do whatever.' (Walt) was a creative man and he understood and appreciated creativity."

The *Cinderella* score, featuring Perry Como's million-selling, "A Dream Is a Wish Your Heart Makes," backed with his Oscar-nominated "Bibbidi-Bobbidi-Boo," plus the Andrews Sisters' "The Work Song," followed, with the soundtrack album selling 750,000 copies the first year. At one point, all three were on the Hit Parade, with both of Como's singles sharing the two top spots.

Fred brought in songwriter Sammy Fain to work on *Alice in Wonderland*, resulting in Fain/Hilliard's "I'm Late" and "Very Good Advice." The David/Livingston/Hoffman team also hit with "The Unbirthday Song," and the entire score was lauded in *Time* and *Newsweek*.

Next came *Peter Pan*, in 1953, with "You Can Fly! You Can Fly! You Can Fly!" and "The Second Star to the Right," both by Sammy Cahn and Sammy Fain, and "Never Smile at a Crocodile," by Frank Churchill and Jack Lawrence, among others.

Fred also brought in outside songs from his regular contacts among songwriters, such as Harold (Hal) Spina (*Annie Doesn't Live Here Anymore*) and the late, great Bob Russell ("He Ain't Heavy, He's My Brother," "Don't Get Around Much Anymore," "You Came a Long Way from St. Louis").

According to Lila Blackburn-Eubanks, Fred's head secretary from 1950 to 1954, "his door was always open to new people." She recalled the time a young Cajun man happened by the office to pick up his date, started strumming on his zither and singing "Shrimp boats is a-comin', there's dancin' tonight!" Fred brought the tune to Paul Weston at Capitol Records to finish. "Shrimp Boats" became a #2 hit for Jo Stafford with husband Weston and his Orchestra in 1951.

Although he was not there to see the movie releases, Fred worked with artist Peggy Lee on the score for *Lady and the Tramp* (1955), and worked on *Sleeping Beauty* (1959). In 1952, he suffered a major heart attack, but after a short hiatus, continued his work. In 1954, desirous of more autonomy as a publisher, Fred resigned to form his own company, Fred Raphael Music, with producer Joe Pasternak and songwriters Jack Lawrence and Sylvia Fine, who was the songwriter wife of Danny Kaye.

Among the new company's successes were Jack Lawrence's Oscar-nominated "Hold My Hand," from the movie *Susan Slept Here*; Ernest Gold's soundtrack score from *On the Beach*; *Anatomy of a Murder*, produced in partnership with Otto Preminger and featuring Duke Ellington's first film score; and *The Five Pennies*, featuring Bobby Troup, Ray Anthony, and the "Five Pennies Saints" duet with Danny Kaye and Louis Armstrong. There was also Otto Preminger's *St. Joan* in 1957. Perhaps best known was the groundbreaking jazz score for *Man with the Golden Arm*, written after Fred brought fledgling composer Elmer Bernstein to meet Preminger.

Fred also formed Dena Music with Kaye, Golden Music with Ernest Gold, and London Music with Bobby Troup. The Troup-penned "Their Hearts Were Full of Spring" was recorded by the Four Freshmen, and then by the Beach Boys, first as "A Young Man Is Gone" (about the death of James Dean), and later in its original form for their 1967 live album.

Q: What was the Hollywood music business like in those days?
A: Well, the late Lee Zhito, who founded and edited *Billboard* for fifty years, called the Sunset and Vine of the era "a golden musical cross-roads." You had ABC, NBC, Capitol Records, Music City, all around there. It was adventurous and cheap to gamble, and fun. Or as Mitch Miller told me, "No lawyers!" The late Seymour Heller, Frankie Laine's manager, told me how he hired an actual mule train to drive down Sunset to get disk jockey Al Jarvis's attention! There were famous song pluggers who told tall tales just to get in to see publishers. Stan Ross, who cofounded Gold Star Studios, tells me he quit the business when it stopped being fun. I get the feeling that it was kind of like a Wild West, the way the '60s felt to my generation.
Q: Your dad signifies the transition where the American songbook and the songwriter-publisher model gradually made some room for the emerging rock 'n' roll sounds that started showing up in 1950s films and TV shows.
A: Well, Dad loved pop music best, but he saw the writing on the wall, and he got into very early rock. His catalogue included such songs as "Hot Rod Rock," by Hal Levy and Alexander Courage (who wrote the theme for *Star Trek* and the movie, *Shake, Rattle and Rock!*), and

so much else. "Hot Rod Rock" was featured in the 1957 movie, *Hot Rod Girl*, starring Lori Nelson and Chuck Connors. And "Graduation Dance," from 1957. I also found in his administrator's office, a 45 rpm on Cadence Records, 1956, called "Stop! Look and Run!" with Alan Freed and his Rock and Roll Band.

Q: He also had a relationship with jazz scores.

A: That's where he really was ahead of his time, with these dark, moody, cutting-edge jazz scores—typical of that late '50s era. Like "Jocko's Theme," from the 1957 movie scored by Kenyon Hopkins, *The Strange One*, which starred a young Ben Gazzara and George Peppard. And Leith Stevens' jazz score for *Hell to Eternity*, whose cast included Jeffrey Hunter, David Janssen, Vic Damone, Patricia Owens, and Richard Eyer. Dad worked with Stevens on a ton of TV shows. This all followed *Man with the Golden Arm*.

Q: Did he ever make any attempts or inroads to embrace the music of the mid-'60s?

A: Well, in 1964 to 1965 I was in film school at UCLA, and my classmates were Jim Morrison and Ray Manzarek, who were just forming the Doors. Dad was in management by then. He said, "Ask them if they have a manager." That excited me that he was interested in my peers. But Ray disappointed me and said they had someone acting as manager. Dad would have been great.

Q: I know your dad had a hand in helping a young Frank Sinatra into the entertainment business.

A: Mother says the first time Dad ever saw Frank at some street concert, he said, "That guy's going to be a big star someday. He has a fantastic voice." Dad had this knack for spotting talent early. According to my mother, Dad chose Frank Sinatra and the Hoboken Boys to be on *The Major Bowes Amateur Hour*—which was kind of the forerunner of *The Ed Sullivan Show*—after seeing him at that street concert. They won, and Sinatra went on to pursue a musical career.

Q: Your father was also around for the growth of the music-on-screen relationship.

A: I think he had a real role in it. As you know, he started out at the Capitol Theater—then owned by Metro Goldwyn Mayer—so one of his tasks was to find classical music and buy synch rights for the Metro movies. And he taught himself all about music law. Mom says studios had large banks of lawyers for that! So when he went to work for Bourne and Shapiro-Bernstein in New York, he got the idea to do movie songs—to get songwriters to write them. That's what got him out to Hollywood. He worked with RKO, 20th Century Fox, MGM, Republic Studios, and Desilu, at Paramount. I hear there's correspondence in the David O. Selznick files with Dad trying to arrange rights to adapt Debussy's "Afternoon of a Fawn" for 20th Century Fox's 1948 movie, *Portrait of Jennie*.

Q: And his contributions and work on behalf of Walt Disney were very important.

A: Before he went to Disney, it never occurred to them that you could make money publishing your own music! They were just giving it away to Saintly-Joy and Bourne. No movie studio published its own scores then. The late Hal Spina had a funny story about being on staff at Irving Berlin Co., and being given fifty pages of Mickey Mouse music to make a song from! Dad made Disney Music a real contender.

And look at what happened with those 1950s Disney soundtracks. Not just the hit songs, but the RCA *Cinderella* album was #1 on the *Billboard* pop charts—something few children's albums ever achieve—and an Oscar nominee. The *Alice in Wonderland* score was a cover story for *Time* and *Newsweek*.

Q: How was your dad as a promoter?

A: You're right—publishers then had to promote as well as get the records. My brother Byron says that *The Jack Benny Show* was one of the biggest plugs you could get at the time. If Dennis Day sang your song, it would be a hit. Dad (and Phil Kahl, his plugger) got him to do "A Dream Is a Wish Your Heart Makes," and it took off from there. Byron used to hang around the office as a teenager, and he remembers Sammy Fain—whose "I Can Dream, Can't I?" was a monster hit—coming in and saying, "Fred, between you and me, we control two-thirds of the music business right here in this room!"

Q: Let's talk about the non-soundtrack Disney hits. Did he work with writers?

A: Yes. He had all these contacts from his New York days, and he knew music. Mother says when a song became public domain, he would take it to a writer and ask him to write a lyric to it. He loved Chopin's "Etude No. 3 in E, Opus 10," and took it to songwriter Bob Russell. Then Russell and Paul Weston turned it into "No Other Love," a 1950 hit for Jo Stafford and Paul Weston. Mother says she would scream at Dad to put his name on the songs, to take credit! Everybody else did. He never would—he kept saying, "I'm not a writer, I'm a publisher."

Q: The music and film worlds were a lot different than today. Tell me about that period.

A: It was just so much more informal. I remember Hal Spina telling me that Dad asked him to come over one night and bring "a couple of things." That's how they did it in those days, very small-time, very social, lunches, dinners, cocktail parties. Spina said actress Signe Hasso and Peter Lorre were there. Dad picked out an "unlikely" Italian tango, and asked Spina to come up with a lyric. Spina was stumped, but, by chance, good old Bob Russell happened by his house that night, and had it by morning. That became "Would I Love You," a million seller for Patti Page in 1950.

You didn't have "appointments" per se. For instance, Jay Lowy, former president of NARAS, told me that they had A&R days at Capitol Records where you could come and play your demos, and executives—Voyle Gilmore, Dave Cavanaugh—would pick them up and even pick the artists on the spot.

Q: Did your dad ever work with public domain material, a common practice with songs that were old enough, not protected, and open for use and exploitation?

A: All the time. Mom and Dad were in Italy in 1956 after he formed his own company, and he heard this great folk song on the radio, "Guaglione" (which means "street boy" or "street man"), and arranged for U.S. rights to it. It's been recorded by *everybody*, from Dean Martin—who had a hit with it as "The Man with the Mandolino" in 1956—to Perez Prado, whose version you probably heard in the Guinness Ale TV commercial in 1994. The song was also featured in the soundtrack of *The Talented Mr. Ripley* in 1999. It's become our biggest moneymaker!

Q: What was your dad's relationship with Walt Disney like?

A: It was good. Right after "Mule Train" hit, according to my brother, Dad went to Walt and asked him if he'd heard that new #1 song. Walt said, "Yes, I hear it all the time." Dad said, "That's our song!" Walt threw his arms around him and said, "Keep it up!" One time he even said to Dad, "Without you, we wouldn't have any of this!" Walt didn't know music—everyone said that—but he trusted creativity.

Q: Man, I've heard some tales, from old school music veterans, and innuendo about Walt and his company . . . How did it affect your dad?

A: Well, Walt himself was OK—he was the creative part of Disney and had little to do with the business. But those around him were jealous of Dad's relationship with him. That's why Dad's office was in

Hollywood, far away from the studios, because one CEO didn't want him too close. They would "forget" to invite him to meetings. His secretaries told us they would call him "Walt's boy."

Q: And what about the then-alleged anti-Semitic climate at that studio? Is it really true some people at Disney got mad when your dad took a day off for a Jewish holiday?

A: It all ties in with the way they treated him. My brother says that one Disney executive—who is still on the Board, by the way—called the house screaming at the top of his lungs because Dad wasn't in the office on Yom Kippur, and threatening, "If you don't work on the High Holidays, you're fired!" They called him "the company Jew" behind his back. He would come home so shaken, Mother says.

When I talked by phone to Mitch Miller in 2000 for an interview, he even offered a funny but sad observation about visiting the Disney lot with Dad decades earlier, which I don't want to repeat here. Mitch remembers Dad as very low-key, never raised his voice. They made his life miserable.

Q: How did he finally leave?

A: He was making millions for Disney, but was just kept on salary. He asked for stock, but Disney did not give stock away. So he asked for a partnership, and he was turned down. Around our house, stories about Disney firings were legion—Disney had fired an animator just a year before his retirement. Daddy was afraid that would happen to him. So he left. Walt protested—he offered Dad a lot of money to stay. We might have become very rich!

Q: And then he went into business on his own with Fred Raphael Music?

A: Yes. He really worked very hard. He had all these great movie scores: Duke Ellington's *Anatomy of a Murder*; *On the Beach*, by Ernest Gold, with the wonderful "Waltzing Matilda" woven in; the Preminger films.

But it was bad timing. By the late '50s, artists were demanding their own publishing, and so were the studios. One of the big things publishers still made money on at the time was sheet music sales, but when rock 'n' roll really hit, it killed that. So this all became the death knell for the small, independent publisher like my father.

Barbara Bireley Haskell, a former secretary of Dad's and the wife of arranger Jimmy Haskell, said it bothered him—"dealing with schmucks"—that it didn't happen for him the way it had with Disney. She'd come into his office one day and his fist was down on the desk—next to the golden arm logo of the company he'd made with Elmer Bernstein.

He had to fight with Otto Preminger and Frank Sinatra to retain the rights to the score of *Man with the Golden Arm*. After he'd introduced Bernstein to Preminger, worked the score, and gotten a cut with Billy May! Sinatra finally said, "Oh, let Freddie have it! A background score has no hit potential!" Of course, it became the first-ever background score to be a hit! (*laughs*). It was the first jazz movie score.

When I was arranging the tribute to my Dad for the Vine Street dinner in 2000, Jack Lawrence, composer of all these standards ("Linda," "Tenderly," "If I Didn't Care," "No One but You," "Sleepy Lagoon"), wrote to me: "Although your dad had many good contacts in the business, it was still a tough row to hoe . . . getting records in that world of payola was difficult if you didn't have the wherewithal to schmear. I helped with what I could, and when I managed to get a couple of songs into my friend Harriet Parsons' film, *Susan Slept Here*, naturally, I turned them over to Fred Raphael Music. And we almost got the Oscar that year for "Hold My Hand!" It lost to "Three Coins in a Fountain." After all, we couldn't match the 20th Century Fox campaign and publicity."

Q: Your dad seemed to be such an honest person, from what I've researched.

A: Yes, Dad would get purple with fury if anyone suggested something shady! He was once offered ten thousand dollars and he brought it home, because he felt it would be wrong to deny us all that kind of money, but Mom talked him out of it. My brother says he once got infuriated when one of his pluggers accepted a bottle of champagne. He had old-fashioned integrity.

Bob Grabeau, the onetime "demo king" of Sunset and Vine, said he was one man you never heard making any kind of a deal that would hurt anybody.

And he was helpful. The late Tess Russell, formerly head of the Singers Society, told me how Dad encouraged her when she first started out as a record librarian with DJ and talent scout Al Jarvis. She was lost, and Dad told her, "Not to worry. I used to be in radio. I will give you all kinds of ideas." And when she got engaged to composer George Russell, Dad left a record of Jo Stafford's "No Other Love" on her desk, with a note saying, "This could be your theme song." The song was inscribed on her wedding band.

Q: Tell me what you learned in your research of the last couple of decades and conducting a series of published interviews with the real music industry veterans of the '40s and '50s.

A: That it was hard, but exciting. There were no playlists. If a disc jockey liked your song, he would play it. Sessions were live—artists like Dean Martin would cut an album in three to four days, in between golf games. Berle Adams, who's done it all—founded Mercury Records, been an MCA executive and a publisher—says that outside of "the big guns at Chappell, everybody was scuffling." He told me, "You were trying to get the good writers to come to you, to get the record company guy and the artist to like the song . . . you had to romance the guy . . . take him to dinner . . . talk to people you wanted to befriend and introduce them to the songs and hope they'd record them. You had no automatic entrée to people."

That tells me everything about the way my Dad worked. That's also why we always had artists at our house for dinner, and why Dad was always at Nickodell's having lunch with somebody. That was such a great place, with its red vinyl booths and dignified waiters. I'd get all excited as these guys in three-piece suits with cigars stopped by the table to talk to my Dad—A&R guys, from Capitol up the street. We went to Laguna for Thanksgiving with the Disney songwriters and their families. My parents would go out to openings at the Coconut Grove, to see Lena Horne open.

Q: What is a Hollywood memory you have of your dad, the music, and the movies?

A: His sweet letters to me at camp on *Alice* stationery, with enclosed sheet music for the girls, 8 x 10s of him at Disney—or back to WHN Radio in the '40s, holding the mike for Ed Wynn, or Fanny Hurst, or Kitty Carlisle—just getting to be a part of that world. The Academy was on Sunset Boulevard, and our family went to premieres there. Dad would also take me to MGM or to Republic Studios, or to RKO, where I got to sit and watch *Susan Slept Here* being filmed with Debbie Reynolds in 1954.

That's the kind of father he was. He involved the whole family in the business. From the time we were very young, he would bring home demos to spin, and ask, "Well, kids, is that a hit or a miss?" I can still see the script for *The Man with the Golden Arm*, stamped with the golden arm logo, lying around the house. And we all always followed the music.

＊

Fred Raphael opened Disney Music Company in 1949. Fred Raphael Music is still active, in Cathedral City, California and is administered by MizMo Music in Burbank, California.

Judy Raphael attended Hamilton High School in West Los Angeles. She received a B.A. in Theater Arts at UCLA, and did graduate work in film from 1963–1965, studying with director Jean Renoir and documentary filmmaker Alberto Cavalcanti. She has published works in *L.A. Weekly*, *Los Angeles Times*, *Los Angeles Herald-Examiner*, *Los Angeles Reader*, *Los Angeles Daily News*, as well as *Music Connection* and *New Country Magazine*, and is a contributor to *HollyWord*, a spoken word album compilation.

ANDREW LOOG OLDHAM

ANDREW LOOG OLDHAM, AUTHOR of two autobiographies, *Stoned* and
2Stoned, was a featured interview subject in my book, *This Is Rebel Music*.

ALO was the manager, producer, and publisher of the Rolling Stones,
their rise to superstardom choreographed, during their riotous 1963–1967
years, under his watchful direction. Please read Andrew's liner notes on
the Stones' album jackets from that epochal period.

Andrew earned honorary Hollywood citizen status many years ago just
for producing and guiding the Rolling Stones' recording output from RCA
Studios on Sunset Boulevard, in addition to his extensive music and movie
knowledge of the lure and lore of Hollywood.

In 1997, the popular band The Verve took Oldham's original release of
"The Last Time," from *The Rolling Stones Songbook* by the Andrew Oldham
Orchestra, and looped its backing tracks to inform their own "Bittersweet
Symphony" chart hit. On February 5, 2006, at Superbowl XL, the Seattle
Seahawks entered the football field to the taped sounds of "Bittersweet
Symphony." And the Rolling Stones provided the half-time entertainment.

Since 2004, Andrew has hosted his own weekly four-hour show, airing
twice each weekend, on Sirius Satellite Radio's Channel 25, *Underground
Garage*, the channel produced by E. Street Band guitarist and cast member
of *The Sopranos*, "Little Steven" Van Zandt.

Andrew Loog Oldham giving the keynote address at the
New Music Reporter Convention, Roosevelt Hotel, Hollywood,
California, March 2003. Photo by Heather Harris.

Andrew was a keynote speaker in Austin, Texas at the 2004 South by Southwest music conference, his appearance sponsored by the British Phonograph Industry. The same year, he lectured and gave a wonderful Question and Answer discussion in Europe, the United States, and Canada while screening the Rolling Stones' 1965 black-and-white tour documentary, *Charlie Is My Darling*, which featured Andrew in a prominent role.

Also in 2004, instrumental tracks from the album, *The Rolling Stones Songbook* by the Andrew Loog Oldham Orchestra—now rereleased by Universal Records—were used in the critically-acclaimed new BBC drama, *The Long Firm*, while in 2005, Oldham's production of the Stones' "Complicated" was featured in a national television advertising campaign for Lexmark. Additionally, an excerpt from the ALO-produced Rolling Stones recording of "Play with Fire" was played in a March 2005 episode of *American Dreams*.

Andrew is a dear friend, walking pop culture historian, a product of all the sounds and films he has digested, and a teacher.

After *This Is Rebel Music* was published, Andrew gave me some advice that he actually received from actor and author Terrence Stamp when his own *Stoned* volume was in the marketplace. "In the future, more about you and less about them." And, as *Hollywood Shack Job* was being constructed and written, Andrew then personally offered, "It's about time you learned—instead of watching the movie, be in the movie."

Visit his website at www.andrewloogoldham.com.

Q: When did you first see and hear rock 'n' roll on the big screen?

A: The first movie that did me in was *Moulin Rouge* in 1953, '54, '55. I got a guy to take me in the front of the theater, because a minor had to be accompanied by an adult. I mean, I saw one of the first films in Cinemascope with all these women with their legs kicking up—if you look carefully it can make you gay! It was traumatic!

Q: In your autobiographies you've cited *The Man with the Golden Arm*, *Expresso Bongo*, and *Sweet Smell of Success* as seminal mixtures of movies and music.

A: And the *Johnny Staccato* TV show with John Cassavetes was fantastic. Plus, *The Girl Can't Help It* film, but there's no soundtrack album to it. Amazing. The Gene Vincent and Eddie Cochran sequences aren't just slotted-in videos. I saw it before I saw Eddie play live. I saw them on-screen, and later at a personal appearance. Both galvanized me. Dark-haired guys didn't interest me, only blondes, because I could be it.

Also the main thing that drew me in for *The Man with the Golden Arm* was designer Saul Bass. If you think of a film, he was like the label of the film. You can put a lot of shit in a movie like *Walk on the Wild Side* after a Saul Bass credit. Movie posters and film graphics also had an impact on me. You could basically say to the world, "Hold whatever plans you've got for me, I have plans of my own because I've seen the visuals." Mind you, *The Man with the Golden Arm* blew my mind—drug addiction, and it's only two or three years later I see Ray Charles huddled on a rock at the Antibes Jazz Festival shivering from smack. So I'm getting all these early warnings, but never fell into smack until my own leisure time. I never nodded on the job. And Kim Novak was pure heroin to look at. Even at that age you knew that. We didn't know Frank (Sinatra) was doing it in one take. It was all pretty good. And the music was the thing, and you get the idea the film was cut to the music.

Expresso Bongo had career impact on me. It was subject specific to the world I was drafted into. My mind was really blown by seeing a Rolls Royce on television, and later taking the Rolls Royce home. My mother took me to the theater and we went to see *Expresso Bongo*. The Laurence Harvey part was played by Paul Scofield. Two years before the movie was made. The Cliff Richard part was played by an English Tab Hunter type thing, which is why it has this *Bye Bye Birdie* connotation. "You mean I'm not the only one thinking like this? You can actually do this?"

The film was like a having a version you could take home forever. I liked "From now on, Bongo, you get fifty percent of everything you earn."

It showed you how to do it. I took it chapter and verse. He walks in and gets a deal for Bongo. I walk in and get a deal for the Rolling Stones. It's as simple as that. See, the stage play only has religious moments. The film was the floor plan.

With *Sweet Smell of Success*, I didn't mind the jazz. But I liked the energy of Tony Curtis. I love the evilness of Burt Lancaster and the energy and beauty of Susan Harrison. The Brill Building. The dialogue. I wanted to be in the industry after seeing that movie, and I had written a song earlier. The dialogue from *Expresso Bongo*, the dialogue from *Sweet Smell of Success*, I knew I could handle that. I remember thinking jazz and fashion were the only cool things on earth.

Q: I know what impact movie posters and film had on you as a budding music producer. You nicked the name "John Paul Jones" from the Warner Bros. film with Robert Stack, and gave it to a young musician you were working with, John Baldwin, who eventually became a member of Led Zeppelin after doing some session and arranging work for you.

A: I had no idea that John Paul Jones actually existed. I never saw the movie—*Untamed Youth*. Great poster. That's got an Eddie Cochran song in it. Mamie Van Doren. I wasn't the type of geezer who would see a movie and then immediately go out and buy the soundtrack or the title song on 45 rpm. You're speaking of a time period where girls were mostly the buying public. Although I did go to the Chelsea football ground. As far as I remember, it would have been too "Nancy" for a guy to have even had one of those little ten pound plastic record players. I think the first record that I really got impressed with was the LP, *Beauty and the Beat*. George Shearing Quintet and Peggy Lee. It was cinematic.

Q: What about Elvis Presley on-screen?

A: Man of hope, dreams, and glory. You must remember that Elvis only toured the U.K. on the screen and on vinyl; therefore, he had the first and last word and the best audio and lighting. This was also the era when TV was a black-and-white affair—afforded by the few—that ran from 5 P.M. to 10 P.M. and did not feature the likes of Elvis. I think *King Creole*, *Jailhouse Rock*, and *Flaming Star* were best; I loved the interplay; loved him with Carolyn Jones in *King Creole*. Elvis seemed to have these great confrontations with older ladies in his flicks, Lizabeth Scott in *Loving You*. The images that I remember best are Elvis singing "Crawfish" on a balcony in New Orleans, which is just classic; singing "Baby, I Don't Care" poolside in *Jailhouse Rock* in those great Zoot Suit pants, cable-knit sweater with the pure Armani neck, and those black-and-white loafers to die for. Elvis gave us hope and attitude.

Q: Let's discuss British rock music TV shows in the '60s, like *Ready, Steady, Go!*

A: By this time I was working. *RSG!* represented the time when we were in the business we wanted to be in and *RSG!* on a Friday night, in the Green Room, was the meeting place of all those similarly blessed. Vicki Wickham booked the show from late 1963 to December 1967. Michael Lindsay-Hogg directed it, and tried new techniques like stop action and freeze frame while the band was on camera. Save to say I still communicate with both of them so that tells you the lot. You were dealing with nice people. None of the people had an agenda. Their background was not really show business. They had no attachment to it. We were still in an era of "I'll help you. I'll give you a leg up. You're not that good but you're passable. I'll take pleasure and I'll use you being around." On the show, the visuals propelled the music.

Q: Were there any early Rolling Stones TV appearances that stand out in your mind?

A: There are a couple of amazing performances by Mick Jagger where I was probably too socially intertwined and pissed, whereas the *Arthur Haynes Show* with them doing "You Better Move On" was one of the most sexual. Black-and-white definitely helped. Less zits. Black-and-white left more for the imagination. Mick Jagger had a relationship with the camera. He must have. Who else could have gotten away with those clothes?

Q: What about *Top of the Pops*? Acts plugging their new singles.

A: Hated the show, its very idea and the people who deigned to run it. It does not work to have snobs running a stall.

Q: What do you remember about being on the set of *The Ed Sullivan Show* when your band appeared a few times?

A: Preproduction where you let Sullivan, or Robert Precht, know to start with. One of the things I was trying to get over with was letting them know that you don't film the bass string and guitar solo. It was the rhythm. So one wouldn't look stupid. Because if you're being filmed stupid, you feel stupid. So one doesn't need the Rolling Stones feeling stupid. They worked good on color. They were getting loaded, they would go shopping, and it worked. Keith's army jacket, Brian's red cords, and his shoes. There you have the happy times of drugs. The songs selected were usually the singles that were just being released. "Let's Spend the Night Together" for me is still one of the best tracks they ever cut, 'cause it doesn't do anything—it just sits there.

Q: You've seen and heard a lot of the songs you produced for the Rolling Stones from 1964 to 1967 used in movies, and now soundtrack albums and other new formats.

A: First great use of "Satisfaction" was in *Apocalypse Now*, with a young Laurence Fishburne on the boat. I knew from Allen Klein it was licensed and a payday.

Q: Director Hal Ashby has to be noted for his use of Stones music in *Coming Home*, including your productions of "Out of Time," "Ruby Tuesday," and a cover of "My Girl."

A: "Out of Time" I love. It's used twice in the movie. On the initial recording it's Mick Jagger pulling off Jimmy Ruffin. It was also Mick's first production with me of singer Chris Farlowe for my label, Immediate.

The only reason we got to produce was to do things that the Beatles hadn't done. At the time, we all felt we could do nothing wrong. I do remember—we all have our way of looking at it, survival mode—I am sure I reached Hal Ashby outside the cinema. I got (producer) Lou Adler, who knew him, to connect me. "I want you to hear me while I still have a lump in my throat. Great. You just blew me away . . ."

Not like I had never been moved. I've had a moment that will be with me forever. The double use of "Out of Time" as a political statement and a love statement was just incredible. Hal was on location and I reached him. If a piece of art has affected you like that, you either want the person to see your eyes or hear the sound of your voice, and I was able to do it. "My Girl" is only just marginally worse than the Mamas and the Papas version. Maybe he got a rate when using songs.

I remember the sessions for *Aftermath*, where "I Am Waiting" sprang from. There's incredible clarity to what they were doing. It was like a linear thing. "Filmic." They were vivid, and the key to that vividness was Brian Jones. The organ on "She Smiled Sweetly" by Brian is just amazing. I like "She Smiled Sweetly" more than "Lady Jane" and "Ruby Tuesday." "Sweetly" was boy/girl, living on the same floor. Whereas both those other songs have a *To the Manor Born* quality to them. Trying to write and evoke. And Mick's vocals . . . Remember, he's an actor. He can't sing. He acts the words. There you go. *Between the Buttons* and *Aftermath*, without a doubt quite a few harried moments. And we did it in Hollywood at RCA.

Aftermath works. They wrote every song on the record. It's like when you go see a stage show or see a movie that works, one of the keys is "beside the fact that it's not me onstage, that's me." So there is a sense of humor with the songs and the records. But not a lot of the other stuff. My life would never be that grungy. "Paint It Black" in *Full Metal Jacket* was terrific. I knew it was gonna be in it. "Paint It Black" was also in *Devil's Advocate*. It closes it.

The session for "Paint It Black" was nearly not done! Bill (Wyman) started futzing around with the pedals of the Hammond B3 organ, basically imitating Eric Easton (The Stones early comanager), who used to play organ on the pier at Blackpool. And Brian's sitar on the song. It was a visual instrument. The fun times were the work. We're in Hollywood. Some of Hollywood came through the door and I'm one of the conduits dragging it in.

Q: Did you love Scorsese's *Mean Streets*? You had a song production, "Tell Me," in the movie.

A: Well first, there was Phil Spector's "Be My Baby" at the opening. You never hear these songs originally thinking they will be at the cinema. Yet, it's cinematic within its own refined audio. I mean, I had a relationship with the catalogue of Phil. One time we were at the studio on Ivar in Hollywood, and someone was delivering Hal Blaine's drums! This is real life! We're in Hollywood! This is life in heaven and we're in Hollywood. And Hal Blaine's drums at the beginning of that song were monstrous. *Mean Streets* was given to me in a culture that didn't behave like that. "Tell Me," which I did with the Stones, was used. I remember being flattered, but not worth holding a scorecard. I remember it standing up to "Be My Baby."

We did it at Regent Street Studio. Keith's guitar leaked throughout the bass drum because there weren't enough microphones to go around. And you have to remember it was basically the first song Mick and Keith wrote together that they recorded for themselves. "Tell Me" was sexy. I just remember the relationship between the drum kit and the acoustic guitar. You could only overdub once more, mono to mono, or otherwise you'd get ala "Under the Boardwalk." OK. You can hear the leakage. Martin Scorsese knows how to put music in his movies. "Long Long While" is in another Scorsese movie, *Casino* or *Goodfellas*. I thought it was amazing. It was a B-side originally. A great vocal. Bette Midler should do it. Jack Nitzsche is on it.

Hey—it's when everything worked. We had a set-up and nothing basically had to be adjusted. We had a huge sigh of relief through those two records, 'cause Mick and Keith had passed the audition with the rest of the band in terms of writing. I still get impacted when I hear the songs on-screen. When something that you made has another perfect use.

Also, I wasn't surprised when our friend Jack Nitzsche had movie score success with *Performance* and his other pieces. Early on, his single, "The Lonely Surfer" was cinematic in arrangement and production.

Q: What are your thoughts on *The T.A.M.I. Show*? The Rolling Stones, Chuck Berry, James Brown, the Beach Boys, Marvin Gaye, Jan and Dean, Lesley Gore, the Supremes, the Barbarians, Gerry and the Pacemakers, Billy J. Kramer and the Dakotas, filmed in October of 1964. Many people were exposed to these groups and bands in the movie theater when the show had its initial release. You met Lou Adler that

Keith Richards and Jack Nitzsche rehearsing for *The T.A.M.I. Show*, Santa Monica Civic Auditorium, California, 1964. Photo courtesy of Steve Binder.

day, who managed and produced Jan and Dean, a close friendship that continues forty years later. *T.A.M.I.* was filmed in "Electronovision."

A: Why it works for me is the fear and loathing in Santa Monica. There you go. Come on man, it's a magic moment. The Stones were becoming successful and getting good, and—wait a minute—we gotta follow James Brown? The other insult was every other British act got twenty-five grand each there, and we thought we had some Stones muscle. But it was a package deal with General Artists Corporation. Seeing the Motown acts was terrific. Seeing Jack Nitzsche and Dave Hassinger. It was the film within the film. Isn't it nice to be in this business? Everyone is working together for one thing. The Beach Boys' shirts were horrendous. Isn't it nice we're all here? Bill Sargent did it. He did the black-and-white Electronovision *Harlow* with actress Carol Linley.

Q: Didn't you try and hustle Carol in London once?

A: I once met Carol at a hotel in London, and my only way to chat her up was to record her. I was besotted with this woman. I will never forget the way she laughed at me, as if she knew what I was about. I asked her if she could sing.

Q: There's an early film of the Rolling Stones done in Ireland circa 1965, *Charlie Is My Darling*.

A: It's the Rolling Stones, we have to make a movie, let's get in the mood. Three or four days in the mood for business, Peter Whitehead filmed it.

And Peter did our video, "Have You Seen Your Mother, Baby, Standing in the Shadow?" live at the Royal Albert Hall. It's an extension of having to be involved with *Charlie Is My Darling*.

I was at the time starting Immediate Records, dressing up in a suit. I was Stephen Boyd in *The Oscar*, with the De Voss collar. Videos were a way of keeping the Stones focused and commercial. You do have to create work for the act. And sometimes you deserve to be filmed.

Showing *Charlie Is My Darling* in 2004, at film festivals in Scotland and Ireland, was an interesting learning curve. It really accentuated the dividing line between the two parts of the '60s. The natural black-and-white, speed-propelled burst of innocence, versus the " been there, got that" slightly jaded Cinemascope and color wide-screen, wide-hatted, bigger-shaded affair that was the "kandy-kolored," acid-enhanced royal affair that became rock pomp. *Charlie* captures the end of the innocence and is quite darling and sweet for just that.

Q: You also participated in the movie *Tonite Let's All Make Love in London*. Did you, or do you, like being on camera?

A: I do now, because I understand the game and the food machine. At that time all food did was give me spots. If you look at the culture we had, one of them was quite Dick Lester-ish. There were some Stones songs, not Stones records. I bankrolled it for Immediate because I got the soundtrack.

Q: The Monterey International Pop Festival? You were on the board of directors and at the festival.

A: We had an office on Sunset Boulevard. I remember having a quick chat with Steve Stills about management of Buffalo Springfield. Lou Adler asked me, what acts did they need from England. I smiled and said, "Easy. The Who and Jimi Hendrix." Lou said to John Phillips, "That's exactly what McCartney said—who do we call?" "I'll do the Who, Kit [Lambert] and Chris [Stamp]." Monterey also meant to me another reason to buy a new wardrobe. Lou and I also flew to San Francisco to explain the festival to [writer] Ralph J. Gleason and to return to L.A. with his approval, which would help us deal with the very necessary groups from the Bay Area. The new San Francisco acts. I didn't like the bands; to me they weren't stars. Unoriginal, fueled by drugs and liquor. I couldn't understand the attraction. I like my stars to behave like stars.

Q: Did any memorable TV shows or documentaries—then or now—have a big impact on you where music was involved?

A: Adam Faith on John Freeman's *Face to Face*, a U.K., in-depth, in your face interview program, not unlike *HARDtalk*, that featured the very eloquent John Freeman and, in this particular interview, Adam Faith, showing his street smarts and standing up for all of us. Anything the journalist Kenneth Alsop hosted. *Free Speech*, an ITV political left versus right show that helped you form some opinions. I was thirteen when that show came on. More recently I was bowled over by the BBC's *Real Blow-Up*, put together so well by Elaine Shepherd. Just a wonderful look at the '50s and '60s and the real art behind the photographic art, music, and film. Most of the documentaries end up fucking over the music.

Q: You really liked the movie *Almost Famous*. I seem to recall something you said, that it was really good because you weren't around for that decade.

A: I kinda missed a professional '70s, so (writer-director) Cameron Crowe filled in the gaps in a wonderful George Cukor/*Terms of Endearment* kind of way.

Q: The music or documentary DVD product. Do you feel all the data and added info packed into these products "deconstructs" or lessens the vibe, or the original statement?

A: DVDs and the extra data are just finding their way. They'll be winners and losers but in total we'll be the winners. Anyway the worst of it is still better than the E! Channel.

Q: Do you own or listen to soundtrack albums? Any favorites?

A: Right now, the movie I saw last night, Spike Lee's *25th Hour* with Edward Norton. Great hair, Ed. Anyway, the music by Terence Blanchard is superb. See if you can find the soundtrack of Robert Towne's *Tequila Sunrise*. Dave Grusin, with a great Duran Duran track that never appeared anywhere else.

I think the best James Bond title song was Duran Duran's "A View to a Kill." I love their videos.

One of the reasons that the theme song of *A View to a Kill* worked was that James Bond—to those in the know at the time—would always appear out of date. But Duran Duran hold themselves down so the foot fits the shoe. They measured themselves well for what it's all about, whereas Madonna did not and neither did Sheena Easton.

I love "Goldfinger," sung by Shirley Bassey. I knew her. Most of the time it's the right person, right gig. It's a club. I like the Carly Simon one, "Nobody Does It Better."

Paul McCartney, Capitol Records Studio, Hollywood, California, 1989.
Photo by Henry Diltz.

And I do like the Paul McCartney thing, "Live and Let Die." It was very clever and Paul did his homework. He had this and that to remind him of earlier things with Bond. He had the tonal space. I like the title tune Garbage did.

One of my favorite videos is the Enriqué Iglesias song with Mickey Rourke in the video. It was almost his comeback. A white guy out of Miami did it. The first music video was "True Love" from *High Society*, with Bing Crosby and Grace Kelly. I like the Who track on the *CSI* TV show.

Q: Did you see the Jim Jarmusch Neil Young tour documentary, *Year of the Horse*?

A: Yes I did. In that style that was accomplished for me by *Sexy Beast* and *Breathless*, the Richard Gere one, and scenes of *Reservoir Dogs*. *Pulp Fiction* in twenty years time will be *The Godfather*. Quentin T. was the right guy with the right movie. John Travolta was a great casting choice. The music—he raised the bar and then he stretched the bar.

Q: *West Side Story*. Blow you away?

A: On-screen, the credits; onstage, the very idea; and in both, George Chakiris.

Q: What rock and pop celluloid appearances hit home?

A: Gene Vincent, Little Richard, and Eddie Cochran in *The Girl Can't Help It*; the aforementioned Elvis appearances; Paul Jones in *Privilege* I liked at the time; *Stardust* with David Essex; Johnny Hallyday in *Man on a Train*; David Bowie in *Blue Jean*; and Sting on a scooter in *Quadrophenia*. I love U2's video shot on the roof in Los Angeles, "Where the Streets Have No Name." That's incredible. The way it was cut. There's a way of putting film, a way of being ahead of the beat, otherwise it's not gonna work. I love the Warren Beatty scenes in Madonna's *Truth or Dare*.

Q: *Blow-Up?* The Yardbirds are in it.

A: It was OK. That's a painting. How can I love them when none of them manage to make these people have the rhythm and the resonance that they had on a record or onstage? Willie Nelson in *Wag the Dog*—there's an example of where it's working.

Q: Any comments on MTV, VH1, or what direction music on TV—as well as rock music in film—will be going?

A: MTV is responsible in some ways for the under-fifty artists not having the same resources as the Stones, Bruce, Dylan. I mean Blondie and Duran Duran is pretty Jimmy Bowen Trio when it all comes down to stagecraft. U2 and Steve Earle are the only exceptions that come to mind. When I say responsible I mean that the road stopped being the building process for an all-important while when record companies seized the video as the selling tool. I saw Duran Duran in the summer of '82 in a London club when they were a vital live band. Then, as they should have, given the time, they concentrated on the videos and the cost is some core ability to be more than a magazine cover onstage. Sorry guys, but that's what I saw.

Q: Trends for film and music?

A: Songs in movie trailers, but not on the screen. Entertainment only mirrors a cult that you mother. There's no morality out in the world. So why should the business be any different?

§

Andrew Loog Oldham discovered, managed, and produced the Rolling Stones from 1963 to 1967. The late '50s films *Expresso Bongo* and *The Sweet*

Smell of Success told him who he wanted to be and he became it. In the '60s he also discovered Marianne Faithfull and via his Immediate Records with Tony Calder he scored with the Small Faces, Eric Clapton, Jimmy Page, John Mayall, Humble Pie, the Nice, and Nico. He has published two volumes of autobiography, *Stoned* and *2Stoned*. He produced and appeared in the 1965 Rolling Stones documentary *Charlie Is My Darling* and 1967's *Tonite Let's All Make Love in London*, directed by Peter Whitehead, and has been seen recently in a number of major music documentaries including *The Real Blow-Up* and *Pop Svengalis*. He was a recent keynote speaker at South by Southwest, North by Northeast, the Triptych Festival in Scotland, AAA in Stockholm, and the Kerry Film Festival in Ireland. He lives with his wife, Colombian actress Esther Farfan, in Bogotá, Colombia, and Vancouver, B.C., Canada, and is currently working on his third book, titled *On Hustling*. He was an extra in Martin Scorsese's *King of Comedy* and proud of it.

MEL STUART

I SAW MEL STUART speak in front of a packed house at the ArcLight Theater in Hollywood, for the premiere screening of the rereleased *Wattstax*, in spring, 2003, and later made arrangements to interview him at his office in Los Angeles.

Mel Stuart was born in New York and graduated from New York University. In 1960, David L. Wolper asked him to join the newly formed Wolper Organization, and for the next seventeen years Stuart served as one of its key executives. During that time he produced and directed dozens of documentaries, among them *The Making of the President*, *Rise and Fall of the Third Reich*, *Four Days in November*, *Love from A to Z*, with Liza Minnelli and Charles Aznavour, *Cary Grant: A Celebration*, with Michael Caine, and *Wattstax*, now rereleased for a 2003 movie audience.

Stuart also directed various features including *Willy Wonka and the Chocolate Factory* and *If It's Tuesday, This Must Be Belgium*. Since 1977 he has been an independent producer and director. His productions have been the documentaries *Man Ray: Prophet of the Avant-Garde* and *Billy Wilder: The Human Comedy* for PBS, *AFI's 100 Years . . . 100 Movies*, *Inside the KGB*, and the reality series, *Ripley's Believe It or Not*.

Mel Stuart served as President of the International Documentary Association for two years and has been the recipient of four Emmy

Los Angeles Coliseum during Wattstax.
Photo ©1972 The Saul Zaentz Company.

Awards, a Peabody Award, and an Oscar nomination. In November 2002, Stuart published *Pure Imagination: The Making of "Willy Wonka and the Chocolate Factory."*

I've always felt the *Wattstax* concert documentary has been overlooked by music and film historians. In 2003 Stax Records made available a three-CD set of forty-seven tracks from the festival and documentary, including seventeen not previously released, and in 2004, the Special Edition *Wattstax* DVD was released by Warner Home Video, including commentary from Stuart, Isaac Hayes, Al Bell, and Chuck D., formerly of Public Enemy, who is an avid *Wattstax* fan. The DVD's restored soundtrack will now—finally—include Hayes' "Theme from *Shaft*," that was in limbo for years because MGM would not allow Hayes to include the movie theme originally. Stax/Fantasy has also issued a fifteen-song collection, *Wattstax: Highlights from the Soundtrack.*

I remember hearing the original FM radio broadcast from the downtown L.A. event. I've had a relationship not only with the music of the

Stax Records label but with the stadium venue that housed the soul exhibition and also with the entire downtown L.A. neighborhood.

In the late 1950s I went to Coliseum Street Elementary School. I learned to swim at the Dorsey High School pool, and later spent a grade at Muirfield Elementary in Crenshaw Village, when it was still known as Crenshaw Town.

The Los Angeles Coliseum is one of my shrines. It was there I saw Sandy Koufax and Don Drysdale take the mound, Dick Bass and Anthony Davis cut off left tackle, and Mott the Hoople galvanize the landmark.

Q: Can you discuss the initial concept, production, and execution of the *Wattstax* concert documentary you directed and coproduced at the Los Angeles Coliseum in August, 1972, which some critics have described as the "Woodstock of Soul"?

A: It started when Stax Records wanted to do a big concert at the Los Angeles Coliseum to recognize the Watts Riots of summer 1965, and they also wanted to show off all their artists in a big concert that would go on for nine hours. Al Bell, then the Stax Organization's board chairman, got in touch with David Wolper, who I worked with, and he had some connections at Columbia Pictures, and through Dave, Stax, and Columbia, they decided to shoot a documentary that would play in the theaters.

I had done a lot of features work with Wolper Productions, and had just done *Willy Wonka and the Chocolate Factory*. I had made many documentaries, *The Making of the President*, *The Rise and Fall of the Third Reich*, and they felt I should supervise it. [Watts native, Forest Hamilton, son of jazz drummer/percussionist Chico Hamilton and Stax L.A. office head, arranged for Al Bell to meet Wolper, who subsequently suggested Stuart for the job.]

What I did was meet with the Stax people, and basically, the way I wanted to work was to be the only white person. [Forty-five black technicians were employed and discovered by Hollywood that day.] And everybody else would be black. The way it would work is the way I wanted it to work. Everybody who would advise me, be around me, guide me, would be black, because they would understand that what we were trying to do was create some kind of personification of the way black people felt at a particular time. I made sure that we hired all black crews, because at the time they didn't get a chance to get jobs.

Some great people came out of that: Richard Wells, Roderick Young [*Bush Mama*], Larry Clark [*Passing Through*]. John Alonso [*Lady Sings the Blues* and *Chinatown*] was there, too, as supervisor of photography. And if I remember correctly, I gave John his first job years before as a cameraman. I needed him and needed one guy who knew about lighting a big stage. And so what we did was put this whole thing together, and we were ready to shoot, and knew we had one shot at it.

I don't do storyboards. I've done too many documentaries and just follow my brain.

We had Melvin Van Peebles to help with the crowd control, because we had eighty thousand people. [Some of the band came from Melvin's film, *Sweet Sweetback's Baadasssss Song*, including Al McKay and Verdine White, founders of Earth, Wind & Fire.] The Stax people lined up all their talent that was available. A very important factor later. And they had Jesse Jackson there, and the Watts community.

[Tickets were ninety-nine cents. Proceeds benefited the Sickle Cell Anemia Foundation, the Martin Luther King Hospital, and the Watts Summer Festival. The entertainer expenses, the equipment, the promotion, and the advertising were all paid by Stax in conjunction with the Schlitz Brewing Company. The performers in *Wattstax* included the Staple Singers, Albert King, Carla Thomas, the Rance Allen Group, the Emotions, Johnnie Taylor, the Bar Kays, Little Milton, Jimmy Jones, Mel & Tim, Rufus Thomas, Luther Ingram, Isaac Hayes. Look closely on "Old Time Religion" and you can get glimpses of William Bell, Eddie Floyd, Eric Mercury, Little Sonny, and Frederick Knight.]

Q: You also had an advantage by working with one record label securing you talent. It was less of a headache and more a saving of countless hours than if it had been a collaboration with several record labels and music managers.

A: Absolutely! I don't ever want to do a concert with a lot of groups. We had one thing: Stax said, "Be there." They were there. I didn't have to worry about all the nonsense that goes with any kind of performer. You know it's going to happen and they had to be there on time. That worked well. And [the late] Larry Shaw [the VP of marketing for Stax] was my main confidant. An historian. He understood the black spirit more than anyone I've ever met. Not from a hothead dumb level, but from a big level.

I knew the first thing we had to do was cover all the acts. As important on that day was having the crews go into the stands and talk to people, and get shots of people reacting to the music. Not so much talk, but reaction shots of the crowd.

We shot everything and got it together, sort of a rough cut. And then I said, "Oh my God, all I have is a newsreel." I don't do newsreels. I hate most of those rock concert things where the people are clapping their hands and that's the show.

I said, "That's not a show—we don't learn anything from this." They said, "What do you want to do?" "I want to take the crews, led by me and other people, and go into the streets and get how people feel, and get an understanding, or have an understanding on how people feel about the music and the life around them."

So we sent some of the better cameramen out into the streets; I went sometimes, sometimes I didn't—I couldn't do it all, to barber shops, beauty parlors, the streets of Watts, funky little restaurants, churches, wherever they appeared, and asked people how they felt. So that was a very big part of what the show is about. Like that wonderful gentleman who talked about the lady who left him, "My nose is open." Sheer poetry. Sheer poetry.

I decided to protect ourselves, because I didn't know how good it was going to be, to have some actors at the time, because maybe they'd be a little more articulate. So we cast, and when Ted Lange [future star of *The Love Boat*] came in, and I heard him start speaking, I said "That's the main man as far as the actors go." And you notice I put him in the middle of the table, not on the side, because I knew I would get the best stuff from him.

Q: I noticed you also incorporated some regional music performances for *Wattstax*, away from the Coliseum setting.

A: I was also fortunate, because three or four acts that day couldn't make it, and I had the Emotions and I could shoot on location in a church, shoot Johnnie Taylor in a funky club, and film Little Milton out by the railroad tracks. Those were the three best.

It was a blessing. If I ever had to do it again I would not do it at a concert setting. I would get all the artists on location, close to the people, getting the feeling, the back and forth emotions. I think concerts to me are a minor way of making a film.

And it's interesting, but the three people I had, the Emotions, Johnnie Taylor, and Little Milton . . . Little Milton's chord structures of the blues . . . What they laid down behind them as far as I'm concerned was better than any blues around. I'm not big on blues being simple blues. We've moved on. It's a hundred years. I want to see an overlay of chordal structure that says "Hey, we're gonna improve the blues and move on." And simplistic blues, I understand it's power and everything else, but I need more as a musician. I have to have more than joy. The Emotions—the chordal structure of their songs is unbelievable. So I enjoy that.

And Johnnie Taylor doing "Jody's Got Your Girl and Gone." It was shot at a club in south central L.A. The feeling and the intimacy of that club, and the heat generated by this guy. The girls laughing and everything else. I was lucky enough to find Rufus Thomas saying something about "Jody" from another piece of film, and so I could put that in to make a whole thing about "Jody." I love the sequence, I love the band, and I liked cutting it. He did very well for me. He's such a hot performer!

Q: In *Wattstax*, the performance I loved the most was Luther Ingram singing "(If Lovin' You Is Wrong) I Don't Want to Be Right."

A: Man, I love that song. I think that song is so "on." I used the entire full version. We had the ability to use full pieces and go all the way through them. I cut short some of the stuff on the stage because again, you don't get the same intensity as when you shoot on location. On a real location with real people, and not at a concert where everybody is sitting in the stands. It's OK, and the musical performances were wonderful. The Bar Kays. But it's not like being on location.

Q: And the aerial footage of the Coliseum was some beautiful stuff. The aerial shot of the Watts Towers that opens the film with the Dramatics singing "Whatcha See Is Whatcha Get" to the montage of L.A. culture and political footage. Man, I also grooved on seeing Albert King because there is so little of him available on celluloid. Albert had a great presence on the screen.

A: Yes. Right.

Q: And Rufus Thomas blew my mind. His "Funky Chicken" was telegenic and rocking!

A: Certain people have star quality. And you can't get it. You either have it or you can't acquire it. You have it or you don't have it. Rufus Thomas has great star quality and you see it. You're fascinated by that sequence. And his ability to project. It's a marvelous sequence.

Q: There was an inherent sense of politics within the film, and even around the repertoire that day.

A: A big moment for me was when Kim Weston got up and sang "The

Rufus Thomas performing at Wattstax. Photo ©1972 The Saul Zaentz Company.

Star Spangled Banner" and nobody stood. A lot of people don't get it, but I left it in there particularly. I didn't have to play "The Star Spangled Banner" in this film, but I thought it was such an incredible statement that nobody out of eighty thousand people stood up. And they really stood up for Jesse Jackson's "I Am Somebody." That was the spirit of the time. That was the way it was and I think I captured something. [Weston also led the audience in the Black National Anthem, "Lift Every Voice and Sing."]

Q: And after you filmed the live concert, integrated the community dialogues and talk sequences, I know you felt you needed another central ingredient to make this movie really swing and move.

A: The final element was, once we got all that together, then they came to get me: "How we doin' over there? Are we done?" "No. What we need is an idea that Shakespeare had in *Henry V*, and that was the idea of a chorus." They were familiar with the play, but I said, "There's a man who tells you what's going to go on, because the subject is so big that you can't show it on that little stage. We have the same problem, we have the feeling of the black community, and we've got to get somebody who can be a chorus and sort of sympathize with what people feel, and comment on it. And you have to give me somebody who can also be very amusing."

And they said to me, "There's this guy in this club," and I went to this club and there's Richard Pryor onstage. I realized within three minutes I was in the presence of one of America's great comic geniuses. It was just something. So we came back the next day, and I just sat at the end of the bar and I said to him, "Gospel"; "Blues"; "Women." No matter what I said to him I got fifteen minutes. Off the top of his head. It was the most unbelievable moment of my life as a director! That any man can improvise in the way that he did. He didn't know what was coming.

I definitely felt something was needed to tie this together. You know what? Aristotle is not wrong. You need the three unities: The beginning, middle, and end. And it is not going to change, MTV notwithstanding, you've got to follow certain rules of structure—not that people know it. They know it if they feel it, but it's up to me to make it feel so that they get it. So people come to the film at the beginning, and Isaac Hayes is at the end. And there's a climax, and you have a middle. You have to follow the old rules or you're going to have a piece of garbage.

In those days, the very early '70s, I had to go into the movie house, I didn't have HDTV. I didn't have the equipment then. Everybody ran a 16mm camera.

Q: What about editing such a big concert movie? A bunch of editors were involved that you supervised.

A: You gotta understand, on any main show, I'm the main editor. I grew up as an editor. If someone works for me they better be very good. Every editor I've ever worked with always goes on to be very successful. Bob Lambert now does features. He was the main editor. It was such a big project that you had to have a few more editors just to get it going and get it done on time.

Personally, I much prefer shooting on tape, certainly editing-wise, but also shooting it on film costs a great deal more when you're doing a documentary.

Now in this particular case, we were shooting for a theatrical release, so we knew from the beginning this wasn't aimed for television. And it never did get on television because of the language. And I hope someday we can get on HBO or Showtime so a lot of people can see it.

Q: What was the initial reaction when it was released?

A: It debuted at the Cannes Festival in 1973. [It was nominated for a best documentary, and a Golden Globe followed the next year.] The people loved the music, but we're talking about a basic French audience. They didn't understand a lot of the language and the nuances. Pryor's use of "Get Down." I think people enjoyed the spectacle, but they didn't understand the black experience at that time. You have to realize it was only a few years before, in the mid-'60s, that President Johnson passed the civil rights bill. The movie did well, and people liked it. It wasn't like today, it would be a different experience.

When it came back here it played in the theaters and did very well in the black neighborhoods. Again, it was a bit too early and a little ahead of its time in those days. Either they didn't push it for a white area or . . .

I mean, you've got to remember that times change, and in 1973, playing this kinda black expression of music and the people, the talk in the streets, it was a different era. And so it did very, very well, and made a big profit for Columbia at that time. The whole trick, the whole thing, regarding the longevity of a film is whether it plays on television.

My film *Willy Wonka* is on every week on some cable channel. It's just sheer repetition for people to like the film, and it has to have something that the audience wants to see, provided you're on television—there's no longevity to a feature. I mean, where else are you going to see it?

Now this picture, because of language, especially in those days— you can't use the word "Motherfucker," so it hasn't played. It might have gotten a few spots but hasn't really played.

Q: I wanted to discuss the shelf life of the film. The Stax Records label then was a roots music record label. Their catalogue enhanced this documentary that you filmed, and two separate double-disc soundtrack albums were issued just after the film was originally released. It wasn't available, it seemed, for years at a time.

And now a DVD has been made available in 2003 for the retail market. Plus, Fantasy Records released in 2003 a CD of Isaac Hayes' hour-long *Wattstax* performance that coincided with the opening of the Stax Museum of American Soul Music in Memphis, Tennessee.

A: In the long run we'll be around a lot longer. There are people coming to see it now who weren't born when the movie was made. By the way, the audience gets more and more white. It's become a thing. At the Sundance Festival they were all white and they really enjoyed it and they loved it. I think people have a much greater understanding for the black experience today than they had then.

My son a few years back wanted [rapper-actor] Ice-T to play the narrator and general host of a show he was developing, which he did do in England, called *Jive Ass TV*. They did a whole bunch of shows. To me Ice-T is so hip, an unbelievable performer. You can't get any better with his laid back manner. And my son went to him, and at first, Ice-T was a little reluctant. "What's this? England?" "My daddy made *Wattstax*," and then that sorta melted Ice-T, and he said, "OK, I'll do it."

Q: A lot of your early work was in black-and-white. And now the last few decades all in color. Were there any differences in doing black-and-white and color?

A: The newspapers we read and the books we read are in black-and-white. And most of the great photos. I just did a film, *Photos of the 20th Century: 20 Memorable Photos*, and the ones we remember are in black-and-white. I did *The Making of the President* in 1960 in black-and-white and *The Making of the President in 1964* in black-and-white.

Then color became popular on television in 1968. I didn't like the color in those days. But I didn't want to do *Willy Wonka* in black-and-white, or *Wattstax* in black-and-white. You'd miss all the costumes and excitement.

※

Mel Stuart: Select Filmography
The Making of the President
Rise and Fall of the Third Reich
Four Days in November
Love from A to Z
Cary Grant: a Celebration
Wattstax
Willy Wonka and the Chocolate Factory
If It's Tuesday, This Must Be Belgium
Man Ray: Prophet of the Avant-Garde
Billy Wilder: The Human Comedy
AFI's 100 Years . . . 100 Movies
Inside the KGB
Ripley's Believe It or Not

MELVIN VAN PEEBLES

RENAISSANCE MAN MELVIN VAN PEEBLES has often been called "the god-father of black film," for his groundbreaking work in movies. He was born in Chicago, Illinois.

Van Peebles' 1971 feature film, *Sweet Sweetback's Baadasssss Song*, which he wrote, acted in, directed, scored, and produced, was shot in L.A.'s Watts community, and featured a black stud as its protagonist in the face of white adversity. Some scenes took place in the Crenshaw Village area.

Melvin Van Peebles debuted with a bang when his first film, the French language *La Permission* (*The Story of a Three-Day Pass*) earned the Critics' Choice award at the San Francisco Film Festival. He subsequently directed *Watermelon Man*, starring Godfrey Cambridge, and *Identity Crisis*. Van Peebles used some of his *Watermelon Man* salary to help finance *Sweetback*.

Van Peebles appeared on-screen in the music documentary *Wattstax*, made in Los Angeles.

Years later, he directed the video of Houdini's influential rap song, "White Lines."

More recently, Van Peebles coproduced the mid-'90s film *Panther*,

Melvin Van Peebles. Photo courtesy of
Melvin Van Peebles and Water Records.

which he adapted from his novel on the Black Panther Party. His son Mario, an actor, directed it.

Van Peebles has also composed music for various film soundtracks, as well as two Broadway musicals. His *Ain't Supposed to Die a Natural Death* is often credited for "changing" modern American theater. In addition, that 1973 cast album earned him two Grammy nominations as producer and composer.

In 2003 Water Records issued the CD of Van Peebles' album, *What the . . . You Mean I Can't Sing?* originally released by Atlantic Records in 1974. MVP sings passionate reflections on the state of 1970s black culture and politics over some very funky grooves with strings and orchestration (think of the soundtracks to any Pam Grier flick). Harold Wheeler arranged the music.

In 2005, the life and work of Van Peebles was the subject of a biographical documentary film by director Joe Angio, called *How to Eat Your Watermelon in White Company (and Enjoy It)*. In late 2005, Van Peebles had a recurring acting role in the UPN TV sitcom, *Girlfriends*. Melvin has published thirteen novels, and currently hosts a syndicated NPR radio show.

I interviewed Van Peebles in Los Angeles in the mid-'90s, when he was in town for a series of meetings around his *Panther* film and the launch of *Ghetto Gothic*, his most recent album on Capitol Records. He penned all the lyrics and music on *Ghetto Gothic*, producing the recording with associate producers William "Spaceman" Patterson and Dunn Pearson.

This is the man who kicked open the bolted movie studio doors for a whole slew of writers, directors, and producers after the *Sweetback* revenue and ownership earned him long overdue green carpet entry to the Hollywood cinema picnic.

In 2004 Van Peebles received a Lifetime Achievement Award in Los Angeles at the Pan African Film and Arts Festival.

That same year, his son Mario Van Peebles recreated the filming of *Sweet Sweetback's Baadasssss Song* for his independent feature, *Baadasssss!* wherein he portrays his father from the 1971 effort in the starring performance. *Baadasssss!* mixed actors, real people, drama, fiction, and documentary style cinematography. Melvin and I sat down to talk at Mario's house in Studio City, California, after enjoying a delightful meal on nearby Ventura Boulevard.

Q: *Ghetto Gothic* was your ninth album, but there is a link that extends back to your debut record, *Brer' Soul*, which was the basic blueprint for rap.

A: When I came back to the States [from Paris] in '67 or '68, I was very surprised, especially at all the protests that were going on. But I felt that urban music didn't really mirror this lifestyle or anything to a great extent. Not only did it not discuss the protests that were going on, but what was called "black music" had really been boiled down to such a very narrow sexual formula. It didn't encompass any of the other aspects of the human experience. However, the form that was available to me at that time—just the normal rhythm and blues, gospel, etc.—didn't really allow for the words the way I wanted to use them. So, I devised my own form, and that form later became known as, or evolved into, rap.

Now, I'm from the south side of Chicago. It's very interesting that my singing was later called "spoken word," early on, because to me, it sounded like a lot of guys I knew, like Blind Lemon Jefferson. My influences go way back to the older forms of black music, like Jefferson and the field hollers. I was also influenced by the spoken word styles from Germany that I encountered when I lived in France. Too many black artists are encouraged not to eat from the entire cornucopia of creative and technical options. But I'm black, so what I do is always black. Once you don't worry about that, you're free to manifest your artistry however you see it. Back then, '67, '68, what happened was black singers had been relegated to a certain formula type, and when you heard a different type voice, it sounded so foreign. But you could still hear this voice if you went deep down into the South. So I did those early albums and they became benchmarks. Then later came the Last Poets, Gil Scott-Heron, etcetera.

It's interesting to see what I have done in cinema. What I did cinematically, I did the same thing on Broadway. I changed the face of theater.

But also musically the disco formula didn't really allow for the words the way I wanted to use them. So I devised my own form, which later evolved into rap. What I did was construct a platform for the vignettes. I made a conscious decision to downplay the music and accentuate the voice. That's what happened. I did the music for *Sweetback*, and my Broadway musicals.

Q: You adapted the screenplay for *Panther* from your novel on the Black Panther Party. Talk to me about this film.

A: I had always been interested in the Panthers. I used to do benefit concerts for them. In fact, on my first album, for A&M Records [*Brer'*

Soul], before anybody else, I had an author's comment, "Free Huey." Huey [Newton] was still in jail. I was the first one who came out and stood up for him. And this was before the African-American bourgeoisie (*laughs*). So, I've been working on this for fifteen years. Let me tell you the funny part of the story: I showed the next-to-last draft to my son, Mario. He said, "It would make a great movie!" But I thought they'd never let us get away with this. Mario said, "I'll stand with you." And Mario did. So Mario and I, with one other person, put the movie together.

Q: Did you have to pitch it and the whole bit to the studios?

A: Oh, yeah. The whole deal. And I had to revise the script because they wanted to make some politically unacceptable changes. You know, the whole schmear. But what had happened was all the books about the Panthers that I'd read over the years were usually bullshit. But the specific books, written by the Panthers themselves, were usually extremely interesting. And always true. But those were just trees, and I wanted to deal with the forest. So, I worked out a format that made it possible to see the forest. And that's our movie!

Q: You graduated from Ohio Wesleyan with a degree in history. Then a stint as a navigator/bombardier in the Strategic Air Command, and later invited to France by the Cinemathéque because of the several distinguished film shorts you did in San Francisco.

Then your first feature, the French language *La Permission*, a love story about an American soldier and a French girl, took first prize at the San Francisco Film Festival. You had come back to the states as a French delegate, but they didn't know you were American—let alone black—and that created a furor because there were no black directors in the United States.

A: What happened was I discovered there was a French law that said a foreign writer could have a temporary director's card to do his own work if he could raise the money. I'd taught myself French and published five novels in France. But it took me nine years to put it all together. I asked for a temporary [director's] card, and they gave it to me. So I made the film. Then I met the curator of the San Francisco Festival, who told me I was going to be one of the people invited.

So, I get off the plane in San Francisco, walk around the airport, and people have welcome signs. This little woman was standing there with blue hair. "Melvin Van Peebles? Melvin Van Peebles?" In San Francisco, what they did was farm you out to one of these society people who'd take you around. So I said, "Hey, lady." And she kept saying "Melvin Van Peebles? Melvin Van Peebles?" So I had to raise my voice! "Hey lady, I'm Melvin Van Peebles!" She freaked. It's 1967. "You're Melvin Van Peebles?" "Yes. *Parlez vous Français?*" We get in the car—a long limo. We're driving out of the airport, and I see a brother with a purple hat. "Hey, man, stop. Want a ride? Get in, brother." I figured this wasn't going to last long, so fuck it.

So about now, the lady really starts freakin'. It was great. So we get in town, drop this guy off, come up California Street, and the woman says the delegation office is at the Fairmont Hotel, but I wouldn't be staying there. She said, "You're at the Mark Hopkins." Well, they didn't allow niggers in the Mark Hopkins when I left [the States], so I get to the Mark Hopkins in the long limo. This Irish-lookin' doorman sees me dressed in blue jeans, ya know, Levi jacket. And you could see the guy thinking, "Oh, no . . . There goes the neighborhood." The look on his face! So I get in, and they got me the top floor penthouse suite! Food. Not just fruit. So I eat all this fuckin' food and go to sleep, because I just know they're gonna throw me out when I come down. Or find some excuse. I slept wonderfully, packed all my stuff, got it ready. Then I come downstairs and go to the Fairmont. Walk in the Fairmont, the film delegates' office is in the lobby. I walk in, and everybody is really friendly: "Hi. Hello. How are you?" So I say to myself, "This is great." Then someone says, "Aren't you here to fix the lights?" I swear to God! By this time, I got my game together. "I'm the French director." (*laughs*)

Q: And you took first prize at the festival!

A: I won the Critics' Award. Watched it play in an auditorium. Applause, not a dry eye in the crowd. The *New York Times* writes, "The shame of America is that the only Black American filmmaker needs the French to direct it because . . ." Then, in America, what happened was the chase for the Great Black Hope was finally on!

Q: What kind of work were you offered after that?

A: If I had taken any of those offers, they would have had the one black threat under wraps. So I didn't have a job. But I wouldn't take it. It then turned into a political embarrassment; they had to find black directors. So they discovered two guys who were older than I was, who had been around and boasted many more credits, guys like Gordon Parks and Ossie Davis. Gordon Parks got to make *The Learning Tree*.

Q: But when *Sweetback* was released, didn't it generate work for you?

A: I was never offered a job as a director. Nobody asked me for shit. The movie is great. But what I expected with *Sweetback* came to pass. I said, "Look, once these guys see that my shit is bad, I'm in trouble!" They prefer to have someone they can control.

Q: You are cited by several influential directors as an inspiration.

A: What has happened is an understanding of the globalness of just what I've done. You know, we're just talkin', but I changed the face and I did it all by my fuckin' self . . . You understand?

I started my own company for these things. The *Sweetback* book went into four printings long ago. For example, *Ain't Supposed to Die a Natural Death* was the *Sweetback* of theater, but it has never been done as a revival. Why? Because I own it. And no one has ever come to me because of the provinciality of racism. *Sweetback* has never been distributed in foreign territories.

See, one of the downsides to what I do is that I don't work as an artist within a major infrastructure. Let me backtrack and tell you the most wonderful thing about me. The most wonderful thing about me is that I never expect justice.

I had to hire a white guy to act as a front to sell *Sweetback*, just to get it distributed in towns to get it seen by black people! To this day, I walk into a studio, and it's "Where's your package?" "I'm not a package. I'm here to see the president [of the studio]!" But it's just a knee-jerk reaction. And my work, somehow, is still offensive in many ways to a whole group of people.

Q: When *Sweetback* first came out in the very early '70s, we had to search for it at drive-ins and dollar theaters. I know it was a bitch and a struggle to even get it made in a time of anti-war protests and racial tensions. I even heard you raised your own money and hocked your motorcycle to make it happen.

A: The problem is the decision makers who say, if you don't go through their structure, they won't give you a fair shake. For example, when *Sweetback* first came out, everybody said, "Flawed." When Rodney King happened, I'd said it twenty-five years ago. What are you talkin' about? If I can't find it, then I cook it myself. If I'd seen *Sweetback* on-screen, I wouldn't have made it. I didn't, so I went out and made it myself.

Q: A lot of younger cats are working in the film industry because of your efforts.

A: I've heard, "You'll never work in this town again." But I'm ahead of the game. When I started, I didn't have a coat. I got a coat. For these kids to get an opportunity to be all that they can be is the important thing. I didn't give for them to be my clones. They're not me. Why should they be? You know what I mean? I'm me and he's him. What's the big deal?

※

Melvin Van Peebles: Select Filmography
Gang in Blue
Calm at Sunset
Panther
Fist of the North Star
Terminal Velocity
Last Action Hero
Posse
Boomerang
True Identity
Identity Crisis
America
Sophisticated Gents
Sweet Sweetback's Baadasssss Song
Watermelon Man

COMPOSER
Sophisticated Gents (song "Greased Lightning")
Just an Old Sweet Song (theme song)
Don't Play Us Cheap
Sweet Sweetback's Baadasssss Song
Watermelon Man
Story of a Three-Day Pass

TELEVISION GUEST APPEARANCES
Homicide: Life on the Street
Living Single
In the Heat of the Night
Girlfriends (Recurring role)

PART TWO
BUSINESS
[AS USUAL]

Kim Fowley, Redlands, California, 2005.
Photo by Roy Swedeen, courtesy of Kim Fowley.

KIM FOWLEY

KIM FOWLEY—THE NAMES of his music and production companies define him: Bad Boy Music, Rare Magnetism, and Living Legend.

Kim Fowley is a child of Hollywood. Both his parents were actors. His dad, Douglas Fowley, did a lot of episodic television, including a regular part as Doc Holliday on the ABC-TV series, *The Life and Legend of Wyatt Earp*, and appeared in dozens of movies, including *Battleground*, *Mighty Joe Young*, and *Singing in the Rain*, in which he portrayed the director. Doug was under contract to several studios during his sixty-five-year career. Kim's mother, Shelby Payne, had a cameo as the cigarette girl in *The Big Sleep*, starring Humphrey Bogart and Lauren Bacall.

Kim has had his own songs in over forty movies and television shows. His career as a music producer, songwriter, and publisher has yielded over 102 Gold and Platinum Record credits, starting in 1960 when he coproduced "Alley-Oop" by the Hollywood Argyles.

No one gets with the *Hollywood Shack Job* program, from social politics, hustle, room-working, creativity, talent discovery, the country club rules, religion (not as faith but as entry and business opportunity), competition, replacement, networking, belief, betrayal, scamming, industry racism and reverse racism, sexism, producing, and licensing rock 'n' roll music content, to the current use of songs in TV, film, DVD, or new media, quite like "the human jukebox," Kim Vincent Fowley.

He was there in 1959 at American International Pictures (A.I.P.), and along the way, has had revenue streams from *American Graffiti*, *Ciao Manhattan*, *Dazed and Confused*, *The Butcher Boy*, *Big Momma's House*, and *E.T.*

In the last decade, Fowley has appeared on network and cable TV in many episodes of *E! True Hollywood Story*, VH1's *Behind the Music*, Court TV, BBC Scotland, MTV (U.K.), and the *Pop Odyssey* documentary in Germany (ZDF).

In 2005 he coproduced, codirected, and costarred in his own independent documentary film, *Jukebox California*, Fowley's dusty music saga on his life in the 909 area code that features his own original music.

This is a character who in 1959 was a DJ on KGEM-AM in Boise, Idaho, broadcasting from the Boy Howdy Drive-In during his Air Force National Guard summer camp. These days, Fowley also serves as a host and DJ on Sirius Satellite Radio's *Underground Garage*, the 24-hour streaming channel produced by "Little Steven" Van Zandt.

Today, musicians and groups like KISS, the Byrds, Cat Stevens, the Runaways, Nirvana, Leon Russell, Gene Vincent, Chris Darrow, Ben Vaughn, Alice Cooper, Blue Oyster Cult, Rocket, BMX Bandits, Emerson, Lake & Palmer, and others continue to earn him money and expose material he's collaborated on and owns.

In spring 2006, the song "Cherry Bomb" that Fowley cowrote (with Joan Jett) and produced for the Runaways was used in director Barry Sonnenfeld's movie *RV*, starring Robin Williams and Cheryl Hines. On May 4, 2006, the same recording was featured in the soundtrack of that evening's episode of the nationally popular Fox TV Network primetime series, *The O.C.*

Visit his website, www.kimfowley.com.

Fowley has always supported the underdog, the rookie, the small label recording artist, and the discarded music veteran in their quest to make a dollar and to get their music heard, especially in a film or on a TV show.

Kim's observations on the evolution of the music and film pairing in *Hollywood Shack Job* are insightful, viable, valid, pathetic, incredible, awful, sad, terrific, and heartbreaking. Just like a good movie.

Q: Your step-grandfather was composer Rudolph Friml, one of the cofounders of ASCAP, the American Society of Composers, Authors and Publishers. I know you had a brief part in a Tim Holt movie when you were a kid.

A: Film music didn't get going in the rock 'n' roll sense until *Rock Around the Clock* and *Blackboard Jungle*, which came along and made everyone go wild.

Because I spent my "Sh-Boom" summer in the Bronx, part of New York City, the music sounded like the streets of New York. By the time it got to *Rock Around the Clock*, it was old white guys doing black music with a country push. I heard Spade Cooley and "Sh-Boom" all together on that Bill Haley and the Comets record.

And of course the visual hit me because I was the child of a B-movie actor and actress. It wasn't a big revelation to me. It was business and a product.

All of a sudden Sam Katzman showed up. Katzman jumped in there, with some other people who put up these "ten day movies" where they would get all the people who had one chart hit and then stick them into a black-and-white movie with a tiny story line. DJ and personality Alan Freed had a bunch of them, like *Mr. Rock 'n' Roll*.

I remember Katzman's movies, and also the shorts that actually started back in the 1930s into 1950s that were under-three-minute versions of current songs, lip-synched in bad black-and-white. While Bettie Page was running around naked, people were making these strange things that were shown in movie theaters, and the black ones were the best. You couldn't find them in the white neighborhood.

In the late 1950s I attended University High—not too far from MGM and 20th Century Fox Studios—which had a lot of students, including myself, that went on to make records and have songs in films: Nancy Sinatra, Sandra Dee, James Brolin, Ryan O'Neal, Bruce Johnston, Jan and Arnie/Jan and Dean, Canned Heat's Henry Vestine, Randy Newman.

Music and movie business parents always intermingled. I went to church and saw Frank Sinatra and Bing Crosby in the same Mass at Good Shepherd in Beverly Hills, where they later held Frank Sinatra's funeral services.

In 1959, I got to enter Hollywood on February 3rd, "the day the music died," when Ritchie Valens, the Big Bopper, and Buddy Holly, along with their pilot, crashed in South Dakota.

Q: What was your first record?

A: That was the day I ran away from home and Willis College of Business to Hollywood. Within three months I produced "Charge," b/w "Geronimo," by the Renegades, in the American International Pictures film, *Ghost of Dragstrip Hollow*.

I got the gig by taking ten dollars a week working for Jimmie Maddin at American International Pictures. Jimmie also owned a supper club, then known as The Summit, that later became Club Lingerie, and I slept on the floor with the cook and his grandson and had one steak dinner a night. Plus, I threw shows for radio station KRLA and their teenage nightclub on Sunday matinees. Artists like Eddie Cochran, Eugene Church, and all the Doo Wop and Rockabilly guys, would alternate with jazz, and we'd have Terry Gibbs and Gerry Mulligan in there, and I'd share the MC duties with a KRLA DJ, Frosty Harris.

I got to work over at American International in a record company, and Jimmie Madden was head of A&R, and I was the smart kid in the office in the morning when he wasn't there. So I appointed myself record producer. The members of the Renegades included Richard Podolor on guitar and bass, who later coproduced Steppenwolf ("Born to Be Wild" in *Easy Rider*) and Three Dog Night. The other guys were Sandy Nelson, the drummer of "Teen Beat" fame; Bruce Johnston, later a Beach Boy from 1966 on; and Nik Venet, who had album production credits earlier with Bobby Darin and later with the Beach Boys. Nik was the writer of those songs. Kim was the producer. The song got in the movie.

They only showed this stuff in the Midwest and the South. None of us ever saw the movie. They gave me five hundred records and I drove up and down Sunset Boulevard in my father's car, handing them out and impressing lots of girls. My father was away in Brazil, making a movie with June Wilkinson, *Macumba Love*.

Q: What was your next movie credit?

A: *Diary of a High School Bride* (A.I.P.). Our singer was Tony Casanova, who was Ritchie Valens' first cousin. He distinguished himself in rock history when he tried—out of jealousy—to run over Ritchie earlier with a truck, at the Rainbow Roller Rink. When we later did a sock hop for Lou Stumpo at Pacific Bandstand, Tony looked at the Pacific Ocean and said, "What's that river?"

Before they hired me, A.I.P. had a lot of mid-to-late 1950s movies, and Eddie Cochran and his cowriter/producer Jerry Capeheart participated in these movies, and John Ashley was the star, and they tried to make a singer out of him. The social life of B-movie actors and rock 'n' roll were one and the same. All at the same parties. All had the same girlfriends. I was a goy schmuck but I grew up with Jews so I was cool. There wasn't such an apartheid atmosphere in entertainment or the arts then.

It was a time when there were no music supervisors, when not everyone was "marrying in" for deals, not a lot of lawyers, not as much nepotism, cocaine wasn't around. It was "Hi. I need this. Have it ready in the morning." "OK."

The year 1960 rolled around and I was on my way to my next movie-to-music gig for Doris Day and Marty Melcher. Their office in Beverly Hills comprised Arwin Records, Daywin Music (BMI), Artist Music (ASCAP), a division of Arwin Productions owned by Doris Day and Marty Melcher. I started off as a food runner, office boy, PR assistant, then up to A&R there, bringing artists in. When I arrived, the project was *Pillow Talk* with Doris Day and Rock Hudson. Joe Lubin was there, producing records. He cowrote "Tutti Frutti" for Little Richard, so there was a slight rock 'n' roll vibe in the office. Black people played on Doris Day records. Doris had come out of a swing band with Les Brown many years earlier. I knew the synergy could happen with film and music, and rock 'n' roll, but you didn't hang out with Doris Day. You greeted her with "Good morning, Mrs. Melcher."

The first artist I brought in was future Beach Boy, Bruce Johnston. Terry Melcher, who inherited all these rights from his stepfather, Marty Melcher, and Doris Day, kept Bruce Johnston under contract for many years. Terry went on to produce the original Byrds—lots of their songs are now in movies and TV shows—and please note that Bruce Johnston wrote "I Write the Songs" that Barry Manilow covered, a huge success published by Artist Music. So I brought in a writer who lasted over twenty years with the company.

One of the things I was assigned to do with the *Pillow Talk* songs was to get R&B covers to come out on Arwin. Milt Grayson sang one and someone else did "Rolly Polly." Grayson, who was at one time a member of Billy Ward and the Dominoes, sang with Duke Ellington. And there was a merger of rock 'n' roll and the film world looming. Hadda Brooks was on Arwin. The two worlds coexisted. The same musicians were on all the records, but the same photos were not on all the artwork. In *West Side Story*, around the same time, it was Marni Nixon doing the ghost singing for actress Natalie Wood.

I wasn't a visionary, but I was making fifty dollars a week and happy to be there. And I was getting laid. Even at eighteen I lived with a thirty-seven-year-old woman, while every one else was in the twelfth grade, hardly necking.

The records from Arwin all failed. I left there and then quickly had "Alley-Oop," that I coproduced and copublished, by the Hollywood Argyles. I also got half of the artist royalties. Funny thing is, that song has never been in a movie, even though it outsold "Are You Lonesome Tonight?" by Elvis Presley.

Ironically, from the time of "Alley-Oop" in 1960 to "Nut Rocker" in 1962, there were movie companies who suddenly had rock 'n' roll divisions. United Artists had one, MGM had one, almost every film company tried to have a record company.

They had no idea what to put out. So we used to use those guys as pigeons. We would visit their offices, do "Jewish Schtick," and pimp our black artists that nobody else wanted on these morons and they would buy them from us. We'd unload all our C-team black talent, including some guys who were sorta talented, but liked any deal, no matter how lame.

I had a ghetto pass before Kid Rock was born. I was a 6'5" white dude who loved to fuck, just like some of the brothers in downtown L.A.

I gave them gigs, paid them, and treated them equally. I was like Harriet Tubman and the Underground Railway.

Q: I also saw Oma Heard, a legendary session vocalist years ago, treat you like Nelson Mandela at a session one night at Larrabee Studios, when we were sharing a studio with the Rev. James Cleveland in 1978. "Are you Kim from 1961?" She almost fainted when she saw you!

In your multicultural independent recording journey all through the early '60s, you extended to both the Negro and Mexican community for talent and recording.

That always impressed me 'cause you were this tall, vanilla weirdo who could work Beverly Hills, East L.A., and Watts, and always supported R&B music. I also learned many years ago not to be on a dance floor if you were there.

A: Don't put this rap into a Kennedy Center Honors Program or NAACP tribute, but I know what you mean. The fact is I also had polio, and Bloods pushed me in a wheelchair into supermarkets and liquor stores and I would cop candy under my polio blankets, since the owners would always watch the Negroes, not me, and then we all had sugar for the day!

I met Roy Hamilton, and was befriended by B. B. King and his wife during his Kent Records period. They treated me to a Sunday after-noon dinner cooked by B. B. himself at his home.

I also ran errands for Dee Clark when he was in L.A., from the Watkins Hotel near Adams Blvd.

I don't have to tell you a member of the Hollywood Flames was a player on "Alley-Oop." Gaynel Hodge worked for me and he co-wrote "Earth Angel" by the Penguins. Sandy Nelson played cans on the record. Harper Cosby, who was the first guy to teach Don Cherry chord changes, came from Johnny Otis and he was on the date. Harper is on "Hand Jive," which I just heard in the movie *The Shawshank Redemption*. And a guy named Ronnie Silco was the drummer, who played on "Big Boy Pete" by the Olympics. You had to have black people on the tracks for the groove.

I did the record with my then partner, Gary Paxton, for ninety-two dollars.

It was a Dallas Frazier song I discovered when I was sleeping in my cot at Happy's Gas Station on Sunset Boulevard in Hollywood. Dallas was an early hippie, and sang me a song, "Alley-Oop." I said, "This is a hit!" Gary said, "Let's book time!" Gary sang with some other people. I was living on Hollywood and Argyle, hence the name of the act. I didn't care what people thought of me and did whatever I wanted with whomever I wanted to, in writing or in the studio. I was fuckin' pumping money into the black economy and got little or no credit. I was in a Jewish/Negro mafia world and few white suburb people were around, and it pissed some people off.

Q: In the early 1960s in the music-publishing world, did you ever feel any sort of racism or religious divide when trying to work or exist?

A: I was a white Negro, even though my dad had a beach club member-ship and my mother was a debutante. Someone said, "A black man can't help it. He's born black. But you're trying to do business in a Jewish business world. What's your excuse?" I could have worked exclusively in West L.A., but I was attracted to the crosstown talent in urban street Hollywood, and what downtown L.A. offered.

In the mid- and late '50s, if there was a fire or a natural disaster in a neighborhood, the brothers and I would do second story jobs and clip golf clubs and wait for the fence guy to take the golf clubs from us. I also got to know brothers and tried to help their talent get heard.

Maybe that was one of the reasons I was hired as the first white employee of Motown in 1960 on the West Coast. I also put Negroes in administrative positions in the early '60s. The woman who ran my office then was Sugar Hall, [arranger and session musician] Rene Hall's wife, and Rene was all over the Ritchie Valens and Sam Cooke records you now hear in movies. Lois Duncan, my secretary, was married to Cleve Duncan, lead singer of the Penguins, of "Earth Angel" fame.

Jews didn't freeze me out, but it depends on the Jew. There are many tribes of Israel, aren't there? In between Arwin and "Alley-Oop," I worked for DJ Alan Freed in 1960, when he was doing radio in L.A. I was his food runner, and he treated me as a human being. Blacks, Browns, Goys, Jews, all were the same to him. There were Jewish people who let me in, like Alan Freed. He let me borrow his car once to get laid. Leonard Chess and Paul Gayten were also gentlemen to me, and helped teach me music, and also let me tag along once in a while when they noshed.

I didn't have Jewish problems like other Goys. I had a step-grandfather, Rudolph Friml, who was Jewish, so I knew the dietary laws, and I know the difference between a schmuck and a *sheenie*. Please use that quote.

Then I hit with "Nut Rocker." I was the publisher and songwriter. It was a boogie-woogie version of "The Nutcracker Suite." Last century this was done in the days of instrumentals with phony names. You could get some middle-aged white and black guys. It was generally black people who did jazz and blues who could read music and white guys who were old or ugly. That's why session guys like Earl Palmer, Rene Hall, Al Hazan, and Ernie Freeman were on records.

"Nut Rocker" came out in 1962 and it was a hit in America—Top Twenty, but around the world it was much more successful, to the extent that it has been used multiple times in the last forty-two years, and the last time it was used was in the movie *Big Momma's House*, starring Martin Lawrence. That filmed grossed $118 million. "Nut Rocker" was also used in *Butcher Boy*. I still have writing and publishing revenue streams from it.

Q: So you have seen your song placed in a black movie, *Big Momma's House*, and an Irish movie, *Butcher Boy*. Yet when you did the song you had no idea of its life expectancy or a target demographic market.

A: It was also in *Poisoner's Handbook,* with David Hemmings. It had a previous movie life. The song gets itself in the movie. I knew it was a visual and it was my arrangement and adaptation of a public domain song. I knew I was going to get laid and paid. It was written to make money short-term and long-term.

Accountants called me when it was utilized for *Butcher Boy,* and I got laid in Ireland when I went there.

I got the call for *Big Momma's House* from the movie production company. The song was used in the aerobics scene. Ironically, they called me in New Orleans thinking I was an African-American, on some Lil' Kim level. I was the only white person who had a song in that movie. Sometimes it pays not to go to the parties . . .

At that time I was living in New Orleans and the music supervisor's office assumed I was black. This race shit works for and against you. My name worked for me, whereas my skin color might possibly have worked against me on the music-in-movies playing field.

Q: And your knowledge and experience on the record charts also paid dividends when you went to England in 1964, just after producing the *Record World* #1 hit, "Popsicles and Icicles" by the Murmaids, also #3 in *Billboard.* Just before the Beatles conquered America, you gave the first break to a young songwriter in 1963, David Gates, later of Bread fame. Gates inked to Screen Gems publishing, and then he later supplied tunes for the Monkees' TV series, including "Saturday's Child."

A: A big, important development in the evolution of the rock song in movies was the movie soundtrack as a retail item, a stand-alone product by itself. It was in 1964 when Murray Deutsch came in from United Artists—they didn't care about the Beatles' movie, *A Hard Day's Night,* they just wanted a soundtrack override—that's what he said to me. Mike Stewart of United Artists Records in America got the rights domestically, even though as you know, the Beatles were on Capitol Records.

Q: I met Walter Shenson, who produced the Beatles' movie. He produced *A Hard Day's Night* and owned it in all formats. The parent movie house let him own the master negative and rights. The company didn't really realize the long-term shelf life of rock 'n' roll and the initial "British Invasion" acts. U.A. "borrowed" the Beatles away from Capitol Records, who held their North American recording agreement.

What about the rock soundtrack album as a product in the retail world?

A: The soundtrack world wasn't that cut-and-dried at the time. Get rid of all the romance that you and so many other consumers and record collectors bring to the music table. It was just, "Let's put these quickly written and recorded throwaway songs out and we'll make some override money without investing anything. We'll get in on some Beatles songs because it will be in the movie. Ha-ha-ha!"

In 1965, the movie business really got into "the music business" for the first time with the Byrds at Ciro's nightclub. The liner notes for the Byrds' *Mr. Tambourine Man* album were written by Billy James, who was an ex-actor from New York before he was a record label executive at Columbia and Elektra.

He explains how actors like Michael J. Pollard started coming down every night to see the Byrds, and pretty soon you had Dennis Hopper and Peter Fonda checking out rock 'n' roll. Fonda got in with the Byrds—"Ballad of Easy Rider"—and later Jack Nicholson got in with the Monkees, and cowrote their *Head* feature film. At Ciro's, that was the first time seeds were really planted, even though there were movies around like earlier A.I.P. and Sam Katzman stuff.

Social, conceptual, and "drug brother"-type themes really fell together in 1965.

In 1966, it really got going when [actor] Steve McQueen announced to the world that Johnny Rivers playing the Whisky A Go Go was God. Rivers was his favorite band at the Whisky, and with this sort of endorsement, with global media coverage, more stars came to the Whisky to dance every night and hang around that vibe. Then, a while later, *Shampoo*—which was years after *Easy Rider*—came along with rock 'n' roll in it, guaranteeing lucrative licensing fees for the use of the Beach Boys' "Wouldn't It Be Nice."

The real big moment for the music and movie soundtrack can be tied to 1968, when *Easy Rider* used individual singles and songs as the elements of the soundtrack, along with album tracks like Jimi Hendrix's "If 6 Were 9" and something by the Electric Prunes.

There were no "Elmer Bernstein" or "Bernard Herrmann" composers in the vehicle. Not even a Johnny Mercer figure.

Q: The *Easy Rider* soundtrack was culled from the record collections of both Peter Fonda and Dennis Hopper. Hopper, who directed the movie, spent a lot of time in the editing room and ended up using a lot of the songs that were "temp tracks," like the Byrds' "Wasn't Born to Follow" and the Hendrix song. I know Fonda screened the movie for

Kim Fowley at Elysian Park Love-In, Los Angeles, California, 1967. Photo by Henry Diltz.

John Kay of Steppenwolf, who then gave him the approval for "Born to Be Wild."

A: I sang with the Fraternity of Man, who had "Don't Bogart that Joint" on the soundtrack. *Easy Rider* was the first time that the record business and the film industry both discovered that they had a new outlet for old product. Everyone forgets a lot of the songs on the *Easy Rider* soundtrack had been previously issued. None of it was really introduced in the movie, except the title song that Bob Dylan and Roger McGuinn cowrote, which Dylan offered McGuinn after a rough cut screening, with some handwritten lyrics that became the title track. I still record with John York, the bassist on that song. John is a musician, actor, singer, and cowriter in my 2004 movie, *Jukebox California*.

The *Easy Rider* songs were sitting there, and a year or two later, the movie came out. And to a lesser degree there were soundtracks to things like the movie *Candy*, that had the Byrds, and even before that, *Beach Ball* with McGuinn and early Walker Brothers, long before they grew their hair and relocated to England.

There were other films that had music, or spotlighted bands, like *The Trip*, and some of the soundtracks that Mike Curb was putting out showed up later in movies about the '60s. Like a U.K. film by Peter Whitehead, *Popcorn*, which had Jimi Hendrix, Otis Redding, the Rolling Stones, and John Lennon. That movie came out again a few years ago as *Backstage Pass*. Whitehead and Andrew Loog Oldham also put together the Stones' first movie, *Charlie Is My Darling*. And "The Trip" was even included in the seminal box-set collection of Punk and Garage Rock, *Nuggets*.

Q: And I also seem to recall you had an earlier life around musicians and composers, because your mother—after her marriage to Doug Fowley ended in divorce—married musician and pianist William Friml, the son of operetta composer Rudolph Friml. The elder Friml was one of the eleven founders of ASCAP and a well-regarded composer, who wrote *The Firefly*, *The Vagabond King*, and *The Three Musketeers*. And when film was ready to go the talking route, *The Vagabond King* was lensed in 1930 with Nelson Eddy and Jeanette McDonald singing songs of his. Rudolph Friml's best-known songs were "Indian Love Call," and "Rosemarie," and much later he wrote more music for the movies.

A: I met Rudolph when I was fourteen. He gave me a bicycle. And William Friml was a good arranger and played piano. My mother married William after meeting him during the World War II period, when she was on the Hollywood Stage Canteen at nights, after doing "Rosie-the-Riveter" factory work during the day.

In the early '50s I watched people like Johnny Bradford and Bill Friml doing special material with Dinah Shore, and Jack Cathcart was around, who married one of Judy Garland's sisters. You had some second-stringers like singer Roberta Linn and all four of Bing Crosby's sons—especially Gary—in the orbit doing some Las Vegas act, and that's where I learned about music. They kept mentioning the name Paul Gregory, an agent, a hustler, who packaged people and talent and got in on the action as well. So around 1954 I kinda knew what I wanted to be. Gregory booked a tour with actor Charles Laughton and some "Shakespeare" people, and worked them on a hundred-city tour of *Don Juan in Hell*.

I did meet music composer-arranger Lionel Newman one day. I

was allowed to watch him in his office, and then on the soundstage at 20th Century Fox, conducting an orchestra, and he tore new assholes and yelled, screamed, and blasted his string players. The guy was like Rod Steiger on steroids! He made sure it came in on budget. The next time I saw someone like him was Gene Simmons of KISS, who ran a tight ship, and also Marilyn Manson. I watched him rehearse his band. Those two guys were like Lionel Newman.

I had a song in the KISS film, *Detroit Rock City*. It was a Kim Fowley and Joan Jett song called "School Days." It was lyric-specific and decade-specific. It was a Runaways tune from their third studio album. The *Detroit Rock City* soundtrack charted in *Billboard* and I was the producer and cowriter. Other KISS songs that I cowrote, "Do You Love Me?" and "King of the Night Time World," have been used on fourteen different KISS products since 1975, including the first KISS movie with Paul Lynde, and on various DVDs and videos [*Unplugged* and *Live*].

I also had "Do You Love Me?" in the TV show *Freaks and Geeks* a few years ago. I didn't see the episode. I just got the money. It's also been covered by Nirvana—that hopefully will be in their box set.

I also have "Cherry Bomb" in the *Boston Public* TV program. Not the Runaways' version, but by 1&1, a brother and sister new wave disco act on the *Billboard* Dance Charts, who covered "Cherry Bomb" on Elektra Records.

The songs become automated, self-contained and self-generating. Songs have a life of their own and they wander into all kinds of opportunities.

For instance, I worked with the Rivingtons, who hit big with "Papa-Oom-Mow-Mow." Gaynel Hodge brought me some of his fellow Black Muslims in the group, and I schlepped them over to Pan-Or Productions, the in-house production company at Beechwood Music, which later evolved into EMI Music. I delivered the Rivingtons to them, and they gave me a "royalty override" on the record, which later was incorporated into the Steven Spielberg movie, *E.T.*

Q: Around 1973, you worked on *American Graffiti* for director George Lucas. I love the Beach Boys' "All Summer Long" blaring over the end credits on-screen.

A: Peter Rachtman, who was the comanager of Firesign Theater and Barbra Streisand at the time, hired me to produce new music sequences for *American Graffiti*. His daughter, Karyn, was later the music supervisor for *Pulp Fiction* and *Boogie Nights*. The story there was that George Lucas, right out of USC Film School, had scored this "Cinderella deal" with Francis Ford Coppola as executive producer.

My deal on *American Graffiti* was royalties on the soundtrack, no fees, because he had spent all his money licensing old hits and was three songs short. So I was hired to produce Flash Cadillac and the Continental Kids, who were in the movie and were managed by Peter Rachtman. He represented me and to this day I still get royalties. The thing to remember is that *American Graffiti* outsold *Easy Rider*. It sold more records. By then the album soundtrack format was a bigger piece of software for the industry.

On the set we did three songs in three hours and forty-five minutes. I covered "At the Hop" and "Louie Louie," because we couldn't get the original masters, and I snuck in the only original song in the movie, "She's So Fine," that Flash Cadillac wrote.

Lucas came there when we did the sequence, and I asked him, "What's your next project?" And he said, "*Apocalypse Now*". "Anything else?" "A thing called *Star Wars*."

I asked, "Who is going to produce the music?" "I am." "Who taught you?" "You just did . . ."

So he said to me, "You went to the gymnasium where we were shooting and figured out that there were three scenes in the movie, one where there was hardly anyone in the gym, then one where the gym is half full, and then finally full, and you altered the room sound for each song, and you rehearsed the group, and you had a real good engineer in a real good studio, and you sat there and barked and it sounds great. Thank you. But I want to ask you a question. How come you're doing this for no front money and just points?" And I looked him in the eye and said, "If you're good enough to be produced by Francis Ford Coppola after *Godfather*, I'll bet on him. You'll probably make it, Mr. Lucas."

When you see the movie, Kim Fowley's name is at the top of the music credits. I was the only guy who didn't ream him on front money walking in and I gambled and we sold ten million units. I also had producer royalties, and because of the honesty of Peter Rachtman and George Lucas, I get paid to this day. George Lucas's production company pays Peter and Peter pays Kim.

Q: You also had songs in *Ciao Manhattan*.

A: Right. They wanted to get the Byrds' version of "Citizen Kane," and then they found out my friend and collaborator, bassist Skip Battin, wasn't under contract to Columbia but was just a Byrd for hire. So we recreated the Byrds at the time, minus Roger McGuinn, with me producing. Clarence White, Skip Battin, Gene Parsons, and Kim Fowley. It's just come out as a twenty-fifth anniversary DVD version. The significance was that Edie Sedgwick was the only woman that Andy Warhol ever loved. In some parts of the world that movie is as big as *The Rocky Horror Picture Show*. They made a book later on, *Edie*, which was a best seller by George Plimpton.

I also cowrote a song with Doug Sahm of Sir Douglas Quintet fame, "Michoacan," that was in the movie *Cisco Pike*, Kris Kristofferson's film debut. I was living in Sweden at the time, ran into Kris there, and Red Rhodes, his steel player in 1970, at a festival. Elton John was in Blue Mink at that time, and we chatted. I wished him well as he was preparing to come to America. Three Dog Night had covered one of his songs. Its founding member Danny Hutton used to be my driver, a list that also included Mark Lindsay of Paul Revere and the Raiders and Warren Zevon. "Michoacan" was the last single Sir Douglas did on Smash Records and they covered us.

Now, in 2004, you don't make a living anymore in the record industry. All the guys who came out of vinyl and mono who still have a heartbeat are making music for film, TV, sports, and commercials, because homey hasn't figured out how to download it yet for free. But my stuff is music that teenagers download, and I don't get paid. On the music for adults over thirty-five I get paid. Reissues and soundtracks provide the only income that is real solid in the music industry now, unless you do *American Idol* format groups, because four-year-olds and their grandparents don't download.

A big movie for me was Richard Linklater's *Dazed and Confused*. I had "Cherry Bomb" on the soundtrack that went platinum in 1996. I heard that the director saw the Runaways as a high school student when the band came through Austin, Texas, and he remembered it and got it in there. I was invited to see the screening. I collected. This was a situation where something I cowrote, produced, and initially published in North Hollywood, ended up in a Hollywood movie. It was a teenage slacker movie that made a lot of sense to me, especially since I started at American International Pictures (A.I.P.) in 1959.

Q: What is the best use of rock 'n' roll in a movie you've ever seen?

A: *Easy Rider*. Because it was the first time. *Rock Around the Clock* was just one song. *Easy Rider* was every song. *Easy Rider* had the rock songs used in a narrative way. There were no people dancing in the theater when I saw it. It was song against action on the screen.

I think the music in *Watermelon Man* was terrific. I'm a big fan of Godfrey Cambridge, who starred in it.

I liked *Urban Cowboy*, but also all the Gene Autry and Roy Rogers singing stuff. My actor father, Doug Fowley, was the first man to ever kiss Dale Evans on the screen.

The worst use of music in a movie was in Mel Gibson's *Road Warrior*. It didn't have rock 'n' roll in it. Shame on you guys who never figured that out! No rock 'n' roll in the ultimate rock 'n' roll movie! There was orchestral music, but don't tell me those biker dudes in that flick weren't down with some sort of apocalyptic crazed rock music. Another lame thing I saw on the screen was James Brown singing snow lyrics in *Ski Party*.

Q: What have you noticed the last ten years in the merger of film and music?

A: A trend? This goes back to at least the last decade, but the director and screenwriter are involved more in the picking of songs for their movies. They might like a new band, have an import, a friend who is in a group, some classic rock favorites that they even wrote the script to.

In 2004 I had a song in the *Mayor of the Sunset Strip* documentary about DJ Rodney Bingenheimer. I also acted in the film, along with Cher, Brian Wilson, David Bowie, Ray Manzarek, and Gwen Stefani. I'm also in *Edgeplay*, a documentary about the Runaways directed by former Runaways member Vicki Blue. I'm an actor in that too. My singing voice was heard in Rhino Films' *My Dinner with Jimi*, a film about Jimi Hendrix. My recording of "The Trip" is in that movie. I also have some action in a movie being developed at Paramount, a movie about Mötley Crüe. I have publishing rights on one song with Nikki Sixx.

Roy Swedeen and I have also just finished my own documentary, *Jukebox California*. I created and selected all the music in that project. All this past year I've been in constant rotation on a few *E! True Hollywood Story* and *Behind the Music* episodes, including a two-hour show on Cher, Sonny Bono, and the Sunset Strip, as well as being on the BBC and Channel 4 in England, on shows about Phil Spector.

I also appeared on the VH1 *Bad Girls of Rock 'n' Roll* show, talking about the Runaways, with my songs being played in the background. Plus an on camera role on both Alan Freed and Mötley Crüe programs on MTV and VH1. And Court TV's show on John Phillips of the Mamas and the Papas fame. In June of 2004 I appeared on camera in *Secret Maps of Hollywood* (BBC). They are also using six songs I cowrote with Roy Swedeen.

Most recently, Kim Fowley and Roy Swedeen got a special feature piece of music included in the *Friends* tenth season DVD. And the beat goes on.

Q: But you've even had an ongoing relationship with TV music shows for many decades. I know you were the first guest on Lloyd Thaxton's local L.A. music and dance TV show in 1962.

A: I was promoting "Nut Rocker" when I did the *Thaxton* program. In 1988, I appeared on MTV in the U.K., on a show with Bunny Wailer. I was a dancer on *Beat Room*, which was on BBC2 in 1964. I was the featured male dancer on a Tommy Tune level every Tuesday. It got me a recording session with Mickie Most producing and Peter Grant doing the coordination. I appeared on *Ready, Steady, Go!* on Rediffusion TV. I sang on *RSG*. I made my English single on CBS, and I appeared on the show with the Small Faces, Los Bravos, and the Troggs. In 1964, on the day I got to England, P. J. Proby, whom I handled as a PR and musical advisor, appeared on *Juke Box Jury*.

That's where I met a young Rod Stewart in the green room. Rod had a song out called "Good Morning Little School Girl."

On *RSG* you would go down there every Friday, do business, get laid, go to parties, dinner. It was quite an event. Vicky Wickham was the one who picked all the music and she knew the hues and cues. She was a genius. Burt Bacharach used to fall by when he was in London for business and hustle songs down there afterward. It was a "green room" scene, before and after the show, and going off to dinner, dancing, and bedrooms. Post-pill, pre-AIDS world. Some of the time I wore Neil Young/Stephen Stills Laurel Canyon buckskin onstage. Green rooms, boardrooms, and bedrooms.

Motown was always popular on the movie set and in that environment. Even to this day, like in recent Julia Roberts movies, there are always various Motown oldies or Jobete Music copyrights for the white people to connect with. *The Big Chill* is their Torah. Instead of two tablets they have two CDs, in the 2004 rerelease model.

On the Mickie Most single, my backing group was Jimmy Page

and John Paul Jones, later of Led Zeppelin. We covered a Tom Rush version of Bo Diddley's "Who Do You Love?" That came as a result of being a dancer on the television tube.

Q: You were also on the *Upbeat* TV show from Cleveland, Ohio, hosted by Don Webster.

A: I was between the Miracles with Smokey Robinson and the Left Banke the afternoon I was on. I hung with the guy Michael [Brown] who sang "Walk Away Renee."

Upbeat was corn-fed morons trying to be Dick Clark with no budget. They tried. In contrast, *RSG* was innovative culture.

On the same tour the next day I was at the Atlantic Steel Pier live between Gene "Duke of Earl" Chandler and Shirley "Nitty Gritty" Ellis. You try working an eight thousand crowd in New Jersey, in 1968, sharing a stage with Gene Chandler, a Vee-Jay artist. I stuffed my pants with a wire coat hanger so I appeared to have a huge penis and all the black girls rushed the stage for whitey.

Q: Good Lord . . . How do you get songs in movies?

A: First lesson is not to write music for people who say it's a shoe-in and then you get stuck with a master that no one wants, that they conned you to do on spec. So if you happen to coincidentally have it, then send it and maybe it can find a home. You answer the telephone, look at your e-mails and you go to music conferences and parties, and people ask you about material. I really don't know how music supervisors and song pickers in the twenty-first century do it, I don't think anybody knows, and if they do, they have conflicting stories.

I believe the music is the last thing that is used for a movie. They do everything and in the last hour somebody decides to put a soundtrack together. Generally, the movie has been cut to the record collection of the director who has been placing Rolling Stones, Doors, Beatles, Neil Young, and Motown songs against the screen. Then he or she finds out the masters and publishing rates are too cost prohibitive to get the Beatles, Stones, Doors, or Neil Young. Then they say, "Get me something that sounds like this, that we can afford, and I want an all-in deal where we can own the master and they own the publishing, and we do a one-stop-shop deal."

That's how you get in there. The new independent music supervisors, who act like the old indie promotion guys in the early '60s, play buddy-buddy with the guys in the studios who don't have time to be pitched by Kim Fowley types, so they call up these guys who act as middlemen between Kim Fowley and them and say, "OK, we need a song about a bulldog and a frog."

There are also situations where the music supervisor will find stuff creatively and bring it to the director, or the director yells a song title, and they get something that sounds like it.

There's a new breed that is emerging. The street level middle-man. He or she takes a share of it and you retain your publishing. An administrator-plugger, but he or she is not affiliated with a record company or label.

If you don't find one of those, you send sound files of verse and chorus and aim at your target. So, if I go to a party, and I hear that someone is looking for a specific tune, the next morning I go to the studio, go online, find his or her address, and without being invited I send over a song like it, if I happen to have it in my catalogue, with a little note that says "we own all the rights. One stop shopping." Sometimes we place things that way.

There is no mailroom anymore, no power lunch. All of a sudden the guy comes to work and it's there in the morning waiting for him. We send our stuff out at night after they go home. We don't even ask permission. We just send it.

They either buy or don't buy. If they don't buy you're not there to be ridiculed. And if they buy it they send you paperwork. You send it over by messenger, not by mail. Try to use a girl with big tits or a mafia guy, or someone related to someone sorta famous. And if the music supervisor is gay, send your office boy over with an open shirt and they can chat about *Queer as Folk*.

Q: What other ways have you acquired to work copyrights and at least get to the submission desk?

A: I also know how to work the Jewish High Holy Days.

Q: I thought it was supposed to be a time of rest and reflection?

A: If you can't talk to a C.E.O. or music supervisor or record label head in their office the previous week or "campus environment," and you don't have kids that hang with theirs at the Cross Roads School, or the Ohev Beth Shalom, position yourself at a temple outing over Passover or Yom Kippur. Even hustle at the Purim carnival.

Q: My mother is in Hadassah. I never got this in the playbook!

A: Learn. Here's the code. Pay attention. Dish out three hundred dollars and get a real good seat and location in the power row at the temple. I don't even go, I'm at a disadvantage as a gentile, so I have a guy who worked for me, Desi, a Sephardic Jew, who wears a Star of David around his neck, and he hands out my business card after the services are completed. There's always a yenta banter curb and valet parking lot scene.

Desi sometimes comes back with some leads and direct numbers from executives who are making movies, and what kind of songs might be in the properties they are developing. I also have him pre-programmed like the character Laurence Harvey portrays in *The Manchurian Candidate*. Desi is instructed to give out my website address, and that's proving to be a real good method.

Once you check my website out and see my forty-five-year career, you're hooked for at least a phone call, or you'll want to meet me. Old school people especially know I'm reliable, and new money is intrigued. Plus, they have albums I'm on, and have seen movies I'm involved with.

I've acquired this "elder cool" stature that Chris Darrow suggests, like the way Johnny Cash was positioned in the last decade.

Harvey, people like you and Chris Darrow have made some mistakes in the arena. You guys still think the entertainment world is a fair and equal marketplace and talent is the only thing that matters. Remember, when you go out in public you are also sometimes judged by the woman on your arm, when it comes to any possible deal.

I learned that mixing race and religion can sometimes make potential money nervous, even the decision makers, limo liberals, who front for five, or pretend they're down with rap music.

Then there's also the current white world in Tennessee that I saw up close last decade.

Let me tell you about the last time I went to Nashville for an ASCAP dinner, to work songs and tunes for movies, about ten years ago. I tried to introduce myself in the country music world, even though in 1960 I coproduced Bonnie Owens, and won the Best New Country Music Newcomer award in *Billboard*. People at the function kept asking me what church I belonged to.

Later, the first company I dialed for a business-meeting visit was the House of Cash. The administrative secretary who answered the phone when I called rather matter-of-factly responded, "Sir, are you a New York Jew or a Hollywood Hustler?"

My mind was so blown I immediately picked up the phone and booked a flight back to Los Angeles.

Q: Hmmm . . . How else do you get product licensed now?

A: I go to a lot of music, film, and TV conventions. Sometimes I'm on a panel and I exchange business cards. In 1965 I was on a panel at Walter E. Hurst's Business School class at UCLA, with Burt Sugarman, now married to Mary Hart of *Entertainment Tonight*. He had a record label then, and in front of the class I hustled him for a singles deal and got it! Later, in the 1970s, Burt produced the *Midnight Special* TV series.

Q: What about this potential conflict where DJs on the radio—and I'm speaking more of National Public Radio—serve as music supervisors. Is it a conflict that they play songs that end up in TV or movies that they also get paid on?

A: There's no conflict when money can be made. This is Show Business. As your guy Frank Sinatra used to say, "Show Business: You show up and it's all business." Enemies do business in Hollywood.

People who do business are sexual icons of the mind.

I've had music in soft-core porn movies and have never seen them. The check cleared. "We need ten songs that girls and guys can grunt to." "OK. Use this."

There's also more politics and egos at play this century than in the '60s and '70s, when it comes to song placement and film soundtrack inclusion.

At the music conferences that are tied to film and TV song placement, "Hollywood shack job" is the perfect description, since the romance or sex—in this case, the song sound "rental"—is temporary, three, five, eight years, or in perpetuity.

No one is trying to get their band signed, and the worst guy in the room has a home studio. Small music conference, big people speaking, being available to be hustled. This is how I like the temperature for the potential intro and possible deal. See, everyone hides their motives in print interviews or in the music business or at conferences.

Q: What about the future of rock 'n' roll and music in film and on TV?

A: Rock 'n' roll died with Elvis Presley, rock died with John Lennon, and now in a post-MTV-Britney Spears-Brad Pitt world, it was best explained to me by an employee of Bug Music, whose name escapes me. This was said in 1998 when I visited the company. They administer some of my material. The executive said, "In this town there are two hundred feature films a year, plus two hundred features for TV a year. That's four hundred chances for you to get your music in four hundred separate films. And guess what? Four hundred bands didn't get four hundred record deals in Hollywood this year, did they?"

That was the day I realized that the music business was over for people like Kim Fowley.

Break patterns in two patterns—and reinvent. Bring on film, TV, sports, commercials, video games, and the ringtone pie, and move your tunes. The future's here . . . until school kids can download movies for free. Then the dark and desperate days will come again.

Here's something more interesting. We're in this Britney Spears-Brad Pitt universe, and the media keeps driving these people into our screens, but Britney Spears' music, as we speak, isn't used in other people's movies. Ironically, a lot of pre-1975 music is used, because it hooks in the older viewer. You can't make everything Jay-Z or Justin Timberlake, because part of your film and TV audience is often over thirty-five, and they want to hear music from their era—even if it's from this era, but has earlier elements in the production or the tonality of the piece.

It used to be the music business, with the emphasis on the word music. Now it's the music business with emphasis on the word business. Everyone still loses their job, don't they?

I live in Redlands, California, which is Palm Springs without movie stars. I go to the bank for my residuals, my soundtrack reissue checks, my license money, and I talk to the other characters in line, who have Social Security and golden parachute trips.

None of them do as well per month as I do, because my songs become a piece of my pension. It's mailbox money.

As my wonderful rock 'n' roll lawyer, the late Walter E. Hurst once said—and for years he had Dorsey and Johnny Burnette, Brenton Wood, Sam Cooke, Eddie Cochran, and Bobby Womack as clients, and also did some property work for the Beatles—"When the bands break up, the pension begins." Because it just becomes "Greatest Hits" and "Best of . . ." packages, and live concerts now available in addition to catalogue heard on-screen and integrated in the visual media for retail.

Q: Have you benefited from the DVD format, as well as things like Sony's PlayStation 2? Songs used on the computer screen?

A: DVD will become the future of closet "bedroom-garage" people, because it's too late for them to start their own record label and get ripped-off by distributors before a major label picks it up. And they can't tour anymore because all the rock 'n' roll places have been torn down for discos. So why not go to college where you're about to flunk out of and get some guys from the audio-visual department and have them make rock videos from rehearsals of you in the garage, with your girlfriends, you know, interviewing the band having a food fight. Go sell a thousand DVDs and make some money. The rappers are already doing it.

That's the future on how to break bands. The new Beatles, the new Steven Spielberg and the new Jenna Jameson will come from it. All of them can have careers launched on the same weekend.

The music supervisors also have an impact on the DVD. Today they're just like music directors and program directors of Top Forty radio in the pre-Beatles '60s. They were the ones who decided what got in or out in the old days, played by the DJs. Today they are the ones who get it in the movie or keep it in the movie.

That's the game in the twenty-first century. Sure you meet and know a lot of people, film and music folks who care about the pairing of music and screen, and even the souvenir CD sale item, but it's not the soundtrack world sonic scrapbook you envision, collect or document as a music historian, writer, and author.

I've participated in the Hollywood shack job. I was both pimp and whore in the bordello.

※

Kim Fowley: Select Filmography and Discography
FILM

Cowrote, coproduced, codirected, costarred in, and solely financed his theatrical feature film, *Jukebox California*. (2005)

CABLE AND TELEVISION APPEARANCES

E! True Hollywood Story; *Behind The Music* (VH1); MTV and MTV2; Court TV; BBC Scotland; MTV (U.K.); Channel 4/Principal Films (U.K.), actor and creator-vocalist of main theme: *The Phil Spector Story*; ITV-Granada Prime Time News Hour (U.K., 2004): Spokesperson, *In the City* music conference; *Pop Odyssey* (ZDF) documentary in Germany.

SOUNDTRACKS

American Graffiti (MCA-Universal): Producer of New Music Sequences; *Big Momma's House* (20th Century Fox): Composer and publisher of one selection; *Dazed and Confused* (PolyGram Pictures): Producer and cowriter of one selection; *The Butcher Boy* (Warner Bros./Geffen Pictures): Composer and publisher of one selection; *Ciao Manhattan* (independent): Producer, cowriter, and copublisher of one selection; *The Hawk Is Dying* (Paul Giamatti) (independent): Cowriter, copublisher, vocalist, one selection.

RADIO

Host, DJ, and content writer on Sirius Satellite Radio Network's *Underground Garage* Channel 25

Songs written or published by Kim Fowley have been recorded by:

KISS, The Byrds, Cat Stevens, Manfred Mann, The Runaways, Nirvana, Leon Russell, Helen Reddy, Wayne Newton, Marty Balin, Alice Cooper, The Hollywood Argyles, The Murmaids, Van Halen, Venus and the Razorblades, Slade, The Dead Boys, Paul Revere and the Raiders, The Seeds, Fabian, NRPS (New Riders of the Purple Sage), Flying Burrito Brothers, Blue Cheer, Steppenwolf, Stars on 45, Blue Oyster Cult, BMX Bandits, Teenage Fanclub, Emerson, Lake & Palmer, Andy White, Chris Darrow, and Ben Vaughn.

LARRY KING

LARRY KING HAS BEEN in the retail record business since the winter of 1978. For twenty-five years he's been affiliated with Tower Records, and is currently one of the lead buyers as well as product manager of the legendary store on Hollywood's Sunset Strip for nearly three decades.

I went to college with King in the '70s at San Diego State University, and also remember going with him to a campus showing of Dennis Hopper's *The Last Movie*. We also saw D. A. Pennebaker's *Don't Look Back* portrait of Bob Dylan at the Ken Theater in Normal Heights one night after a downtown San Diego record-seeking mission at Arcade Music.

King is also an avid vinyl collector, an expert on the folk and bluegrass genres, and for years wrote a monthly column in *Tower Pulse!* magazine, where he interviewed Bill Monroe, Alison Krauss, and Jimmie Dale Gilmore.

For decades he's observed and participated in the retail foot traffic and floor space changes to accommodate Tower's demanding clientele. He offers some original observations on the consumer and current climate of soundtrack product.

In his tenure, King has witnessed and developed the once small soundtrack section at the fabled Sunset Boulevard location, a section that now has expanded to multiple aisles, while even across the street there

Left to right, standing: Elton John, Bernie Taupin, and longtime Tower executive Howard Krumholtz, with Larry King at Tower Records on Sunset Boulevard, West Hollywood, California, 1995. Photo courtesy of Larry King.

is another Tower store, originally created to house home videos and now carrying DVD product.

Q: Has the chain changed in the positioning and evolution of the soundtrack album?

A: You have to always remember, up until the home video market, even before laser discs and DVD format, you had to buy the soundtrack LP, then the cassette, and now the CD, in order to hear the music from the movies.

Today, it seems almost mandatory that every film released has a soundtrack album, or an edition with bonus tracks, or an expanded two-CD set, or sometimes, a whole other album produced, generated, or inspired by the movie.

Now we're at the stage where they have two soundtracks: one with the music and the songs, the other with the score, and a few, like *Sleepless in Seattle*, where they come up with a sequel, with additional songs that *could* have been in the movie; music included in and inspired by *8 Mile* or *Moulin Rouge*.

Screenwriters, partly due to cable TV, have been empowered to write for the medium, and also have a lot more to do with the music in the films and the soundtracks. A lot of these guys were in bands, or have friends in music groups.

Q: In a world before the Internet, downloading, file swapping, and music sharing, and other record chains, a city was partially defined by mom and pop shops.

A: People and consumers come to the store today for a variety of reasons, especially the working professionals in the entertainment field. They do research, sometimes they are collectors, sometimes they are spying on friends, or supporting friends.

Q: Soundtracks where music and film collide.

A: The best one that ever did that was *The Harder They Come*, which unlocked the gates to reggae music in the United States. A mind-blowing soundtrack. The movie was something else, but for every person in the U.S. who saw that movie, a hundred people had the record. What a soundtrack.

Last decade, there was a similar trend, or situation, where a movie didn't do well—*The Mambo Kings*—but the soundtrack did better and went on to glory, and really had a significant impact on tropical and salsa music to new ears. The soundtrack really was on the charts in the urban centers like Miami, L.A., and New York for a long time.

And this extended to the *Buena Vista Social Club*, where you had some of the artists chronicled in the original documentary and concert footage actually come to the U.S. and play live. And, even going back to *Alice's Restaurant*, which might have been a small budget movie, but an enormous soundtrack that helped expose Arlo Guthrie. Even though Guthrie had no camera presence, he opened up an entirely new avenue for pop stars—the music icon as a film star. Remember, when Sinatra was getting kudos, deservedly so, as an actor, his singing career had tanked for the most part. Nowadays, recording stars like Bon Jovi or Ice Cube or David Bowie have lucrative film careers as well.

Q: In the '70s, the soundtrack was a souvenir of the movie. A take-home item.

A: And the film and music industries made attempts to work together, or at least market the music in film together, and pitch it to me. Years ago, our staff would be invited to advance screenings because of the music and film tie-in. Even today I was invited to see a documentary about how South African music helped the freedom movement. Many years ago it was not like that.

When you were in A&R at MCA Records, I remember—in 1978, 1979—I'd see you at *Animal House* or *The Best Little Whorehouse in Texas* screenings and events, where the parent company, Universal, had the product on its music label subsidiary, MCA Records. Where the label was a division of a film company, a companion soundtrack was always in the offing. There were some real masterpieces in the mix in those days. Ry Cooder and Captain Beefheart's work comes to mind, on director-screenwriter Paul Schrader's neglected but influential *Blue Collar*, which Jack Nitzsche was involved with. Back then, they were glorified compilation records, and some of them were afterthoughts, with a degree of back scratching—"Hey, we have a publishing deal with someone, let's throw it on the soundtrack." *American Graffiti* was different, and it was a two record set.

There was always a traditional soundtrack bin or section. In the '60s it would display *South Pacific* or *Oklahoma*. A vinyl universe, always a soundtrack section, but we would always in the last twenty years have discussions about whether to split it into two sections, "theatrical shows and musicals," and "movie soundtracks."

The world consists of splitters and lumpers. There are always people trying to split, but others lumping them together. "Where are the Broadway shows?" "They are mixed in with the soundtracks." You have to say it like that. The drama divas are still very cognizant of that. "Gotta have *Paint Your Wagon*," the Broadway one and the movie one.

Q: In the '70s, the soundtrack section was often at the back of the store. It created revenue, and things like *West Side Story* and *Hair* would sell. Tower's early stockings would be things like *Oklahoma*.

A: You have to remember, the soundtrack world includes Broadway shows, which over the last decade, have incorporated rock 'n' roll. *Hair Spray* and *Aida* and *The Graduate*, as stage plays, with soundtrack albums not owing hardly anything to the original birth mother. Then

Chicago, and the territorial productions of shows with songs and music. In the record store this was a larger section before catalogue orders, in a pre-Internet and eBay world. In the traditional vinyl world.

Saturday Night Fever turned it all around, and people realized there was gold in them there hills. Eventually, however, the bloom fell off the rose. Now you saw *Sgt. Pepper* and *Times Square* that shipped platinum and returned double platinum.

FM radio influenced the soundtrack audience and the hip record buyer a few decades ago. In the '70s we were still coming out of underground radio into the approaching mid-'70s, long before the new conglomerates of radio and more restricted play lists. And keep in mind, the *Easy Rider* soundtrack was unavailable for years on CD, as well as *Candy*, or *Blue Collar*. As imports, sure, but not domestically.

When the studio was 20th Century, with their record label, or when Paramount Pictures had a label, they took care of business, but then the studio vanishes and the takeover entity loses sight of what it has and the record library turns into a glorified collector's item. They get lost. They could have been catalogue generators but sometimes the companies weren't fast in picking them up.

Q: Then how did the climate change for the soundtrack album in the '80s?

A: The world started swelling. You started seeing music supervisors picking songs not just from catalogue or publishers and libraries, they started commissioning artists like Jackson Browne for a movie slot, akin to the way some of Paul Simon's songs were fused into *The Graduate*. Or going back to *Midnight Cowboy*, a few people then being introduced to the talents of Fred Neil, who wrote "Everybody's Talkin'" that Harry Nilsson sang. As a product buyer I could find reissues from as far away as Japan or the U.K., and I could bring them in because I knew the studio libraries would snatch them up as they have such an interest there.

In the '80s there was more concern and more aggressive techniques were used by companies to acquire end cap room, counter space, lobby cards, point of purchase items, and a wider section devoted to soundtracks.

Tower, like other record stores, is a place where movie studios distribute free tickets and early screening tickets, sometimes with a tag in the advertising, or to draw awareness to an existing soundtrack. Let's face it, the music market and the movie market pretty much overlap.

Q: Over the decades, you've seen a move away from the composer scores on soundtrack albums toward product stuffed with rock songs, but the composer is still living.

A: It used to be composer-oriented, and there is a slight return to where consumers are buying Jerry Goldsmith, Henry Mancini, and Morricone, now seeing people want the songs.

For many years—and this was more obvious in the early and mid-'70s—sometimes there was dialogue and film narrative on the vinyl, like *Taxi Driver* and *The Wild Bunch*. I like that as a record collector. *Five Easy Pieces* with some great Jack Nicholson narrative. What was cool about *Five Easy Pieces* is that it's a play on the five girls in the film and it's also five classical pieces. On the one vinyl side of the record are Tammy Wynette songs and on the other side the record is classical. Talk about a bad marketing idea! At that time those audiences could not bear one another, which come to think about it, was a key plot point near the movie's end.

Q: But it's also reflective of the whole stance of BBS films. They made bold movies and strong musical choices when it came to their releases like *Easy Rider*, *Head*, *The Last Picture Show*, and *Carnal Knowledge*.

A: Yes. You'll see, as you examine the soundtrack world over the decades, that there are economics at work, it's like we're now down to five major distributors, and when they figure out [mergers of] EMI and WEA or Sony and Bertelsmann, there's going to be three or four. The same thing happened with the studios. One by one they are merging into other things, and you are seeing a consolidation.

Q: And then the '90s.

A: We did have a technological "Go Go" nineties. People realize what a compact disc can do. Instead of coming out with a bad transfer, there's more time on the disc, and more things you can do with it. They go to town on it. There's a reissue of one of my favorite soundtracks, which I saw with you at school, *Zabriskie Point*. A whole other disc from the original vinyl album, as well as extensive liner notes.

Q: But do the expanded liner notes, the bonus materials, the outtakes, the jams and instrumentals impact, harm, or demystify the original intention of the music collection listening experience for you?

A: You get to keep the original thing together, and then you have a supplemental disc. That's how you get around that.

For example, you'll have jazz masterpieces, and then they'll come out years later, and sometimes they put takes one, two, three, and four, and they will jumble up the sequence and chronology of the original record. You know what I mean? That's wrong. The alternate takes are fine, and I'm glad to hear them, but not at the expense of going from song two to song three on the original.

Q: Sometimes the soundtrack album is sort of a misrepresentation, besides the fact that they quickly go out of print. Like with *Easy Rider*, on-screen you hear The Band do "The Weight," but on the soundtrack it's by Smith.

Q: Ironically, in spring 2004, out came the *Easy Rider* deluxe edition that now includes that original version of "The Weight" by The Band, which was denied for use on the late '60s-issued album.

A: You know inherently there were some contract negotiations and management issues that defined the exclusion from the original collection.

Q: The second disc of the 2004 *Easy Rider* rerelease has a set of nineteen tracks, titled *Something in the Air*, featuring songs that filled the new rock radio airwaves "and spoke to the Woodstock generation." But, you know, due to licensing issues, the first CD release of the *Easy Rider* soundtrack was relatively recent, in 2000.

And also out in spring 2004 is the *Big Chill* deluxe edition that in 1983 was a six-times-platinum, blockbuster soundtrack. The new version contains the film's brief instrumental interludes, including the theme to the fictional TV program, *J. T. Lancer*, and nineteen favorites "of the era." The second disc is aptly titled *Bigger Chill: Music of a Generation*.

A: There are a lot more soundtracks now. More indie bands given slots, and educated music supervisors incorporating their choices and cult bands and artists into the soundtrack product.

In the last ten years we've got some music guys calling the shots, like the director Curtis Hanson. See, you don't hear me complaining about doing two hours on the register, because it's put me back in touch with things. It's kind of neat, getting the interaction with the consumer. Like I don't know visually what most of these directors look like—I know the pop stars—but when they hand you their credit cards, you connect the face, and it sometimes leads to a whole discussion. This way, I've chatted up Alan Parker, John Sayles, Michael Cimino, Monte Hellman. These guys are so into their projects that they buy *tonnage* of music for them. You can tell that for them it's a labor of love. I did strike out with one of them once, to my eternal regret. It was the late Paul Bartel, and he was looking for the Communist Party anthem, the *"Internationale,"* for what would become *Scenes from the Class Struggle in Beverly Hills*. I tore the store apart looking for that one, I knew it was on Warren Beatty's *Reds*, but that is another lost masterpiece. Conversely, I was able to track down the original version of "Only You" by the Platters, from a host of bogus rerecordings, for another film of his. The funny thing is if a director-type pays cash, more often than not I have no idea who they are. My point is really that most of these directors, who are often screenwriters as well, are executive producers of their soundtracks, so they are really aware of the music in film relationship.

Then again, and I've heard this from a few different people, from fans to executives, to other music and film people, and maybe it's mentioned or revealed on the DVD: the making of Nick Hornby's *High Fidelity* was pretty much a breeze, but apparently it got bloody when they put the soundtrack together. Because he had all the creative people going, "I want this song . . ." and there was only so much room they could put in that soundtrack.

There's one thing, and I need to unwind, and I'm speaking as a fan, and a purist. I'm watching this movie, based on an Evelyn Waugh novel *A Handful of Dust*. They were using Andean panpipe music in the score, but it's set in a tropical rain forest. I hate it when they mess up things chronologically or geographically. I can give you another example, one of the biggest soundtracks in history, *The Sting*. I think *The Sting* was set in the Roaring Twenties, but the soundtrack is ragtime music from the 1890s, and it just sold millions and revived a type of music, just like Jimmy Cliff's *The Harder They Come* did with reggae. Watching *The Sting* used to make me cringe. Like you and me watching *American Graffiti*, and the guy decided to put Glenn Miller music in it!

Then there are other good rock examples. I hated the movie *Forrest Gump*, but they did a good job on the soundtrack album. I thought the movie was mean-spirited, but its music, like the times, soared.

Q: Who buys soundtracks?

A: That's the beauty of it. It's the exact cross section of the consuming public, plus lots of people who actually saw the movie. You might think it would be the other way around, but that in a nutshell is how the marketing folks have changed the dynamics of the mass-merchandised soundtrack.

Q: Are the prices a little more expensive on soundtrack albums? And why?

A: Yes they are. For many years—and I'm going back to Beatles records at $5.99 for a regular LP—soundtracks would often be priced a dollar more. *A Hard Day's Night* would have been $6.99. That was the norm all the way through. I always wondered about it, and the story I heard was that the studios wanted a take. An override.

Q: What about country music in movies and soundtracks?

A: It's really about how country music and country artists are used in films and soundtracks. I mean, *Rio Bravo* just with Ricky Nelson was good, or the Faron Young song "Hello Walls" in that Larry Flynt movie was excellent usage where the song met the screen. Candi Staton doing "Stand by Your Man" in *Five Easy Pieces* really serves the action well. Country music cues and portions of songs get used all the time, but they don't usually fly. Here's why, and it has to do with the soundtracks of the '70s and the soundtrack now. If you don't think it through, you are corrupting the marketplace, and someone will pick up the record, and it will have "Stand by Your Man" *and* a piece by Horace Silver. That's not going to fly. Sure, our record collections are varied and not segregated like a lot of other people's, but the casual buyers and fans don't need that kind of an aural adventure.

The record world, radio stations, and charts don't want it diverse. They want it specialized. When I see these labels put out a disc from their movie and expect the audience to pay their lunch money to hear a Bee Gees song and a Johnny Cash song, I can only wonder what they're thinking. It doesn't work that way. You can have one, you can have the other, but you can't mix them. I'm only talking about the business, not aesthetics.

It could be mixed if they did their homework. A movie like *Forrest Gump*, which had lots of songs, a diverse time period and various regions, works effectively as one song would segue into the next one. It was conceptualized, or thought through. Perhaps they could have gone deeper into the catalogues of the Jefferson Airplane or the Doors, but it really worked.

Q: Who is the consumer these days who likes music and film product?

A: We've had twenty years of music videos, where the artist records the song, a visual is added, and the whole perception of the song is changed. People come to the register or information booth and describe the video they've seen to buy the song. That's promotion and marketing.

The labels look at it in terms of the music being introduced by the video. And there are a lot of consumers these days that don't even care about liner notes or packaging information.

Lots of people come up to me and say, "Do you have *Jerry McGuire*?" They bark the film title, and don't even ask about specific songs. It is a souvenir of the experience. And I do get a lot of different people asking for it. Like even with the *Frida* soundtrack. It's selling. You get the college coeds, the intellectuals, the Latinos, older women, art heads. The kind of people you'd like to hang out with. It has a little extra going for it, as opposed to *Jerry McGuire*.

I mean, for years you were one of the few guys who would call or come to the store and ask if Jimmy Miller or Nitzsche had produced any new records. You asked about the producer and the arranger. No one really seeks it out that way these days.

There's always room for new genres and catalogue reissues, like the soundtracks of black exploitation movies. Sometimes they use the same cover on the soundtrack album as the new DVD. One of the best items is the rerelease of Curtis Mayfield's *Superfly* soundtrack. This is a case where the composer was given props and his motives detailed in the liner notes and deluxe packaging.

I also have to add, if two white guys like you and me could get our hands on the BET channel, it would be *Putney Swope*, man.

We do have debates in the store about the physical display of music, whether it be oldies or rap music. One manager insists that rap is the minstrel music for the twenty-first century. He got in trouble for being quoted in the media describing it that way, although some of the best rappers are from the strata that W. E. B. Du Bois referred to as "the talented tenth" and not the thugs from the street. Let's face it, you have to be really together to have any kind of a long-lived music career these days. I crossed paths with Tupac Shakur one time at the shop and two things really stood out about him: he was small, I mean diminutive, and he was humble and self-effacing in a really quiet way. He's been dead for some time now, but this was a guy who really, really worked, and he is *still* putting out records—even a soundtrack!

Q: There is a proliferation of rap music and new urban soundtracks. They have a quick burn, don't they? But a lot of people get involved on various levels.

A: You know what, this has been happening for a while. Earlier today, a woman came into the store, and I was helping an editor-type for the movie *Solaris*, with George Clooney. And she said, "I'm going against two competitors, trying to get the music for the trailer." I said to her, "You're putting together the music for the film, and you have a rough edit of the film, and since you don't have the rights yet, you need to show the movie to some of the executives and you need to have some type of mood in the movie, right?" And she said, "No, somebody else is doing that. I have to do it for the trailer." I started thinking, "Man, this is really new to me." Look, it's all above board, everyone gets their check and royalty, but I can also see a master song used simply as a promotional tool and income. I still think you'll have some artists not allowing songs for commercials and TV use when it's not tied to something they are in.

Q: As a fan with a quarter of a century in record store trenches, and an ardent record collector, what are the soundtracks you keep returning to, and that you notice have a steady stream of sales?

A: *Performance*. The premise of the story is this omnipotent, all-seeing musician, so musically it really had to deliver the goods. Mick Jagger supplied the vocal on "Memo from Turner," and it helped that Nitzsche had all this studio history with the Rolling Stones. And the inclusion of Randy Newman singing his guts out and Buffy Sainte-Marie on Jew's harp. And the Last Poets. I don't think a week goes by where I don't think about their track on the soundtrack.

I like *Pat Garrett and Billy the Kid*. The Dylan songs and atmosphere. Bob Dylan was foisted on the director, Sam Peckinpah, who wanted Neil Diamond. I'm also a fan of Robert Altman and his films and soundtracks. The overlapping of dialogue into music. I know people who hate it. It sort of makes you sit forward and really strain to hear everything.

I like Bob Dylan on-screen. He has this charisma in the sense that he holds something back, and you want him to put out, and you anticipate, and he lets you see a little more. He teases you. The Charlie Chaplin mannerisms. I heard his voice on the new movie, *Masked and Anonymous*. You hear him and he stops singing, and you go, "Wow."

I love the Stones' *Rock and Roll Circus*. It is well paced and it really segues from one song to the next really well. It just moves. Pacing is really important in these soundtracks.

I bought the DVD of *A Hard Day's Night* the day it came out. I haven't done something like that in a long time. As soundtracks go, it's probably as close to perfection as you can get, don't you think? I like *Help!*—a weak plot, but the song selections were better than the cinema. And in the first one they are just flawless. I like *Let It Be.* I like seeing the process and the deconstruction.

I like the soundtrack to *Blow-Up* that Herbie Hancock did as a jazz soundtrack, but it has a rock song by the Yardbirds. It's kind of the exception to the rule—my rule that you should not mix genres, even though this was thirty-five years ago. More politics and factions would get in the way these days for that to even get made.

Q: What about the collision and merger of music and film?

A: I hate to be a cynic—follow the money, man. You've got these two powerhouses, and instead of sucking it up and being partners, they just go to the bank.

The next trend, video games, video arcades, there are many volumes to all of them. *WWF* five volumes, soundtracks to extreme sports, whatever you do you have a soundtrack to your life. It's a commodification lifestyle. So you were a surfer, and the music just grew up out of that culture, like rocket scientists in the south bay and their children who did such a great job creating a hard-core punk hybrid of British angst and surfer zeal. Now, everything is commodified. This is the key word. The marketplace is going to sell you the lifestyle and the soundtrack with it, you see. The soundtrack of *your* life! Better yet, the life that their accountants and psychologists *think* that you should have.

Even George Orwell couldn't have dreamed up something so diabolical. You want the tattoo? We're gonna give you the music to get the tattoo by. Or the Super Bowl, we're going to give you a soundtrack to get plastered to, ya know?

Q: What about technology? You've been around long enough, from the seven-inch single to the DVD to the SACD format.

A: I've always had somewhat of a reservation with what I call the technophiles. They are more interested in the process and the engineering than they are in the spirit of the enterprise.

Let's face it. Would you rather listen to a scratchy 45 or an eight-track cartridge? And if it delivers the goods, we don't care about the pops and scratches.

Now with downloading, Napster, the phasing out of retail record chains, the direct buyer from the world wide web, partially fueled by the internet, you'll probably download a film and make your own soundtrack to the movie.

For twenty years, Larry King has been a product manager/buyer at the Tower Records flagship store on the legendary Sunset Strip. During the advent of digital technology and the rise of an alternative, independent music scene, he served as a spokesperson to the print media and television outlets such as CNN and MTV on matters relating to recording artists and their musical offerings. For two decades he wrote about music for *Tower Pulse!* magazine, the company's acclaimed musical publication, on subjects as diverse as bluegrass, holiday music, klezmer bands, Celtic groups, western swing, and folk. In that capacity he interviewed and published stories about Alison Krauss, Bill Monroe, the Flatlanders, and Keith Whitley.

King has also authored liner notes for folksinger Ed McCurdy and funk masters The Meters, and he has been used as a source for other CD productions. He is a participant in the yearly *Village Voice* survey of the best in popular music, the prestigious *Pazz and Jop* poll.

RANDALL POSTER

Randall Poster has been the music supervisor for Wes Anderson's movies, *Bottle Rocket* and *Rushmore*, and most recently, *The Royal Tenenbaums*. Poster has also matched songs to other films: *Jesus' Son*, *Rounders*, *Velvet Goldmine*, *I Shot Andy Warhol*, *Kids*, and *Meet the Parents*.

I conducted a phone interview with Poster when he was in Beverly Hills on business around the promotion of *The Royal Tenenbaums*.

Q: What is the role of the music supervisor?

A: The music supervisor's role is to help establish a vocabulary that the primary participants can share in referencing music, and then the other goal is to help define the musical logic of the movie. Sometimes that can be by connecting sounds, sometimes it can be by connecting a musical legacy, sometimes it can be by drawing contrast or confluence in a musical arrangement and style. Sometimes it can be by connecting an instrument throughout the course of the movie. If you think about it, there's a trombone that becomes *The Royal Tenenbaums'* signature.

Q: Describe the process of working with Wes Anderson and the record label in creating the *Royal Tenenbaums* soundtrack.

A: Wes and I first started working on the movie when the movie was a one-sentence idea. We basically went from *Rushmore* to the new movie. We just go back and forth with songs, listening to them, and discuss them back and forth with each other. It's a very organic process, and I would say we had seventy-five percent of the songs picked out and licensed before we even started shooting the movie. They weren't detailed in the script.

There's a process of discovery in the course of making the movie but, for the most part, we basically did our exploration prior to shooting. It's a great way to do it.

This way, Wes could choreograph certain sequences knowing that he had certain pieces of music. What I try to do is find the logic, pinpoint it, and then pursue it as aggressively as we can.

We're guys who love music. I don't make suggestions to Wes, I sorta expose him to the music, or show something that by virtue of juxtaposition with another song gives it a kind of life credibility.

What's interesting about this soundtrack, and kind of fun, is that John Cale plays not only on the Nico and Velvet Underground songs, but he's also on the Nick Drake piece. So those are the types of connections and the currency that we work on; where those kind of connections really mean a lot to us, and you see how the music connects.

Q: You and Wes have always included a vintage era Andrew Loog Oldham-produced Rolling Stones song in all three of your films. In *The Royal Tenenbaums* there is even a scene where their original *Between the Buttons* red label London Records vinyl is displayed to "She Smiled Sweetly." Who has the Stones jones or digs the work of arranger-session man Jack Nitzsche on those classic tracks?

A: Everybody owns those records, and Wes has had a Rolling Stones song in all three of his movies. I think Wes has an abiding connection to that music, and I know at least in *Rushmore*—and maybe it carries through to *The Royal Tenenbaums*—the image of the Stones in that era, with the Edwardian suits and ties, the spirit is just soaring. So I think that's an element and a connection to the music that somehow transcends the music, and tunes into a cultural touchstone.

In this business you have to keep yourself in check. One of my truth tests is that I always say to a friend of mine, Marq Roswell, a music supervisor, "What would (Jack) 'Specs' (Nitzsche) say?" Or, "What would 'Specs' do? How would 'Specs' handle this? How do we mine the real musical truth of this thing?"

Q: Is it easier for soundtracks to be constructed these days?

A: I think that people like managers and A&R people are really persistent and they see it as an opportunity, so they basically are very aggressive in getting me material and making themselves available. As much as they can get the information, even during casting. They have vague notions that there's a movie being readied from reading the trades, and there are people who are better at walking in the door than others.

Funnily enough, Jason Schwartzman, who was the star of *Rushmore*, turned Wes and I on to Emitt Rhodes, who has a cut on the *Royal Tenenbaums* soundtrack.

Q: I also think your teaming with Wes, as well as his writing a glowing liner note underscoring Mark Mothersbaugh's work as a composer on *The Royal Tenenbaums*, might signal a new trend where the composer doesn't always get dumped off of the soundtrack product.

A: We've been kind of unconventional in the way we use so much score on the records. A lot of times when you see these records, there's the eight songs, and then they have a piece of the score at the end of the record. We just felt it captured the spirit of the movie by interspersing songs with Mark Mothersbaugh's score pieces. I think that score is so unique. We may not sell as many records as some soundtracks, but I would say our audience, our collectors and fans are more devoted to our records than anybody. I would put them up against anybody. Soundtracks do different things for different kinds of movies.

Q: What about dealing with estates like Nico and Nick Drake, and new copyright holders who populate your *Royal Tenenbaums* soundtrack; people as owners who were not even around when the original songs were written and produced?

A: One of the joys of my job working with Wes Anderson is that we're tight and we spend a lot of time together, so it's very informal.

I just love good songs. Wes is so decisive and he's so committed to our ideas. Like we used a track from Vince Guaraldi in *Rushmore*, and also in *The Royal Tenenbaums*.

When we were mixing *Rushmore*, we would listen to Nico and the Velvet Underground while driving through Berkeley.

Regarding soundtracks and estates, new copyright owners, there's no hard and fast rule. Sometimes it makes it more complicated, sometimes more simple. A lot of times there are all sorts of complications with songs. Sometimes the artists don't have any control of a song at all. We've licensed from some of the most notoriously difficult people. That's why we really try and get in there early, so we know where we stand, and we're relentless.

Q: What about working with record labels in putting a soundtrack together. Have there been situations where labels lean for the inclusion of artists on their label if the soundtrack is being done for them or a parent company?

A: I'm lucky at this point in what I'm doing, in that people want me involved by virtue of my total commitment to making sure the music in the movie is enhancing the movie. I haven't been involved in that many confrontational situations with labels.

In certain movies, it's easy enough to do. Certain movies are more porous than others as far as being adaptable to other types of music.

As far as the *Rushmore* and *Tenenbaums* soundtracks are concerned, I have some interaction with the label who put them out. These people really respond to the material, especially with *Tenenbaums* following *Rushmore*, it's a rare breed. I don't think they would try and make it something it wasn't. I'm always open to working with the label and the A&R person.

There are certain labels and executives that really feel, if one of their bands is working a record, or a single, they don't want to see them have the distraction of that track being available anywhere else.

Then there are other people who say, "Any exposure that I can get for this artist, I'm gonna take, so I'm not going to be that precious about it."

You see, the growing trend is that there are very few career artists. A lot of times they need every opportunity to expose the band, through a movie, to whatever audience might not be reached otherwise.

Q: Is it more complicated in 2002 to secure songs for movies and soundtracks?

A: Yes. Conglomerates. Fewer owners. The proliferation of songs in commercials. I think it raises people's expectations as far as money goes. And competition for songs. There are more moviemakers who see the opportunity—whether true or not—of tying in with music to promote their movie, or it being an ancillary form of income. With certain pop artists, there's a lot of competition, so that raises the price.

Q: What about when you can't get a clearance or a license for a movie, because the artist or manager says no?

A: As long as they say no to your face and don't do something weird at the end. I've been doing this for ten years and have a body of work.

I don't play that fast game, and I'm very passionate about the movies I work on. So either they get it or they don't get it. You know what? There's nothing I can really do. And if the manager wants to interfere, and the thing in my mind has to happen, we'll just keep at it and do whatever we can to involve the people who we think will support us and respond to the passion.

Q: Does it ever bother you? Are you emotionally attached to the possibility of inclusion?

A: I let it fly off my back. I don't worry about it. If it's not meant to be, it's not meant to be. One day we'll put together our box set, or compile all our records, and we'll try again to get those records.

Q: Where do you see the role or roles of music in film and the role of the music supervisor going in the future?

A: Sometimes you need to have leverage to get the record company to allow you to do it. I love doing what I do, and it's all I want to do. I don't hanker to transcend that role. I just want to work with people who are nice to me and let me have fun making the movie. As I've said before, my feeling about it is, it's not your movie, it's our movie. So work with people who go into it with that spirit and keep putting in great songs, and that combination of music and image can be transcendent.

Some new films are using blues music. Unfortunately, a lot of times with music in the movies, music is often the last thing that has any elasticity to it in the process. So a song, or the music or the theme, needs to do what it can to compensate for what is there or not there in the scene. Sometimes it's by virtue of the piece itself, or having a steady rhythm rather than an erratic rhythm, or that there are times in movies where certain instruments at a certain point become very tiresome. I don't think there are any rules to these things. I think people are always looking to put the music they love into their movies.

※

Randall Poster: Music Supervisor
The Pink Panther (2006)
Jarhead (2005)
Bad News Bears (2005)
The Aviator (2004)
The Life Aquatic with Steve Zissou (2004)
The Stepford Wives (2004)

Starsky & Hutch (2004)
Along Came Polly (2004)
Mona Lisa Smile (2003)
Bottle Rocket
Rushmore
The Royal Tenenbaums
Jesus' Son
Rounders
Velvet Goldmine
I Shot Andy Warhol
Kids
Meet the Parents
(. . . and more)

GARY CALAMAR

Gary Calamar, along with Thomas Golubic, produced the Grammy-nominated *Six Feet Under* soundtrack, music from the HBO original series, released on the Universal/UMG Sound Track label. Alan Ball and Alan Poul served as the soundtrack executive producers.

The soundtrack is a varied assortment of new bands, world music, classic rock nuggets, and three variations of the title theme by composer Thomas Newman. The CD includes Peggy Lee, Shuggie Otis, PJ Harvey, Classics IV, the Dandy Warhols, Zero 7, Beta Band, and others. There's even a bonus selection tucked deep inside the package—a Julie London track produced by Tommy Oliver. The dark humor and funeral home atmosphere of the series does not exclusively permeate the positive pop veneer of a lot of the music within the episodes. It's a very uplifting compilation of new, now music.

Calamar also has a weekly Sunday evening program, *The Open Road*, on National Public Radio's Santa Monica-based affiliate, while also hosting a show for the musical skies of Delta Airlines and consulting and overseeing the extensive music library of AOL Music.

It was in 1998 that Calamar met veteran music supervisor G. Marq Roswell, and the two jointly supervised the music for *Varsity Blues*, resulting in a #1 box office hit and a gold soundtrack album. They

Gary Calamar (right) with actor Federico Diaz, who portrays
Freddy Rodriguez in HBO's *Six Feet Under*.
Photo by Alice Calamar, courtesy of Gary Calamar.

quickly followed up with *Slums of Beverly Hills,* before the New York-born Calamar struck out on his own, going on to supervise the music of the critically acclaimed *Panic* in 1999.

This century he joined forces with friend and fellow music supervisor Thomas Golubic to form SuperMusicVision. Their collaboration on the *Six Feet Under* soundtrack followed.

Q: Is there a different mindset when you are supervising music for feature films like *Varsity Blues*, as opposed to assembling the music for *Six Feet Under*?

A: The main difference, just talking mechanics, is the pace of TV. I mean, it's just relentless. You do one show, "Great—we've got twelve more to go." You really have to work fast, and clear and license music fast. You just have to be on your toes. With film, obviously you still put in a lot of work, and talent is very important, but it seems to go at a bit more leisurely pace. Sometimes you'll have a couple of months to nail down the right songs and clear them. With TV, and I'm speaking of *Six Feet Under*, sometimes we'll have just a few days to get a song cleared and get it on the show.

Q: Do you work closely with Alan Ball of *Six Feet Under*, who wrote the movie *American Beauty*?

A: Absolutely. I worked closely with him on our soundtrack and he's at every music meeting. He's very hands-on and collaborative. In putting together the soundtrack for the series, he made some suggestions that were implemented in the collection. He picked a song by the Devlins that ended the pilot show.

It's not unusual for a song to be written into the script and make it onto the show. A lot of times it doesn't happen, though. Writers will put a song in the script, thinking that it might work on the page, and we'll end up changing it. Sometimes the song starts right at the script level. From what I understand, the writers will be listening to music as they are writing the script, and that helps them and makes it more organic if it makes it to the show.

Q: Tell me about *Six Feet Under*. I heard your soundtrack and got curious to see the visuals and hear the writing in the show.

A: No one really thought about a soundtrack album very early on. Everybody was just hoping. I read the script, saw the pilot, and was very optimistic that it was going to catch on. But no one was thinking about a soundtrack album until the end of the first season, when the show got to be popular. Even when we started shopping the soundtrack around, my partner Thomas Golubic and I assumed a small independent label might pick it up. We were not seeking major labels. The music was interesting, and eventually the soundtrack did get picked up by Universal. I won't call it a bidding war, but there were several major labels interested in it.

Q: Have you noticed in the last five years or so, putting on your radio DJ hat, an increase in soundtracks coming to you at the station? Or even as a music supervisor, seeing more soundtrack compilations or tunes from other arenas, like DVD or samplers, in the retail outlets you frequent?

A: I have noticed things like black exploitation and TV show soundtracks that have escalated a little bit. Since the late 1970s with *Saturday Night Fever*, *Grease*, and *Urban Cowboy*, it seems like everything's been rolling from there.

Then you had record labels working with the movie companies, and it actually got to a certain point where the cart was leading the horse. It felt as if the studios wanted to have a hit soundtrack just to promote the movie. One of the reasons was for the soundtrack to get on the radio the week before the movie came out, and to have it as a marketing tool. Now it survives independently as its own thing. But the studios still want it to market their movie.

Q: Tell me how you work with your partner Thomas, with Alan Ball, and in licensing music for *Six Feet Under*. You wear a lot of hats in relation to the music in the series.

A: Yes. A lot of music supervisors do not clear or license their songs. Thomas and I do. It was part of the gig. Sometimes people will give us a real high price and that will exclude them from being considered. Neil Young declined, he just doesn't do TV.

Q: What about some of the songs on the soundtrack? Were you looking for items that were theme-oriented and connected very obviously to the topic of the series? In the liner notes to your soundtrack, Alan Ball says, "Music plays an integral role and we employ a wide variety of both source and score in an attempt to create an environment that is contemporary, yet somehow timeless." And the package starts out with the group named Lamb doing "Heaven."

A: The song "Heaven" of course has sort of the lyrical connection, and often Alan Ball likes to stay away from that, but sometimes the song just works. I was a fan of their previous record, and actually this new Lamb album came in and it was never released in the United States. So it's kind of an exclusive track. Craig Armstrong, whom you might know from his music in Baz Luhrmann's movies, is on the soundtrack. "Let's Go Out Tonight." He's part of the Massive Attack crew, and in addition to composing for films he's put out some albums with songs on them, and the song in our show features Paul Buchanan of Blue Nile. That song came originally from a Blue Nile album and he reworked it.

We think of the characters all the time and consider what they would be playing in the script or scene. We don't have the power to say a specific song is going in the show, but it gets filtered through us.

Early on, we work out rough ideas of what these characters might be listening to. We do it for Clair, Ruth, Nate, and the mom. All of them.

We had a lot of freedom putting this soundtrack album together. Since we assembled it before we went to labels for distribution, we weren't locked or governed by their existing catalogue. That was part of the deal when we were talking to labels. Whatever makes it on the soundtrack album has to be something that was actually in the show. It's not going to be an "inspired by" album. In order to make it in the show, it's just got to work. Alan Ball and the producers and Thomas and I just need to believe that it works in the show. We're not going to put something in because we want it to be on the soundtrack. Cuts like Stereo MC's "Deep Down & Dirty" came from our record collections. A scene called for upbeat, party music and we placed it in there. Thomas and I have some shorthand going when we do the music, but we also butt heads from time to time. We have our different strengths. He is very strong in DJ culture, jams, hip-hop, and things like that. I may be stronger in pop and songs, but that's not to say I won't come up with an electronic song for a scene and he won't come up with a pop song for a scene. I'm a little older than he is and we cover a lot of ground.

As far as music supervision is concerned, you're basically serving the production, serving the director and the producers. It shouldn't be my particular favorite songs, but it's always nice when it works out that way.

Q: What are the steps in the process of putting together music for the series?

A: We work off the script initially. Wild brainstorming at that point and deciding where music might be.

Alan and the writer sometimes will put in a song that he or she thinks is gonna work in the script, and we'll go chase it.

Actually, Elmer Bernstein told me in our radio interview that "you can't really tell if a song is going to work from the script. You have to see the picture and get the vibes."

After the script is read, it varies. We have the script several weeks or a month before we see a rough cut, and we have a session with Alan Ball and the production team. Thomas and I will have put together a presentation for them. Maybe five songs per scene that will work, or the direction that we will take it. And we play it for them, and then we go clear them.

People talk about HBO and the freedom given, and with this

production it's true. We can look at a scene, think about the character and "what is he listening to?" Maybe some old soul music or an oldies station; and we slotted Shuggie Otis into the show. His "Inspiration Information" made an impression on me, along with an Italian band, the Dining Rooms, an instrumental electronic band. Very atmospheric. There's an album of theirs out in the U.S. on the Guidance label, and several albums out in Italy. It was sent to us, came across our desk and we loved it.

Comparing it to *Varsity Blues*, where there was so much politics, that was an MTV production, and they were working with Paramount at the time. But there were a lot of people to please. Hollywood Records was putting out the soundtrack, they had their interests. Paramount. This was going to be a hit soundtrack and played on MTV. No Steve Earle and Wilco, but Foo Fighters. *Slums of Beverly Hills* was before *Varsity Blues*, and that was kind of an indie project with Fox Searchlight. Very low budget, compared to *Varsity Blues*, and that was relatively no politics, but free to use.

Q: What are the trends for the future regarding the soundtrack album from a TV series? I see young bands and unsigned groups getting some network and cable visibility that didn't exist all that much in the past.

A: For labels and young artists it's a fantastic vehicle, but for the most part these young artists aren't getting any airplay and they generally work inexpensively, which I think is certainly a factor, but there is a lot of great talent out there that's just not getting exposed any other way. I'm all for them getting on these TV shows and hopefully onto albums as well.

§

In 1994, Gary Calamar started as a volunteer at National Public Radio's KCRW-FM and was given the opportunity to pilot *The Red Eye* each Saturday night-Sunday morning from one to 5 A.M. *The Open Road* currently airs Sunday nights from nine to midnight. Through the years Gary has hosted live performances and interviews with musical greats ranging from Brian Wilson and Elmer Bernstein to Wilco and the Flaming Lips. In 1998, Gary collaborated with music supervisor G. Marq Roswell and the two supervised the movie *Varsity Blues*, resulting in a #1 box office hit and a soundtrack album certified gold, and *Slums of Beverly Hills*.

Striking out on his own, Gary went on to music supervise the critically acclaimed *Panic* in 1999. In 2001 Gary joined forces with friend and fellow KCRW DJ Thomas Golubic to form SuperMusicVision. The duo supplied the music for the HBO original series *Six Feet Under*, and have recently produced Volume Two of the soundtrack album, which was released in June 2005 on Astralwerks Records. Gary and Thomas were nominated for a Grammy for producing Volume One of the *Six Feet Under* soundtrack.

Gary currently teaches the Music Supervision class at UCLA Extension.

MARTIN BRUESTLE

MARTIN BRUESTLE IS THE producer who, along with creator-writer David Chase and music editor Kathryn Dayak, is in charge of postproduction music supervision on the HBO cable TV series, *The Sopranos*. He also directed the episode "Do Not Resuscitate" in the second season of the series.

After graduating from the University of Minnesota in 1987, Bruestle was selected to participate in the Academy of Television Arts and Sciences Internship Program on the television series, *Thirtysomething*.

In 1990 he was on the series *Northern Exposure* as associate producer or coproducer for all five seasons of the series, and helped produce two soundtrack albums.

In the summer of 1997, Bruestle began work on the *Sopranos* pilot. He and show creator David Chase have been nominated twice for Grammy Awards for the show's soundtracks, released by Sony Music.

Steven Van Zandt, a.k.a. Little Steven, who acts on *The Sopranos*, suggested I definitely had to talk to Bruestle for *Hollywood Shack Job*, and put me in touch with him.

Bruestle is now in his fifth season working very intensively on *The Sopranos* out of their Santa Monica production office in California. Ten

Martin Bruestle. Photo courtesy of *The Sopranos*-HBO.

years ago, I recorded new *Sopranos* cast member Patti D'Arbanville for an album I produced, *HollyWord*.

Q: I've read that you and David Chase are not fans of the big scoring action in *The Sopranos* because the orchestrations and cues can sometimes create anticipation and warn the story.

A: They can. Traditional score can be very manipulative. Music manipulates your impression of something, whether it be a piece of underscore written for a scene, or something you have dropped a needle on. Music will affect how you perceive a scene. But we sit and have these spotting sessions and say, "Where should the score start?" You're essentially picking a place where you want the underscore to go in. When you use music for the most part as source music, then the music is coming from a space and will play from the first frame of the scene to the last frame of the scene. It's wall-to-wall in the scene. On *The Sopranos*, we predominantly use source music. So we don't watch the scene and say, "Where can we start the score?" Sometimes a score tells you what to feel. Music will bring an emotion to it.

Q: Is it a different vibe and situation, doing music for a network show versus a cable one?

A: I would say, in the beginning of *Northern Exposure*, we would only clear songs for five years. That's very common when a show is new. If my memory is correct, that's what they did in the first season of *The Sopranos*. After *Northern Exposure* took off and got picked up for fifty episodes after the first or second year, Universal realized that this thing was going to make enough to go to syndication, so they changed the rights to perpetuity. In that process they realized how expensive the first few years of *Northern Exposure* were for going back and making deals for perpetuity on all the music that was in it. As a result, the music budget for *Northern Exposure*, when the rights changed, became a period when it was doing well, in the top ten, on the cover of *TV Guide*, so there weren't quite as many questions about how much we were spending on music in the show. Like all series that go into their later years, they look to where they can save the money. And there was a considerable reduction of our total licensing budget toward the end of the last two seasons.

Q: But with *The Sopranos*, the dynamic of songs in the show and on the soundtrack albums is a whole different trip. I know you and David sit around and really think about what you want heard in the series. And you get everything from classic rock like Them's "Mystic Eyes" to a Keith Richards and the Rolling Stones track, "Through and Through."

I was on the last Stones tour, and I talked briefly to Keith about "Through and Through," from their *Voodoo Lounge* album, that you have in *The Sopranos*, and Keith even ended up including it on several stage dates. He told me he played it one night in New York at Madison

Square Garden and thanked the producers onstage, since it was a tune he had kinda forgotten about, and it came around again when it aired on *The Sopranos*.

A: Yeah! That was fantastic. We don't want to feel we're dropping hit songs on scenes. The hit song isn't gonna make the scene better. David picked that Stones Keith song that he actually wrote into the script, as he had that song in mind for the episode. It also goes back to David thinking of the use of music as something like a Greek chorus in our storytelling. Music tells a story. If you look at "Through and Through," it's applicable to the imagery at the end of the show as they were showing guys on the street selling phone cards, loading a garbage truck. David thought of that song on a script level, played it to the director, John Patterson, and they really used it in two places.

Q: I've read, and even heard through our friend, Little Steven [who portrays club owner Silvio Dante in *The Sopranos*], that not only is *The Sopranos* principal David Chase a big music fan, but he "puts pins in the scripts" for tunes to use. Explain this process to me.

A: Yes. "Put a pin in it" is an expression that David uses when there is a song that we know we like or it's a good piece of music, and we don't have a scene in our current run of shows that we're working on, where it would work. So "put a pin in it" means "this is good, save this for the future."

Q: What is the craziest way a tune has found its way to *The Sopranos*?

A: Some of the selections come from my own collection. The thing that's been great about *The Sopranos* is the licensing end and artist approval has been fantastic. We have gotten answers on clearances from publishers and record companies in twenty-four hours. Quick turnarounds. Releasing a soundtrack that has a Frank Sinatra song, a Rolling Stones song, and a Bob Dylan song on it is difficult. Some high-end acts, when you put in a request for a TV show, they usually do two things: they give a quote that is so astronomically high that you're going to say no, or they don't even respond to the request.

Q: I have to say the two Sony Music soundtrack albums aren't loaded up with Sony artists.

A: You're right. When we met with different labels and different people, when we did the first one, there was a buzz on us doing a soundtrack album, based on the volume of music we were using per episode. It was something where David and I—music lovers that we are—said,

"Let's do an album. We're not in a band, but we can do an album. We're in a TV show!" It was something we wanted to do, and people were aware, the show had been airing for a year, the use of music in the show was a natural fit for an album. In that process, whoever we met with, conceptualizing a soundtrack album, we were very clear it was not going to be the tail wagging the dog.

In the beginning of the show we were picking selections in a vacuum, because the show hadn't aired yet, but we were mixing the shows, so you had to be really on the music clearances to make sure it was happening. It wasn't a thing where we had a "festival clearance" like an indie movie that may air at a festival. It was, "We have shows that are going to air on HBO in January '99 so they have to get cleared." David was very clear from the pilot how much he wanted to use music, and I wasn't in the conversations he had with HBO, but I know he expressed to them how much music he wanted to use in the show. In the beginning it was a vacuum, we had to explain to people what *The Sopranos* was all about, talk about David's previous credits, and get permissions. And we did. People have music they want to sell and they can.

Q: I know, because I've talked to some of the artists or their reps, that they didn't play hardball and do a lot of power or traditional business maneuvers when you and David wanted to have some of their material. No demands for full versions, no restrictions on placements and product positioning.

A: You know, you asked a question earlier about the difference between network and cable shows. On both kinds of shows I've been blessed with the opportunity to work very independently, and—other than running selections by executive producers, who are ultimately responsible and running the show—there's never a situation where we will show the CD cover at the end of the episode, the promo tie-in. The recording artists and rights holders know whom they are getting into bed with when the music is requested for *The Sopranos*. There's a language freedom.

Q: What about music supporting dialogue?

A: If we're in a scene in a bar, the music will be played very loud in the scene. I generally try to find the instrumental bridge in a song placing that, when you place the song, instead of starting and going right into the hook or something, find out where the instrumental bridge is because the truth is we're having people in rooms talking to each other and you have to hear the words that they are saying, otherwise you're not going to get what the story is about.

I try to find a song that has an instrumental section or a vocal- or dialogue-friendly section in the song and try placing that in the process so it's not killing the dialogue, for lack of a better word.

There is a conscious effort in the mixing process, and this is kinda fun, if we're in the Bada Bing room, we're not going to lay the CD music on top of the dialogue. Last year in the back room, adjacent to the dance floor portion of the Bada Bing, we tended to spike up the music when people entered the room, but when we mixed things we'd tell the dubber on the mixing stage, "Bottom end. Through the walls." Because it's mixing the music and being truthful to the space you are in.

Little Steven has gotten involved in the show's music. The weekly in and out selection of music is done by myself, David Chase, and Kathryn Dayak, the music editor on the show. Steven makes suggestions. The character of Adrianna now owns a New Jersey bar called the Crazy Horse, and we've had two different situations with live bands playing in the club, and both of them were recommendations we've gotten from Steven. I also had a private tutorial with Steven with a VHS cassette of our pilot show of *The Sopranos* and spent the evening eating food from the Brooklyn Diner. We did five or six hours in his office and he played different tracks against scenes and presented music. He wasn't territorial and knows this world very well. It was a great evening and hearing his ideas was special. He also has a track on one of the soundtracks.

Q: What is the genesis of the Bruce Springsteen song used in *The Sopranos*?

A: I love Bruce's *Nebraska* album. "State Trooper" is one of those "put a pin in it" songs. We tried it before, at the end of Episode 10 or 11. David Chase is also from New Jersey. It came into the last episode. The license cleared quite easily.

The first time you approach Bruce Springsteen for a song in the show, you are concerned. "Will it clear? Will it clear?"

And it did. We've been very fortunate, partially because we've been a very musician- and artist-friendly show.

Q: Do any of the cast offer you feedback on the music in *The Sopranos*?

A: Yes. I've gotten comments and plenty of positive response from cast members saying they really like the music. Lorraine Bracco really responded to the music. I remember her coming up to me when we were looping in New York and saying, "I love the music!"

HBO gives us incredible independence. We've never ever in the history of the show gotten a musical note or memo from HBO. Their concerns are that everything is covered with paper prior to broadcast and that clearances and proper publishing have been established. What's really nice about being on HBO is that we run our end credits right after the show like a feature film. Whereas on *Northern Exposure* we would end the show with a piece of music, but there would come up a four second executive producer credit and we're fading to black. The song is over and the show is over. On this show we get to run for a minute and thirty seconds after the show is over, right into the end credits.

Q: Have the rates for licensing gone up over the duration of the show?

A: Yes. Music is expensive to license. It goes up, but we knew from the get-go there was going to be a big number needed to cover the show. Sometimes we use a song twice in an episode. We call it bookending the show.

Q: What have you learned about the relationship between rock music and the screen?

A: A lot of it goes back to the idea that you have to play the music with the film. I think too often great songs are horribly used, just thrown on top of scenes. And you have to sit down and spend the time playing the music against the film. Songs can be great on their own but they have to work with the film. It works with not only being considerate of the dialogue and what is going on in the scene, but you can get into the tapestry and the movements that are going on. Is something moving visually? Flashing light bulbs that you could grab an element of; something that is working as a background secondary instrument in the arrangement in a piece of music, but it has something working with the flashing light bulbs in the back. It's finding movement and life that exists in the scene or not existing in the scene.

A lot of times we'll have a scene that frankly needs a little of that existence. So a Metallica song with bottom end through the wall could help create a little more danger and a forbidding quality going on in the scene. A lot of it for me goes back to turning my TV on, and turning the volume off and playing albums.

The basic rule when we are mixing these things is if people aren't talking, you can play music louder. We're not that "paint by number."

It all starts with a strong script. We were done with eight shows prior to the first show airing. You can't sit there and predict, but what I reacted to was really liking David's sensibilities in filmmaking. Not just music but filmmaking. He's very smart in the editorial process of putting these things together on a pacing level.

Q: How does the actual workweek of *The Sopranos* happen?

A: We work on multiple episodes. We get a script. Another is in prep, one is in filming, one is in editor's cut, one in director's cut, and David's cut. So they all are in different phases. David finishes and locks the show, and then we go into all the postproduction work, where I'm predominantly responsible.

David is involved from the first word on the page to the playback, to the final mix of the show. It's a David Chase creation. Music at the beginning of the editorial process is basically an annoyance to David. He doesn't want to hear what is playing in Meadow's bedroom in a dialogue scene. I don't even introduce music into the shows until I feel David is approaching a little bit of editing on the show.

It's a matter of looking at what space we're in. If we're in the Bada Bing strip club, there's a general feeling of what can work in the strip club. Away from that we can be a little more experimental with time warp music. We used a Led Zeppelin song in a pizza place. Before then Led Zeppelin had never licensed a song to a TV show. And we didn't use it over a chase scene or someone hitting someone. It was low in the background in a pizza place over a speaker. It was very expensive.

Q: There are two soundtrack albums out in retail from *The Sopranos*. There are songs heard in the series that didn't make the two CD collections. How are the albums assembled?

A: We licensed the music independently of the soundtrack albums.

I think what we keep doing is having a clean slate for each episode. There is no composer and no recurring theme, just a main title song. And that main title—David heard a song on his car radio by a group, A3, and eventually we used a different mix, the urban takeover mix, available on an EP with five or six mixes of "Woke Up This Morning." It was played against the images, after we did an edit and took out the rap portion of the song, and the rest is history. Earlier we had thought of having revolving main title songs, with the concept of every song from Tony's car radio.

The music is all licensed prior to the compilation of the soundtrack. For the first soundtrack, I took a list of every piece of music we licensed, ten to twelve tracks an episode. I made a list and we just did a process of elimination, narrowing it down to twenty tracks we were fond of. Then I had those burned onto a CD, no order, as songs, because we were making a soundtrack album versus playing music on a TV show. You want it to be representative of a TV show, and we had to listen from beginning to end, to see how they would live on a soundtrack album. We had songs like Cream's "I Feel Free" and Bob Dylan's "You Gotta Serve Somebody."

For our second album, *Peppers and Eggs*, Dylan recorded a second version of "Return to Me" and that's only available on the second soundtrack album. He did that for the show. He is a Columbia artist, and it was arranged. The actual production was done by Sony Music. We had his "You Gotta Serve Somebody" in the first season, and Sony approached Dylan for participation for the second soundtrack and at that time he was interested in doing a cover of "Return to Me." Bob Dylan presented the idea himself of doing the cover. It came time for the second soundtrack, and they asked if he still was interested, and he said yes. It was presented to us, we liked it and it was used at the end of one of the episodes.

You have to buy the album to hear that song. We don't talk in terms of things like cross promotion, record promotions, or making a single. We first make a TV show with music, and soundtracks emerge from that. We don't have talks with Sony about strategic marketing, but they'll send us things for consideration. "Mystic Eyes" by Them was used in a flashback scene. David picked that one. "I Feel Free" I selected for the end of the Isabella episode. When we worked on the second soundtrack, more time had passed, so we had more episodes to choose from, and more songs that were used.

Q: Was there any discussion about not branding or employing more of a *Sopranos* logo to the second CD collection?

A: I was adamant that it not be called *More Music from 'The Sopranos'* or *Sopranos 2*. We wanted it to have a distinct identity. It was culled from two more seasons and Sony Music wanted the second soundtrack to be a double album. It lined up to be not twelve, but twenty-six or twenty-eight tracks, on two CDs. I grew up listening to albums, with the whole concept of sides, two sides, in my mind. In my head more time had passed, more tunes to be chosen from. The first one went Gold. And the soundtracks, even more in the second one, have a variety of different music genres: R&B, Gospel, Rock.

Q: Was there ever a situation where you or David Chase was a fan of someone, or had an existing music or song relationship with a band or recording artist, that helped secure them into the series or one of the soundtracks?

A: David Chase has an earlier TV relationship with the music of Elvis Costello. David created a series in 1988 for CBS, *Almost Grown*, which used Elvis Costello's "(What's So Funny 'Bout) Peace, Love and Understanding?"

In the *Sopranos* series and subsequent soundtracks, we've used Costello's "Complicated Shadows" and "High Fidelity." David is a major Elvis fan.

▒

Martin Bruestle: Filmography

The Sopranos (1999) TV Series (coproducer)

The Sopranos (1999) TV Series (coproducer, director, episode "Do Not Resuscitate")

Cupid (1998) TV Series (associate producer)

Northern Exposure (1990) TV Series (associate producer)

ROY TRAKIN

Roy Trakin has been the Senior Editor of *HITS* magazine, a weekly radio and music trade periodical and tip sheet, since 1986.

He holds a Master of Fine Arts degree in film from Columbia University in New York, where he studied under the author and critic, Andrew Sarris, the originator of the auteur theory, and Raymond Durgnat, the British editor of *Sight and Sound* and noted Alfred Hitchcock scholar. Roy was also responsible for the long-lost student film *Mystery Girls*, based on the New York Dolls song of the same name. Durgnat praised the effort as "looking like a dog had directed it."

Trakin eventually became the lead singer of the New York-based punk-rock group The Geeks and played CBGBs.

I've known him for over twenty-five years, since the '70s, when we both wrote for *Melody Maker*.

Over the years Trakin has been receptive to my suggestions and story ideas involving music and film for *HITS*. Some of those "directors on music and soundtrack" assignments are displayed in expanded versions here in *Hollywood Shack Job*.

It was in 2003 that I started seriously considering writing and compiling a book on the movie and TV music and soundtrack world. My concept started to pick up more momentum when Trakin told me a couple of freelance scribes had begun griping to him about the amount of space and regularity (every four months, mind you) I managed to get for these director interviews and movie music industry profiles in *HITS*.

This is Hollywood in 2004!

Trakin has written two books: *Sting and the Police* and *Tom Hanks: Journey to Stardom*.

Trakin is also heard Sunday nights on the KLSX-FM radio show *Media Whores* and writes weekly for Music Snobs.com, a "dia-blog" with Bud Scoppa for Sony Connect.

He hosted the world's first online interactive pop music chat show and pickup area, *Rant & Roll*, for Prodigy, and America Online's *L.A. Digital City*. Trakin was previously chief copywriter for MTV's Corporate Relations Department and Director of PR for the R.I.A.A. (Recording Industry Association of America).

Trakin, part scholar, part pundit, has been on VH1's *The List*, Court TV, E! Entertainment, and CNN, and conducted an on-camera interview with Nick Lachey of the MTV reality show, *The Newlyweds*. I've also seen Trakin on A&E's *City Confidential*, reflecting on the plight of murdered record company promo man Charlie Minor. I watched that program just to hear the narration by actor Paul Winfield, a graduate of Manual Arts High School.

Q: What future trends do you see for music in soundtracks and movies?

A: There was, of course, a golden age of the soundtrack, in terms of commercial viability, coming out of *Saturday Night Fever*, *Grease*, and *Urban Cowboy*. Then there was another one with *Titanic* in the late '90s as well. The DVD format and the continued evolution of digital sound in the home—the growing home theater thing—is absolutely going to make the whole melding of sound and vision increasingly important. These two are working hand in hand.

Music is now wall-to-wall. It's not just plastered in the back of films. Look at commercials, TV shows and the electronic gaming industry. People walking the streets with their iPods. You walk through the landscape like it's a movie with its own soundtrack. There are people who haven't spent a moment without a wallpaper of music backing what they do, from the car to walking to the office, to working at their computer.

With the consolidation of radio and the fact that airplay rotations are so tight, publishers and artists have been forced to look for alternatives to place or attach their music. You now have music on cell phones, on hold buttons, XM and Sirius in your car. The soundtrack album is part of that cycle.

Q: What about the growth of the music supervisor and the soundtrack unit?

A: The fact of the matter is, there have been people who have developed these jobs and have been able to go out and pick the right music for a situation and then follow up by securing the necessary licensing and clearances. Is this a job that has developed over the past ten or fifteen years? Yes. And have people gotten very good at it? Yes. There are two keys: There is effective music within the film situation when you see it in the theater, and there are effective soundtracks, and they are not necessarily the same thing. There are two very distinct forms. The music itself that exists in the theatrical and home setting, and the soundtrack, which derives from the cinematic experience, that can include the actual music included in the movie and other songs inspired by it. We've seen the two grow side by side.

We all know when we've seen a movie whose use of music knocks us out. From *Pulp Fiction* to the use of "The End" in *Apocalypse Now*. Simon & Garfunkel's music in *The Graduate*. Tangerine Dream's electronic score for *The Thief*. All the way to the music of the Magnetic Fields' Stephin Merritt in *Pieces of April*. The movie becomes a whole marketing tool for the soundtrack album.

Q: And some record labels now have film soundtrack divisions.

A: More and more we are seeing that so-called synergy. Spearheaded by Sony buying Columbia Records and Columbia film studios. Have everything under the same corporate roof. It's standard format these days. That's certainly been the trend for the past ten to fifteen years. We will see if that continues. Universal has just sold their film division, while holding on to the music division. Warner Bros., which has a film studio, just sold its record division. I have always thought that music and movies belong together.

Silent movies began, not silent, but with music accompanying them. Music and image are the most powerful means of expression available for reaching a person's inner psyche.

MTV is the single biggest influence on filmmaking and TV today. The cumulative influence of its twenty-three years is out there affecting the ways movies and commercials are produced. From reality TV to *American Idol*. What we are seeing now is programming directed at the kids raised by MTV. That's the audience everyone is making movies and records for.

Q: I've really noticed the expansion of the electronic gaming industry and the incorporation of songs in these new soundtrack venues, like Sony's PlayStation 2 and Electronic Arts' Madden football games.

A: Games are a six billion dollar-a-year industry. The songs play often. You will get more impressions than you would on Top 40 radio ultimately. It's the new soundtrack.

It's a Jean-Luc Godard world out there, and the song on the soundtrack, PlayStation 2, or TV show, is the boutique item these days. Aural signals connecting with one another. Follow the signal. "Where do I download?" Or, if you are an old-timer, "Where do I buy the album?"

Q: What about the consumer and the soundtrack album?

A: Well, if you're a collector or a record geek, you care about the information, the liner notes and, especially, the credits. The image of Robert De Niro on the cover of the *Taxi Driver* original soundtrack LP was very powerful. But the new breed of kids really don't give a fuck about the data and the information. Sure they want the sounds, but we're moving from a possession-oriented society of material goods to one that wants access and service, where you don't actually own CDs or books but the ability to access them when you want.

Essentially we are about to revert to a medieval society, where we rent, but don't own. It's a high-tech fiefdom, where the visuals are there, the soundtrack is there, either on your wristwatch, Palm Pilot or BlackBerry, but you don't own the fuckin' stuff you listen to or absorb, you're just leasing. You are paying to access content, like a twenty-first century jukebox, where everything is pay-per-view. And you know what? The consolidated corporations want that to happen. They don't want you to own the fuckin' thing. They own the copyright. They want to be the gatekeepers. They want to be the guys you dial up when you want something.

Everybody knows the CD is just a T-shirt with less of a margin. Just another piece of merch. That's what the Internet wants. It wants content to be free. For content to be free, someone has to step forward and pay for it.

Q: What about trends regarding the merger of music and visuals?

A: iTunes, Kazaa. One of the things I'd like to see happen is for the TiVo or DVR device to create customized programming that allows you to order a song, or a piece of merchandise, directly from the screen by clicking a mouse, which gives you the ability to download, stream, or order it. I believe in the micro-payment system. I think weaving commercials and product placements within the intellectual property is the way it's going to go.

If you're going to use the music, let people find out what it is. Give them an opportunity to click and buy the thing, or hear it again. That can be extended to brands being worn by people onscreen.

The soundtrack album still has a presence, but it's decreasing. The soundtrack album will become more of a market for the true score albums, which you can't get anywhere else. With DVD being more readily available and with quicker releases, the soundtrack album is rather superfluous. You can get the original music piece itself on DVD. This book of yours might well turn out to be a chronicle of the soundtrack's demise. However, you are seeing more TV show soundtracks being issued. *The Sopranos, Six Feet Under*. The Who's "Won't Get Fooled Again" at the top of *CSI* every week.

It's marketing. Trying to brand name it and share the demo audience and provide a memento, a shared experience, from the show. Practically everyone is a music snob these days.

Q: What about the evolution of the technology around the sight and sound business?

A: Computer speakers are getting better and better and it's now increasingly becoming the way that people will be capturing music. The computer represents a potential jukebox on everybody's desktop. I love music, but it's like candy. You can have too much. The problem is the industry has created too many gadgets, with not enough people to buy them. The vanishing middle class doesn't have the disposable income to keep up with the advances. We now have a technology hurtling into the future faster than the economy can support it. That's the problem.

The business of entertainment and film and TV music is five to seven years ahead of the public, which has to catch up, and that's going to be a painful transformation. The Internet is the worm at the heart of the economy. It eats away at the middle people between the vendor and the buying public. There used to be discussion and dialogue when you went to a record shop, or even a chain record store, about a new album or a movie in general release, and if there was a soundtrack available. That conversation doesn't happen very often these days. The world is now filled with flat screen TVs, digital sound

5.1 speakers, and relatively few people can actually afford it. Though the beauty of it is that these items will become cheaper and cheaper.

The new media industry business is growing in the fiscal end, but the traditional music world of shippers and pressers are under siege. It's a business being torn apart right from the middle.

Even as there's more music and film product than ever available.

Audio and video streaming is the future, and when broadband really gets out there, it will be mind-boggling. That's the new soundtrack.

Q: What are some trends regarding recording artists and filmmakers?

A: Today's kids, both in bands and behind the camera, are very media-savvy. They are the by-products of a visually obsessed society. They come into the game with more knowledge from the get-go. Look at the credits. Most of these kids are repped by ASCAP, BMI, or publishing companies even before they sign with a record label. There will be more fashion and lifestyle corporate sponsorship. Look, acts have always been signed based on how they look visually. It's always been part and parcel, going back to the start of the teen idol as recording artist.

Q: What about censorship in the media and the current state of radio?

A: There's a bit of a timid climate out there. Gun-shyness. But as you know, that only spurs a virulent, angry reaction from the real underground. As a matter of fact, the seeds for a counterculture are out there. The kids can turn against the prevailing materialism and have their own sensibility. You see that. And the live concert experience is still very valid in discovering bands. In radio, there are some witch hunts going on; no one is happy with the hegemony that Clear Channel has forged, linking airplay on their stations with appearances at their live music venues. Radio now has more restrictive playlists than ever.

Some of the classic albums and soundtracks you were introduced to and eventually explored I'm sure got some initial airplay when the hip underground promo man from the record label gave the program director a joint to play it. But not anymore. Radio is now a high-stakes game with decisions that used to be made on a local level now being made on the corporate level.

Satellite radio outlets like XM and Sirius have a shot in this climate. If they continue to become standard equipment in new car purchases, the days of terrestrial radio are numbered. Radio listeners will eventually require deep catalogue and these new formats and places are gearing and delivering to those people.

Lifestyle marketing will also continue. The major record companies supported by corporations with other interests, which means more movie and music tie-ins.

Q: I just saw the ad for the *Mean Girls* movie and the soundtrack and music were plugged as "available exclusively at iTunes" and "the single performed by Kathy Rose."

A: Exactly. We might be moving more into the middle age, where companies are proud to put their names on rock tours, like "Anheuser Beer presents the Rolling Stones." And eventually, the home theater gets cheaper, until everybody can afford to have five speakers and a DVD player.

Soundtracks still have great sound and will always be a carry-around item. You can't schlep your DVD player with you all the time.

Meanwhile, cable TV is starting to tackle music in film in a creative way, with exceptional documentaries on IFC, Bravo, and Trio. Showtime has some interesting programming. With two hundred channels, you can see anything you want.

※

Roy Trakin has previously written the biographies *Sting and the Police* (Ballantine Books, 1984), *Tom Hanks: Journey to Stardom* (St. Martin's Press, 1995), and *Jim Carrey Unmasked* (St. Martin's Press, 1995). He also served as an editorial assistant on *John Lennon Remembered: Strawberry Fields Forever* (Bantam Books, 1980), with Vic Garbarini and Barbara Graustark. He penned Malcolm McLaren's famed speech at the New Music Seminar in 1984, and has written speeches for the likes of Virgin's Richard Branson.

Trakin has been Senior Editor at *HITS* magazine for two decades and received an M.F.A. in film at Columbia University. Max Ophuls, Alfred Hitchcock, Alan Vega, and Marty Rev are among his all-time idols.

He has also been quoted extensively as a music and entertainment business expert on CNN, A&E, VH1, and MTV. Roy also was an on-air music correspondent for E! Entertainment and covered West Coast news stories as a segment producer for MTV.

Trakin also hosted the world's first online interactive pop music chat show/pickup area, *Rant & Roll*, for Prodigy, as well as America Online's *L.A. Digital City*, which *USA Today* called one of the new wave of online talk shows.

His ambition is to appear as a Claymation character alongside Mötley Crüe in the upcoming motion picture, *Disaster! The Movie.*

BOB LEFSETZ

Bob Lefsetz hosts a Sunday evening radio show on KLSX-FM, focusing on the music business, rock 'n' roll, new media, film, and sound toys. He's in a number of magazines, on a website, "Celebrity Access," and formerly contributed to VH1.com.

Lefsetz went to Middlebury College in Vermont, and later obtained a law degree from Southwestern Law School in L.A. Lefsetz formerly ran the U.S. office of Sanctuary Music before he initiated *The Lefsetz Letter*, and began publishing it electronically. It started in 1986 and went online in 2000. It's an e-mail newsletter, which started out as an industry play, word-of-mouth thing and has blown up with a truly global traffic pattern.

Lefsetz is a guy who wears his heart on his sleeve and has a passion for rock 'n' roll and film.

I've discovered bands, movie soundtracks, and educational knowledge about men and women and relationships in his missives that remind me at times of Charles Bukowski on the prowl. "The newsletter is my own personal truth outlet," he explained to me one sunny afternoon from Santa Monica, California. To subscribe to *The Lefsetz Letter*, visit lefsetz.com.

Q: What is the current climate like for the soundtrack album?

A: It used to be, in the old days, where the movie company literally took the album. And before that, it was really the Broadway albums, and they made those into movies, and it really wasn't until *Footloose* that the record companies really started to develop—1982 to 1990—more successful soundtracks, and saw this as a way to make money.

Then they started to use the soundtrack album as a way to break their acts, like a group on the *Punisher* soundtrack.

Years ago there was also a time where the record soundtrack could be successful even though the movie was not. Then the terms were so onerous that there were changes in the business, and these projects stopped earning back their advances. That has happened in the last couple of years. Therefore, it is now where you want a successful one, but you don't want to run out and make every deal. And I really think it's about picking and choosing and using what has been learned the last twenty years, both peppering with known acts and putting in some acts you want to break as a result of this particular movie.

You can still discover a band or a song from a movie. I love a tune from Pablo Cruise I first heard on the *Unmarried Woman.* soundtrack.

But you also had situations like the *Dirty Dancing* soundtrack. The first one was so successful they did another one that had similar music that wasn't even in the movie.

Q: Has DVD eradicated the soundtrack album?

A: Not whatsoever. That's really about P2P [peer-to-peer] piracy. The bottom line is frequently it costs more to buy the soundtrack album than it does for the DVD with all the music in it. However, most movies don't have the complete songs, nor do they even have the same songs. It's just an argument from people who are arguing about record pricing.

When we first heard the '50s and '60s in *American Graffiti*, that's one thing. Then we heard it again in *Dirty Dancing* and *Forrest Gump*. So they burned out all these genres.

Q: MTV has boiled down the mentality from the forty-six-minute album to the three-minute single.

A: MTV ruined music. The premise of MTV and what it has become now has always been the same: "We're selling advertising."

At first it was a train wreck. When you went to somebody's house and they had it, like a car wreck on the freeway, everyone looks. Same deal. But what happened as the years went by, prior to 1990, people realized music is something you hear, not something you see, and that is when MTV changed its programming and became more of a clubhouse. Because if you get TV exposure, reaching so many people, you are going to sell records. Generally speaking, the record companies are in cahoots, have blinders on, and want to sell tonnage, even though they play no music. However they have MTV2, and other deep cable channels, but the format itself is burned out. Basically, visual image is about narrative and we explore special effects. And it's ultimately unsatisfying to the viewer.

Q: The soundtrack market now?

A: When you're looking at the indie scene, unless you have the one movie a year that breaks through, if that, they're buying the soundtracks the same way people bought soundtracks prior to *Flashdance*. The same way somebody buys a T-shirt, a poster, a photo book at a gig. It's purely a souvenir.

Q: Trends?

A: We will continue to see more music in movies for a number of reasons. It's very successful across the board and we live in a culture inundated with music, and people are no longer reluctant to license. They have a price, but they will license. Whereas in the old days people didn't want to be in the movies. As much as we think music is ubiquitous at this particular time, it's actually being held back. We're going to experience something akin to cable television. What we have now is P2P, and the rest of the public doesn't use P2P services. The bottom line is that the promise of online music is for more people to have more music. Inherently, this is good for music itself. It's irrelevant to movies.

We are led to believe that music works best in two different circumstances. When we know it, or when it's a perfect placement. That's not what we see normally. Now we see a film director throwing in the assets of a particular record company, therefore you are buying it as a record. When you went to see *The Graduate*, the only new song was "Mrs. Robinson." The perfect vibe songs are rare.

Q: How desperate, horrific and political is the scene for managers and agents to get their people and bands into movies, and especially soundtracks?

A: Unbelievably desperate. We're talking about exposure. And the real story is the synergy of music video and DVD.

Now DVD has superceded music video, the classic story being *Eddie and the Cruisers*. A very lightly successful movie that sold a certain number of soundtrack albums. When it hit HBO, the record started to fly out of the stores because so many more people saw it on HBO than at the theater. So if you have an unknown act, now more than ever, with the tightness of radio and MTV, it's really about exposure.

Unfortunately in most cases, there is no exposure. For every act that breaks off a soundtrack there is a priority, never mind the fill-in acts, there has to be a hundred that don't. That's one of the reasons the whole thing has become of less value. By the same token, there are fewer powerful managers than ever before, so it becomes about having powerful managers manipulating for a movie to hit and have a good placement.

Q: More catalogue than ever in movies and soundtracks?

A: Just the opposite.

Q: Because we've heard "God Only Knows" in six different movies already?

A: Exactly. The other thing, it behooves the record releasing company to have an act that can sell a separate piece of product. With "God Only Knows," the odds of everybody running out and buying every Beach Boys album is low. But a new Jet song—buy the other records by Jet!

Q: What directors or movies with music have impressed you lately?

A: With the lowering of standards in film in general, you have to ask yourself, how many times do you walk out of the theater feeling really impacted by the music? *American Beauty*. The movie was so stark, but when tracks played it was great.

Then sometimes there is the issue of hearing one of your favorite songs that you don't think anyone knows, and it's prominent.

It is a rare auteur who can reach down and pick those songs and put them in their films.

Q: The music supervisor?

A: They don't have anywhere near the power they tell you they do. Bottom line, the image is that these people run around, collect new stuff, and get it into movies. As a practical matter, they get that stuff with a handful of people. The labels, the movie companies, and the director are basically a conduit to the major labels for the stuff they want to hype. The director—or the studio—has the clout, because they have the power. The music supervisor doesn't have it.

Q: Songs in commercials?

A: It's like the stock market. You have a period of time when this stuff is valuable. The Who had this comeback, the 9/11 tribute show, and a few other things, but when they first started to license things, if they didn't license then, the music would have been worthless. Because very soon no one would know it. I personally believe it should not be done at all, but there's interesting songs, forgotten one-hit wonders that are used, and then the act gets a whole new life.

Q: Like the Nick Drake song in a commercial in England, and Brad Pitt being quoted in articles about him and a Hollywood film being made of his life.

A: But that's a good thing. I'm a purist. It's like using the Mona Lisa to sell something. Isn't anything sacred? We have a completely sold-out culture. When I'm lying in bed, some chick doesn't say she's fucking me 'cause she's doing it for Jergen's Hand Lotion. It's between the two of us. And I feel the same way about the music.

Q: If you ran the world?

A: If I were king, everything would be a licensed P2P. Distribute the money like ASCAP or BMI. As far as music in movies, I wish there was an edict that the music should serve the movie and should not be a business enterprise.

  The bottom line is that the music should be in service to the movie, but the record company is still saying, we want this in and that in, and we all know—and I don't care what anybody says—the more singular the vision, the better the artistic work.

Q: Trends. Music and the screen meeting each other.

A: The luxury the movie studios have is that they control exhibition. As an independent it is very costly to get your movie distributed. However, the main outlet presently is DVD. So therefore there is an explosion, as we speak, of a number of films shot on digital videotape, like 8 Days Later was. Therefore, just like in music, the power is going to the maker, rather than the banker. They have much more creative control and therefore it is healthy for this after it happens.

Q: What about music and movies on the computer screen?

A: First of all, a computer screen has a much better resolution than a TV screen. So if you're watching a DVD, it looks better on your computer screen. Speaker size is a nonissue. For a hundred-and-fifty dollars you can get shit that sounds great. I do not want to see my act perform on a regular basis. Access to trailers and footage and complete works, I'm not convinced.

  We have a culture where we no longer need to travel to a city center. It's now into the home theater element. If you didn't have to leave the house and do all sorts of fucked-up things with the opposite sex and your buddies, the movie theaters would have died a long time ago. So the dominant exhibition area will be the home. If you like the soundtrack, it will be instantly available, whether it be downloaded or included on the disc you are watching. There will be much easier access, but you will pay for that privilege. Hopefully it will be a lesser hurdle, so that more people will consume more product and the overall growth will be larger with the individual price being lower.

We learned in the '80s that vertical integration doesn't work, where you own everything from beginning to end. CBS *used to own* record stores. So we know *that* is not the trend for the future.

Q: People are discovering bands and music products by new means these days.

A: Because the means of production is in the hands of the *proletariat*. Everyone and every band will have a movie, footage on the web that will surpass the movie business. The film business would like to control everything and sell you a DVD, but that's not going to last forever.

The web homepage has become the key element, so that you can develop a niche that can be self-sustaining and will fly under the radar, and not give a fuck.

§

Santa Monica, California-based Bob Lefsetz is the author of the e-mail newsletter, *The Lefsetz Letter* (http://www.lefsetz.com). In the publication, and formerly on his KLSX-FM radio show, Lefsetz reaches deep into the core of the music business: downloading, new distribution outlets, copy protection, pricing, and the music itself. He always has an opinion. Bob writes a column for the *Encore* publication and *The Hit Sheet* in the U.K. Lefsetz's insights are fueled by his stints as an entertainment business attorney, majordomo of Sanctuary Music's American division and a consultant to major labels.

PART THREE
MUSICIANS ON
THE REAL TO REEL

Robbie Robertson outside The Palace,
Hollywood, California, November 1988. Photo by Jim Roup.

ROBBIE ROBERTSON

United Artists, MGM Home Entertainment, and Warner Bros./Rhino issued a Special Edition DVD and 4-CD boxed set of The Band and director Martin Scorsese's *The Last Waltz* in 2002, to celebrate the twenty-fifth anniversary of the concert documentary's limited theatrical release.

Scorsese, with director of photography Michael Chapman and a team of seven cameramen, recorded the Thanksgiving Day 1976 concert event that was produced by rock promoter Bill Graham at Winterland in San Francisco.

The Last Waltz captured The Band's final live performance, sharing the stage with Eric Clapton, Bob Dylan, Van Morrison, Ringo Starr, Muddy Waters, Emmylou Harris, Neil Young, Joni Mitchell, Neil Diamond, Ronnie Hawkins, the Staple Singers, Ron Wood, Paul Butterfield, Dr. John, Stephen Stills, and others.

The film and soundtrack set were digitally remixed and remastered and personally supervised by The Band's Robbie Robertson. The audio collection has all thirty tracks from the original 1978 soundtrack, plus twenty-four previously unreleased performances and rehearsals from the concert and film.

The Special Edition DVD also features never-before-seen "jam footage" of the performers, new interviews with and commentary from Scorsese and Robertson, along with additional commentary from remaining Band members Levon Helm and Garth Hudson, plus Ronnie Hawkins and Mavis Staples, and much more.

The roots of *The Last Waltz* began when Jonathan Taplin, executive producer of the film, who had been The Band's road manager for four years and had produced Scorsese's breakout film, *Mean Streets*, introduced Robertson to Scorsese, who had edited *Woodstock* and *Elvis on Tour*. "I couldn't let the opportunity pass," Scorsese explained. "It was this crazy desire to get it on film, to be a part of it."

Scorsese's concert film included a photography team with Laszlo Kovacs and Vilmos Zsigmond. "The idea was to get the most complete coverage possible, so our 35mm cameras were scanning and zooming for the action," Scorsese stated. "When Bob Dylan shifts from 'Forever Young' to 'Baby Let Me Follow You Down,' the film truly documents how Robertson, Helm, Hudson, and Danko adjust and play on."

Robertson recalls, "I remember Marty saying, 'This is something you never see—you're never in on this.'"

The film became the first concert documentary to be shot in 35mm, and influenced future music documentaries. "We live so emotionally and powerfully through those moments," Scorsese felt. "The picture, for us, was so powerful. And it was bringing these emotions to us, creating the psychological atmosphere that I couldn't verbalize then. But it was pretty scary. As exciting and creatively fulfilling as it was, it was extremely frightening."

The Band (Robertson, Levon Helm, Rick Danko, Garth Hudson, and Richard Manuel) had a vision to create a concert and a film that would mark not only the end of their run together, but would magnify an end to a roots and blues rock era that would be followed by punk rock. "There was something about this period from the '60s through the '70s, everybody had a pretty good run," Robertson offers. "When you watch these things over and over again, and how stirring these performances were, you're almost seeing inside the whole era."

In 1977 I interviewed Rick Danko, the bassist of The Band, for *Melody Maker* in the Century City office of Arista Records, when he had just released his debut solo album, *Rick Danko*.

During that conversation, we chatted about *The Last Waltz* and touring the world with Bob Dylan in 1966 and the United States in 1974:

The cameras didn't inhibit anyone. We wanted to feed five thousand people a gourmet dinner, and I think we also gave 'em a good show," he winked. "You were there. You saw the concert. Wasn't it terrific? We had people stashed behind the curtains giving us hand signals. The movie is a labor of love. At the start, The Band had to raise a few hundred thousand bucks so this event could become a reality. We were taking a chance—we almost hocked our houses.

We were the perfect house band. Even the rehearsals were incredible. It cost $125,000 to renovate Winterland. I hate to keep relating to money, but I want to show you how important it was for us to have the theme and décor amplify the mood of the celebration. It was a special night.

Preparing for the gig was a trip in itself. For four days we did nothing but play music. We finished *Islands*, our last album for Capitol, and then nonstop rehearsal for *The Last Waltz*.

The Band really came alive that night. We were cruising the last year and it was obvious. We were onstage for six hours and The Band worked until 5 A.M. that morning. We rehearsed with Bob [Dylan] at the hotel. We played for sixteen hours before the gig. The Band has always been into precision, like a fine car. We didn't take it easy during preparation. I think that will show in the movie. No split screen stuff and very little backstage footage. No way was I gonna walk out onstage and wing it next to Joni Mitchell. And Muddy Waters—wait till you see Muddy in the film. We also did a version of "Mannish Boy" at the hotel and nobody had a tape recorder. I was playing next to him and got chills. I think for Muddy and for Ronnie Hawkins, they arrived at the high point in their lives that night.

Days before the *Last Waltz* concert, Scorsese had put together a three hundred-page shooting script which choreographed every camera movement to lyric and music changes. "No matter how prepared you are, you're going to be subject to chance, to fate, to luck," Scorsese stated.

Jaime Robbie Robertson was born in Toronto, Canada on July 5, 1943. Father from Toronto, mother—of Mohawk descent—born and raised on the Six Nations Reservation. He learned guitar from relatives while visiting the reservation during summer months. He is still active in Native American rights and still creating awareness to free Leonard Peltier from prison.

In 2002 he performed in the Native American ceremonial spectacular at the opening ceremonies of the XIX Olympic Winter Games in Salt Lake

City, Utah. The same year he was the music supervisor of Scorsese's *The Gangs of New York*.

In 2000 and 2001, Robertson oversaw Capitol Records' reissue campaign of all eight of The Band's original albums.

In 1994 The Band was inducted into the Rock and Roll Hall of Fame.

"Everyone was so incredible about wanting to be involved with *The Last Waltz*, come hell or high water," Robertson exclaims. "No one had to think about it; they just said they'd do it."

Robertson talked to me in 2002 from his hotel room in Austin, Texas, where he keynoted the South by Southwest music conference and screened *The Last Waltz*.

Q: What was your first reaction on viewing the new cut of *The Last Waltz* and hearing the music?

A: Well, it's pretty extraordinary to be able to see this better than it's ever been seen, and to hear it better than it's ever been heard, and for it to be so much more encompassing—the whole experience. Because now, with what you can do with technology, just the way that it looks is richer, the blacks are blacker, the colors are warmer, and when I was working on sound for it, they had a thing where you could A/B what it was—the old mix of it—against the new Surround Sound on it, and the difference was overwhelming. And the way that I did this was to put the viewer in the best seat in the house—in the audience, so you can hear people around you, y'know, breathing, and screaming and carrying on. It really is such a different feeling from what it's ever been and such a tremendous improvement.

Q: Did you ever have any concerns while revisiting *The Last Waltz* that you might turn out a soundtrack using the new technology without hiss and noise, which is part of rock 'n' roll, and that you might have too sterile and too clean a soundtrack in this new model?

A: Yeah. But with something like this, there are certain things that are part of the characteristic of it, and I think you have to be careful when you go in. This is not doing surgery and trying to fix something that isn't broken. I think that some of that can actually be complementary and musical, just the same way that vinyl can be. It's just getting it so it's under control and it's not overwhelming what the heart of the whole thing is.

Q: Does your own life flash in front of you when you see the new print?

A: No, it doesn't do that to me. I go into an automatic mode of doing the work. I go to a place of "here's what needs to be done," "here's what we have to address now," "I want to remember to get this right."

I don't go down memory lane at all in these things. I really look at it like the work that needs to be done, or the work that was done, and how is it in this setting? Things like that. I automatically go there. And I don't know if I'm cheating myself by not affording myself the pleasure of doing that, but it's just not my nature to sit back and, y'know, light up a pipe and just enjoy the experience for what it is.

Q: I know there was a short rehearsal time before the actual gig and subsequent film and original soundtrack album. I've always felt that those couple of days—instead of an extended preproduction and lengthy rehearsal—added to the existing vibe and execution of the show, and a lot of politics and factors didn't get a chance to enter the equation, because you kept the original focus on the music and short-term preparation. Like the rehearsals included on the new CD set.

A: Yeah, yeah. That's great. The rehearsals were a wonderful surprise for me. Because I didn't know that any of these rehearsals were even taped. What they were doing was testing the equipment and just taping some of these things to make sure everything was working, and then they were judging whether they were using the right microphones for certain things. That kind of stuff. So that was just a lovely surprise to hear and also to hear the difference in what somebody might do when they're working the thing out, and what they would do when the audience is there and the lights go on.

Q: When did *The Last Waltz* concert go into the planning stages? I know when we talked in 1976, for *Crawdaddy!* magazine, you admitted then you were tired of a routine of "album, tour, album, tour." Did this begin to bubble in summer of 1976? Did the seeds of the event go back earlier?

A: No it didn't. The idea came around probably in September. Then I needed to talk to everybody about it and it had to germinate, the whole thing. When you come up with something so right, it takes on a life of its own. And when I started thinking that we were going to do this and who we were going to invite, we had only talked about Bob Dylan and Ronnie Hawkins. And then there were other people who had been so supportive and that we respected so much musically, that we said, if we're gonna invite them, we shouldn't forget Eric [Clapton]. Over the years I saw him a lot. The same thing with Van [Morrison]. And then there's our countrymen from Canada; Joni and

Neil—and the whole thing just snowballed in a way and it was almost like your job, a good portion of the time, was to get out of the way.

Like rock 'n' roll, it's definitely call and response. And that's what happened. After I had an idea of the people we felt should be a part of this, and I reached the point of thinking about the musical people of that generation, and who had been so influential to that generation, y'know—talking about Muddy Waters and the Staple Singers—and all the parts and all of these flavors of music played into the whole picture, then it became really important to me that the horizon had such depth and such different flavors to it, and to hope that we could display all of that. That's one of the reasons we went back later with Marty, shooting on the MGM soundstages for three songs: "The Weight" with the Staples; "Evangeline" with Emmylou Harris; and "The Theme from *The Last Waltz*."

We had done *The Last Waltz* and never paid that same kind of respect to the music that came down from the mountains, or whether it would be gospel or country or even the *Last Waltz* theme, which was so traditional and me just being a movie buff, y'know. I wanted to have something that was thematic to it and was absolutely as lovely as what Scorsese and [production designer] Boris Leven and the cinematographers and everyone were trying to do. People kept using the words, "beautiful," and "that's so warm," that you wanted to just go with that whole thing and everybody feeding off all of those different energies.

So, with the preparation for it, by the time I got to Marty, it was probably six weeks away when I talked to him about it. That's what I'm remembering. The timing wasn't great for him, but it was something that he was so passionately wanting to do, he made it work.

Q: You've seen it all from your own group's gigs to dates with Sonny Boy Williamson in the early '60s in a club where a single white spotlight was on the singer.

Then, cut to *The Last Waltz*, where you have lots of cameras, additional lights, the possible intrusion of chandeliers hanging above and around the stage at Winterland. The stuff had to be there to help document everything. At the time, at the event, were you aware of the camera and sound relationship? Did it inhibit your performance? You know you are being filmed.

A: Yeah, but I thought that it was important to know when to get out of the way, too. And when Marty invited Boris Leven, the production designer, to help us out with this, with such respect to the guy who had done *West Side Story* and *The Sound of Music*, and *Giant*.

Q: You were still going to film school then.

A: Yes. That was part of my passion that I had great admiration for. This work, and what he had been involved with. So, when he sat down and talked with Marty about this, he had all kinds of ideas that were way too ambitious for us 'cause we didn't have any financing for this, so we were just reeling him in on that. Never was there an idea though that we thought was just silly and out of context. When he said, "I'm getting these chandeliers from *Gone with the Wind*, and this set from *La Traviata*," because we can get them for no money at all from the San Francisco Opera Company 'cause we're in San Francisco—it was just him operating on whatever those skills were under those circumstances. And we said, "Chandeliers?" And he said, "This is *The Last Waltz*." And Marty and I said, "Excuse us Boris, we forgot ourselves there for a minute." He said, "This has to be so elegant."

Q: And Marty brings in some heavyweights like Michael Chapman as director of photography. Heritage film people at the helm, and not exclusively recent film school graduates and rookies who've done two music videos and then get a major feature film gig. And this is added to people like yourself and Jonathan Taplin [The Band's road manager and executive producer of the film], who truly emerged out of rock 'n' roll. That's healthy.

A: For sure, but you know what? I think the healthiest thing is when you mix those worlds together and—whether you're mixing different elements of music together and coming up with something fresh, or whether you're doing the same thing with film, or mixing music and film together in this case—it's all about going somewhere that neither one of you would have gone on your own, and accepting God's favor. And I'm just not gonna sit around and judge every element that comes along. I asked Martin Scorsese to do this because I have great respect for him, and he has great respect for the music, and I'm just gonna let him do everything that his instincts tell him and he's gonna let me do everything that my instincts tell me on my end.

Everybody [The Band] was overwhelmed by how this thing caught fire. How exciting this was seeing this thing come together. And just being surrounded by such brilliance. So everybody was having a great time with that. Like all movies—and like any project this big that has so many people involved—it was "committee art," y'know.

This was not one person doing anything. It was many, many people participating.

Q: Did you have discussions about subject-specific things, like not having a whole film of just close-ups, or the camera fixed on the guitarist's fingers?

A: We had conversations about just the approach of what we didn't like about things that had happened in the past, where we just didn't want to do that. We wanted to do this in a much tastier fashion, in a classic fashion. And Marty was so in tune with that, and he said, "I worked on *Woodstock*, and that movie was about the audience. This movie is about the music." And this is getting people together who will never be together in our lifetime. And an event that will never happen again. And he said, "I want to do this in a way that shows how much I care about what's happening here, and how grateful I am to be part of this." And that's where those choices were made. And we talked about things and how they would be shot, where the cameras would be. He went over that 'cause he's a very generous artistic person, plus he wanted everybody to be on the same page, so we'd all be in a position to do whatever we possibly could.

Q: There's extra footage of Bob Dylan and his songs on the soundtrack discs.

When we talked in 1976 about The Band playing with Dylan on the 1974 tour, you remarked, "At least this past time we weren't booed." I still have a hard time comprehending Dylan and your group being booed on the world tour of 1966, when what I remember about the 1974 shows I saw is that everyone was totally digging the blend onstage.

A: Well, one of the things I'm excited about on the [new] *Last Waltz* is that we got to use this other Dylan song, "Hazel." We had to make sacrifices originally, obviously, in the movie, because it's a movie, and you have to edit a movie so it plays. But on the record we had a limited amount of space, too. And I was always taken by Bob's performance on "Hazel." I thought he did an amazing performance on it and poured such passion into this song.

Q: And you were on the original studio version of "Hazel" on *Planet Waves*.

A: Yeah! And I remember when I was putting this whole [new] thing together, "Hazel" was really good, too. I'm glad to hear I wasn't alone in that.

Getting back to your question about The Band and Bob onstage. There was a thing that happened between Bob and The Band that when we played together, we would just go into a certain gear automatically. It was like instinctual, like you smelled something in the air, you know, and it made you hungry. (*laughs*) It was that instinctual. And the way we played music together was very much that way. And, whether we were playing in 1966 or 1976, or when we did the tour together in 1974, we would go to a certain place where we just pulled the trigger. It was like, "Just burn down the doors, 'cause we're coming through." And it was a whole other place than we played when we weren't playing with him. It was a whole other place than he played when he wasn't playing with us, so it was like putting a flame and oil together, or something. I don't know.

When we did the Dylan and Band tour in '74, we went and did a lot of the same things we did back in '66, and the people's response was "This is the shit and I knew it all along." It was like you weren't really there all along. It's interesting and it's one of the things I talked about in my keynote speech that I had to make at this SXSW conference. It's really a very interesting experiment to see, or to go from something where people were so adamantly against this music, and that we didn't change anything, and the world revolved, and everybody came around and said, "This is brilliant." That was very interesting, to see everything else change around you.

Q: Did you have some interaction with Dylan about repertoire before the show? Song selection?

A: Oh for sure. "Forever Young." We all threw our thoughts into the hat and then we would try stuff, and if it felt right, then we just did it. It was one of those things like letting some higher power make the decision, because the proof was in the pudding. And, "Let's play that song and see how it feels." We would play it and say, "That was fun. Let's do that." But Bob wanted to do stuff that was connected with our origins together, which is why we did "Baby Let Me Follow You Down," which we played back then; and "I Don't Believe You (She Acts Like We Never Had Met)"; and obviously "Hazel" and "Forever Young," because of us working together on the *Planet Waves* thing. So it was about trying to find a connection, and not just doing something that had nothing to do with anything. We wanted it to have had some thought.

Q: Robbie, Muddy Waters in *The Last Waltz* was incredible. He leaps out of the screen. When you were taking a look at this new print, and putting the soundtrack together, with two of his tracks, did he blow your mind, too, maybe because you captured something that people will never be able to physically see and experience.

A: More so. Because now, when I'm watching it, I'm also hearing it that way. And the power of it. Because you look at this man and say, "This guy . . . I don't know what the Rolling Stones would have done, or how much music wouldn't have existed, if it hadn't been for this guy." And look at him—can't you see why? It is one of the high points for me in this. Just talking about pedal to the metal, and pulling the trigger—he must have been about sixty-five or so, he came out and he was the daddy of the whole Delta Blues scene for sure, but such a gentleman. He came out there with people who are so large with their own music, and held his own, and didn't take a step backward. There's a true master.

Q: You know, previously, I had seen Muddy in clubs like The Ash Grove. At *The Last Waltz*, Muddy had the best sound, the best lights, a huge stage, and lots of people behind him. Muddy brought something to the party. I left Winterland afterward feeling I could rock 'n' roll to age eighty, like many other people in the room.

A: Yep. Well you know, there's something to the idea that when all these people are in this place, and you're coming out and doing one song, or two songs, or whatever you're doing, and then there's all these people who've been out before you, and all these people coming after you—all of that—it makes everybody just rise to the occasion musically and spiritually in a way that sometimes you don't even know you have in yourself. That's one of the things where I think, "Thank God this was captured in such a beautiful way, too." And that you can really see this and really go inside it, and really feel a part of the whole thing. Because it's a movie. It isn't just a video of something, where you're looking at it and saying, "Is this fake?" "Is this real?" "Is this being fluffed up like a television commercial?"

This is the real thing, in a setting of such respectful elegance that, when I was working on it, I did think, "My God, I've known Van Morrison for all these years, I've seen him perform many, many times, and I never saw him do what he did." Muddy Waters coming out there between all of these people and rocking the very foundation of music in that whole place that night. This was like an outstanding experience. Sometimes I had to just catch myself, not to be standing there with my mouth open.

Well, that's why I spent five and a half months doing this, and even the DVD audio of this is astounding, because it's not goofy, where things are over here and over there for no reason. It's done in a way that draws you. You're no longer sitting in the audience in this thing. You are sitting right up on the stage, in front of the music. And it just wraps around you. It's really quite beautifully done.

Q: When you hear The Band's music on the speakers, what do you think when it's coming back at you? Is it a joyous experience? Is it a sad experience?

A: I just feel extremely proud in the choice that we made to work together. I absolutely feel there are moments when I think, "Whew . . . he's the business. What talent. What an amazing emotional musical choice was made right there." I do feel those things.

Q: Do you have a different relationship to the film and music merger now, after working on *The Last Waltz*?

A: Well, I don't know. I think the big difference for me is that I hope I never have to do it again, because it was such an undertaking (*laughs*). I just wasn't thinking. After we were at mix number 154, we were mixing this whole record, right? Then, it had to be mixed in DVD-A. And then we had to do the Surround Sound for the movie. And then the 5.1 mixes for the DVD of the movie. It was so much that you thought, "Are we there yet?"

So it was one of those things where I'm doing it and I'm really glad that I did it, and now I'm really glad that it was done. Because it was incredibly time-consuming. But this was something special that needed to be treated with love and affection, and I wanted to do that.

Q: Did you have any doubts or fears, embarking on the *Last Waltz* event?

A: Entering the event, big time, was, "Can we pull this off?" There's a thousand things that can go wrong, and a couple of things that can go right here. "Are we going to nail this?" "Are we gonna pull it off?" "Is the film going to capture it?" "Are they going to say afterward that the recordings we have are a disaster?" There's all those kinds of technical concerns, and just your ability to rise to the occasion at that moment. It wasn't like we were stopping and doing the songs over and over, or that "I think we can do it better." There was none of that.

In March, 2002, Robbie Robertson gave the keynote opening address at the South by Southwest Film and Music Conference in Austin, Texas and screened *The Last Waltz*. That same year, he was the music supervisor on Martin Scorsese's film *The Gangs of New York*, and earlier served as the music supervisor for the movie *The Color of Money*.

In 2000 and 2001, Robertson oversaw Capitol Records' reissue campaign of all eight of The Band's original albums. In addition to supervising the remastering and remixing, he personally selected all previously unreleased material included in the packages. In fall of 2005, Robertson performed similar functions to prepare *The Band: A Musical History*, a box set from EMI/Capitol Records.

In 1994 The Band was inducted into the Rock and Roll Hall of Fame.

STEVEN VAN ZANDT AND CHRIS COLUMBUS

BORN IN MASSACHUSETTS, nurtured in New Jersey, a longtime resident of New York City, and racking up plenty of frequent flier miles to Hollywood and Los Angeles, California, these days, Steven Van Zandt, a.k.a. Little Steven, plays Silvio Dante in HBO's *The Sopranos*, and is also the longtime guitarist in Bruce Springsteen's E Street Band.

He's been in your video store and on your TV screen and home entertainment system for decades. You've watched him in *Bruce Springsteen: The Complete Video Anthology 1978–2000, Blood Brothers: Bruce Springsteen and the E Street Band*, and *Bruce Springsteen: Video Anthology 1978–1988*. He also appeared on *Saturday Night Live* as a musical guest with Bruce Springsteen and the E Street Band.

In addition to his fulltime acting job, Steven joined his old friend Springsteen for a record-breaking international tour with the E Street Band to promote the album, *The Rising*, during 2002 and 2003. Van Zandt has also released five solo albums.

In 2004 video products, Little Steven was included in *Ramones Raw* and participated in *Out of Our Dens: The Richard and the Young Lions Story*. On VH1 he was a talking head in the *Behind the Music* episode on Bon Jovi.

You've also seen him on the television screen, on *The Late Show with David Letterman, Jimmy Kimmel Live*, and *Late Night with Conan O'Brien*.

Festival poster. Courtesy of Renegade Nation.

Steven Van Zandt was at the epicenter of the political and musical recording and video, *Sun City/The Making of Sun City*, producing the Artists United Against Apartheid compilation.

Van Zandt is a distinguished record producer of artists such as Bruce Springsteen and the E Street Band, Southside Johnny and the Asbury Jukes, Darlene Love, Lone Justice, Gary U.S. Bonds, Michael Monroe, Lords of the New Church, the Arc Angels, the Charms, Tina Sugandh, Davie Allan and the Arrows, Jean Beauvoir, and the Chesterfield Kings.

In my book, *This Is Rebel Music*, I conducted a lengthy interview with Steven that chronicled our thirty-year friendship and discussed his own music, *The Sopranos*, and his recent radio endeavors. I'm a consultant to his weekly two-hour syndicated radio show, *Little Steven's Underground Garage*, which launched with twenty-three affiliates and now, halfway through its third year, has grown to a remarkable 125 stations in 190 markets across the United States and Canada. The show is also broadcast weekly on the Voice of America Music Mix Channel in forty-three different countries.

In 2004, Little Steven joined Sirius Satellite Radio as creative consultant, creating a twenty-four-hour *Underground Garage* format that launched in July. He is also executive producer of *Outlaw Country*, a new twenty-four-hour format that provides sanctuary for the rebels and renegades of country and rock 'n' roll on Sirius. In addition, he is executive producer of *The Wiseguy Show*, a weekly talk show that features Vinny Pastore and Steve Schirippa, among others.

In March 2005, Little Steven and Sirius Satellite Radio celebrated rock 'n' roll's future on the fiftieth anniversary of the landmark film, *Blackboard Jungle*, directed by Richard Brooks, the film that jump-started rock 'n' roll with its theme song, "Rock Around the Clock."

Previously, Van Zandt served as film music supervisor and soundtrack executive producer for *Christmas with the Kranks*, released in late 2004 by Sony Pictures. The film, based on John Grisham's novel, *Skipping Christmas*, stars Jamie Lee Curtis, Tim Allen, and Dan Aykroyd. The screenplay is by one of the film's coproducers, Chris Columbus.

Little Steven's Renegade Nation produced the most acclaimed rock concert of 2004, "Little Steven's International Underground Garage Festival." Presented by Dunkin' Donuts and held on August 14, 2004, at Randall's Island in New York City, the festival featured forty-five bands, including Iggy Pop and the Stooges, the Fondas, the Electric Prunes, the Strokes, the Pretty Things, the Chesterfield Kings, and the reunited New York Dolls.

Shot in 3-D by director Chris Columbus, a film of the concert is a work in progress that hopefully will see release in the next couple of years.

Little Steven's Rolodex booked a music festival that thankfully is preserved on film. Forty-five acts helped further define the active garage rock genre.

In October of 2004 Steven invited me to a trailer of the in-progress production, shown in an eighteen-minute clip of this event that was shot in 3-D by Paradise FX, based in Van Nuys, California.

The footage is a history and mystery lesson unfolding in front of me. Effective camera sweeps and the revolving band lineup. A daytime-nighttime sound and vision time capsule linked together with stage introductions from Little Steven, *Sopranos* cast members, Bruce Springsteen, Kim Fowley, Martin Lewis, Edd "Kookie" Byrnes, and Chuck Barris—he penned "Palisades Park"—among the hosts. The screening piece was riveting and pulsating; the duality of a new form of rock documentary that combines elements of *Hullabaloo, Shindig!* cosmic Go Go girls, old school, new school, cool shul, global awareness, reflecting from a festival akin to the first generation radio stars who later jumped to the world of television.

It was a brief glimpse of a new way the music and rock form has been presented the last forty years since *The T.A.M.I. Show* and further embodying the earlier fifty years of rock 'n' roll on the silver screen.

Previous music festival movies have all woven the fabric of rock 'n' roll along the way to create the great melodic quilt of dreams. *Woodstock* certainly took it to another place with split screen editing techniques that were legendary. Garage rock united in 3-D is a movie, which is part homage to the past, and in the process creates a new sound and film frontier—the next dance after the last waltz.

It's a tribute to Little Steven's ongoing tough task of programming and broadcasting, on a regular basis, classic garage rock, new bands, veteran rock 'n' roll as well as rock 'n' toll survivors now heard on his syndicated radio network.

The garage rock mix filmed in 3-D brings the viewer a long way from *House of Wax* to this stage of facts. Van Zandt and Columbus with the FX folks have taken us from *13 Ghosts* to a global village of forty-five bands and characters fortified from the sixteen thousand-member audience throng at the venue who braved the threat of rain and nearby hurricane Charlie to witness real-to-reel living history.

One of the reasons this specific merger of garage rock and film grooved so well in the short form rough cut I viewed is that Steven Van Zandt has supervised music in big budget movies and franchise properties. Van Zandt has also seen it all around the globe on the stages of the biggest arenas and mammoth stadiums, playing guitar and singing with Bruce Springsteen & the E Street Band for decades. Underneath it all, Steven has the empathy and understanding of the clubs and alternative venues too—the backbone of the garage rock circuit. Little Steven always remained a fan and record collector: the ideal action poet candidate to take the music, the heritage, and the new sounds to a modern and groovy cinema exhibition.

You see, rock 'n' roll is a religion to Little Steven, and to a lot of us. He's like Gandhi with a Fender guitar walking stick.

Van Zandt and Columbus, along with coproducer Marc Brickman—himself a veteran creator of those stellar Springsteen, Pink Floyd, and Paul McCartney light shows for many, many years—have fashioned their own collective vision of a celluloid universe for inspection: a marriage of rule-breaking aural collage juxtaposition and enriching sensory experience. It all makes sense and is a very logical extension of the fifty-year bedfellows of rock 'n' roll and film.

After our preview, I talked first to Little Steven and later to Chris Columbus.

Q: Steven, in knowing about garage rock and how some of the records of these bands have been used in previous television shows, cable programs, and earlier music compilations, what I've seen in preproduction of your garage music festival on-screen takes it to a whole new level visually, not just sonically.

A: The subject is garage rock, which is a culture where we're discovering and creating fans for a certain thing we know about, a certain reverence for the '50s and '60s, and acknowledging that the renaissance is gonna be cool forever. We are distinctly expressing the timelessness of cool. Taking things out of chronological order and providing a different experience of rock 'n' roll. No film has truly acknowledged that. Not playing a lot of songs all the way through, a different thing happens to your brain.

Part of the contemporary garage rock culture and the reverence for the 1950s and '60s is an aspect of fun that does not exist in any other part of our culture. Part of the 3-D factor, a bit of camp and kitsch, a bit of silliness, a looking back at that aspect of pop culture as purely fun.

Little Steven. Photo courtesy of Renegade Nation.

These days we've gotten to a point of lowest common denominator, especially straight ahead, boring, taking itself way too serious. You look around and you don't see a lot of fun. Garage rock's main sensibility comes from pre-1965 rock 'n' roll, pre-art form rock. Completely ridiculous.

Q: Why did you choose the 3-D format?

A: For this music and these visuals, it lent itself so well. This particular type of music is based on that era—theatrical; it has personality, no limit to that. I wanted to take people right next to the people right on the stage. 'Cause people haven't experienced this stuff in a long time.

I honestly believe the *Underground Garage* format (197 radio stations) is the first format that bridges the generation gap. It's the first thing in music actually to bridge the generation gap, like baseball. Fathers and sons actually enjoy the experience equally. First time that is changing.

Q: So your syndicated radio show is the foundation for the festival, and the next logical extension had to be celluloid?

A: We don't play many songs over three minutes on the radio show. We do that for a reason. It has a cumulative energy that is spectacular. After the show they can't sleep because in most markets we air on Saturday nights. One of the things with my radio show and this movie is to transport people to another place, a surreal aspect of it all. *Ernie Kovacs* meets *Yellow Submarine*, but we don't like to acknowledge time. For me, the icons that we respect are just as vital and relevant as ever, and fun. Some are wise, cool, and important in some combination, like Allen Ginsberg.

We sort of promote that kind of thing—cool, at least looking back over the last fifty years, it's finite. There's a finite number of people that we consider in terms of the rock 'n' roll culture—which is now called the garage rock culture—and those people, I knew the radio show could translate into a visual world. It has concert elements and more than that: the experience—and not just backstage footage. Any expedition is in symbolic form or metaphor form. The person writing this script is the mythical version of Roger Corman somewhere. So when you see a clip of Peter Fonda and Nancy Sinatra from an A.I.P. movie, and then cut to her in 2004 singing "These Boots Are Made for Walkin,'" well, Nancy and Peter were cool then and she's cool now. Amusing to see how people age—or don't age in the case of David Aguilar of the Chocolate Watchband, who moves the exact same way now as he did thirty-five years ago.

As you know, Harvey, there's a global nature and support to this music that integrates fans, freaks, the DIY nation, fanzines, other musicians, and writers. Everyone is connected. And the artists and groups always work, some are on independent labels, others own their labels, there are refugees from major labels, and bands gigging and surviving, partially based on album reissues and CD rereleases, video film clips, while others have been chronicled in documentaries. Some bands have reformed. What remarkable coincidences, something Joseph Campbell says about "happening in a same time thousands of miles apart for no apparent reason." The bands are from England, Finland, Spain, and America. Everywhere. It's inviting and fun.

Q: From what I've seen of this rough stuff, even before editing, it carries the next generation of roots music forward: the garage rock genre on parade.

A: I love *The Last Waltz*, but it implies the last chapter of the book. Let's open a new chapter, and here comes the *Underground Garage* movie, and this becomes the new era of rock 'n' roll. I haven't been a revolutionary and a renegade out of choice. We always end up being innovative because we have to. I tried the normal route, the easier way—it never works for me. What are you gonna do? Not do it?

Marc Brickman is one of the three producers, a legendary lighting designer, and a production designer of the show. How about the genius of lighting done ninety-five percent during the day? What happened was that we designed the Go Go girls to be part of the design. No proven tricks of the last fifty years. The idea was to reinvent the form—very conscious from day one. Didn't really storyboard the event. The designs that Marc came up with are genius. A rotating stage, separation panels, and he got together with Maureen Van Zandt, who choreographed the girls and designed the costumes with Marc. Maureen found rare material and came up with the costumes that became the lights. Marc pointed out that the costumes could solve the huge potential problem of no lights during the day and a bare stage.

All of a sudden you realize, with beach movies, biker flicks, Go Go girls, they all have one thing in common. At first you think it's funny, and then after a little bit, it's funny and a bit cool. It's still cool. I'm actually enjoying it for it's own sake. Not looking at it for nostalgia reasons.

Q: What about your stage hosts?

A: I selected hosts we are associated with across the board: Kim Fowley, Chuck Barris, Edd "Kookie" Byrnes, Martin Lewis, *Sopranos* cast members, Bruce Springsteen—all part of our family of freaks and icons. They move the action. Most of them emerge from the radio ID's you hear on the radio show.

Q: The music and the movie also are a result of your combined efforts with many people, especially Marc Brickman and Chris Columbus, who from day one understood your original vision of translating the radio show to the festival stage and subsequent movie.

A: Right. The thing that has to get you first, even experiencing 3-D in the past, how you remember it: you can't remember it. See it. Wow. It's something your brain cannot remember. Moments of bliss, revelation, and epiphany.

It's the first time ever that six generations of rock 'n' roll are represented, live and on film. Some groups are pretty strict about rock 'n' roll, and it got made without people telling me how to make it.

Q: Tell me about hooking up with director Chris Columbus for this venture.

A: Chris Columbus is a person who loves music and especially rock 'n' roll. Over fifteen years ago he paired me with Darlene Love and I wrote a song for her that was in *Home Alone 2: Lost in New York*.

Q: I remember around 1982 you phoned one night and asked me to join you and Bruce Springsteen to see Darlene perform in West Hollywood at a club. Even then you mentioned she was one of your favorite singers of all time and you hoped to record or produce her in the future.

A: That's right! Lou Adler, who owns the Roxy Theater, invited us that evening. Chris later gave me the chance to work with Darlene Love, a chance that I would otherwise never have gotten. In movies you can do things that don't have any rules; occasionally a movie person likes a hit song that can help sell the movie, but they want something that works for the movie. That's the only criteria besides the emotional connection. That's a wonderful challenge.

A couple of years ago, Chris fell in love with the radio show. That's where it started. I also did the end title song, "The Time of Your Life," for *Nine Months*, another film of his. Again, the radio show—both Chris and his son had something in common with the music. I can't tell you how many fathers come up to me and say, "Thank you for giving me a common ground with my son" or daughter.

So with Chris Columbus we had the relationship, and in trying to communicate the visual version of the radio show, we needed to have a surreal element and take it out of time and place if possible. That's where the animation comes in, and who better to do that than Chris Columbus? Like he did with *Home Alone*, it's not a real place, but from a kid's mind. Of course he did it with *Harry Potter* in a much more literal way, where you are literally in another place. The element of showing fantasy to better explain reality is sort of our thing—with a lot of energy.

Hailing from Pennsylvania and raised in Ohio, Chris Columbus is helming the feature-length movie culled from Little Steven's *Underground Garage Festival*. Columbus' film industry career brings a wealth of dazzling and commercial movie achievements to this groundbreaking musical and cinematic collaboration.

His own 2005 and 2006 movie plans are like the NBA basketball playoff schedule. When I talked to Chris he was in production with Little Steven and in preproduction for the filmed adaptation of the Broadway musical *Rent*. In 2005, he also begins production of *NFL Dad*.

In this decade, Columbus is best known for his direction of two Harry Potter feature films, *Harry Potter and the Sorcerer's Stone* and *Harry Potter and the Chamber of Secrets*. He also produced *Harry Potter and the Prisoner of Azkaban* in 2004.

As a writer, producer, and director, some of Chris's movie work includes *Bicentennial Man, Stepmom, Nine Months, Mrs. Doubtfire, Home Alone, Home Alone 2: Lost in New York, Heartbreak Hotel*, and *Adventures in Babysitting*. Columbus is also producing the *Fantastic Four* movie in 2005.

As a writer, he has penned more scripts than you probably realize, and been behind plenty of movies and DVDs you've rented. Chris is toiling on *Rent*, and just finished *Christmas with the Kranks*, that came out in late 2004. Previous Columbus writing credits and screenplays are *Nine Months, Little Nemo: Adventures in Slumberland, Only the Lonely, Gremlins 2: The New Batch, Heartbreak Hotel, Young Sherlock Holmes, Goonies, Gremlins*, and *Reckless*.

Chris Columbus, since entering the movie business from jump street, has constantly put his passion for rock 'n' roll, blues, R&B, and classic English '60s rock into his own movies and soundtrack albums.

In his debut film in 1987, he licensed the Rolling Stones' "Gimme Shelter" for *Adventures in Babysitting* I remember another motion picture of his had a key scene where a Tyrone Davis record played.

Trust me, and especially believe Little Steven. He would not hand over the direction of his collective garage festival effort to Chris Columbus if the multitalented filmmaker didn't understand the magic of rock 'n' roll and believe in it as well.

Chris Columbus.
Photo by Zade
Rosenthal,
courtesy of
Revolution
Studios.

Q: Chris, what about music and rock 'n' roll in film?

A: When I first saw *Mean Streets* and heard the Stones' "Jumpin' Jack Flash" in a sequence, it moved me so much, it was striking. I said to myself, "Someday I want to be able to use music in film like this. I want to be able to find the perfect partnership between the visuals and rock 'n' roll." More than score. A lot of filmmakers I talk to, like Steven Spielberg and George Lucas and guys I've known for years, always have at their fingertips this vast knowledge of people who do scores. I don't have that. The only knowledge I have at my fingertips is the songs in the back of my head that someday I'd like to use in a film that I've just never been able to.

Q: I was sort of stunned when the Stones' "Gimme Shelter" was in your first film, *Adventures in Babysitting*. I know there was a club scene with Elisabeth Shue singing, and Albert Collins leading the band.

A: That movie was a walk through my record collection at that time. It's like rock 'n' roll itself. If you think about it too much before you make the movie, you may sometimes find that you can't fit it in the movie, or it feels like it's been thought about too much. The key is that when you see the movie and see what you've done, you go back through the iPod that is your head, and you go through the countless songs that may work and may fit, and then you take them all and put them up against the picture. "Gimme Shelter" was put up against the picture.

When I first went to Chicago, my wife and I were very young at the time, and we would be going out at night and staying out until four in the morning. To get to the bars in Chicago you had to go through Lower Wacker Drive, which at the time was a smoky tunnel underground through Chicago lit by green light. It was a surreal place and I was obsessed with putting "Gimme Shelter" in *Adventures in Babysitting*. When the kids descend into the bowels of Lower Wacker Drive, what better song than "Gimme Shelter"? What is more haunting? Like you're stepping into another world. Some songs stay in your head. There's no notebook. You can't prepare for it. You just know in the back of your head that someday you're gonna pull out Dobie Gray's "Drift Away." I used that in the movie, *Heartbreak Hotel*. I designed a scene around "Drift Away." I didn't shoot it with that in mind, but I designed it in the editing room.

Q: I know you are a fan of Little Steven's *Underground Garage* radio show. You and your son check it out together. What about the challenge of shooting and directing a rock 'n' roll festival in the 3-D format? The challenge of 3-D capturing live garage rock bands? Does 3-D lend itself to the live music experience?

A: Unless I'm wrong—maybe there was a rock 'n' roll film in the 1950s shot in 3-D—this is the first time a 3-D concert film has ever been shot. For me the idea was to let the audience feel like they're actually experiencing these bands for the first time. Steven has a philosophy that 3-D fits under the *Underground Garage* banner of everything that was cool in the '50s and '60s, which is great, and it fits into that idea. For me, 3-D at its best takes the audience into the performance, and these are bands that they are not all familiar with. It makes the audience immediately familiar with the bands and it's the only thing that can sort of capture the feeling of being at a live show. So I was intrigued by that. For me it's like going back and seeing *The Last Waltz* in 3-D. As much as I love that movie, if there was a version in 3-D, then that would take me into it, onstage with those guys . . .

I did some test footage in 3-D of the New York Dolls, from the festival, on the song "You Can't Put Your Arms Around a Memory." I swear to you, I felt the night air blowing through that screening room and it was because the 3-D was so effective. It felt like I was onstage with them.

Q: How does the 3-D actually serve the angles of a rock song?

A: It bends the music in a way that makes you feel as if you're actually taking in this concert. The cool thing is to think of it as an underground garage stylistic gimmick in the '50s and '60s, but 3-D is so sophisticated now—we've come a long way from *The Creature from the Black Lagoon.*

I really struggled with the idea of shooting *Rent* in 3-D, thinking I could bring the audience onto the stage with these actors. I'm not going to do it, due to time limitations. What 3-D really does is make bands that are not known to the general audience immediately accessible. I love that. The potential for it is that you can take a band that you really know, like U2 or the Rolling Stones, and suddenly bring people closer to that band. The world of videos themselves, rock videos, was never that interesting to me. It felt odd but I can't put my finger on it. They very rarely capture the essence of what the band is about live.

Q: We talked before, and I know the *Hullabaloo* TV series and the Beatles' *A Hard Day's Night* blew your mind. Some elements of *Hullabaloo* and the Beatles' movie influence this current production. I'm talking about being brought inside the rhythms of the music.

A: Yes, definitely. *A Hard Day's Night* to me is the only real record we have of the Beatles' performance of the time. The Shea Stadium movie sound quality is horrendous and there's no feeling of Beatlemania— the excitement of being around those guys at the time. We look at it now through some rose-colored glasses because we want to believe Beatlemania was like that, but *A Hard Day's Night* actually captured the feeling we had when we listened to those records. There are very few rock 'n' roll movies that can do that. *Hullabaloo* was a forerunner of garage rock, and the point of this film is that we don't want to take ourselves too seriously.

Q: A unique aspect about garage rock—and I'm especially talking about the festival and subsequent movie you're working on—is that the performers' ages are from twenty to seventy-two.

A: To me, garage rock is one of the truly timeless things about our culture. It continues to move forward. Whether people are buying the records doesn't matter at this point. The music continues to be made all over the world. If anything, the underground garage stuff will prove there are acts in Scotland, Sweden, Spain, Detroit, England, and Australia. People are making this music and that's what draws me to it. It's the most global sort of music in a weird way. It's world music that everyone can relate to.

Q: Here's my own *Harry Potter* theory and how it applies to you as a director, in relation to this garage rock movie you've made. Part of the appeal and durability of *Harry Potter* is that it was literary and book-birthed. Some of the garage rock bands, the principals like Iggy Pop or David Johansen, are lyric-driven even though their music obviously is throbbing. Is there a relationship between *Potter* and this movie? What carries over from your work in the *Harry Potter* films that informs this garage rock collaboration?

A: Hmmm. It's a difficult connection, but it's the sense of youth probably. *Harry Potter* to me was always a story about hope. Here's a kid that lived in the suburbs in a dreary lifestyle and basically was sleeping in a cupboard under the stairs. One day he gets a letter inviting him to Hogwarts School of Witchcraft and Wizardry, enabling him to escape from his dreary world. Right? Rock 'n' roll has always been about escape, and to me the ultimate form of rock 'n' roll is escape from your dreary world or suburbia. Harry Potter lives in the most dreary section of suburban England that you can imagine; a colorless cookie-cutter world. For me, that embodies the spirit of rock 'n' roll and garage rock. It embodies the spirit of every great rock 'n' roll song I've ever loved, from the Animals to the Rolling Stones to Bruce Springsteen. Everything. It's all part of escape and it all goes back to my own personal reason for getting into the film business, which was leaving my small factory town in Ohio to get out and escape. So it's all connected, and the very heart of *Harry Potter* is connected to the spirit of rock 'n' roll.

Q: In this garage rock movie, you see people of all ages. Most of the music videos and rock concert films use a lot of makeup and cover-up to hide aging and always gear the resulting product for the youth market. There's an age barrier for talent to be filmed. In your movie, Nancy

Sinatra is over age sixty. So what! Bo Diddley is over age seventy. Iggy is pushing sixty. Big deal. A lot of the footage I've seen is shot in the morning and afternoon. Not the nighttime concert movie stuff or arena trip with lighting bathing or soaking everyone performing.

A: You don't see this in prepackaged MTV rock 'n' roll. The timelessness is just that everybody can do it at anytime. There's nothing so odd about anyone at age sixty still playing or trying—like the Chocolate Watchband. The lead singer still moves the same and still has the same amount of passion from thirty-five years ago, and you see what drove him there from the beginning. There's nothing sad about it, and there's something really invigorating, really life affirming, about it.

Q: You've also cast Little Steven in an animated character role. It adds the element of fantasy, an area you are very versed in, cinematically. You and Steven have also integrated various B-movie clips, black-and-white interstitial footage.

A: Well, it has to do with the idea that we're trying to create a movie that embodies the feeling of rock 'n' roll and listening to maybe twenty great 45s in a row. Because of that, the only way to capture that feeling is the use of clips. I was dressed as Groucho Marx this past Halloween, and few people—kids and forty-year-olds—knew who I was.

There's a part of our culture that is getting lost. We have so much information at our fingertips, but what we don't have at our fingertips is the ability to access any information that is cool and valid, from the 1930s through the 1960s. This stuff is dying and slowly fading away. So what we are trying to show here is that everything has a reason for existing, and just because it existed thirty, forty, and fifty years ago, it still is pretty great and cool.

The use of the clips serves the action and creates a feeling of what I'd like people to bring away from this movie. It would be as if they'd seen—subconsciously—a history lesson of rock 'n' roll. It's not that they will walk away with facts in their heads, but with feelings in their heads. The clips help you with the emotional history of rock 'n' roll, and the animation brings you into this world to explain what the umbrella definition of the underground garage is. People say to us, "What possible connection is there between Nancy Sinatra and Iggy Pop?" The idea is that there is a feeling and it feels right. There are a lot of pieces of culture from that time period that wouldn't work in the underground garage banner.

The idea of animated characters is that these rock 'n' roll personalities live forever and are part of your life. They exist in your mind forever. Steven in this movie is an icon and an animated form.

They help lead you through this world and explain it to you.

Q: You're also putting together a nation of unity on display.

A: Right. It's not the Rock and Roll Hall of Fame. One song buys you a ticket into an eternity of garage rock. That's it. That's what does it. You want to go back and find these bands. It means a lot to all of us.

Q: What about the challenge of shooting outdoors in the morning and the daytime so that it also blends into the bands that performed at night. Is it tricky?

A: It's got to feel more real than what's been shoved down our throats over the past twenty years, and MTV is responsible for that. MTV is responsible for creating an image for people. I think when you strip away a lot of that, suddenly the music feels as real as the day it was conceived. That happens in the bright daylight. That's what I look for. When these bands are onstage, there is nothing there to protect them. They are there in high definition 3-D. These are people like you.

The best part of rock 'n' roll for me—and I know it doesn't exist like this for everyone, and you can't expect to convert everyone—the best part of rock 'n' roll for me has always been the idea that the guy onstage is not only entertaining me and moving me emotionally by singing, but he can also potentially be my best friend. He could also be a guy I grew up with. It could be me up there.

That ties into the whole fantasy and the *Harry Potter* side of it. "I can do that. That can be me." When that wall is put up between the band and the audience, that's when I have a problem with rock 'n' roll. This takes down the wall. Daylight takes down the wall. 3-D takes down the wall. Suddenly you have accessibility to the performers. You're there with them. You're like the fifth member of the band.

Q: Let's discuss rock 'n' roll in music videos and the DVD format.

A: It does work on DVD, but it never works better than it does in a theater. It always takes you by surprise. You never know when it will move you and affect you. It could be a not-particularly-great film. Sometimes I think, well, maybe the filmmaker got lucky and they found a song that worked, but just because you have Aretha Franklin's "Respect" at your fingertips doesn't necessarily mean that when you put it up against a picture it's gonna work. If it's not the right image, you are going to be doing a disservice to the song and to your film. You have to make absolutely certain it feels right. I think the biggest problem that people fall into is that sometimes they let the music do the work for them. That's a huge mistake when the music doesn't work really well.

Q: What about director D. A. Pennebaker's *Monterey International Pop Festival* documentary?

A: Amazing. Amazing. Blew my mind. You don't get better than that, except maybe *The Last Waltz*. The key is to be brought in and not feel intrusive—the absolute key. Don't be intrusive and don't let your style influence your audience's enjoyment of the subject matter. Pennebaker is a documentarian. He doesn't intrude and by not intruding he invites the audience into the world.

There are very few feature films that are as emotionally involving as *Monterey Pop* or *Don't Look Back*. The black-and-white helps on *Don't Look Back*, and there's a theory that comedies are much better in black-and-white. That's Roger Ebert. *Don't Look Back* kicked me in the ass because Pennebaker captured a moment in time. These are rock 'n' roll snapshots. *A Hard Day's Night*. Go to Jonathan Demme and his Talking Heads' film, *Stop Making Sense*. Again, he's not intrusive with his style. He brings you into that world.

Q: What do you want to see in music films where a song hits the screen?

A: It's in a real dangerous situation. When I was using "Gimme Shelter" in 1987, it was still a little new compared to now, where every great Motown song has been bastardized by a credit card commercial. So where do you stop? How can you tell the difference between someone who believes the song works so well with their film, as opposed to someone who is just picking up a Motown greatest hits album and tossing in "I Heard It Through the Grapevine" for no reason? That's the trend that is scary to me: people who are using these songs over and over and over just because they play nicely over a chase scene. Then it suddenly becomes something corporate as opposed to something you believe in. Our 3-D movie is the antithesis of this.

Q: I'm speaking to you while you're in the early production phase of this garage festival effort and also in preproduction with a movie version of the Broadway musical *Rent*. In both movies—no matter how they end up on the big screen—both projects and properties are about people chasing dreams.

A: They all sing like their lives depend on it. In *Rent* they didn't have long to live. People tell me *Rent* isn't really rock 'n' roll. Of course it's rock 'n' roll. It's the heart of rock 'n' roll. You've got a year to live and how are you going to deal with it? What rock 'n' roll has always said to me is, no matter how much time you've got in this world, take the time you've got and run with it and have a great time.

The garage bands for a moment, one three-minute song from ten, twenty, thirty, or forty years ago, they wanted to be heard as well. You know what? You can say *Rent* is a Broadway show and it doesn't have it's heart in the origins of rock 'n' roll, but you look at a song, "One Song Glory," and that is all this character wants—"One song before I go."

Garage bands are the antithesis of that. The Electric Prunes' "I Had Too Much to Dream Last Night." Those guys don't have to do anything else. They did that.

It all collides together and it has to have a purpose. That's the interesting thing about art—that you can continue to use it, because pop art exists—we've had it for fifty or sixty years—and it will exist forever. When we figure out a way to preserve everything, you can constantly use it, reuse it, bend it, and change it. That's what we are trying to do with this garage festival film.

≈

Steven Van Zandt

Founder and host of the weekly two-hour syndicated radio show, *Little Steven's Underground Garage*, who in 2004 also created the *Underground Garage* 24-hour format for Sirius Satellite Radio. Actor, portraying Silvio Dante in HBO's *The Sopranos*. Guitarist with Bruce Springsteen and the E Street Band.

Film and television appearances with Springsteen and the band include *Bruce Springsteen: The Complete Video Anthology 1978–2000*; *Blood Brothers: Bruce Springsteen and the E Street Band*; *Bruce Springsteen: Video Anthology 1978–1988*.

Little Steven TV appearances include *The Late Show with David Letterman*; *Jimmy Kimmel Live*; *Late Night with Conan O'Brien*.

Van Zandt produced the recording and video *Sun City/The Making of Sun City*, producing the Artists United Against Apartheid compilation. He also participated in VH1's *Behind the Music* episode on Bon Jovi. In 2005 he served as music supervisor for the feature film, *Christmas with the Kranks*, now out on DVD. Van Zandt has released five solo albums.

Chris Columbus: Select Filmography

Rent
NFL Dad
Harry Potter and the Chamber of Secrets
Harry Potter and the Sorcerer's Stone
Harry Potter and the Goblet of Fire
Bicentennial Man
Stepmom
Nine Months
Mrs. Doubtfire
Home Alone
Home Alone 2: Lost in New York
Heartbreak Hotel
Adventures in Babysitting
Little Nemo: Adventures in Slumberland
Only the Lonely
Gremlins
Gremlins 2
Young Sherlock Holmes
Goonies
Reckless

CLEM BURKE

CLEM BURKE IS THE cofounder and drummer of Blondie. The band has sold millions of records and still tours the world. In 2002 and 2003 they were profiled on the BBC for the *Bravo* series, and on VH1's *Behind the Music*. In 2006 they were inducted into the Rock and Roll Hall of Fame.

I first met Clem on Blondie's first U.S. tour when they debuted at the Whisky A Go Go nightclub in Hollywood in 1977. We went out and saw another band at Madame Wong's in Chinatown after the show, as I recall. Burke is as vital to Blondie's sound as Charlie Watts is to the Rolling Stones. The New Jersey-born, New York-raised Burke is now a neighbor of mine, and is a true and passionate fan of music. He's still a student of rock 'n' roll and a record collector.

I ran into Clem at Brian Wilson's *Pet Sounds* concert at the Hollywood Bowl in 2002, at Phil Spector's yearly bowling party in 2002, and then once more at the Hollywood Roosevelt Hotel for the *New Music Reporter* seminar which Andrew Loog Oldham keynoted in 2003, that I helped produce.

Q: Over the last quarter of a century, your group Blondie has had songs in TV commercials and over a dozen tunes placed in feature-length movies. "Call Me" was the title song of *American Gigolo*, "Atomic"

Clem Burke at Electric Lady Studios, West 8th Street,
New York City, August 1998. Photo courtesy of Clem Burke.

was in this year's *Bend It like Beckham,* and last decade was covered by Sleeper in *Trainspotting. The Last American Virgin* showcased "In the Flesh," while "One Way or Another" was placed in *Little Darlings.* Blondie music has been integral in *Gia,* an HBO film, while I know your "Rapture" has also been heard on-screen as well. You even danced in the music video Blondie did for "Rapture." And in 2004, "Rapture" was in an episode of Fox's *Nip/Tuck* TV series.

What are your feelings about the relationship between music and film, and the use of your recording and publishing catalogue?

A: A lot of our songs are lush and the imagery is basically cinematic. We've always been influenced by film and, obviously, Andy Warhol.

And the visual arts have always been an influence on us. I mean, in our song, "Fade Away and Radiate," Debbie (Harry) sings, "My dream is on the screen." Our song, "Platinum Blonde"—the only movie I believe that was in has been Amos Poe's *The Blank Generation*.

Q: I know when you recorded with Blondie, especially in the early years, you never knew some of these songs would have a life independent of the album they were initially recorded for. I was at the Whisky A Go Go when Blondie was being filmed for a few days by John Cassavetes.

A: But Blondie appealed to screenwriters and film directors. And Debbie has been cast in many movies. Again, in "Platinum Blonde," she sings about Marilyn Monroe, Jean Harlow, Marlene Dietrich—and that's a very early Blondie song. And don't forget, one of our biggest influences was composer Nino Rota. We were put in the "New Wave" category, but we knew the term from French movies of the 1950s. Our music gets licensed through Chrysalis Publishing. We share, and they actually do control the licensing. We did have a meeting coincidentally, last December, about them asking too much money for certain films. We told them to ease up on that because there were certain films we wanted to be involved with. For example, for the 2003 documentary on [DJ] Rodney Bingenheimer, we asked them to give a break on "Dreaming" that's on the soundtrack. We had a song in *Gia*. A lot of the music was representative of a certain time and place, although it seems to have transcended that. Particularly when you are doing period movies. Like I knew the real Gia. She was a friend of mine. Firsthand. The whole thing is kinda like a dream sequence really when you start seeing the stuff on TV and the big screen. Films about people that you know.

One of my favorite uses of our music was in the film *Muriel's Wedding*. A soundtrack that is exclusively ABBA songs and two Blondie songs. ABBA is one of my all-time favorite groups, and hearing our music with theirs was fabulous. As I was saying before, the whole Andy Warhol philosophy within the band, obviously he was not adverse to commercial use of his art. Turning the commonplace into iconic significance is a really brilliant thing, and I think maybe there's a bit of that in Blondie as far as his influence goes.

Q: "Call Me" was the opening title track for the movie *American Gigolo*.

A: That was the only song that was actually written for a film. [Producer] Giorgio Moroder originally approached us to do one of his songs that he'd completely written, called "Man Machine." It was a basic boogie, a more stripped-down song, and then Debbie wrote the lyrics to "Call Me," which was more from a woman's perspective. The recording process with Giorgio Moroder was a little different, and he was a bit more particular how the track would go down and how it was recorded. And so in that respect I played a little differently because I was working with a different producer, and I try and work with the producer, not against the producer. So I did probably play a little differently on that. The weird thing about "Call Me" was that, after we did it, I forgot about it and went on tour for six months and came back. I remember getting picked up at the airport, and the radio got turned on and there was this song that came on and sounded kind of familiar, and I wasn't really sure, and it was "Call Me." That was like a real one-off experience. In the studio for one day recording that track. Richard Gere came down to the studio when we were recording it and that was cool. He's a good guy. He was doing the play *Bent* onstage at the time. It's amazing how many actors are musicians, and he's one of them.

Q: What are your feelings about music videos in general?

A: It took me a long time to latch on to conceptual music videos. I like lip-synching. I like the Monkees. I like all that kind of stuff. Many bands lip-synched on *Ed Sullivan*.

Performing in front of the camera as a pop musician I thought was cool. It stands to reason that a lot of the aesthetics involved in the whole Blondie setup are somewhat "out-of-the-box" compared to the norm of what punk rock was supposed to be. It had a lot to do with our commercial success. Because we never really shunned commercial success, we kind of embraced it, as well as the whole Warholian aesthetic of art as commerce. And especially in England and Europe we were more active in music videos and TV music shows where our music was on the screen.

We were sort of bailing out when MTV first hit. If anything, it was probably one of the worst business moves we ever made, as the band was fragmenting right with the advent of MTV. Had we been there, who knows? MTV came to us early on. The band's in their ads. "I want my MTV" and all that. I thought live performance where you weren't lip-synching would be the best medium for video, capturing a specific live performance, like *The Last Waltz*, or *Don't Look Back*. Something that preserved an honest performance, as opposed to a storyboarded thing.

Our first couple of videos were directed by rock photographer Bob

Gruen, who took John Lennon's passport visa shot. We were also on the British chart show *Top of the Pops* quite a bit. At that particular time they refused to use video. It shows you how much times have changed. They wanted you in the studio, and you were actually supposed to rerecord your track in a studio in Great Britain. We had several "pretend" recording sessions for *Top of the Pops*, where an actual member of the British Musicians Union would be sitting there in the control room, and we'd be in the studio pretending to record the song, when in fact we were using the multitrack of the actual song. One of the most embarrassing things was a song called "Denis," a number one song from our second album. It's all out of time, and when you isolate the tracks it's very obviously out of time, for instance, the handclaps and the foot stomps that were on it. So we were out in the studio going, "We gotta get that right." But in fact it was the hit record we were pretending to be rerecording, and everything was out of time on the hit. So that was an embarrassing situation.

Q: What about songs in television commercials? You and the band don't seem to be so righteous and afraid of the corporate tie-in when lending your music to overt commercials for products.

A: We've licensed "Atomic" to Pepsi, "One Way or Another" for Mazda, and—irony of all ironies—the I.R.S. Various members of the band have had serious tax problems over the years. The I.R.S. licensed "One Way or Another," which has the line, "We're gonna get you." (*laughs*)

From our point of view, we've never had the big meeting about songs for commercials. It's kinda like pop art. I think that having the Ramones song, "Blitzkrieg Bop," in the Mobil commercial is tremendous. They come to us. There is a "pitching geek" within the whole approach to the band to consider songs for placement. We're not Bruce Springsteen. I respect that. We don't have the kind of money he has. Our management did demographic research about all of that stuff to pitch everything. It's amazing how much of our stuff has been utilized in films.

Q: And Blondie has appeared in movies. Like *Roadie*, where you perform a version of Johnny Cash's "Ring of Fire" that June Carter Cash co-wrote with Merle Kilgore.

A: That was definitely, in my opinion, way ahead of its time, doing "Ring of Fire." The tune wasn't in the script—it came from the band. Debbie has always come up with some interesting ideas for covers: "Denis," "The Tide Is High."

Q: Blondie has been widely documented and filmed over the decades, and was a recent subject of the infamous VH1 *Behind the Music* series. I have some real issues with that program. I watched it back-to-back with the BBC documentary on your band, and it seemed like two different sets of people were being chronicled. Too many bummers and sad moments in *Behind the Music*. The romantic breakups, the drug problems, money trips, the pending terminal illness, legal and management problems. You know, "Don't do blow, monitor your dough" lessons. Predictable story lines. What about the music?

I did an interview with Patti Smith last year, and we talked a bit about *Behind the Music*, 'cause I get calls from them for archival research. Patti has always balked at participating in the series and told me, "I don't have any sob stories for those guys." I want to see music shows about music, not heroin or rehab, the deconstruction of rock 'n' roll bands in tales veering away from the actual music and songs. But I also know it's a tremendous promotional vehicle, and I've heard the bands are really involved in producing the show, hence some cool early home movie footage and childhood photos. And naturally some involvement in editorial control. But reality TV and tabloid mentality has filtered through VH1 and some MTV programming that has very little to do with the music. Look, I also know the viewers don't want on their TV screen an examination of the chord structure of your composition, "Rip Her to Shreds"!

A: Well, the *Behind the Music* was a double-edged sword for us, but it was very much needed as a promotional tool to highlight the resurgence of the band. We had the *Behind the Music* thing in the pipeline, as far as knowing we'd be able to use it to promote the *No Exit* record.

Q: Is it true that the bands have creative control and are very active in materials included in the show?

A: You get to see it and make suggestions and edit, and if there is something you don't like you work with them. Chris [Stein] is usually at odds with most people he needs to work with to begin with. (*laughs*) Yeah, there was definite control by the band, and an obvious "sob story" involved Chris's illness. But there's a certain misnomer—that we've been completely ripped off—which is not true to the extent that gets portrayed by some people. It has more to do with people not really being particularly responsible with their money. With the *Behind the Music*, there was some reticence by some people in the band to expose things, but at the same time we knew we needed *Behind the Music* to promote the new album and the resurgence of the band. But the contrast between that and the BBC *Omnibus* TV program came much more from a place of respect for the band, and not from the angle that is involved with the heart-wrenching sob story. I don't think the BBC were really out for that. I mean the BBC show begins with images of Albert Einstein, John Lennon, Khruschev. *Omnibus* is their version of our A&E *Biography*. They are not looking for scandal but human history.

To really answer your question, about scandals in music documentaries and portions of *Behind the Music*, I know both of us would like more archive film footage and rare photos in the program, and no, I don't want to know more about the scandals behind the music, which is why it's called that. I think it kinda dilutes the persona of the band and feeds the cliché of "do you really want to meet your heroes and be disappointed." But I think you are exposed to that, and Blondie was as guilty as anyone who was seeking publicity at that point.

Q: Why does Blondie work well in the visual medium?

A: There's a younger fan base discovering us, and one of the main attributes is that Debbie has a really huge head. That's almost rule number one for being a TV or movie star, y'know. There's that whole thing of "I thought they'd be much taller than that." It's not the height, but the dimensions of the head, Debbie has probably one of the biggest heads in the business and I don't mean that facetiously. She does. The band just has a charisma in general and a lot of that is attributed to Debbie as well.

Q: What are the music documentaries and rock movies that delivered and really impressed you?

A: I like the ABBA documentary. Bob Dylan's *Don't Look Back*, with Dylan being himself. The whole cinema verité concept. You kind of got the feeling you were a fly on the wall and Pennebaker had access. I really liked Madonna's *Truth or Dare*. She went for it, and it's very parallel to *Don't Look Back*. And there was a lot of black-and-white and only the music concert scenes were in color. It was very much a road picture. Madonna let us into her world as much as she wanted to, but she was very aware of the camera. The things with her dad. I remember enjoying it at the time, but it's not something I could quote verbatim.

The Last Waltz was great. I went to see a screening of it at The New School when it first came out, and Martin Scorsese and Robbie

Robertson spoke at it. That is getting back to what I thought music videos should be. There you have great performances captured for posterity. You have a moment in time that should have been captured. All those artists together in one place. Levon Helm blew my mind. I liked *Bangladesh* but no behind-the-scenes stuff at all—just about performance.

There's a lot of movies that capture the mood of what it is like to be in a rock band or what it's like to be on the road. *Still Crazy*. You know what movie really captured it, and I hate to say it?—*Rock Star*. I think it was very out of vogue when it was made, and I think the music was the least enjoyable aspect in it. Also the film was released right next to 9/11. *Boogie Nights*? Come on! The guy who directed it, Paul Thomas Anderson, then did *Magnolia*, one of the greatest films last decade. Fabulous soundtrack. The music was integral, and the use of Supertramp in that movie made me rethink that band. I mean, I like those Supertramp songs now. Profound philosophical songs that carried the movie, with the original Aimee Mann songs in the soundtrack. And I really like Jon Brion's scores. I dig Anderson's *Hard Eight*, and the opening is sorta like an homage to *Goodfellas*.

Scorsese is the original music-in-film guy as far as putting songs in movies. "Be My Baby" opening *Mean Streets*. See, that's the thing. He took music almost out of context to what's going on. Here's a movie about the mob and "Be My Baby" is playing. I like when Scorsese does a wall-to-wall thing with music packed in his films. I like the juxtaposition when a song in the film has nothing to do with what is happening on the screen in my opinion. I kind of enjoy that. I guess what he's doing is trying to capture an era, but lyrically. You see somebody getting their head bashed in and hearing Cream's "Tales of Brave Ulysses," and it's kinda wild.

Q: What are some of the soundtracks that you own?
A: *Superfly* by Curtis Mayfield. Amazing soundtrack and amazing record.

Privilege is a great movie and a great soundtrack. Paul Jones in the movie, and the songs Mike Leander arranged for it. "Free Me" and "I've Been a Bad, Bad Boy." It was probably viewed as controversial because it mixed religion and music. Sort of like Bono now. *High Fidelity* was an entertaining movie. We understood that.

Hands down, my favorite soundtrack of all time would be *Blow-Up*. Herbie Hancock. *Blow-Up* is an endless source of inspiration. The

Yardbirds doing "Stroll On." Then in *Performance*, there's "Memo from Turner"—what about the first time you heard something like that? Really great. Jack Nitzsche was making great music for films.

West Side Story is one of my favorite movies and soundtrack albums. The songs—what a glimpse into New York City street life. The Nice did "America," and P. J. Proby covered "Somewhere" from it.

That Thing You Do is really a great movie that captures what it's like being in a band. The cast. *Backbeat* was great. I cried at the end.

The Beatles' *A Hard Day's Night* blew my mind. The most enduring thing about that movie was seeing the Beatles as human beings. Walking, talking, and eating. Funny human beings. I loved the way the Marx Brothers incorporated music into their films way before rock 'n' roll. I liked *Help!* a lot, too. For me, I like the songs better than *A Hard Day's Night*. *Let It Be* is essential viewing for anybody in a rock band. I think you have to be in a band or involved in the music business to really get the dynamics of what is going on in that film and all the baggage on display. I saw *Let It Be* before I was ever in Blondie. *Let It Be* is a learning tool. Art is really there to learn from generally, especially if you are in the arts. That movie evolves as you evolve as a human being.

I like *Monterey Pop*, if nothing else for the Who, [Jimi] Hendrix and Otis Redding footage. I liked *Woodstock* at the time, but it's not a film that I go back over and over to watch, like *Performance*, *Privilege*, *Don't Look Back*, *Bangladesh*, or *The Last Waltz*. The music of the *Woodstock* era has not endured for me the same way Iggy Pop or David Bowie have. The Monkees' *Head* was hard for me to watch. I loved their TV show. More concise and edited. It was under control. Maybe with *Head* they all were out to destroy the Monkees. *The Harder They Come* is a great movie about the music business. A phenomenal reggae music soundtrack. The Who's *Quadrophenia* was terrific. The soundtrack is just as good as the film.

I really like *The T.A.M.I. Show* and *The Big T.N.T.* The black-and-white concert films. *T.A.M.I.* had James Brown, the Supremes, Chuck Berry, the Rolling Stones. *T.N.T.* had the Byrds, the Lovin' Spoonful, the Ronettes, Ray Charles, Donovan. I really like the Frank Sinatra movie, *The Man with the Golden Arm*, with its Elmer Bernstein score. That's brilliant.

8 Mile is great. Eminem was good onscreen. I'm very familiar with that part of the country. Eminem walked off the street into my friend's studio.

Left to right: Mick Jagger, Bill Wyman, Toni Basil, Jack Nitzsche (foreground), and Steve Binder, rehearsing for *The T.A.M.I. Show*, Santa Monica Civic Auditorium, California, 1964. Photo courtesy of Steve Binder.

Elvis Presley—*Jailhouse Rock, King Creole,* and *Kid Galahad*. The only one that is horrible is *Change of Habit. Viva Las Vegas* was a great movie. Just Elvis' sexuality and all his interaction with all those cool chicks in it. His movies were microcosms of an era too, and although out of synch with the times, in some ways they still kinda reflect the period, at the same time. The songs in those movies. I really liked his concert movies. *The Way It Is*. He didn't seem larger than life, because in some ways he was before my time in a way. I think people that are in one's time seem to become much larger than life, more so than people that are more kind of mythical. Elvis was cool and had one of the best voices. His films were movies inside of movies, in a way. I think the only time Elvis seemed bigger to me was when he died in 1977. The whole punk rock thing was going on, and it added an extra meaning to me. Like all of a sudden there was no Elvis Presley, only Elvis Costello, which was kinda strange.

Q: What has been your best movie and music collaboration?

A: Actually the soundtrack I'm probably the most proud of is *Repo Man*. It's Chequered Past, my old band during a break from Blondie, minus Michael des Barres, with Iggy Pop. On the record we're listed, but not in the film. We did the title song with Iggy, who just blasted out the lyrics. I know I didn't get paid and we got the studio for free. I think, in general, movie soundtracks—for the creators, artists, and composers—are more of an outlet, more of a free rein to be more creative, especially if you get to see the film and let your imagination run wild and create music for a particular scene. There's also some background music that you can expand.

I'm like Phil Spector: I like to hear things coming out of a little five inch mono speaker—coming out of the radio, anyway.

Q: Is looking at music films a different experience now, since you've been a professional musician and involved in an influential global music band for decades?

A: With any film that is about the entertainment business, you're able to say, "This is genuine," or "This is not a real experience—this is too corny."

Q: It must bum you out to hear wrong song placements in movies. When the songs are not time-specific for scenes.

A: That's really bad. It's weird enough when you see a 1985 Fender head stack in a scene about a blues musician in 1964. Or when you see drums that obviously weren't around in the '60s. I think our generation has come of age, and we are in control, for better or worse. I think you see less of that.

The archival stuff—it's gonna be a while before the next generation picks up on it. Like compact discs, there's gonna be less interest in it. Less interest in catalogue. Less interest in Blondie. Maybe not the Beatles. It might skip a generation until after our generation has bought the CDs and seen all the DVDs.

The evolution of pop music needs to be explained as time goes on, and how it's all connected.

Between working with Blondie, I'm doing some live shows with Nancy Sinatra, which is a lot of fun. [Keyboardist] Don Randi is in the band. She sings her theme song to the James Bond movie *You Only Live Twice*. So I'm around and involved with movie and music tunes.

Clem Burke has drummed on the entire recorded catalogue of his band, Blondie, in nearly thirty years, including the albums *Blondie*, *Plastic Letters*, *Parallel Lines*, *Eat to the Beat*, *Auto American*, *The Hunter*, and *Curse of Blondie*. Burke plays the drums on "Call Me," the theme from *American Gigolo*, and is also heard on three Eurythmics albums, *In the Garden*, *Revenge* and *Eurythmics Live*, as well as Chequered Past's self-titled debut LP, Iggy Pop's *Zombie Bird House*, Dramarama's *Hi-Fi Sci-Fi*, Pete Townshend's *White City*, Bob Dylan's *Knocked Out Loaded*, *Kool Trash* by the Plimsouls, the Romantics' *61/49*, *Green Man* from Mark Owen, and recent sessions with guitarist Denny Freeman.

Between recording and tour stints with Blondie, Burke also performs with Nancy Sinatra, and in spring of 2005 was behind the skins on her month-long European engagement.

In 2006 Clem's band, Blondie, was inducted into the Rock and Roll Hall of Fame.

MARK MOTHERSBAUGH

MARK MOTHERSBAUGH IS A songwriter-composer and founding member of Devo.

In the last twenty-five years he has been an award-winning film and TV composer. He's scored *Thirteen*, *200 Cigarettes*, *Envy*, *Rushmore*, *The Royal Tenenbaums*, *Pee-wee's Playhouse*, and *Rugrats*.

In May 2004 he was the top honoree at BMI's Film and Television Awards, held in Beverly Hills, where he received the Richard Kirk Award for career achievement for his compositions in film, TV, interactive media, and commercials.

Wes Anderson's liner notes for *The Royal Tenenbaums* reflect the role of composer Mothersbaugh's score in a film soundtrack stocked with pop song gems. Of Mothersbaugh's participation, Anderson wrote, "I felt we needed the music to feel magical in order to support the characters. But as we started working on it, the goal changed. Mark can quickly bring a magical feeling to a score, but his desire, and mine, became more and more about deepening the movie. His music was more ambitious for this film than the two previous."

I caught up with Mark one afternoon by telephone at his Mutato Muzika office, a composing and editing company he co-owns on Sunset Strip in West Hollywood.

Q: How did you begin working with Wes Anderson?

A: I was asked by someone at Sony to look at a film that Owen [Wilson] and Wes wrote together, *Bottle Rocket*. I saw a screening and thought it was much more interesting than other movies made about this generation.

I said I'd like to do music for this that had nothing to do with rock 'n' roll or current trends or MTV. I was offered the score. I met with Wes and we talked, which later led to *Rushmore* and *Tenenbaums*. Now we have a vocabulary when we work. Since we had done two films, he was calling me when he was writing the script for *The Tenenbaums*, so we were talking back then, trading music over a year before the movie came out.

Q: What about the process of the composer working with the record label for soundtracks?

A: Labels don't really care about composers. That's the truth. Generally speaking, a label is simply looking for a way to sell. They look at the movie as a poster, a commercial for their talent that they've signed and don't know what do with, and they try and pick up movies that they think they can stick their songs into, and don't care where or how, usually.

Most movies do not care about the underscore when it comes to a soundtrack album because, from a numbers point of view, it's a rare soundtrack that sells numbers that are exciting to a record company.

With my pieces on *Tenenbaums*, it's Wes's call. He was very adamant about the score being on the soundtrack. That's the only reason it's there. The movie is Wes's vision. He's an artist.

Now movies are made with a lot of lawyers in the middle, and there's a lot of focus, depending on your focus group, either sixteen-year-old boys in Encino or twelve-year-old kids in Pasadena.

Typically they tell you how much money they have for a music budget and from the get-go Wes knew he wanted some of these songs.

Q: You've been the artist with Devo—what's the best way for the composer to work with a director and music supervisor?

A: It took me a while to get there. I always looked at music supervisors as being unnecessary and meddlesome and over-credited. I think you have to try and understand everybody's motivations and why they are there in the first place.

The most important thing for me is helping a director achieve his vision. You're given the limitations of what the film company thinks you're worth, you have that many dollars to use toward that goal, and a lot of the time directors don't have a clue about a soundtrack album.

In the case of Wes, it was quite different. Every single piece of this movie is important to him. He sat with me while I was writing music for the film and scoring, and we talked constantly during the process. Most times directors get nervous, or are too busy to do that, or they're already on to the next project. He sat in the back room. He's probably the most hands-on director I've ever worked with.

In this case, I wrote cues while temp music was already in place. It's very common that the songs are in place before the film gets to a composer. But unlike our previous collaborations, this is the first time he called me to discuss music as he was putting the script together. So I was writing sketches based on early drafts of the script and then sending them to him. That allowed him to listen to the music as he was filming. Actually I was writing music when he gave me the first draft of his script back in November of last year.

Q: What drew you to Wes?

A: His temp music was one of the reasons I wanted to work with him from the very beginning. Even in *Bottle Rocket*. In that one, he used the Rolling Stones' "2000 Man," which I really like. I thought, "What an odd choice, but it was a perfect choice." How interesting that he would go there instead of doing something from MTV. That's what made me want to meet him in the first place. This is somebody who needs somebody to protect him and to help him create his vision. He has interesting tastes and makes a lot of his choices intellectually, but they always resonate with what he's doing. He picks things that complement his picture. I've worked on movies where the producers made a deal with a company or label before they finished filming, and it didn't matter to the label who they were, and at a certain point it didn't matter to the filmmakers either, they just wanted an album and they were all hoping and fishing for a hit song. And if it related to the movie, all the better, but if it didn't they quite honestly couldn't care less.

By the time we mixed the movie, we backed off from some of the score simply because there were so many songs in the audio, you didn't want to distract anybody. But that's a balance you find as you are going along and it becomes determined what songs are going or staying.

Q: What about scoring for movies and directors who might like your band. Does it help?

A: You know what, maybe a little bit, but I wouldn't overrate that. I don't think it's necessarily a plus to come from a band. The reality is that there's a lot of people who were in bands that tried to get into composing and it didn't work. It's a totally different monster. I think the writers that have the most success are the ones that are empathetic. First of all, you have to understand what your job is, and it's to help the director's vision come to fruition. When you're in a band, that's not really what your job is at all. You have your own vision and your own story to tell, and pity the person who tries to fuck with that.

Q: What about Devo and the songs in films and soundtracks?

A: Jerry [Casale] and I are both kind of active in that, and the other Devo members all work with me at Mutato, so sometimes they'll be working on a project, like Bob has done a couple of movies for MTV where he's been able to suggest things. There's some involvement.

Regarding music videos, we thought we were doing something different and bigger when we were making our films. We thought we were creating a new art form that was going to eclipse rock 'n' roll, believe it or not. That's what our intentions were.

Unfortunately, MTV came along. We had ideas earlier about music television and sound and vision eclipsing rock 'n' roll to where visual audio artists—people who were multimedia artists—would become more prominent in pop culture. But I think, because it didn't happen early enough, the lawyers had already started to figure out a way to turn it into Home Shopping Network. What we were doing was sort of reduced to baby pictures for record companies. Just a three-and-a-half minute commercial.

Q: What does music add to movies?

A: I think composers know better than anybody what their music brings to a movie, because when you are in the process of writing things, you don't always write what finally goes on the screen. It's probably not always the first thing that you write. In my case, sometimes it's the third, fourth, or fifth thing I've written for a scene, instead of the first.

Q: There seems to be a trend where directors are really involved in the music in their films and hands-on in music and songs on soundtracks, and maybe music informs the script. How do you see the role or roles of the soundtracks as far as the composers in the future, and music on the screen, are concerned?

A: I think scores showing up on CDs only relate to the economic viability of it, if they can figure out a way to do it and just hit the niche market that wants it. I don't think you're ever going to talk the general public into thinking that underscores should be listened to without the movie. There'll be moments when the underscore catches someone's fancy, like a Henry Mancini theme that actually becomes a song that's part of the movie. Stuff like that does happen. Rock music has been around so long now, it's like the classical music of our time in a way.

※

Songwriter-composer-producer Mark Mothersbaugh is a founding member of Devo. In the last twenty-five years he has been an award-winning film and TV composer. He's scored *Herbie: Fully Loaded*, *Lords of Dogtown*, *The Big White*, *The Life Aquatic with Steve Zissou*, *Confessions of a Teenage Drama Queen*, *Thirteen*, *200 Cigarettes*, *Power Puff Girls*, *Envy*, *Rushmore*, *The Royal Tenenbaums*, *Pee Wee's Playhouse*, *Rugrats*, and countless others.

In May 2004, Mark was honored at BMI's Film and Television Awards, held in Beverly Hills, where he was given the Richard Kirk Award for career achievement for his compositions in film, TV, interactive media, and commercials. Mothersbaugh operates Mutato Muzika, a composing and editing company he co-owns on Sunset Boulevard in West Hollywood.

PART FOUR
SIGHT AND SOUND NEW MASTERS

Mansion party behind the Beverly Hills Hotel, 1977, a real-life precursor of *Boogie Nights.* Photo by Brad Elterman.

PAUL THOMAS ANDERSON

PAUL THOMAS ANDERSON'S NEW Line Cinema production of *Boogie Nights*, which garnered three Academy Award nominations including Best Supporting Actress (Julianne Moore), Best Supporting Actor (Burt Reynolds), and Best Original Screenplay (Anderson), demonstrated the arrival of a talented and music-driven director.

Boogie Nights was the twenty-seven-year-old writer-director-producer's study of the adult movie business in the 1977 to 1984 era, starring Mark Wahlberg, Moore, Don Cheadle, William H. Macy, John C. Reilly, and Reynolds. In April 1998, New Line Home Video marketed a special Platinum Edition DVD version of the movie.

Capitol Records released *Boogie Nights: Music from the Original Motion Picture*, the initial soundtrack, featuring the dance floor pump of McFadden and Whitehead's hit, "Ain't No Stopping Us Now," and "Best of My Love," the pop-soul smash from the Emotions, coupled with the dreamy psychedelic whimsy of Eric Burdon & War's "Spill the Wine," as well as Marvin Gaye's "Got to Give It Up." The disc really put the audio to the visual focus on the porn world, as the soundtrack captured the decadence and innocence of that era.

Capitol Records later shipped *Boogie Nights #2: Music from the Original Motion Picture*, which continued its examination of pop music evolution from the '70s into the '80s. Take a listen and digest the tribal, pre-disco R&B of the 1969 soul-funk chart topper, "Do Your Thing," by local Los Angeles artists Charles Wright & the Watts 103rd Street Rhythm Band. Along the way, Anderson really did his homework and unearthed some goodies like "Boogie Shoes" by KC and the Sunshine Band (the original B-side of "Shake Your Booty"), and Three Dog Night's 1970 #1 cover of Randy Newman's "Mama Told Me Not to Come." Anderson's selections for the movie and subsequent soundtracks, stuffed with disco-era jams, are not only integral to the fabric of the movie, but also serve as commentary.

Paul Thomas Anderson was born and raised in Studio City, California. At seventeen, still a high schooler in Van Nuys, he made a half hour movie, *The Dirk Diggler Story*, that laid the blueprint for the expanded *Boogie Nights* he would write and direct nearly a decade later. He did two semesters as an English major at Emerson College, and split after two days at NYU Film School. At age twenty-two he shot his debut film in color, a twenty-four-minute short called *Cigarettes and Coffee*, which was accepted at the 1993 Sundance Film Festival. His first feature film was *Hard Eight*, with Gwyneth Paltrow and Samuel L. Jackson, which screened in competition at both the 1996 Sundance and Cannes Film Festivals.

How could you not want to root for a newcomer who worshipped *Putney Swope*, hired its director, Robert Downey, Sr., as a record executive in *Boogie Nights*, could probably talk for hours about John Cassavetes and recite dialogue from *Bad Day at Black Rock*?

I looked forward to talking to Anderson. I attended the recording session when the Commodores tracked "Brick House" at the Motown studio in Hollywood. I never proclaimed "Death to Disco" either, when the phrase and declaration was fashionable. The San Fernando Valley has always been my own back lot as well. Anderson even filmed the donut shop on Sherman Way in Reseda for *Boogie Nights*.

Over the phone from New York, during a promotional tour for *Boogie Nights*, PTA seemed delighted just to talk about the music and songs that he picked for both volumes of *Boogie Nights* soundtracks, and the relationship of that music to his big-budget flick.

Q: When you were writing the screenplay to *Boogie Nights*, did you already have certain songs and tunes picked out for scenes and the soundtracks?

A: Totally. One hundred percent, and like to a freakish extent. For a bunch of different reasons, obviously, I mean I'm a fan of all the music that's in the movie. That's stuff in my record collection, you know what I mean? It's built in because of the story that's gonna take place 1977 to '84. So OK, great. I get to put all this music I love in the movie. And I would write (the screenplay) to music. I write generally with music playing. CDs, LPs, and the radio. For the longest time I only had *Boogie Nights* #2's "Feel Too Good" on LP, so I would have to listen to it on vinyl. But I finally found it on CD, so I was OK there. And so I was planning sequences out to music as I was writing. But, on top of that, I was also doing it because I kind of freakishly prepare the movie beforehand. Really where the music is going to be.

Q: Did you know, even during preproduction and before, in the initial writing stage, that there was going to be a whole lot of music and songs in *Boogie Nights*?

A: Yes. There were going to be about fifty or sixty music tunes in this movie. I knew it was a good idea to let [music supervisor] Karyn Rachtman know pretty early, so she could then help with knowing how much money to set aside, so I wouldn't plan a sequence out to music, get to the editing room and find out, "You don't have enough money to get this song" or that song.

It wasn't like I was going to her for advice on what music to put in my movie, 'cause I already knew. Some directors need her to tell them what songs should be in a movie. I was going to her with the music already there and needing her expertise in clearing and getting songs that were hard to find.

Q: Were there any situations where songs you loved weren't available because the licensing or leasing of the tracks was too costly?

A: I'm sure, but the thing was I avoided that situation on this movie by preparing so far ahead of time. I didn't want to get my heart broken by planning a sequence out and then not having that song available.

There's so much music that I thought in terms of commercial appeal for the first one. But the second one, I got to really think in terms of, "Wow! I get to make a soundtrack where I can put the full version of the Move's 'Feel Too Good' on there. I get to put Charles Wright & the Watts 103rd Street Rhythm Band's 'Do Your Thing' on, and it's stuff you normally wouldn't get on a soundtrack." That's hard-to-find stuff.

Q: But I also know disco people and the majority of the dancers in the '77 to '84 era just wanted to dance and groove. No real hard rock and social messages and heavy lyrics. Right?

A: Pretty true. You've got disco scenes. And believe me, some of my taste does tend more toward the rock stuff. But I had to service the movie and a couple of times put my personal taste on the side. Not that I don't love every song that is in the movie. But I gotta tell you, usually it's great when a song kind of lyrically works thematically with the movie, but I threw that out the window on this. I was like, OK, I want to shamelessly go for vibe. Just vibe and vibe alone. That's my criteria for picking songs. Does it feel right? Just do it. Sometimes it's cool when a song does work lyrically and links with the movie, like "Mama Told Me Not to Come."

Q: So now, what do Volume 1 and Volume 2 of *Boogie Nights* feel like to you when you hear the soundtracks and remove yourself as the writer-director and co-executive producer of the music selected?

A: Volume 1 actually feels like a souvenir of the movie to me. If you're a fan of the movie, and you want to have something to take home and put on to remind you of the overall experience of watching the movie, you get that from Volume 1. You get it too because it's book-ended with a little dialogue from the movie, and you get an overall sense of the motion picture. Volume 2 is like a cool record. It's like a cool compilation record. And it may not necessarily spark a lot of memories of the movie, because a lot of those cues are more hidden in the movie. A lot of the cues from Volume 1 are really prominent songs in the movie. Volume 2 is stuff that was hidden by dialogue or sound effects, or something like that. But to me, great, great songs.

Q: The use of "Spill the Wine," which chronologically preceded the era, since it originally came out around 1970, and is now integrated years later in the film, really further illustrates how a tune can even expand a scene.

A: Exactly. That song *had* to be in the movie. I love the rambling narrative.

Getting back to your earlier question, like with "Jessie's Girl" [on Volume 2], that really meant something to me. I was thirteen and had a crush on a girl. I like that I can look at Mark [Wahlberg] in that scene and hear "Jessie's Girl" and be selfish and personal about my attachment to it. It's one of those personal attraction songs, I hate to admit that. (*laughs*)

Q: I was aware that some regional artists, like Charles Wright, are also heard in the soundtrack, and naturally the Beach Boys. I think the regional things added to the film. Although I know most consumers and fans aren't aware of the almost geo-piety aspects of the song-and-film collaboration.

A: You're absolutely right, and I actually wish that could have been more of a theme, and I could have worked that in more, but the truth is, a lot of the sort of California singer-songwriter vibe at that time wasn't actually fitting with the movie in a lot of places. I wish some Jackson Browne stuff was in there, but I couldn't get it in.

Q: Did you add songs to the film, once you were shooting the movie? I know you got a lot of things taken care of thirty, sixty, ninety days before lensing.

A: No, not while we were shooting. After the fact in editing, I'd say four or five cues, a lot of the smaller, more background, source cues, coming-from-the-radio type of thing, changed in my mind. Like "Afternoon Delight" was played very low on the radio in the background; it was an afterthought. The Juice Newton cue was also an afterthought. A couple of cues that I thought would work didn't work. So I changed those around. The one thing that I do miss is that the movie focuses itself on this transition of porno from film to video. When I'd written the script—and it was actually longer at one time—I felt I wanted to take advantage of that in music as well. So all this great R&B and funk stuff was played by wonderful musicians on real instruments. And then also get into the more synthesizer-dominated bad '80s stuff. That's there in a small way. I wish I had been able to do that in a bigger way. But it didn't lend itself to that and I could only tack on what two-and-a-half hours would let me, in the movie, you know.

Q: With *Boogie Nights*, all sorts of people and industry types are really leaning on you to incorporate songs in the film and soundtracks. That's part of their job. But how do you deal with all the vested interests? I honestly feel every track on these discs is something you wanted heard. And people have legitimate reasons for material.

A: It's a good question, but a real simple answer: I'm aware that that stuff is there, OK, 'cause of stories I've heard. And that's half the reason why I planned this stuff out so far in advance. So I don't enter into any situation that is ever like that. I don't give anybody the opportunity to be able to make suggestions, fortunately or unfortunately, that are gonna be coming from a business perspective. It's like, these are the songs in the movie. These are the ones that I want. If you are very specific and everybody knows that and sees that, then there's no way to crowbar in on suggestions. Like, "Why don't we have Pearl Jam do a cover of 'Spill the Wine' and then we'll sell more records?" That kind of thing doesn't happen if you can be real specific. That situation is gonna crop up for a director who isn't really specific. In this business, if people see a moment of weakness in a filmmaker, they are gonna jump on it and attack, and that filmmaker is gonna be like a ladybug on its back.

Q: Am I correct to assume the sound editor on *Boogie Nights* might really be even more important to this film than most films where music plays such a vital part, because the editing and cuts often are done around dance and beat-driven music?

A: That's a good question. The picture editor, Dylan Tichenor, is also the music editor because we cut the whole movie to music. It had been planned out beforehand and all the music edits that do happen are Dylan. It's like one and the same. The picture cuts are the same as the music cuts.

Q: You mean, on some Alfred Hitchcock level, it's storyboarded?

A: Exactly. It saves time. Especially in four or five scenes, there is no other choice. Like, if you have a drug deal scene where Alfred Molina is singing along to a song, you can't just wing that, or improvise, you gotta know.

Q: So editing the film and having the music in place must be easier.

A: Totally. Because you know where it becomes easier—not just in editing, but easy the whole way through. Because I can play a song—like when the actors are in a nightclub, I can play that song for the actors and the extras on the set and go, "This is the vibe." It's not going to be an after-thought. They can hear what the groove is and where the beats are and kind of tailor their performances and all the movements to that song. Which is great. It's great for Heather Graham to know that her theme song is basically "Brand New Key" by Melanie.

Q: Did you match music or songs to certain actors, even in preproduction?

A: Yeah. Definitely. It's not that each character has that, but Roller Girl sort of lends herself to that quality of needing her theme music. Much of the celebratory '70s music and anthems are Dirk music. It's all Dirk music. So everyone kind of gets their little song. Again, whether or not it's in the music, I could give songs to actors and say, "This song reminds me of your character." There are songs I gave to John Reilly that reminded me of him and his weirdness and magic show stuff that we didn't use in the movie, but were cool to give him as an actor.

Q: Does it help that some of the principals in the movie, like Mark

Wahlberg and, to a lesser extent, John Reilly, are really into music? Wahlberg was a music personality and performer first, and then the acting emerged. Is it an asset for a movie with a strong music content that some of your actors have a music jones?

A: It isn't mandatory, but it certainly helps, you know what I mean? That has to do more with sort of an acting style, too. Look, when you're shooting a disco scene in a nightclub, you can have playback on the set, but you can't have that playback while the actors are doing their dialogue. But what you can do is play the song, right, and keep the beat in your head, or your performance and your body movements register along with the beat. Great actors who have a musical sense can kind of tailor their performance to that beat, so you're playing "Boogie Shoes" by KC and the Sunshine Band, and then you stop the playback and you go, "Action," but keep that same kind of beat in your head. And they can do that. And when you match that up with the film in the editing process, their movements all sort of reference what happens in the song, because they keep the song in their head and throw their performance through the music.

Q: In constructing the film and the eventual soundtracks, were you at all concerned about blending disco tunes with singer-songwriter verse and chorus songs? You don't often get "God Only Knows" by the Beach Boys matched with "Machine Gun" from the Commodores. Except maybe in my world.

A: The bigger concern was smashing together Michael Penn's score with the kind of feel-good disco stuff. That was trying to go with the bigger clash of style.

Like with *Hard Eight*, I had already shot the movie and cut it and he had to make the score to fit the movie. The situation with *Boogie Nights* was different, in that we could talk about it at the script stage, during the shooting, talk about it through the first cut, and I could tailor cuts to kind of accommodate his score. I could get his score early in the editing process, so I could trim around his score if I needed to. It was much more of a collaboration. On *Hard Eight* he had to try and fit a circle into a square sometimes, and he did it beautifully. The truth is, now I'm in the middle of writing my next movie and we're already talking about the music. I can think the same way I wrote down all the cues for *Boogie Nights*, in the writing process. So the writing process and the scoring process are coming together already for us, and it's a beautiful thing.

Q: Is there a deeper effort made when you look for ballads to place in your film and soundtrack in relationship to the dance and more often heard disco oldies songs?

A: Not really. "Magnet and Steel" on Volume 1 is such a gem. It hasn't been on a lot of other soundtracks, I'm sure, so that is certainly helpful, and that's a tricky thing when you're setting up a movie that takes place from '77 to '84. There's been a lot of this music that's been used. The thing is, at the end of the day, I wanted the right song. I certainly did have this surface level thing where I didn't want songs that were used in other movies. But I felt like, if this song crops up in another movie while I'm in the middle of the editing process, and I hear about it, I'm not going to change my ways. I don't mind that "You Sexy Thing" by Hot Chocolate is also in *The Full Monty*. I'd heard that it was gonna be, but fuck it. I didn't want to change what worked, just because I had heard it was going to be in another movie.

Q: I liked the fact that on Volume 1 you utilized an ELO track, "Livin' Thing," and now on the new Volume 2 you integrated the Move's "Feel Too Good." And Jeff Lynne and Roy Wood of the Move helped form ELO.

A: Jeff Lynne of ELO allowed me to use "Livin' Thing" only after seeing the film and calling it "Brilliant." The Move song—I had been a Move fan, you know, "Message from the Country," "Brontosaurus," and just a Roy Wood fan, and a Jeff Lynne fan.

I always liked the Elvin Bishop song, "Fooled Around and Fell in Love," that's on Volume 2, the vibe and the way it works. The comedic way it sets in the scene. In *Boogie Nights*, the story dictated the time, and it just happened to set itself in a wonderful period of music and fashion.

With some songs, they become stronger when linked to a visual. Like with "Mama Told Me Not to Come," it's done by Three Dog Night. I think there's layer upon layer for why that song works. I think there's the double entendre about "Mama Told Me Not to Come" as some sort of sexual note within the movie. Also the way the movie is cut to that song is a very dramatic, stylish kind of cut. Very cinematic and it fits perfectly there. However, the song continues to play in not the greatest, most obvious way. It plays under a four- or five-page dialogue scene between John Reilly and Mark Wahlberg. It's not "cut, cut, cut," kind of music video style. The song is very groovy and it could have been really massively cinematic, but it almost plays in this kind of anti-groove way that I think just kind of worked wonderfully as an accident.

Q: Does it become even more rewarding when a song ends up on a soundtrack, or even in a movie, that appears because it's a great song, and you don't feel the politics of a label was involved in the selection? To bring it back to Brian Wilson and the Beach Boys, you weren't even born when that song was first recorded and released. And I talk to Brian and even today he is sometimes surprised which of his compositions get requests for movie and TV use.

A: It was a wonderful thing that the Beach Boys were on Capitol, wasn't it? Lucky for me, believe me. Capitol was very happy to hear it 'cause there is no other Capitol master (recording) on the whole soundtrack. I told them, "By the way, the Beach Boys." And they said, "Finally, a Capitol master." (*laughs*)

Q: It underscores the ending in a form of closure.

A: There's certainly that, but I also have to admit that very selfishly I was able to play my favorite song of all time in my movie. To me it's one of the best songs ever written and certainly my favorite.

※

Paul Thomas Anderson's early short, *The Dirk Diggler Story*, evolved nearly ten years later into the theatrical film *Boogie Nights*, which he wrote and directed. His debut short film, *Cigarettes and Coffee*, was accepted at the 1993 Sundance Film Festival. Later, his feature film *Hard Eight* was shown at both the 1996 Sundance and Cannes Film Festivals.

After *Boogie Nights*, Anderson also wrote and directed the movie *Magnolia* and later wrote the screenplay for and directed the Adam Sandler movie, *Punch-Drunk Love*, for which he won the Best Director Award at the Cannes Film Festival in 2002.

ICE CUBE

I TALKED TO ICE CUBE in 1998 in Hollywood, as he was prepping the movie and soundtrack release of his directorial feature film debut, *The Players Club*. We met at the offices of Herb Alpert and Jerry Moss's influential A&M Records, on the company's La Brea Avenue studio lot, originally built as Chaplin Studios in 1917 and used to film all of Charlie Chaplin's classic silent movies through 1939's *The Great Dictator*. Today the location is home to Jim Henson Productions, who brought us Miss Piggy, Kermit the Frog, Big Bird, and the rest of the Muppets.

Ice Cube remains a prolific voice in rap music and one of the most important artists coming out of the West Coast. Behind the board, Ice Cube has produced platinum-selling acts and projects, such as Mack 10 and the groundbreaking Westside Connection, that cross geographic boundaries and offer a universal head-nodding effect.

Ice Cube (O'Shea Jackson) burst on the scene as a hardcore teenager with the seminal rap group NWA in 1986. Some of his solo albums, like *AmeriKKKa's Most Wanted* and *Death Certificate* (reissued with bonus tracks in 2004), are considered classic long-play efforts, having foretold the rage that later erupted in the 1992 L.A. riots uprising.

As an actor, Ice Cube has delivered acclaimed dramatic performances in films such as director John Singleton's *Boyz 'n the Hood*, *Trespass*, *Higher*

Learning, Dangerous Ground, Glass Shield, and *Anaconda.* With the comedy hit, *Friday,* which he cowrote, Ice Cube demonstrated the range of his acting and screenwriting skills.

In *The Players Club,* Ice Cube directed and fashioned a script about an ambitious woman struggling to complete her education while working as a stripper at a popular gentlemen's club. The flick offers an explosive look at the web of crime, money, men, and vulnerability that entangle the lives of those walking in and out of this seedy men's club. The film features Bernie Mac, Jamie Foxx, Alex Thomas, Adele Givens, as well as newcomer Lisa Raye, who told me in a phone call, "I thought the script was sensitive to women, and he was great to work with as a director, because—especially from an actor's point of view—he was a fresh director and really receptive to working with me during the shoot. And he's a regular guy," reflects Raye, who also appeared in the late rapper Tupac Shakur's video, "Toss It Up."

The Players Club is financed by New Line Cinema. "I don't want to be seen simply as a 'rapping director,' or 'the first rapper to direct a major film,'" says Ice Cube, "I just want to be the best."

The soundtrack album that Ice Cube put together includes some of the street's most valuable players, including Master P, Mack 10, Kurupt, Scarface, and Jodeci's Mr. Dalvin. The collection also debuts Ice Cube's much-anticipated protegé, Mr. Short Khop, on a couple of tracks. The street feminism of Mia X's "Shake Whatcha Mama Gave Ya" is also included, along with the five selections that showcase Ice Cube.

Half a decade after I conducted this Ice Cube interview, I talked to music journalist and rap music publicist Phyllis Pollack in May 2004. She heads Def Press. Pollack wrote the liner notes to the reissue of NWA's *Straight Outta Compton,* and Compton's Most Wanted's *When We Wuz Bangin'.* Compton's Most Wanted made a big splash with "Growin' Up in the Hood" from the *Boyz 'n the Hood* soundtrack. Pollack also handled the publicity, in conjunction with Jive Records, for the soundtrack to New Line Cinema's *Menace II Society* feature, directed by Allen and Albert Hughes. "The black movie audience in America is a very important demographic in supporting a film, as well as an essential component in regards to exposure and buying the companion soundtrack album," offers Pollack, who was searched for weapons upon entering the Fairfax Theater in L.A. when she went to a paid showing of *Boyz 'n the Hood* when it was initially released.

Over ten years ago, in an article in *Daily Variety* with reporter Bruce

Haring, Pollack then believed, "It is a misconception that soundtracks that feature a large portion of rap don't have appeal beyond the genre's core audience of fans." At the time she pointed out to Haring that with the Hughes Brothers' *Menace II Society*, their soundtrack album "entered at No. 11 on the pop charts. Now, if there's no white following or white interest, it wouldn't have entered at No. 11. The movie and album transcended race."

"The Hughes Brothers' and Ice Cube's soundtracks have songs that match the screen action," Pollack also told Haring in the same *Daily Variety* article. "With movies like *Wayne's World*, the songs have nothing to do with the plot. With white films, it's more about getting big name recording artists. In some of the [urban] soundtrack albums, the goal is finding songs that illustrate the film, rather than to concentrate on brand-name artists."

Ice Cube has come a long way from graduating Taft High School in Woodland Hills. An enthusiastic fan of director Martin Scorsese, Ice Cube had his head opened up as a teenager after seeing the rapper movie, *Krush Groove*, and viewing *A Clockwork Orange*, one of his all-time favorite films.

Q: You decided to write and direct your own movie and initiate a new record label, Heavyweight Records, distributed through A&M Records. How did the concept for *The Players Club* begin?

A: I decided that if I was going to write this movie, I was going to see it the whole way through, by directing it and putting my whole vision on it. I was talking to [writer-director] John Singleton, and he said, "The only way you will get a movie that you want to do is to write it yourself. But before you write a movie, you want to think of a topic that intrigues people." With me, I'm always thinking of a way to shake things up a little bit.

I wanted to launch my label with a soundtrack album. I wanted to have something that was concrete, a film with a soundtrack that could guarantee some exposure. I wanted to create a soundtrack that is related to the film's plot. It's not just a T&A movie. The club is a backdrop for what's going on. If you really watch the movie, there isn't really that much time spent on the girls' dancing. The message is: Make money, don't let it make you.

Q: Did you write the film and already have specific songs and artists in mind when you were preparing to shoot the movie?

A: I had a mock soundtrack compiled before we ever started filming. I had temp. music. I would call artists up and say, "I have this scene," even in preproduction. Even before I got the artists, what I did with the mock soundtrack was that it was set up for the girls to dance. I had to have the pacing right. Then, as I wrote it, it developed into "Let me see what the movie is turning out to be and I can be more specific with some of these songs." Like the first single, "We Be Clubbin.'" I did it specifically for the movie. I knew it would be the first single. I knew where it was gonna play in the movie, and, in some ways, it made it easier to put things together.

Q: I know you bring in some cinematic influences when you write songs. A lot of your tunes are very graphic and detailed. When you are creating songs for a movie, and not just for an album, do you use additional visual elements in constructing the material?

A: Well, yeah. What I know about writing a song is, you got a topic and I can go all over the place on that topic and by the end of that song I got a hook and a connection and people are happy. See, with a soundtrack you're dealing with A&M's interests. With the movie, you're dealing with New Line's interests and sometimes a song might fit good in a movie but it isn't right when you're playing it as a song. We ran into the problem a couple of times where on the soundtrack we tried to make sure the soundtrack had as much integrity as good soundtracks should have, and that you remember them, like *Saturday Night Fever* and *Car Wash*. Soundtracks that just fit right in with the movie. That's what we tried to do, but we ran into problems where we had to lock the picture before we finished the soundtrack, so we ended up getting some new songs at the finish line and we gotta make it dope, you know what I mean? I'm trying to get better. I'm trying to create.

Q: Let's talk about music. The title track.

A: I knew it was going to be like a club song and would have many levels and layers. A song to fit the movie. I didn't want to do a hardcore song and it didn't fit the movie. That was my inspiration in going to the studio. I knew it had to be a hit. On the music, I wanted an intro and outtro putting it together. I'm working with a new guy, Mr. Short Khop, and he's got two songs in *The Players Club*, "Who Are You Lovin'" and "My Loved One." I also did a remix with DMX on "We Be Clubbin.'" Changing Faces do a slow song that pushes the Blue [Jamie Foxx] and Diamond story along. Kurupt, from the Dogg Pound, had a hot tune, "Under Pressure," that we used. It couldn't make the movie, but it was too good not to make the soundtrack.

Master P and I did a remake of Whodini's "You Know I'm a Ho." Mack 10 and Scarface did a song, "You Delinquent," and that plays around St. Louis and Dollar Bill. Jay-Z featuring Memphis Bleek and Sauce Money gave "From Marcy to Hollywood," 'bout the street and going into a Hollywood-type person. I used Brownstone's "Don't Play Me Wrong" again to drive home the female story. Mia X, a female rapper, is on there with "Shake Whatcha Mama Gave Ya (But Make Sho' Your Niggas Pay Ya)." Public Announcement, who are on the soundtrack, are one of A&M's groups. "Get Mine," by Mr. Dalvin, didn't make the movie, but it's a hot song. Also Emmage, featuring Mr. Short Khop and Li'l Mo, do "Dreamin.'"

In writing a movie like this, a "dramedy,"—a comedy with drama—when you write it, it reads good on paper. The transitions from comedy to dramatic scenes. But when you shoot the film and edit it, sometimes it's hard to be bustin' at the gut at one scene and get real serious. So it felt like a glitch. So what we did was to use the music to help the transitions of the movie, to position the beats and everything to feel right. So some music we hinted to, and some music was used to drive a scene. The story lines and montage. But the music is "acting" in the movie. You are inside a club. It's a natural thing to have music playing in the background. So some of the music we were using was there to help the dialogue along. Sometimes you had to play the hard stuff back so you made sure you could hear the dialogue. Always looking for the perfect balance.

Q: You cowrote the comedy *Friday* and wrote *The Players Club*. Is it different collaborating on a script and then doing one yourself?

A: I enjoy them both. The difference is, with a teammate, when I'm not on the script, somebody else is on. When I don't have all the good ideas, here comes somebody else to pick up the slack, y'know. To bounce off each other. Stuff gets refined quicker, scenes get better quicker, because you have people bouncing off on it. You have two energies working on the same goal, and sometimes you can pump out a script quicker. By yourself, you are relying on your energy, so you have to figure every scene out and make sure your movie beats are right and that it moves along.

Q: You were never trained formally in film as an actor or a director?

A: I would take all my years doing videos to four or five years in somebody's film school. I would rather be right on the set. I learned more that way.

Q: What did you learn from the likes of John Singleton and Walter Hill, two directors you worked with as an actor, and did any of that work prepare or reinforce your new role as a director?

A: Experience and paying attention are factors about really getting involved with a scene or my work as a director. An actor can sit in a trailer and read lines. He only gives a fuck about how he looks. You know what I'm saying? He goes out there and gives a performance and returns to the trailer. I wasn't like that. I would do my thing and work to try and make the scene better for the director and do all the things that we need to do to make sure he had the vision he had. In doin' that, I learned a lot from John Singleton, Walter Hill, F. Gary Gray. I learned how not to treat actors, from certain movies I was in. I've learned the more leeway you give an actor, the more he or she will want to give you. If he or she understands what you need out of a scene, you hired this dude—man, let him or her go!

It was shot in the spirit of *Cooley High* and *Claudine*.

Q: Did you have a sense of restriction since you were mostly location dependent in principal filming? Basically a set, and a lot of the action taking place in the one venue.

A: Any movie can be location dependent. Long as you have a place to shoot every scene. You take a movie like *12 Angry Men*, mostly shot in that room. If you figure out, "I can shoot here by the window," "I can shoot on top of you," then the day you say, "There's no room in here," you gotta go to another location. So with *The Players Club*, the good thing about it was pretty much one location, but we built the set, so before we built anything, I made sure we had enough space by looking at the model, and that I could shoot my scenes within the set.

Q: I know you had some budget concerns, but at times when you could run the floor like the L.A. Lakers, I dug the panning techniques and the sweeps, like in the opening shot. You been watching Martin Scorsese?

A: Oh yeah. Oh yeah. Some of my favorite directors like Scorsese employ those sweeps and look-from-above shots. Where the narration is going and you got a cool look and cool actors doin' cool shit and the camera just floatin.' Scorsese is the best floater around. He has your arm and walks you around. He's Dr. J. with a little of the Ice Man extension, because he's your guide. He has you by the waist and telling you where these people are. Like in *Goodfellas*. I loved it. I loved it.

I wish I had the money and time to do more of those angles you mentioned. Hopefully I will be able to have the chance to explore some of that stuff where I can play with the camera. This is pretty much pop and shoot.

※

The Players Club was Ice Cube's directorial film debut. As an actor, Ice Cube has appeared in *Boyz 'n the Hood, Trespass, Higher Learning, Dangerous Ground, Glass Shield* and *Anaconda,* as well as *Barbershop, Barbershop 2: Back in Business, Torque* and *Ghosts of Mars.* In addition, he produced and acted in *Next Friday, Friday After Next, All About the Benjamins* and *Are We There Yet?* He wrote *All About the Benjamins* and cowrote the original *Friday,* for which he also served as executive producer.

Ice Cube (O'Shea Jackson) began in the rap world with NWA in 1986. Solo albums followed in the early '90s, including *AmeriKKKa's Most Wanted, Death Certificate, The Predator,* and *Lethal Injection.* Between 1994 and 1998, besides his increasing movie work, he stayed busy writing and producing music for other artists, including da Lench Mob, Kam, and the hip-hop supergroup he formed called Westside Connection, which consisted of Ice Cube and fellow gangsta rappers Mack 10 and WC. In 1998 he returned to solo recording with *War & Peace, Vol. 1 (The War Disc)*; its sequel, *War & Peace, Vol. 2 (The Peace Disc),* followed in 2000.

JIM JARMUSCH

DIRECTOR JIM JARMUSCH'S INTIMATE documentary about Neil Young and Crazy Horse, *Year of the Horse*, spans the band's twenty-eight-year history, incorporating footage from tours in 1976, 1986, and their most recent 1996 jaunt around America and Europe.

The Akron, Ohio-born Jarmusch, one of the pioneers of the American independent film boom, is best known for his idiosyncratic movies, *Stranger than Paradise*, *Down by Law* and *Mystery Train*. Music is a big element in all his films, and Jarmusch has cast rock music personalities in his movies, including Screamin' Jay Hawkins and Tom Waits.

The director's relationship with Young began when the rocker did the score for his last film, *Dead Man*, while Neil's own label, Vapor, released the soundtrack album. Jarmusch also directed the video for the song, "Big Time," from the recent Neil Young and Crazy Horse record, *Broken Arrow*.

Year of the Horse is about the band, Neil Young and Crazy Horse—which includes longtime cohorts drummer-vocalist Ralph Molina, bassist-vocalist Billy Talbot, and guitarist-vocalist Frank "Poncho" Sampedro.

Former Neil Young and Crazy Horse producer-arranger Jack Nitzsche is represented in some still photos in the collection, as is Crazy Horse founding member Danny Whitten.

Neil Young at Balboa Stadium, San Diego,
California, 1969. Photo by Henry Diltz.

The live performances, along with the interviews and behind-the-scenes
footage, were filmed in Europe and the United States during the '96 tour,
with some archival material from both the '76 and '86 treks. Most of the
performances were photographed in 16mm, but a large percentage was
captured on Super-8 film by L. A. Johnson and Jarmusch. "We went that
way partly because the small cameras allowed us to easily shoot by ourselves, without a crew," says the white-haired auteur. "But mostly we used
Super-8 because we love the way it looks—the raw beauty of the material
somehow corresponds to the particular quality of the Horse's music."

I talked to Jarmusch in Los Angeles at his hotel room on La Cienega
Boulevard.

Q: How did your relationship with Neil Young begin?

A: Neil and the band liked the results of the video I did for the song, "Big Time," which was shot entirely on Super-8 film in and around Half Moon Bay, California. Neil particularly liked the rough look of the Super-8. He called me up a little while later and said, "Listen, we should do a longer film that looks and feels like the 'Big Time' video!" Neil liked the way we were such a small, portable little crew.

Q: What are you most proud about or happy with, after viewing and living with this movie?

A: I love the contradiction of Super-8 film on a big screen with music that is recorded in forty-track digital Dolby. The combination of high tech sound with a real low-tech image. Somehow that contradiction is very appropriate to this band, because they have this huge transcendent sound that comes out of old amps and a very raw kind of playing approach to the music. Somehow, that raw beauty and bigness and smallness together, I don't know how to explain it, but I think we captured that contradiction on film.

Year of the Horse makes it clear that the band's music comes from the whole band. Neil Young is certainly their navigator, leading them into the soaring territory of their songs, but Ralph, Poncho, and Billy are anything but sidemen. Together they create a singular sound that—in the same way John Coltrane kept jazz alive and evolving with his group's "sheets of sounds"—keeps rock 'n' roll alive through its emotional connection to the musicians who are playing it. I wanted to shoot Super-8, and then we covered the concerts that we shot in the house with 16mm.

Q: One of your film's strong points is the fusion of archival 1976 and 1986 materials shot in 16mm and the utilization of photos blended with the 1996 tours you and the crew captured.

A: Neil had 16mm film material from 1976, and the '86 footage was "stolen" from Bernard Shakey's film, done by Neil himself, *Muddy Track*. The 1986 was high-8 video that Neil and, I guess, [arranger-producer] David Briggs shot.

Q: What did you notice about the '76 and '86 footage? I would imagine even then the camera was mostly on Neil.

A: I tried to keep the crews that shot our 16mm from doing that. Neil is the lead singer, the lead guitar player, and the songwriter, the front man of the group.

Crazy Horse tends to be overshadowed by Neil, not by his own design, but that's just the way it is. One aspect of *Year of the Horse* was to make those guys known as people a little bit, so we understand them as a band, and not just as Neil Young's backup, side musicians.

I began to realize they were a four-piece band when I started shooting "Big Time." I've always been a big fan of Neil, particularly with Crazy Horse on albums like *Tonight's the Night* or *On the Beach*. I like the more dark, rock 'n' roll side of Neil. I think he's a great songwriter, but *Harvest Moon* isn't *Ragged Glory* for me, y'know.

I'm a rock 'n' roller, so I never liked Crosby, Stills and Nash, for example. It's too sweet and light, and doesn't speak to me. I don't respond to that stuff. So, I was always a fan of the Horse. I started realizing that sound comes from these guys and, if you were to replace any of them, you wouldn't have that sound anymore.

Q: Were Neil and the band cooperative interview subjects?

A: We were treated as part of their gang! We were in the same hotels and given the room list. We were able to hang out with them anytime we wanted—with or without a camera. We were very polite—we didn't barge in. They were really gracious. At one show in England, there were sixty thousand people there. Neil's guys allowed L. A. Johnson and me onstage and let us film with total access. We're not supposed to get in Neil's eye line, because he gives a hundred and ten percent when he's onstage. He's there to make music, not to make a movie. You get a slightly different show when they play in small clubs, which they love to do before they go out on tour. Those shows are amazing.

Q: Were you always a Neil Young fan?

A: I've been a big fan since I was a kid and first heard the song, "Broken Arrow," by Buffalo Springfield, which was very visual and dreamlike to me. I didn't know what the lyrics meant, so I invented my own scenario. After that, the next big thing that went right into me was the first Crazy Horse record, *Everybody Knows This Is Nowhere*. So, I've been a big fan all along, but had never seen Neil live until the late '80s. The good stuff always holds up. That's why we listen to Bach.

I was listening constantly to Neil and Crazy Horse while I was writing the script for *Dead Man*, then again during the shooting, which involved a great deal of travel. Crazy Horse even performed in Sedona, Arizona, during the shooting period, and a large number of our crew attended the show.

I wrote *Dead Man* in a little house in the Catskills with Neil's music playing on a boom box.

Q: What did you learn about Crazy Horse's music, and Neil Young as a writer-guitarist?

A: He's a real poet, but not in an extravagant way. I mean, he uses very common language, but it becomes poetic in the economy. Things are not over-explained. What really kind of blew my mind was, after I hung out with Neil at his ranch, I realized certain lyrics that were very abstract to me, I then saw, or had some insight into what, literally, they were all about.

Q: Tell me about the preproduction process.

A: Filming is like going out and collecting material. It's like taking some guys and going out to a rock quarry and you bring back a big chunk of marble, and then you look at it. Say you wanted to have a sculpture of a horse and you bring back the model which you think is the right size and shape, but then while you're looking at it, it tells you

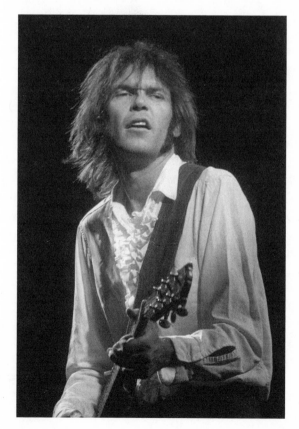

Neil Young performing in Los Angeles, California, 1976. Photo by Henry Diltz.

it should be a deer, or a cow. You have to let the material tell you what it wants to be. That's the way I like to work. There's certainly the "Hitchcock School," where you storyboard everything. Hitchcock said himself that filming was incredibly boring because it was just trying to translate this stuff on paper onto the screen, but I like to be open to the things you can't control. I like to be open and bring something else. Neil is a master of this. Often the best things you do are by accident or by mistake, or things you didn't plan properly. Things out of your control.

Q: Were you impressed by the availability of film and video from earlier tours that you were allowed to use in *Year of the Horse*?

A: Well, it kind of threw me for a loop when I realized all that 1976 footage is a feature-length film. I keep tellin' Neil, "Man, you gotta make that into a feature-length film. Then you'll have *Muddy Track* from '86, *Year of the Horse* from '96 and this other film from '76."

There's a little scene we took out of the movie, after the credits, where Neil and I are in the dressing room and I say to him, "Well Neil, do we do this again in ten years? 2006?" "All right. We'll make another one."

Q: What did you observe about the growth of Crazy Horse and their relationship with Neil over the years?

A: They've become more pure and more loose at the same time. They are more open to letting something take them away into the sky without knowing the destination necessarily. I think they're more courageous in that way. And yet their music is wilder. It's less refined, less careful. Like, there's Neil playing that solo from '76 in "Like a Hurricane," that is a breathtakingly beautiful guitar solo, but it's very clean in a way. It's a different kind of purity. But then you cut to how far he's gone, to this real wild, way-out-there stuff. He's not afraid to go into dark terrain and bring all that experience with him. They are warriors and they've been in more battles and are more violent than ever. But they are also stronger. I agree with Neil's dad in the film when he says, "Their music just seems to get better and better."

Q: It was also interesting to learn about the other members of Crazy Horse. The candid interview segments really educated a lot of people to a band that has played together for twenty-eight years.

A: They are not used to it. It's like people have always gone by them to get to Neil. On one level they probably like that, because they are not thrown into the melee all the time. On another level, they deserve, and know they deserve, respect for their contributions to this "world's greatest garage band," or whatever you want to call them.

Q: It's not often we get to see and hear musicians run down their individual histories around the age of fifty, as they are sort of being introduced to an audience for the first time.

A: They've seen it all. These guys have had people die around them. Tragic things. They've lived through really wild drug experiences and they all survived. Not all of them, but these four.

When I worked on *Dead Man*, I spent a lot of time with native people in the States and Canada. One old guy was saying, "In our culture, to be old is like getting to go to the top of the mountain and looking out." That's a value all the young people respect: a guy who has been able to look out up there. Because in native culture, it's very cool to be old, you know. Their view is from a higher place. That's very valuable to those of us who are catching up to that, who are just starting out our climb up the mountain.

※

Jim Jarmusch: Select Filmography
Broken Flowers
Coffee and Cigarettes
Ghost Dog: The Way of the Samurai
Year of the Horse
Dead Man
Night on Earth
Mystery Train
Down by Law
Stranger than Paradise
Permanent Vacation

BAZ LUHRMANN

INTERSCOPE RECORDS RELEASED the soundtrack, *Music from Baz Luhrmann's Film, 'Moulin Rouge,'* the 20th Century Fox movie.

Previously, the Australian-born Luhrmann directed *Romeo & Juliet* and *Strictly Ballroom*. He had also released on CD *Something for Everybody (Music from the House of Iona)*, a collection of remixed and reinterpreted songs from his films, theater, and opera, including hits from *Romeo & Juliet, Strictly Ballroom*, and *La Bohème*.

Moulin Rouge stars Nicole Kidman, Ewan McGregor, John Leguizamo, Jim Broadbent, and Richard Roxburgh. It was written by Luhrmann and Craig Pearce.

Current cutting-edge artists, lyricists, and composers collaborated closely with writer-director Luhrmann on this soundtrack. *Moulin Rouge* is a period piece musical, underscored with elements of comedy and tragedy, a merger of love and inspiration set in 1900, in the infamous Paris nightclub. Luhrmann threads together text, narration, and speech with modern-era pop tunes, and celebrates many key pop songs of the twentieth century, from Rodgers and Hammerstein to Lennon and McCartney, from Sting to Elton John, from Dolly Parton, Bob Crewe, and Jack Nitzsche to David Bowie.

Bowie sings Eden Ahbez's "Nature Boy," initially made famous by

Nat King Cole, and David reprises it as well with Massive Attack, with "Nature Boy" bookending the compilation. Fatboy Slim offers a new tune, "Because We Can," for the film. Bono, Gavin Friday, and Maurice Seezer cover T-Rex's/Marc Bolan's "Children of the Revolution." José Feliciano and actors McGregor and Jacek Koman team to create a tango version of the Police's "Roxanne," mixed with a classic Argentine tango, "Tanguera," by Mariano Mores. There are other tunes aired in the movie, including some not available in the soundtrack package. Nicole Kidman and Ewan McGregor make their on-screen and soundtrack singing debuts.

Q: It seems your earlier *Something for Everybody (Music from the House of Iona)* album had an impact on *Moulin Rouge* and the subsequent soundtrack album. Narration, spoken word, reinterpreted songs from opera?

A: You know what? It's a good observation and it's real simple. Anton Monsted, my music supervisor, also coproduced a lot of the tracks on the *Music from the House of Iona* album with me. We set out to do that as a practice run for doing the musical, *Moulin Rouge*. Specifically, we were going to do a little charity record for Australia. We wanted to do more hands-on producing, because with all the films I've done, I work very closely in the music, and I worked closely on *Romeo & Juliet* with Nelly Hooper, Marius DeVries, and Craig Armstrong, to actually physically produce the music myself and do that hands-on work. So I was ready, and also this way we could deal with this idea of the eclectic nature of the music that was going to be used in *Moulin Rouge*. So that was the starting point.

Q: The hit, "Everybody's Free (to Wear Sunscreen)." A year after release in the U.K., it pops stateside. Did you know when it was first recorded you had something special? Didn't some people, or music and record industry ears, think you were off your rocker, or doing something out of format?

A: As with all the music that we do, y'know, Harvey, every record I've ever made, including the album for *Romeo & Juliet*, I had a lot of A&R people telling me, "That will never work in the states." "It's too different." "It's too eclectic." That was the whole thing with *R&J*. "Too European." The thing is, this assumption that because I work in Australia, it couldn't be the same here.

Q: But this flow and song mix seems very logical and natural. Is it always a fight?

A: Yes, simply put. No one has ever asked me this before. Yes, it is always a fight. Going back to the first question, yes. It's quite natural to me. It is really the way we see the world.

I've grown up in a very isolated place. I love music. Just great music, whether it's rap, opera, or rock, and the universality of things is what attracts me, not the division. The thought of the need for economics— the strongest in the States—not as a criticism, but just because it's such a vast market to segregate things, to focus things to nail and nail and nail, and so therefore it has turned into a fight, and it's a fight I've had from my very first film. *Romeo & Juliet* sold eight million copies worldwide. "This soundtrack is too eclectic," when I first talked to EMI in marketing. Multiplatinum later on *R&J*. You know what I mean? I got to tell you it's been the reverse at Interscope.

Q: You had made two films before, *Romeo & Juliet* and *Strictly Ballroom*.

A: Do you think any executive was begging me to make those films?

Q: No.

A: Yes, exactly, and so like after the second, which was kind of like, "William Shakespeare? Go back to the ballroom dancing, we know that can be a hit." Eventually it becomes a Bazmark Production: "As long as he doesn't go off his number, what do we know about reinventing the musical," y'know.

With *Moulin Rouge*, we are using traditional break-out-into-song techniques, Greek chorus techniques, post-mod MTV techniques, and some of our own techniques.

Q: You are blending a lot of dialogue, speech and text, music and songs, and along the way you are giving some well-deserved props to the writers and lyricists. It's refreshing to hear on the big screen. So why can't narrative and speech and song be more in demand in film projects?

A: It matters to me. People say, "Oh, you're so daring." And I'm very much of the mind of, "Daring? I'm just saying it's just a natural step. It's going to happen, even if I don't do it." You can feel around you, you can think of people like Dré and people like that, who are reaching their tentacles out for film, or people who write poetry, or spoken word, or language.

This was going to be the last of the "red curtain" films I make, and I will do music cinema again, but sometime next year I want to see a film where someone is using a spoken word or rap-like storytelling in cinema. It's got to happen. It's going to happen.

That's why we've got audiences who clap and cheer at the songs in cinemas. They are not cheering the projectionist. What they are doing is communing with everybody else in the room and saying, "Ha ha ha. I get it too." You know, "We're unified by this experience." Now nothing is more powerful than that in doing music. If you can shackle music to story, not shackle, but display music to story, I know it sounds dramatic, but if you can do that, you unleash a force that is unstoppable. I feel that *Moulin Rouge* is just the first step on that road.

Q: One of your central goals then obviously is to move the story along with music.

A: That's a rule. If you break that rule you are in dire trouble. It only can exist if it advances plot, and there were many musical ideas I had that had to be jettisoned simply because they weren't advancing plot or revealing character.

Q: You also mentioned that, when making *Moulin Rouge*, it was about breaking "the code." It's like a combination of many cinematic languages applied to music numbers.

A: Well, when I say "breaking the code," what I'm talking about is we needed to find a code, if you like, to make it acceptable for people to tell story through song in this moment. Now, while we reference the past, and we look to the future, it's ultimately a potpourri of references and techniques that speak to a person now.

It's just about a deal between the film and the audience that allows the contemporary audience to accept that they know they are in on it. *Moulin Rouge*, and its particular cinematic form, is part of a larger gesture that we started ten years ago and we're concluding now. With the film, we want to do the finest version of this cinematic form.

Q: When you were first writing *Moulin Rouge*, did you already have certain songs, recording artists, and composers in the initial draft? Did you write the script with definite songs and tunes in place?

A: This is what happened. I began with a philosophy. Here's the background: First, I wanted to reinvent the musical. Second, I also wanted a musical where the musical language on one hand had to tell story, on the other hand I wanted the track to it to be eclectic like a modern soundtrack, instead of using one voice. So I just didn't want to work with one voice. Some background notes, Harvey. It's a very old idea in musicals, like when Judy Garland sings "Clang clang clang went the trolley," in *Meet Me in St. Louis*, that's set in 1900. She is singing big band music from the 1940s, the music of her time, to let you into the characters of another time and another place.

The other thing is in an old musical, the audience had a relationship to the music generally before they went in. It was either a Broadway show, or songs move from film to film. So the audience having a pre-existing relationship to at least some of the music was very important. Hence, Craig [Pearce] and I came up with the device of our main character telling the story, and because he was a poet, channeling if you like, the great examples of every kind of music of the last hundred years.

So that's how we began. Then we constructed a very simple story that took a long time to do, based on a few things including *La Bohème*.

So there was a recognizable story for the audience. You're not about revealing plot. Then, we spent a great deal of time scanning, scanning, and scanning songs to identify which song would actually tell a particular moment or reveal a character.

Q: Did "Nature Boy" set the tone early for the film? It's used twice in the available soundtrack, opening and closing the disc.

A: Actually, you know what? I have to tell you honestly that was the one song that came a little later in the process. Eden Ahbez is an Orphic, messianic character. I've always loved "Nature Boy," but when I realized the story of Eden Ahbez while the song was in the body of the film, I realized it reflected the overall structure. I grew that out during the shooting process.

I'll tell you why it came about. I actually began the film with a theme between the father and the son with Cat Stevens' "Father and Son." What happened was that Cat rejected it based on religious beliefs. OK I respect him for that. That left me looking at "How do I clarify the structures?" So coming back to it and having identified the song, then it was about how to get the licensing and people to agree. Honestly, it was just a journey of going to see most of the artists one-on-one. I went to publishing companies and they were enthusiastic, because it represents a new use of popular song, in the grand rite of the musical. But then I met with Elton [John]. I knew Bono. I wrote to Paul McCartney. I met with Dolly Parton. They were really enthusiastic. You know, Harvey, if it were the 1940s, someone like Bono would be writing for movie musicals.

No one stood in our way. It was the opposite. Because we didn't have that much money. I worked with Bowie quite openly on it. Bowie was very supportive in giving us the song, "Heroes." I've got a lot of codes. Subtle signs and symbols. It's like a record. If you play this movie more than once you hear things. Bowie appears through it, and I was going to use Bowie with Massive Attack on the end credits. Bowie and Massive ended up being, in a sense, so dark that we needed to resurrect the audience during the credits. So that's where the idea of "The Bolero" came from, which Steve Hitchcock or then Steve Sharpels composed.

I really enjoyed working with Bowie. He was very giving. You can imagine how he feels about the film.

Q: When did songs start entering the scenes on the pages?

A: They were all driven by "what does this story beat need?" Now I love "Nature Boy," so I was happy that it revealed itself as the right choice. But things were dropped. We had "Under My Thumb" in a kind of rape scene, but we didn't need it in the end. So I missed a Rolling Stones piece. But it wasn't about, "Well, we must have a Rolling Stones piece." It was a story that simply doesn't need it.

Q: What is the secret of getting and working together with music people, labels, publishers, songwriters, to serve the project? Hassles, games, egos?

A: Y'know what, the silver sword to cut through all of that is that the idea is so exciting that it actually diminishes all of those fears.

Other than being an acolyte of that, I personally go and—I hope—enthuse people and explain and involve them, and don't manipulate them and don't make them feel it's a quickie. Our love of what we're making, which is so absolute—transporting that, but finally how often do you get the opportunity to actually work on something where you're reinventing a genre or breaking new ground? People really find that exciting.

Q: The film's songwriting credits, and to a lesser extent, the soundtrack, due to space limitations, have so many names you never see linked together. Paul Stanley of KISS to Rodgers & Hammerstein. Yet radio programmers, print, and electronic media often fail to integrate their names in broadcasts or magazines in the same pages.

A: Exactly, exactly. To me, I'm blind to it, Harvey. I'm blind to it. To me they are great tunes, great popular culture. Popular culture today becomes classical culture tomorrow. Shakespeare was pop of its time. I work in opera. So I know that Puccini was the television of its time. One of the strengths of the piece is that I am captain of collaboration. I am very big on collaborators. I wanted all kinds of musical talents to work together.

Q: "Lady Marmalade" is done in the film with four actors, another character is rapping over it with spoken word, and "Teen Spirit" is being sung at the same time. So it's really a round of three things. Much like an opera. Then Paul Hunter directed a video casting, away from the film, with Christina Aguilera, Lil' Kim, Mya, and Pink.

A: I think it's a very good interpretation of the film. It's not the film, but it captures some moments. We supported him a lot, gave him some stuff. The idea was to say, "Look Paul, don't try and homage the movie, just go and make a gesture that tells what you got from the film."

Q: "Sparkling Diamonds" features Nicole Kidman's vocals.

A: Nicole turned out to be a wonderful singer. She tells story through her voice.

Q: Ewan McGregor has a very pretty singing voice. Really carries a rendition of "Your Song." I know he worked really hard with a vocal coach, and he can sing. It's a pivotal part in the movie, and I'm sure it helps that your leading man can really carry a note.

A: Elton John would agree with you. Ewan worked really hard and he grew into a great singer in front of us, really. He was good, but he became great. When Elton saw the footage of Ewan doing "Your Song," he went, "My God, he really is a singer." There's a recording career ahead of him if he so chooses. That's been one of the great surprises, just how strong he is.

Q: Then there's a T-Rex song, "Children of the Revolution," that pairs Bono, Gavin Friday, and Maurice Seezer. One of the important cues in the film and soundtrack album. Bolan and T-Rex are overlooked in America.

A: T-Rex is bigger for us in Australia. That was a theme for me, "Children of the Revolution." But also again, story. It's about the Bohemians, in a Bohemian revolution. It was about identifying popular song that can unite all of us, that tells story. It's that simple. Marc Bolan is hugely underrated in America.

Bono actually rang me about something else. Bono is such a great supporter of my films, he said, "Anything I can do to help out with Moulin Rouge?" I said, "Well, as a matter of fact . . ." "Maybe I can make a cup of tea." So he went in with Gavin, who worked with us on *Romeo & Juliet*, and Maurice, and he made that track in about a week for us. He was very passionate about it, y'know, as only Bono can be. You're a lucky person if you get to work with Bono, I have to say that.

Q: Was there ever a time when you reviewed songs and tune and artist pairings, looked at something and felt, this is too obvious, or it telegraphs too much?

A: No. I think it's really important that you take the obvious. You take what you might think is the "cheesiest," you take something that is overt and what you do is turn it on its head. Because there is a reason why things are obvious. They have value inside them. The problem is they become rusty from overuse. What we had to do is shake the rust off by inverting it, so I feel what we've done with that piece is invert it by subjecting it to story. You can constantly shake the rust off.

You know, anything that survives time and geography is always worth revisiting.

Q: You had a great say in the casting of the movie. Did you initially look for actors that you thought could work vocally as singers?

A: You know, in my films I have a big say about every single thing. You know what I mean? I looked very extensively, and I had to find actors, and I'd worked with both Nicole and Ewan before, but I had to find actors that could sing the roles. Ultimately, it sounds boring, but they got the jobs because they were best for them, that's really the truth.

Q: That doesn't happen very often in this world.

A: Well, no, but as I say, for all the disadvantages of trying to reinvent the wheel, every time we make a movie, one of the advantages is that you're left alone. It's got to be the right person for the right role.

Q: Don't you think some of the songs were better realized when matched with the visual?

A: Well yes, I think that's very true. I mean, it's storytelling music. If you were creating it just for a sonic experience, you would probably take different roads on certain tracks.

Q: The film at times attacks the senses.

A: Yes. Particularly in the first twenty minutes. It's important that I wake people up. It's not a passive experience. It has to slap you around a bit so that, by the time they break out into song, it becomes quite classical. I hope you surrender to the contract.

Q: Even though you didn't get the use of the Cat Stevens principal theme early on in putting *Moulin Rouge* together for film and soundtrack, and then "Nature Boy" sort of emerged out of the pack to be featured widely in the soundtrack disc and in the movie, it appears often you find out things happen for a reason. Andrew Loog Oldham told me, "There are no accidents."

A: Do you know what? There are no accidents. You are going always to the same place. How you get there is your inventiveness.

Q: Ultimately, you are serving the whole in some sort of Zen capacity.

A: Absolutely. I think the reason for all the crazy ego stuff, the thing that actually makes it a human experience and worthwhile, is that we all finally serve something greater than ourselves. That is the story, the piece you are making. That is the beautiful side of this creative process. What it is, Harvey, it is ultimately fulfilling. That, I can say, is the truth.

Q: Ewan McGregor's singing was as convincing as Marlon Brando in *Guys and Dolls*.

A: I totally agree with you and that's a favorite role of mine. But he [Ewan] has got that absolutely bold face openness to the camera, which you have to have to sing. Singing exposes you on a very deep level. You've got to be able to be that vulnerable, open, and exposed.

Q: The film moves comedy and tragedy forward together.

A: Comedy and tragedy together are not common on our screen, but they should be, because our audience is used to swinging from comedy to tragedy. Now we're so advanced in being aware of manipulation, we can sign the contract that allows us to accept that.

※

Baz Luhrmann: Select Filmography

DIRECTOR:
Moulin Rouge
Romeo & Juliet
Strictly Ballroom
La Bohème (TV)

WRITER:
Moulin Rouge
Romeo & Juliet (screenplay)
Strictly Ballroom (screenplay and idea)

PRODUCER:
Moulin Rouge
Romeo & Juliet

Moulin Rouge (lyricist on two songs, composer on two others, music producer on all songs)

Nominated for Tony Award in 2003 for Best Musical Direction (*La Bohème*)

Nominated for Academy Award in 2002 for Best Picture (*Moulin Rouge*)

JESSIE NELSON

Jessie Nelson is the director and cowriter of *I Am Sam*.

The entire film's soundtrack is comprised of recording artists performing personal renditions of classic Beatles songs. Eddie Vedder covers "You've Got to Hide Your Love Away," while Nick Cave, Sheryl Crow, Heather Nova, Ben Folds Five, Stereophonics, Sarah McLachlan, and others deliver selections from the Lennon-McCartney songbook.

I was initially introduced to the music of *I Am Sam* by KROQ-FM DJ Rodney Bingenheimer, when I heard him track the first spin of the Vines doing "I'm Only Sleeping," and then decided to view the movie.

Jessie Nelson emerged from the avant-garde theater company, Mabou Mines, at the Joseph Papp Public Theater in New York. An actress initially, appearing in television shows like the "Ambush" episode of *ER* in 1994, Nelson directed "My First Time," that gained her acceptance into the American Film Institute's Chanticleer program. Nelson then directed the award-winning *To the Moon, Alice* for Showtime.

Jessie Nelson's feature film directorial debut was *Corrina, Corrina*, starring Whoopi Goldberg, Ray Liotta, and Tina Majorino. She also cowrote and produced with Alan Zweibel *The Story of Us*, directed by Rob Reiner, starring Bruce Willis and Michelle Pfeiffer.

"I've always thought music added an important layer to movies. But

I didn't realize how much until this film," she further explained to me about the Beatles-driven *I Am Sam* soundtrack, one night when she called me on the telephone from her home in Southern California.

Q: When you were working on the screenplay for *I Am Sam* and working on the script, did you already have specific Beatles songs in mind?

A: I had placed twelve songs in the script and I was pretty naïve to be honest, thinking all twelve would be sung by the Beatles, not realizing how sensitive it would be to get the publishing, let alone the Beatles singing them. Some of the songs shifted once we were in the cutting room. Different songs would replace what I had, or new ones worked perfectly.

For me the writing is around the mood and the feeling you want to capture in a scene, and how can a song take it even further, or heighten it.

Q: Were you amazed when you did research for *I Am Sam* at L.A. Goal, a non-profit organization that serves adults with developmental disabilities, that people could communicate through the music and legacy of the Beatles?

A: I did not go into the research thinking that I would be using the Beatles. It was the way that the disabled people loved the Beatles that made me think that would be an interesting thing for Sean Penn's character. Then once we started writing it into Sean's character came the notion of putting the music in. So it really all came through the research.

You know, I think a lot of people with disabilities connect with the Beatles for the same reason we do. You know what I mean? There is something so universal about those songs and the kind of purity of the emotions of them. They're almost like children's songs. Many of the people we met not only loved and idolized the Beatles but looked to them as guides on how to act in life.

It came from working with all these people with disabilities, how they were always singing Beatles' songs and sharing with us how much they loved the Beatles.

Q: How were most of the songs selected for your film and the soundtrack album?

A: A good deal of the songs had been in the screenplay. Some of them in editing, we would try some things: "What would work here?"

Would it be "The Two of Us" or "Across the Universe"? We would throw different songs up against the movie. Then we chose the nine that seemed to resonate the most.

When we had chosen the nine we definitely wanted, then the record company came aboard, and it was almost like the way you cast a movie. We sort of took each song and said, "OK, what voice would really capture the mood of this theme?"

Q: How do you even pick the nine Beatles songs? I know they serve the film.

A: You take a specific moment in the movie, and you have it right there in the script descriptions. Then sometimes a song works beautifully in a scene, but doesn't work for the overall film, and you have to reevaluate it in that context, maybe there's too many songs too close together. So each choice gets made for many reasons.

Q: You were also involved in producing this movie, as well as directing it and cowriting. How did you work with the record label?

A: We had a person at New Line, Erin Scully, who was really supportive of us figuring out a way to get the vision onto a record and then into a movie. And then we had the record company.

Q: The record label didn't really show up until late in the game.

A: Man, they showed up four weeks before the film had to be locked. We shopped it around and everyone flipped out over the idea, but everyone was terrified, not just by business concerns, but also they had so little time to put it together. They thought, "If we're not going to be able to get amazing artists in this short a time, can we really do it, and will it be able to compete in the marketplace that just had *The Beatles 1* album and Paul McCartney doing 'Vanilla Sky'?" All the stuff that's out there. People would get really, really close to doing it and then kind of panic.

But once you stick those songs in a movie, you can't imagine the movie without them. So you just can't imagine getting a "no." You have to fight to get a "yes."

I was really lucky in that Jody Graham, one of the people who controls the publishing at Sony, is someone I grew up with, who was my best friend when I was eleven years old. So she gave us a phenomenal deal and that allowed us to have the nine songs.

You still have to clear the publishing, whether it's the Beatles singing it or Sara McLachlan.

Q: What changed for you when other artists sang the Beatles' songs in the film and subsequent soundtrack? Obviously the intent still translated.

A: Yes, and in a way what we learned was that it allowed the music to reach a whole other group of people because, if we had just had the Beatles singing it, people wouldn't have bought the record in the same way, because they have those songs in their other albums. This collection now exists on its own terms. To get such people as Eddie Vedder and Sarah to do such beautiful interpretations I think allows the music to live longer in a certain way, and kind of reaches this generation.

Michelle Pfeiffer from the very beginning was saying to me, "Don't get the Beatles, get people to cover the Beatles," because she had a wonderful experience on *Dangerous Minds* with that soundtrack and how much it had helped the film, and she felt, "Let a new artist cover the music and let it be really fresh, and let there be videos on MTV and all that comes with that." So it's not like she made phone calls or things like that, that wasn't really necessary, but she supported it so much creatively.

Q: How did you work with Andy Gershon, Kate Hyman, and Jon Sidel of V2 Records, who helped you produce the soundtrack?

A: God bless Andy, because everyday we would have a conference call between my producer, Erin Scully at New Line, myself and Andy and his team, Jon Sidel and Kate Hyman. We would say, "OK. We've got 'You've Got to Hide Your Love Away.' What voice can knock it out of the ballpark?" "Eddie Vedder." "OK. How do we get to Eddie Vedder?" It was literally song-by-song. We would make a list of our first few choices and they never forced us to use anyone we didn't want to use. V2 was so supportive in getting people, and fought just as hard for those people on other labels as for the artists on the V2 label. So they were really committed to the movie, and doing what was right for the movie.

Sean got a beautiful letter from Paul McCartney after he saw the movie telling Sean that he was angry at Sean because he'd given his girlfriend a sinus infection, because she was crying so hard when she saw the movie, and how much they loved the movie—how deeply they were moved by it. The same thing with Yoko Ono's camp. We got very beautiful feedback from her.

V2 saw the movie originally in an interesting way. Our executive producer ending up living next door to Jon Sidel, who had just gotten a job with V2, and she invited him to a screening, and in the eleventh hour, he saw the movie and showed it to Andy. It was totally serendipitous. There was some sort of destiny for this working out.

Q: Had you ever gone through the trials of working with a record label to distribute the music or soundtrack for a film you've done?

A: We had an intense experience on our soundtrack to *Corinna, Corinna*, which was the same thing of trying to find a record label who would take some of those Billie Holiday songs and Bill Evans songs. It was challenging, and ultimately it came together beautifully.

Q: What about when some songs are heard in the movie but don't make the soundtrack? Or on the soundtrack, and not heard in the movie?

A: You know, I think it's a really tricky dance directors have to do between the record company needs and their needs as filmmakers. Sometimes you're lucky enough to have somebody like Andy who says the movie is the priority, and we'll make the soundtrack around the movie. Then sometimes you have other people who say, "Look, if you want the soundtrack you have to make these specific compromises." It's a dance you do, and hopefully you don't have to give up too much to get what you need. I think it depends on what record company you're dealing with and what person you're with. We were lucky to be really in synch in the tastes level with this company. No disagreements.

Q: I was struck by how well the Beatles' songs sound when they're sung by women.

A: What I learned as a writer listening to the Beatles' songs is that they're so well written. The lyrics are so beautiful and the tunes are so tight. You forget in that huge body of work how magnificent so many of the songs are. Listen to the lyrics on "Across the Universe." They are really poets.

To me the music is like the fourth lead character in our film. They are a huge character in our film and the soundtrack album had to have a huge presence in the movie.

※

Jessie Nelson: Select Filmography
Writer:
I Am Sam
The Story of Us
Stepmom (screenplay)
Chicago Hope (TV Series)
Corrina, Corrina

To the Moon, Alice (Showtime TV)
Daniel and the Towers (TV)

PRODUCER:
I Am Sam
The Story of Us
Corrina, Corrina

DIRECTOR:
I Am Sam
Corrina, Corrina
To the Moon, Alice (Showtime TV)

ACTRESS:
The Story of Us
ER (Episode #4.1: "Ambush")
Hoggs' Heaven (TV)
So I Married an Axe Murderer
The Switch (TV)
Tucker: The Man and His Dream

STEPHEN WOOLLEY

LONDON-BORN ROCK 'N' ROLL FAN, movie buff, and heralded filmmaker-producer Stephen Woolley made his directorial movie debut with *Stoned*, released in the United States in spring 2006, a feature length film on the influential multi-instrumentalist and Rolling Stones founder, the late Brian Jones.

Woolley has spent the last ten years researching the events surrounding the musician's death on the night of Wednesday, July 2, 1969. At age twenty-seven, Jones was dead in the deep end of his own swimming pool. Officially, he drowned by misadventure, while under the influence of drink and drugs, at his East Sussex country retreat, Cotchford Farm, the former home of Winnie the Pooh author A. A. Milne.

Stoned was written by Robert Wade and Neal Purvis and based on and inspired by the books *Paint It Black*, by Geoffrey Giuliano; *Who Killed Christopher Robin?* from Terry Rawlings; and Anna Wohlin's *The Murder of Brian Jones*. The *Stoned* screenplay is a mixture of moments using music, words, and flashback memories as connecting and thematic devices.

Woolley had first become intrigued by the controversy involving Jones' physical passing after reading the three different books about him by Giuliano, Rawlings, and Wohlin, which contradicted the coroner's verdict of misadventure.

Director Stephen Woolley (left) on the set of *Stoned* with actors Leo Gregory (as Brian Jones, right foreground) and Monet Mazur (as Anita Pallenberg, center foreground), 2005. Photo courtesy of Number 9 Films.

Woolley and the two screenwriters seriously investigated and examined 1994's *Who Killed Christopher Robin? The Truth behind the Murder of Brian Jones,* by Rawlings. Complete with copies of many of the documents regarding Jones' drowning, including the coroner's findings and the witness statements, Rawlings' study contained a new pathologist's report and reexamined the police evidence.

Director Woolley's *Stoned* celluloid trek traces the 1963–1969 life of Brian Jones individually and with the Rolling Stones. Woolley's ambitious film captures the world of Brian Jones from rebellious teenager to ex-Rolling Stone, the murder of Brian, and the interlocking destinies of the six main characters: Jones, Frank Thorogood, Tom Keylock, Anita Pallenberg, Janet Lawson, and Anna Wohlin.

Actor Leo Gregory portrays Brian Jones. Frank Thorogood is played by Paddy Considine; Tom Keylock by David Morrissey; Anna Wohlin by Tuva Novotny; Janet Lawson by Amelia Warner; and Anita Pallenberg by Monet Mazur.

Composer David Arnold wrote and produced the musical score for *Stoned*. The music from the motion picture soundtrack album was issued on Milan Records.

In 2005, Woolley's latest coproduction, Neil Jordan's *Breakfast on Pluto*, was his twenty-third feature film. In addition, over a twenty-year period, Woolley has been executive-producer on twenty movies. The release of *Breakfast on Pluto* has continued Stephen Woolley's long-term partnership with director Neil Jordan that began with *The Company of Wolves* in 1983. Woolley's collaborations with Jordan include *The Actors* and *The Good Thief*, the Oscar-nominated *The End of the Affair*, *Michael Collins*, *Interview with the Vampire*, and the Oscar-winning *The Crying Game*. Woolley also produced Jordan's delightful *Mona Lisa*, which won numerous international awards. The duo worked together again on *High Spirits*, *The Miracle*, and the stirring *Butcher Boy*.

Stephen Woolley's career began in the summer of 1976 at the Screen on the Green cinema in London, where he tore tickets, sold ice cream, projected films and helped manage the venue. After working with The Other Cinema, he programmed and subsequently owned his own cinema, The Scala, which won acclaim for its diverse, original, and risk-taking program calendar.

The screening schedule at Woolley's theatre encompassed everything from the Howard Koch-directed cult movie classic, *Untamed Youth*, featuring Mamie Van Doren and Eddie Cochran, to early 1960s black-and-white episodic television shows like *The Untouchables*. During this same period, Woolley also wrote film criticism, helped edit a film journal, and produced a TV series for Channel 4 in England, *The Worst of Hollywood*.

In 1982, Woolley launched Palace Video in partnership with Nik Powell, releasing titles such as *Eraserhead* and *Mephisto*. Establishing a theatrical division one year later, Palace Video acquired, marketed, and distributed some two hundred and fifty independent and European movies, from *Diva* to *When Harry Met Sally*.

During this period, Woolley's producing career flourished, first with the musical *Absolute Beginners*, starring David Bowie, Ray Davies, Patsy Kensit, and James Fox, and then the dance comedy *Shag*, for which Bridget Fonda was nominated for a Golden Globe. Next came the absorbing *Scandal*, with star turns by Joanne Whalley-Kilmer, John Hurt, and Bridget Fonda.

After the Producers Guild of America awarded him the 1992 Producer of the Year title for *The Crying Game*, Woolley's first film with his previous company, Scala Productions, was *Backbeat*, a probing story of "fifth Beatle" Stuart Sutcliffe, produced in 1993.

Woolley subsequently executive-produced the charming *Little Voice*, starring Sir Michael Caine and Jane Horrocks. In 2003, he filmed *Intermission* in Ireland, providing Colin Farrell, Kelly MacDonald, and Cillian Murphy with acting jobs.

Until recently, Woolley was Chairman of the BAFTA film committee, where he served for ten years. He is also a member of the American Academy (the Academy of Motion Picture Arts and Sciences).

In early 2002, Woolley started Number 9 Films with partner Elizabeth Karlsen. Number 9 Films produced *Mrs. Harris*, starring Annette Bening and Ben Kingsley.

In 2006, Woolley is in development with Blake Morrison's novel, *When Did You Last See Your Father?* Jonny Lee Miller and David Morrissey, who appeared in *Stoned*, are slated to star in the planned film.

In his movie *Stoned*, Woolley examines the reality of the massively mythologized Brian Jones, a real character in all senses of the word.

Lewis Brian Hopkin-Jones, born on February 28, 1942, in Cheltenham, England, was more than just "a Rolling Stone" or the guitarist in the band. He actually named the band as a founding member in 1962. He emblazoned the early career path of the Stones as their first leader, R&B revival visionary, initial booker, and spokesman, who then colored their sound in the recording studio and onstage. For a few short years, before he was hounded and pounded by authorities, Brian Jones, Pisces, did embody and display a lifestyle, fashion, and musicality combo like few cool school cats of the last fifty years. *Stoned* also sadly shows Jones' 1969 struggle for identity, direction, and companionship.

Stephen Woolley, who grew up in North London, sat down with me in spring 2006 for an interview about *Stoned* in his publicist's office on Wilshire Boulevard in the Miracle Mile district of Los Angeles, California; the same street where I purchased my first Rolling Stones picture-sleeve 45 rpm single.

Q: What initially attracted you to develop and then coproduce, with Finola Dwyer, a film about Brian Jones?

A: I grew up in the '60s with the Beatles and the Rolling Stones. If you liked the Beatles, you weren't supposed to like the Stones. That's as kids. I was always fascinated by the idea of the Beatles, the Stones, and that period. The lyrics and everything else. As a teenager, I discovered punk in 1976. I was lucky enough to see the Sex Pistols seven times, and the Clash. And every night someone would be in London: The Ramones, Television, Talking Heads. Punk had suddenly taken over. I saw the Stones play live for the first time in 1976 at Earl's Court, and found them entertaining, but hardly challenging. I wondered what it was about the Rolling Stones that I thought was so rebellious. I just thought, "Who are these old guys, compared to Joe Strummer and Johnny Rotten?" These guys were lifeless and did not mean anything to me at all.

Q: How did your movie *Backbeat* influence *Stoned*?

A: I made a film called *Backbeat*, which is about the Beatles in Hamburg. And then I realized, while Mick Jagger was at the London School of Economics and Keith Richard[s] was at an art college, there were Paul McCartney and John Lennon taking speed and playing strip clubs, and hanging out with existentialists. That was rock 'n' roll. And the Stones were manufactured. So we thought the Beatles were a manufactured, "I Wanna Hold Your Hand," "Love Me Do" kind of band, and the Stones were the real thing, hard rocking, you know, but in fact it wasn't quite as simple as that. The two kind of merged into one. So when I read the book about Brian Jones, *Fade to Black*, and then followed by another book, *Who Killed Christopher Robin*, I was fascinated, not just by the murder, but by who this Brian Jones was. 'Cause I put two and two together and thought, "Wow. He was the anarchist. He was the extreme one. He was the kind of guy obsessed with this sound, obsessed with Robert Johnson. Obsessed with this Afro-American music. Obsessed with fashion, obsessed with experimenting, obsessed with acid, obsessed with drugs." He was the one Bob Dylan would go up to at parties. He was the one Jimi Hendrix loved. He was the one John Lennon loved. He was the one Pete Townshend loved. He was the one that Janis Joplin loved. It was Brian.

Q: Yet, even in the 1990s you hardly remembered Brian Jones.

A: Here I was in the mid-'90s, having thought of myself as a Rolling Stones fan, knowing nothing about Brian Jones. He was the blonde one, and I kind of vaguely remembered he died, fell into his swimming pool. Who cared? It was Mick and Keith that we loved anyway, you know. And so the icon that was Brian Jones in the mid-'60s when he was at the peak of being Brian Jones, when he was with Anita Pallenberg, and they were the Pete Doherty and Kate Moss of their time . . . Brian and Anita were, you know, sex on legs. They were everything. So what happened? Why did he fade? When you think about Jimi, and you think about Janis, you think about Jim Morrison, his three good friends, who all died at age twenty-seven, just in the same year as Brian almost. And yet, they are still icons. And Brian Jones was the forgotten icon. For me, it wasn't just a murder, which was fascinating, it was just sort of telling a story about someone who was far more important dead and in a sense much more of a catalyst than anyone ever gives him credit for.

Q: Brian was in the Stones for around six years, but had no solo song-writing credits, and that lends to his not being acknowledged or even discovered over the subsequent decades.

A: The reason that he is not remembered is because he didn't write the songs, which became far more crucial as the '60s went on than anyone realized at the beginning. 'Cause when they collectively first wrote songs, sometimes as B-sides, Brian suggested those be credited as (written by) Nanker/Phelge. But [former long-time Rolling Stones bassist] Bill Wyman says this very clearly: "Without Brian Jones there would be no Rolling Stones."

Q: You made it a point to show Jones scoring a film starring Anita Pallenberg, *A Degree of Murder*, released in 1967, directed by Volker Schlöndorff, and later a scene of him recording music with Moroccan villagers for *The Pipes of Pan at Jajouka*.

A: I wanted to show Brian as someone who was into world music before world music existed. And I wanted to show Brian as a composer. He worked with director Volker Schlöndorff, who later went on to win an Oscar for *The Tin Drum*. Brian could have scored Oscar-winning movies. He was at the forefront of world music. Nobody else was doing what Brian was doing at that time.

Q: How was the music chosen for *Stoned*?

A: I had a bible for the music. My bible was Robert Johnson, who meant everything to me. When I discovered Robert Johnson in 1970, I was hugely into the Allman Brothers Band, Taj Mahal, John McLaughlin, Jimi Hendrix.

In the early '70s, somebody gave me that Robert Johnson album, *King of the Delta Blues Singers*, and I thought, "This is everything. Everyone has taken from this guy." This one guy. That slide that he plays. That voice, the haunting melodies. It was like, "My God." And I thought, well, Robert Johnson. Everyone's done Robert Johnson in different ways. And how is that? It's [because] the guy's almost limitless. You know, you've got "Crossroads" by Cream, and you look at "Come on in My Kitchen" by Delaney and Bonnie. You look at the versions of "Stop Breaking Down" and "Love in Vain" that the Stones themselves did. Even in the movie *Performance*, you know, Mick Jagger plays three Robert Johnson songs in *Performance*. And that scene where he plays acoustic guitar—clearly "Come on in My Kitchen." And he plays "Devil Blues," which Led Zeppelin ripped off. He just seemed to me . . . and the fact that he died at the same age, at twenty-seven. I wanted to show how Robert Johnson was timeless— the White Stripes do "Stop Breaking Down"—and that in fact what Brian had discovered was this music, but actually it's just as relevant in 2006 as in 1937, or in 1966.

Q: What about the music groups and composers approving their music and copyrights for *Stoned*?

A: The White Stripes had recorded "Stop Breaking Down." I found the track and they insisted on seeing some of the film before they let me use it. And I showed them where I was going to use it and they came back immediately and they said yes. Same with Dylan. I sent it off to Dylan, and they gave me the rights. And Jefferson Airplane. They had to see some footage.

Q: And there are other really terrific period piece selections like Traffic's "Paper Sun" and Small Faces' "Lazy Sunday" that underscore the movie. And Jefferson Airplane's "White Rabbit" in a segment in 1965, but the song really came out in 1967.

A: It was very important to me that the other music featured in the film was contemporaneous of that time and had a flavor of Brian. "White Rabbit" was used because of the trip that Brian made to the Monterey Pop Festival to introduce Jimi Hendrix in 1967. And he hung out with Nico and Janis, and he loved that acid sound of the West Coast. The San Francisco psychedelic hippie scene. Then I've got to put that in there. Then I wanted a "builder's sound," 'cause it's a time in his life when he is taking acid. Then the house builders' acid sound for the movie. What did we have? So I wanted the Small Faces "Lazy Sunday" to be the sound of the builders. Cockney kind of acid. How wrong was that (*laughs*). With "Paper Sun" by Traffic, I always felt that Traffic, in particular, had a quite sophisticated, quite clever sound, another permutation of the R&B and blues thing. "Paper Sun" to me was the idea of Morocco.

I had all the music before I started the movie. For instance, I had the Bob Dylan song, "Ballad of a Thin Man," a modern version by Kula Shaker. 'Cause Brian Jones always thought that was about him. And Bob Dylan always said it wasn't about him, but whenever Bob saw Brian Jones at a party, he'd come over to him and say, "You know that song is about you" and walk away. Feeding Brian's paranoia.

Q: And with the use of covers by the Bees, Kula Shaker, the White Stripes, the Counterfeit Stones, you brought in new musicians for the soundtrack to balance out the older recordings you licensed. Also the opening track of the Willie Dixon-composed "Little Red Rooster," covered by session musicians, replicated the spine-tingling sound of Brian Jones's slide guitar.

A: I didn't want young people to see this movie and think, "Oh, it's all nostalgia." So the Bees did five tracks for me at the end. I wanted to get the Bees, Kula Shaker, and realize that music has kind of an internal sense. It isn't just of that period. I was excited that the Bees were able to contribute a great version of "Not Fade Away."

Keith Richards and Brian Jones at ABC Television Studios
in Hollywood, California, May 1965, on the set of *Shindig!*
Photo by Jean Marie Périer, courtesy of www.jean-marie-perier.net

My plan was always to interweave these songs into the fabric of the movie, using the originals alongside more contemporary versions. The White Stripes' recent recording of "Stop Breaking Down" is juxtaposed with the original. The Bees provided an updated version of "Stop Breaking Down" for the swimming pool scene, with the characters of Frank and Brian performing, and Hayley Glennie-Smith recorded beautiful, acoustic folk-inspired renditions of "Love in Vain" and "Come on in My Kitchen."

Q: The original rendition of "Time Is on My Side," performed by Irma Thomas, closes the movie.

A: And we were able to use the initial version of "Time Is on My Side" to invoke the legend of Brian Jones. It was very easy to use "Time Is on My Side." You see this face of Brian, with this smile. That's how we'll remember him. Like James Dean or River Phoenix. Time is on *his* side.

Q: Composer David Arnold wrote the musical score for *Stoned* and has the compositions, "Brian's Joint," "Out of Control," "Pool Fight," and "Angel/Devil" on the soundtrack disc.

A: He did not compete with the rock songs and I wanted David to be really character-driven. He's counteracting a lot of what is going on. There are times when the score takes over and is the central theme. David did that in three weeks and I worked so closely with him, because he was doing another big film for proper money and I was swapping midnight with him in his studio in Hampstead. David Arnold created a score both sinister and melodic, to mirror and contrast the narrative and character development. Given the wealth of music used in the film, it was crucial that David Arnold's music should underpin and enhance the dramatic flow of the film, rather than fight with the prerecorded and period music that reflected Brian's state of mind. David's superb compositions and arrangements provide a portal for a modern audience to look back to a world that no longer exists.

I view the story of Brian Jones as a parable for the times. It's Brian's hedonistic world that leads him to this awful, dreadful ending. The '60s were about naivety, optimism, and youth that's slowly ground down by the establishment and finally becomes self-destructive.

Q: What about the influence of the film *Performance* on your movie?

A: You think you can be in there, around someone like Brian Jones, and still be yourself, but you're gonna get dragged in. The sexual fascination by these guys. And that's what the James Fox character does in *Performance*. What was also interesting about *Performance*, from the research—and I'm sure you know this—in Marianne Faithfull's book, she talks about how Mick turned down *Performance* because it was written by their friend, Donald Cammell. And Mick read it—Donald was very clever, he got Marianne to read it first. And Mick read it and said, "This isn't me. I can't play this." And Marianne said, "Of course it's not you. It's Brian. Play Brian." So what Mick is doing in *Performance* is playing Brian. So I wanted to take that central kind of bisexual character that Mick is playing, and that was my kind of influence for the film. But what was also influential for me was that I screened *Performance* for my cast and crew the week before we started shooting.

Q: You've become an educator in a sense with some of the movies you've distributed and produced, and more recently your films like *Scandal* and *Stoned* are also being viewed a lot more by people under age forty.

A: Thank you. I think you have to tell the real story. No one told the real story of Profumo and Stephen Ward. Up until *Scandal* was made, Stephen Ward was thought of as one of the nastiest people in Britain. And Christine Keeler was supposedly one of the most evil women. And I wanted to say, "No, that actually isn't the case." The same with this. I wanted to tell the story of Brian Jones that the Rolling Stones have somehow forgotten about. He seems to have fallen below the surface somehow.

▓

Stephen Woolley: Select Filmography
How to Lose Friends & Alienate People (2006) (announced)
Stoned (2005) (producer, director)
Breakfast on Pluto (2005) (producer)
Intermission (2003) (producer)
The Good Thief (2002) (producer)
The End of the Affair (1999) (producer)
Little Voice (1998) (executive producer)
The Butcher Boy (1997) (producer)
Michael Collins (1996) (producer)
Interview with the Vampire: The Vampire Chronicles (1994) (producer)
Backbeat (1994) (producer)
The Crying Game (1992) (producer)

Dust Devil (1992) (executive producer)
Shag (1989) (producer) — aka *Shag: The Movie*
Scandal (1989) (producer)
Mona Lisa (1986) (producer)
Absolute Beginners (1986) (producer)
Letter to Brezhnev (1985) (executive producer)
The Company of Wolves (1984) (executive producer, producer)
The Worst of Hollywood (1983) TV series (producer)

CURTIS HANSON AND JAMES ELLROY

THE MOVIE, *L.A. Confidential* garnered five Academy Award nominations, including Best Picture, Best Director, and Best Screenplay. The hit film, directed and cowritten by Curtis Hanson (with Brian Helgeland), based on the book by James Ellroy, received rave reviews around the country. Helgeland and Hanson shared the Oscar in 1997 for Best Adapted Screenplay, and under Hanson's direction, Kim Basinger won a Best Supporting Actress Academy Award for her role in the film.

In conjunction with the movie, Restless Records issued a '50s jazz-driven soundtrack selected by Hanson himself as executive producer, with songs from Johnny Mercer, Chet Baker, Gerry Mulligan, Betty Hutton, Dean Martin, Jackie Gleason, and Jerry Goldsmith, who composed the film's theme.

Hanson, best known for his box office hits, *The Hand that Rocks the Cradle*, *The River Wild*, and *Bad Influence*, was born in Reno, Nevada, and raised in the Los Angeles area. He eventually covered music and arts for the Cal State Los Angeles college newspaper. A lifelong film aficionado, Hanson emerged from the pages of *Cinema* magazine, and over the last few decades collaborated with Sam Fuller and Roger Corman, and wrote the screenplay for the 1978 thriller *The Silent Partner*.

In 1999 Hanson became the first chairman of the UCLA Film and Television Archive.

After this interview was conducted, Hanson then directed *Wonder Boys*, where Bob Dylan won an Oscar for his "Things Have Changed" song, and *8 Mile*, the film debut of Eminem, who also garnered an Oscar for his "Lose Yourself" composition.

Los Angeles-born Ellroy is a graduate of Fairfax High School. His L.A. Quartet novels, *The Black Dahlia*, *The Big Nowhere*, *L.A. Confidential*, and *White Jazz*, were worldwide best sellers. Ellroy's novel *American Tabloid* was *Time* magazine's "Best Book of 1995 (Fiction)," and his memoir, *Dark Places*, was a *Time* "Best Book of the Year."

I interviewed Hanson and Ellroy in a phone conference when the *L.A. Confidential* film was first released in 1997, with the focus on the music and the soundtrack album.

Ellroy was living in Kansas City when we talked, but has subsequently relocated to Carmel, California. However, I'm sure his favorite restaurant still remains the Pacific Dining Car on West Sixth Street in downtown L.A.

During the time of our conversation, Ellroy had already appeared in the Los Angeles documentary film, *Shotgun Freeway*, and in this current decade was the subject himself of his own documentary, *Feast of Death*.

Both Hanson and Ellroy worship classic film noir from the '40s and '50s. Hanson and Ellroy did some select joint appearances at bookstores and film-related screenings promoting the movie, the soundtrack, and the new Warner Books edition of the novel. Hanson has remarked that he was thinking about the music a lot while he wrote the script, and it shows. The movie's musical backdrop fits seamlessly with its rat-a-tat-tat narrative, reflecting an L.A. of the '50s that was both a lot more innocent and a lot more corrupt than it is now. Or was it?

Composer Jerry Goldsmith was on the beat for this screen music gig, and his score work along with the song selections on *L.A. Confidential* brings to mind neo-noir *Chinatown* hues and cues in this retro but still topical package, including some pieces handpicked from the vaults of the Liberty, World Pacific, and Capitol Records labels.

Q: What kind of music in movies are you into, and how did some of your selections end up in *L.A. Confidential*?

A: Curtis Hanson: I look on the music and song selection as part of telling the story. Not just to set the period or the mood of a given scene, but to actually help delineate the themes, move the story along, and shed light on the arcs of the various specific characters.

I first found a Lee Wiley album at a Salvation Army thrift shop about twenty years ago, on Liberty Records. She was the first to record the so-called songbook approach to composers. I stumbled upon one of those and heard her voice and went, "Wow! Who is this?" Then I made it my business to keep looking in used record stores until I put a little bit of a collection of her work together. Not with the idea of ever using it, but simply as a music fan. I wouldn't call myself a music collector, but I have a lot of records. Along with using the music in the way I described, I also, obviously, wanted to fill in a tapestry of music that was heard in Los Angeles at that time. By using songs from that immediate period as well as songs from earlier times that one might have heard on a radio jukebox, I also wanted to capture the birth of what is known as Pacific Jazz, or the Pacific sound.

I had picked most of the primary songs before we started shooting, which was good for a couple of reasons. One, I knew that I was creating this musical tapestry and two, I was then able to play some of the songs on the set while we were actually shooting, so the actors could hear the mood that we were ultimately going for.

As often as possible, I used songs that were recorded in or around Los Angeles at that time. Even old standards like Gershwin's "But Not for Me," which was recorded by Jackie Gleason on his first album, *Music for Lovers Only*, in 1953 in Hollywood, literally blocks from where Lynn Bracken's (Kim Basinger's) house was, where you first hear the song.

Putting together the music for this film was so much easier than it had ever been before. I've always cared greatly about the music, and I've always had a battle about it. On this one, I was able to do what I wanted. It meant shouldering a different business responsibility, but it was easier than being creatively frustrated.

The songs helped tell the story, and I wanted the underscoring to help with the emotions and the action. I'd worked with Jerry Goldsmith on *The River Wild*, and he's a fabulous composer. He was my first choice. I screened the film for him with the songs so he would know what he was going to be working with. Jerry loved the use of Harold Arlen and Johnny Mercer's "Ac-Cent-Tchu-Ate the Positive" as the main theme.

A: James Ellroy: I'm much more localized in my interests than Curtis. I love crime movies with a passion, and an occasional documentary. I also love film noir. It's a big fixation of mine and a field of study for me. As far as music goes, I like classical music. I listen to it almost exclusively, mostly the German and Russian romantic composers.

The soundtrack to *L.A. Confidential* doesn't tell you what to think. It allows you to think for yourself. The music rarely intrudes on the dialogue. It's generally not specific to 1952–1953 Los Angeles, with a few exceptions. The two Lee Wiley tunes are standards from previous decades, and the Chet Baker and Gerry Mulligan tunes are reworked in period jazz arrangements. Curtis pulls out all the stops with Kay Starr's "Wheel of Fortune." I may have heard that song two or three times in my life, prior to seeing the film the first time. The way they play it in the montage—after some very dark events transpire—is startling. The Starr song might well become a hit again as a result of the film.

Q: What is your initial reaction to seeing the film adaptation of your book, *L.A. Confidential*?

A: Ellroy: More than anything else, I was simply startled with it. It was a schizophrenic kind of feeling. Here were characters, situations, and an overall milieu that I had created, now brilliantly transposed to a visual form. Here are my characters, embodied by the actors to such an extent that when I read passages from the book to myself, I see their faces saying the words. It was an amazing experience to see this compatible visual form on the screen. And, as I've said a dozen times before, I think the film is both a salutary adaptation of my book, and a wonderful work of art in its own right. On subsequent viewings, it's easy to surrender to its spell. I see new things each time I watch it.

People will tell you my books are visual, and there may be an element of truth to that, but it's all subjectively visual. People bring their own visuals to the books as they read them. Now there is a definitive visual of *L.A. Confidential*.

Q: I've heard that you felt *L.A. Confidential* would be the last of your books to be made into a movie?

A: Ellroy: For one thing, it covers eight entire years and plays out in an almost completely vanished Los Angeles. There are at least eight fully fleshed-out plot lines and over a hundred characters. It's a very difficult adaptation. The first book in my L.A. Quartet, *The Black Dahlia*, would have been a much easier book to do. I thought if any of my books got made into a film, that would be it.

Q: Can you both discuss the multiple character construction and points of view of *L.A. Confidential*?

A: Ellroy: I like movies that let you think for yourself. You have characters playing out their different destinies. It's as if both the book and the film represent horizontal grafts of plot and a vertical graft of character development that almost, because it's so dense, turns into a grid work. What one character doesn't know, the other one does. It keeps people guessing. Part of the miracle of Hanson and Helgeland's adaptation of my book is that they trim plot lines, move characters to the foreground and the background, stress only the most dramatically viable plot lines for the compressed time frame and—this is the key—retain my three-man style.

A: Hanson: As a moviemaker, the opportunity to tell a story with multiple points of view was part of the attraction. What really knocked me out about Ellroy's book was the fact that each of these characters was presented in a complex, fully rounded way, and that each of them prompted in me a correspondingly complex emotional reaction which changed as the story unfolded.

Clarity is something that I place a lot of stake in. We were dealing with a very densely plotted, complex novel. And even though we whittled it down, it ends up being a rather dense narrative. I think audiences like to be engaged, and they like to think, but at the same time, they also like to be rewarded so that when they do apply themselves, it makes sense.

Q: What was your reaction when you first read *L.A. Confidential*?

A: Hanson: I read the book for pleasure. I had read half a dozen of his books prior to that, not looking for movie projects, but because I like to read, and Ellroy is a unique voice in contemporary fiction. When I read *L.A. Confidential* I was knocked out by the characters. And the more I thought about them, the more I thought, "I've got to try to make a movie out of this."

Q: I understand you showed the cast and crew some of your favorite films noirs before shooting began?

A: Hanson: That acted as a bonding process, because it gave us something we could all do and enjoy together, then everyone could talk about it. It allowed the casting director to see what the faces and body types of that period were like, because they're quite different than today. It allowed the actors, Russell Crowe and Guy Pierce, both from Australia, as you know, to hear the language and the rhythms, but I certainly didn't want them to imitate any performances they were seeing. It also showed my collaborators in the art department and my cinematographer the apparently casual way in which street scenes were shot at that time. That was very much the way I wanted to approach our movie. To shoot it as though it were contemporary.

Some of my favorite films noirs which we showed include Robert Aldrich's *Kiss Me Deadly*, Don Siegel's *Private Hell*, *Invasion of the Body Snatchers*, and *The Lineup*. His lean, efficient style always impressed me tremendously; the way he was able to tell stories personally, no matter what the circumstances under which he was working. Sam Fuller's *Crimson Kimono*, *Underworld U.S.A.* and *China Gate*. Vincente Minnelli's *The Bad and the Beautiful* and *Some Came Running*. Nicholas Ray's *In a Lonely Place*.

A: Ellroy: Some of my favorites are Robert Wise's film, *Odds Against Tomorrow*, and Joseph Losey's *The Prowler*, a gem which is unavailable on video in the States. I saw it on TV in France.

Q: After seeing *L.A. Confidential*, I know both you guys were hit hard by episodic black-and-white television of the late '50s and early '60s, like *Naked City* and *The Fugitive*, made out of Hollywood.

A: Hanson: Absolutely. All of those. *M Squad* and *Dragnet*, which I later thought was very bizarre and peculiar. *Perry Mason* too.

A: Ellroy: I was very impressed with the original TV show, *The Fugitive*, which made big impressions on me. It debuted a few months before the Kennedy assassination. I was about fifteen years old then and I watched it religiously. The show, at least the first season, holds up pretty well today. Power figures are all corrupted and there's an undertone of sexual longing throughout it. The women in it are fuckin' astonishing. Wherever the fugitive would go, the grooviest girl in the town would seize upon him. Susan Oliver, Suzanne Pleshette, Madeline Rhue, Patricia Crowley. A young actress at the time named June Harding. The women were tremendous. A true level of longing. The women all reacted to Richard Kimble with a good deal of weariness and hunger. And boy, for a fifteen-year-old kid, it was powerful stuff.

A: Hanson: I loved *Naked City*. And, as you know, Jerry Goldsmith scored

Lineup, the TV series. There were great female parts with those great actresses you just named. Most of them were on *Route 66.*

A: Ellroy: I watched *Route 66* and fell in love with Corvettes—a love affair that lasts to this day!

※

Curtis Hanson: Select Filmography

DIRECTOR:

In Her Shoes
8 Mile
Greg the Bunny (TV series)
Wonder Boys
L.A. Confidential
The River Wild
The Hand That Rocks the Cradle
Bad Influence
The Bedroom Window
The Children of Times Square (TV)
Losin' It
The Little Dragons
Sweet Kill

PRODUCER:

In Her Shoes
8 Mile
Wonder Boys
L.A. Confidential
The Little Dragons (executive producer)
The Silent Partner
Sweet Kill

WRITER:

L.A. Confidential (screenplay); Academy Award winner for Best Adapted Screenplay, 1998
The Bedroom Window
The Children of Times Square (TV)
White Dog
The Silent Partner
Sweet Kill
The Dunwich Horror

In 1999, Hanson became the first chairman of the UCLA Film and Television Archive.

Since 2001 he has been a member of the Board of Governors of the Academy of Motion Picture Arts and Sciences (Directors Branch).

James Ellroy: Select Bibliography & Filmography

WRITER:

Dark Blue (story)

Stay Clean (novel: Killer on the Road)

L.A. Sheriff's Homicide (TV)

Brown's Requiem (novel: Brown's Requiem)

L.A. Confidential (novel: L.A. Confidential)

Fallen Angels TV series (story) (episode "Since I Don't Have You")

Cop (novel: Blood on the Moon)

James Ellroy's L.A. Quartet novels include:

The Black Dahlia

The Big Nowhere

L.A. Confidential

White Jazz

Ellroy's most recent book is *The Cold Six Thousand.*

He also appeared as himself in the 1995 Southern California documentary film, *Shotgun Freeway: Drives Through Lost L.A.* and is the subject of his own documentary, *Feast of Death.*

PART FIVE
A VIEW FROM THE AISLE

Kirk Silsbee (left) with Lionel Hampton in the studio at A&M Records, Hollywood, California, December 1994. Photo by Steve Appleford.

KIRK SILSBEE

KIRK SILSBEE AND I went to different schools together. He grew up in Inglewood, California, a mile away from Brian Wilson. He's been writing about jazz for close to thirty years, for *Downbeat*, *Jazziz*, *L.A. Reader*, and *L.A. CityBeat*.

Like me, Kirk grew up listening to radio stations KRLA, KFWB, and KBLA, with some side damage from KGFJ, XERB, and KPPC along the way.

I was talking to rhythm 'n' blues pioneer Charles Brown one night with Kirk at the Hollywood Cinegrill. Charles asked him, "How do you know so much about this music?" I said, "Why do you think I use him so much?" Charles put the capper on it: "Ain't he tough? Ain't he tough?"

Q: From *Pet Sounds*, the songs "Caroline No," "Wouldn't It Be Nice," and "God Only Knows" have shown up in movies. Is *Pet Sounds* a movie to you?

A: Well, it's a soundtrack to a movie that has yet to be made. "Theme for an Imaginary Western," as it were. *Pet Sounds* is a programmatic album and it's a conceptual statement. Having said that, I never bought "Sloop John B" as part of the album; it always sounded to me like a foreign element or something added as an afterthought. As far as the audio texture and the thematic content of that song, it doesn't work with the rest of the album. And it's a pop song adaptation of a Carl Sandburg poem; not exactly a Brian Wilson wig bubble. So when I dubbed *Pet Sounds* onto cassette for one of my car tapes, I dropped "She Knows Me Too Well" from *The Beach Boys Today* in the place of "Sloop John B." With that small adjustment, *Pet Sounds* makes a lot more audio and conceptual sense to me, but that's just my personal taste.

Q: I've noticed a recurring rotation of a half dozen songs that we all own, that show up in movies. This is the Hollywood shack job. For example, Jefferson Airplane's "Today" and "Comin' Back to Me" from *Surrealistic Pillow* are now in the Platinum Club of being in three different movies. It used to be "Today" was in movies, now it's "Comin' Back to Me." Are those songs just inherently atmospheric copyrights and you're not surprised at all by the longevity of the tunes?

A: Here's what I think is interesting. Even though *Pillow* wasn't a debut album, it was essentially a debut album. Its antecedent, *Jefferson Airplane Takes Off*, got virtually no airplay and not many people knew what was on it. As a debut album, *Pillow* was one of the best of its time. In the summer of '67, it was competing with the first Doors album, another brilliant first statement, and *Sgt. Pepper*, maybe the Beatles' best album. *Pillow* held its mud quite well in the same arena as those two albums, both as music and in sales. All three of those albums are sequenced beautifully and work with a variety of moods and textures throughout. So if filmmakers are getting around to using that music in their movies, it shouldn't be a surprise to anyone.

It's no surprise to me or you that the Doors' music gets continually used and recycled in movies, thereby reaching ever-younger audiences.

Q: Why?

A: Because, as Ray Manzarek says, it was conceived cinematically. Ray and Jim Morrison thought not only in terms of songs and music but also in terms of film and theater. The music was one thing; Morrison's lyrics were probably the most literate and cutting edge for pop music in that era. It's a fascinating combination that made for built-in longevity.

Q: Do you think the Stones have some of that? "Jumpin' Jack Flash" is in *Mean Streets*, and "Gimme Shelter" shows up on-screen as well.

A: I wish the people who pick the music for these movies would get more creative when it comes to the Stones and dig deeper.

Q: Well, the *Rushmore* soundtrack has "I Am Waiting" from *Aftermath*. You want more of that, don't you?

A: I want more of that and I want it deeper. In the right film at the right moment, something like "Miss Amanda Jones" or "Out of Time" could be very pungent.

Q: This is a stretch, but I can justify it. Charlie Watts, because his meatballs are jazz people—including people like Chico Hamilton—does his drumming just lend itself to pictures?

A: I don't know about that, but I do know that because his orientation was jazz, he was able to come up with more inventive figures than the average rock drummer did. Look at the Beatles; look at how limited Ringo Starr was, how monochromatic his playing was. Look at Charlie and how creative he was. The sounds he got out of his trap set and what he was able to play was exceptional for rock drummers. So many of the Stones' records are drum-driven. Not just the flag-wavers like "Paint It Black," "Street Fighting Man," and "19th Nervous Breakdown," but subtle things like "Ruby Tuesday" and "Under My Thumb." He had a wide palette of expression and his cymbals had a lot of variety. They sounded like he was playing on trash can lids on "Parachute Woman" and they splashed on "Mother's Little Helper" and his hi-hat was sharp as a knife on "My Obsession." They mixed his drums to the audio foreground on *Who's Driving Your Plane?* and Charlie held the whole ensemble together with his playing. Remove him and the whole thing would've fallen apart.

Q: Here's a rock 'n' roll situation. Arthur Lee and Love: Arthur's getting bones now in movies. "Emotions" is in *Medium Cool*, now out on DVD. *High Fidelity* has a song from *Four Sail*. "Signed D.C." was used in a show on both HBO and PBS called *Dear America: Letters Home from Vietnam*.

People are discovering Arthur Lee. Possibly because Bryan MacLean was right out of Lerner and Lowe show tunes: "Softly to Me." Hello! There's Lerner and Lowe in there. That's not even to say, "Let's go to the Pix Theatre, look at *What's New, Pussycat?* and afterward record a cover of 'Little Red Book.'" Arthur's jones started on the screen! Are you dazzled by the longevity of Love's catalogue?

A: I look at Love and I consider the cinematic quality of that music, especially what's on *Da Capo* and *Forever Changes*. I look at the film industry and think, "You're all asleep on the music of this band." Why haven't they been using this stuff for the past thirty-five years? Like the Doors, Love's music is so layered and dimensional. You told me that "Stephanie Knows Who" was used in a work print for one of Hal Jepson's surf films. I'd love to see that. Maybe the reason that these things haven't been used in movies more often is that they're little audio movies themselves, rather than just audio wallpaper.

Q: Is the whole *Forever Changes* album just one big movie in your head?

A: Sure it is, because, again, it's a concept album. It's so well programmed and executed that one song just moves beautifully into the next. Each song tells a story and has vivid imagery.

Q: The dawn of the popular soundtrack broke open with *Easy Rider*, which preceded *American Graffiti*. How about the *Easy Rider* soundtrack?

A: I thought "Ballad of Easy Rider" was a good "runnin' down the road" song for the way it was used. As for the soundtrack, I just thought it was a pastiche of songs. As a soundtrack, as a unified statement, I didn't see it as any great landmark.

Q: Let's be realistic. Leiber and Stoller, whether it be walking through the front door doing Elvis songs, or then being the architects behind that humongous copyright, "Stand by Me," there's been a lot of their tunes in movies.

A: You know, the Elvis tunes are just drop-ins in those otherwise stupid movies. Ian Whitcomb has said that the post-Leiber and Stoller Elvis movies like *Tickle Me* or *Wild in the Country* are not movies that hold up as cinema. Rather, you'd do better looking at them as early, extended MTV videos. That's the only way you can sit through those stupid movies.

Q: How about our friends Bacharach and David in the movies, whether it be writing "The Man Who Shot Liberty Valance" or "Theme to *Valley of the Dolls*"?

A: "Liberty Valance" was written after the movie was released. The movie was doing so well, somebody said, "Hey, we need a popular song outta this." "Little Red Book" by Manfred Mann, from *What's New, Pussycat?* is a good use of a pop song in a movie. It's used under the titles and again during a strip club sequence where Woody Allen and Peter O'Toole are hanging out at night, watching these girls dance. Love took that tune, made an adjustment in the rhythm, gave the beat more testosterone and made the tune a rock tune, rather than a quasi-jazz pop tune.

Q: Getting back to jazz, Peggy Lee wrote songs for and sang in and even had a speaking part in *Lady and the Tramp*. Talk a little bit about jazz and animation.

A: Well, the older Disney animated features are great for your kids, because they were full of great people. Roger Miller wrote songs for *Robin Hood* and sang them in the movie. Phil Harris had a part in it. What a great character he was: a Jew from the South with a Southern soul. Phil and Louis Prima were in *Jungle Book* and their songs in that movie are delightful. As a parent, those films provided me with some "teaching moments." Later on I could point to a movie or a record and say, "Remember King Louie in *Jungle Book*? Well that's him in real life." Those Disney films were always well-cast and sometimes the songs were good. You can raise your kids on worse things than Peggy Lee and Phil Harris.

Q: What are some of the other animated movies that use interesting music?

A: Well, the Tex Avery cartoons of the late '40s for MGM are just such masterpieces of surrealism and mayhem. Brilliant gags, fake-outs, resolving scenes in unexpected ways, and characterizations. Long before Jessica Rabbit, those cartoons had the hottest female merchandise ever in American mainstream cartoons. The music in those things is big band jazz fragments, usually snippets and film cues rather than songs, because everything moved so fast. Definitely the Carl Stalling aesthetic that John Zorn picked up on and applied to the downtown New York music scene of the '70s and '80s.

There's a whole body of films made by a husband-and-wife team, Faith and John Hubley. They made art films that were wonderful because they utilized very hip design, mixed media figures and backgrounds that reflected a knowledge of Miró and Kleé and modern art, and they commissioned jazz musicians to provide the soundtracks. Their films were lyrical and poetic and they used Benny Carter, Dizzy Gillespie, and Quincy Jones. These movies were a gas to look at and they always had provocative themes. One of the films was a dialogue between two figures about the perils of nuclear war. The more rational and humanistic voice was Dizzy. The Hubleys worked in the commercial film industry, but they did whatever it took to produce one personal independent film a year.

These movies had a parallel in the films of Charles and Ray Eames, the design team. Their stuff was all live action and often had jazz scores. They'd film the hosing down of a blacktop with soapy water or a bunch of tops spinning in a creative way with instrumental music. Buddy Collette did one with Joe Pass where Buddy wrote out sixteen bars and they just jammed a soundtrack out of it.

Q: These were in general release?

A: I saw them in art school. I don't think they were ever in general release. Then you had the U.P.A. cartoons like *Gerald McBoing-Boing* and *The Three Little Bops*, for Warner Bros., where the soundtracks were West Coast Jazz, written by Shorty Rogers. These were smart cartoons. They may have been for kids but they never dumbed down for kids. The content set the bar high and the movies asked kids to rise to that level. Same thing that *Rocky and Bullwinkle* did later.

Q: Benny Carter did some film music.

A: Yeah, he did a lot of it. He came to L.A. in '42, specifically to write music for movies. Initially he ghosted a lot of film music because black composers weren't given official screen credit for major motion pictures until sometime in the '50s. We'll never know all that Benny really wrote—just as we'll never know all that Phil Moore really wrote—because the nature of ghosting is that you get the work, you're well-paid, but someone else puts their name on it at the end of the day. Benny got an onscreen appearance in '51 in *An American in Paris*, where he led a small band on-screen. Gerald Wilson is in the band. What's remarkable is that Benny and the guys got to play their own music on the soundtrack, rather than white studio players, which was the norm. Dexter Gordon had a part in a '55 movie called *Unchained*, where he played the saxophone but it was ghosted by a studio player! It wasn't until Dexter went to Europe as an expatriate in the '60s that he was actually filmed playing his own music. It was crazy! But Benny wrote for a lot of TV, like *The Alfred Hitchcock Hour* and *Ironside*, and movies like *Too Late Blues* for John Cassavetes.

Q: It's interesting that even on the soundtracks, whether it's *Chicago* or *In the Heat of the Night*, there's always some jazz cats lurking.

A: Sure. In the '50s, when Hollywood started using jazz scores for movies, that meant admitting jazz composers like Gerry Mulligan and Shorty Rogers to the soundtrack studio party, and it meant admitting their jazz-playing buddies. These guys wrote jazz scores and the work demanded that jazz musicians play it: people who could read anything, execute anything, and who could improvise a solo. That was something that Hollywood couldn't get out of an old school studio player who was raised on nothing but classical music.

Ten, twenty years later, when composers like Johnny Mandel, Quincy Jones, J. J. Johnson, and Oliver Nelson were composing and scoring and conducting their soundtracks, they not only wrote but they trusted their musicians to bring something to the table that could be spontaneously added to the music.

Today, it's an entirely different situation. There are very few people writing music for movies who can write for the entire orchestra. John Williams is the standard-bearer in that respect. Soundtracks rely on a lot of synthesizers to approximate the orchestra or specific instruments. There's even one well-known film composer who doesn't read music. He's got somebody to write out his charts for him and do who-knows-how-much ghost writing. I've heard from people who play on his sessions that he walks around the studio lecturing the musicians about how the music's supposed to sound and what musicians they should be trying to imitate. He'll pontificate on Duke Ellington's jungle band to a group of people who can play the entire history of jazz on their instruments. But they don't say anything; they just do their work and do their best to make this little martinet a star.

It's a shame that movie soundtracks these days don't use very much composition, because L.A. has a cadre of tremendous musicians. They come here from all over the world, and they come out of the local colleges and music schools to get work in the studios. Unfortunately, the Golden Age of the L.A. recording studio is about twenty years over. Up into the early '80s, the most valued studio musicians often played on two and three sessions a day. People flew into L.A. to make records here, because they knew that the L.A. studio players would do whatever it took to make their records special. [Pianist] Mike Melvoin told me that he made albums for people who had vowed to never record in New York again. In the New York studios, if an artist asked for something special, maybe some creative input or something spontaneous, the musicians would just stare at them, or maybe flip them off. If it wasn't written in the score, you couldn't expect any extra help.

My friend Don Specht had a very lucrative career from the late '50s to the early '80s, writing for commercials and films. He used jazz players like Shelly Manne, Buddy Collette, Joe Maini, Lou Levy, and he used the best string players too. He's a fine composer who can write for the entire orchestra, including strings, which he understands extremely well. The only work he gets is a very occasional call to ghostwrite something that will save somebody's ass. He'll get a four o'clock call in the afternoon and at nine the next morning he'll have an orchestral piece all ready to be played that he conducts. It's good money but you'll never see his name onscreen. A contractor told him the other day, "Don, you're an anomaly. Nobody uses those instruments anymore in movies."

§

Kirk Silsbee has been writing professionally for thirty years. His work can currently be seen in *Downbeat, Jazziz, L.A. CityBeat, Pasadena Weekly*, and *Senior Life USA*. His primary focus is jazz, especially as it relates to Southern California. A noted jazz historian, his many liner note essays include the box set, *The Complete Pacific Jazz Joe Pass Quartet Sessions* on Mosaic. He has also interviewed subjects for the Grammy Foundation's videotaped oral history archives.

He contributed historic material and written interludes to David Leaf's script for the Verve 50th Anniversary television special. He was executive director for Don McGlynn's documentary, *The Legend of Teddy Edwards*, and contributed on-camera spoken testimony. He can also be seen in Ken Koenig's historical film, *Jazz on The West Coast: The Lighthouse*. Silsbee's cultural awareness stems largely from the Imperial Theatre and Lishon's Records, both a stone's throw from each other in the Imperial Village section of Inglewood, California.

ROGER STEFFENS

Roger Steffens is the cofounder of *The Beat* magazine, North America's oldest and most prestigious reggae and world beat publication, whose annual Bob Marley Collectors' Edition he edits. A former national promotions director of Island Records for reggae and African music, Steffens has been the chairman of the Reggae Grammy Committee since its inception in 1985.

He and Hank Holmes began the award-winning *Reggae Beat* radio show on the NPR outlet in L.A. in 1979, and Bob Marley was their first guest. Later the program was syndicated for four years to 130 stations worldwide.

Roger's reggae collection fills six rooms of his Los Angeles home, floor to ceiling, and is known as Roger Steffens' Reggae Archives, featured in 2001 for eight months in a public exhibition at the Queen Mary, in Long Beach, California. In May 2004, he completed negotiations for his materials to move to Kingston, Jamaica, to become the founding collection of the National Museum of Jamaican Music.

A profile on Roger and his vast archives served as the epilogue in my debut book, *This Is Rebel Music*.

Steffens lectures internationally on "The Life of Bob Marley," using unreleased film and video clips from his extensive archives.

Roger Steffens (left) and Jimmy Cliff at Cliff's home in Kingston, Jamaica,
June 1976. Photo by Mary Steffens, courtesy of Roger Steffens' Reggae Archives.

Performances have taken him to the Smithsonian in Washington, D.C.,
the Schomburg in New York City, the Rock and Roll Hall of Fame and
Museum in Cleveland (where he is the first and most frequent speaker),
the Experience Music Project in Seattle, and to universities and theaters in
Japan, Canada, Australia, France, Holland, England, Martinique, Puerto
Rico, and Jamaica.

He has written several books about Bob Marley, but it is as an actor that he makes his living, primarily doing voice-overs. He has narrated Oscar- and Emmy-winning films, and has been heard in *Forrest Gump*, *Wag the Dog*, and *The American President*, among hundreds of others. He is also himself the subject of a 2005 documentary film called *Livicated*, directed by Erik Crown, and produced by Paul Madelenat. He is married and has two grown children.

Q: I keep returning to the movie, *The Harder They Come*, which starred Jimmy Cliff. It's universally recognized as the most important film ever released in the Caribbean. Who was Jimmy Cliff back in 1972 when the film came out?

A: Well, Jimmy had been one of the earliest people in Jamaica to record Ska music at the dawn of the '60s. He found limited financial success however, and spent a lot of time in places like Brazil, where he wrote "Many Rivers to Cross," and in England. The film's director, Perry Henzell, saw an album cover which had a humble, friendly-looking image of Jimmy on one side and a rather hardened picture on the other, which made him think that he could easily portray the dual sides of the lead character in the film.

Q: What was the initial reaction when the film opened in Kingston?

A: The minute the bus lurches around the bend in the jungle road, almost tipping over on its side as Jimmy Cliff implores, "You Can Get It (If You Really Want)," Perry told me he knew he had the audience. I did an interview with him several years ago for *L.A. Reggae*, my local cable TV show, and he said, "The night we opened in Kingston, 40,000 people surrounded the theater, which was just a 1,500 seat theater, the Carib. And they all go 'round the theater. There was a metal fence, a fifteen-foot metal fence, around the theater and the next day when I went there, it was flat on the ground. The doors were broken down and it was like an assault on the theater.

When the theater was full to overflowing, we rolled the film. When the crowd saw the opening titles they were kind of waiting, and when they saw the bus turn nearly on its side, it's like this scream went up in the theater, like they realized they were safe. You know, an audience wants to feel safe, an audience wants to feel that they can let them- selves relax."

Relax audiences certainly did, sometimes to the point of commu- nal herbal saturation. *The Harder They Come* became the fulcrum on which the twin necessities of political passion and carnal satisfaction

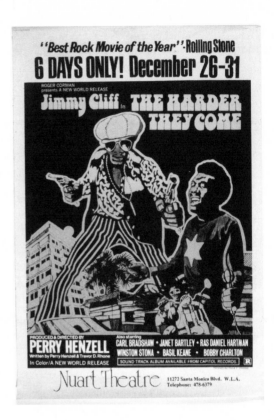

The Harder They Come movie poster, Nuart Theatre, Westwood, California, 1972. Courtesy of Roger Steffens' Reggae Archives.

found a most willing international audience, thereby revealing to the world the hidden wealth of Jamaican culture, music, and religion, all to a beat that was actually, physically, irresistible. Inspired by British and South American avant-garde work, Perry set out to make a film about "this guy [who] has this dream and he's come to town with his dream and he'd rather die than give up the dream."

That's really what it is about. The message that reaches the country boy is so strong that, when he comes to town and finds the reality is different than the dream, he'd rather die than give up the dream. I think "pie in the sky" was like the key phrase in that. Jimmy wrote the song and recorded the title song.

Not since the scintillating, fervid midnight hallucinations of *Black Orpheus*, a decade earlier, had a foreign film touched so many people in America. Not just film aficionados but, slapped silly by vapid disco and gutless rock rants as the '60s slid into the ignominious '70s, music fans also—people who were looking for something new and vital to reignite their passions in a Nixon-ized era of ennui.

Q: You were twelve in 1954, the year we think of as the birth of rock 'n' roll. Was there a similarity between those early rock movies and *The Harder They Come*?

A: As a child also of the '50s, I was one of those eager young teens who filled the suburban New Jersey movie theater in 1954 for a "j.d. pic"— juvenile delinquents in *Blackboard Jungle*. We really didn't care about the lurid film, since it was the opening music that we had all come to experience in a way utterly impossible in all but that darkened flick palace. "One, two, three o'clock, four o'clock rock . . ." the screen blared, ebullient sound pushed to peak volume through those huge old theatrical speakers. The seats rattled, we sang along and looked at each other, eyes agape, as if we were witnessing an actual birth.

This was something new called "rock 'n' roll," and it really pissed off our parents and made us feel like dancing real fast, petticoats swirling as we twirled our gals in whirling abandon in the C.Y.O. church basement, a mad, glad rebellion of duck's ass D.A.s and tight jeans, and smokin' cigarettes under the River Road bridge, talkin' 'bout the great new Chuck Berry single that Alan Freed had played last night on his *Rock 'n' Roll Dance Party* radio show on WINS in New York City, just over the Hudson from our safe Jersey outposts.

When we heard "Rock Around the Clock" in that movie house, it was the equivalent of an atom bomb going off in our ears; to this day it still arouses me, a full fifty years on. Surely Bill Haley and the Comets will fly forward forever on the wings of that one song alone.

In 1970, I was a Vietnam vet of twenty-six months in-country, who had returned to "the world" to find the music business taken over by lawyers and accountants, and the political edge of the best of the previous, peerless decade's work neutered. So when I saw *The Harder They Come*, it was the first time I had had that kind of feeling in twenty years.

Sitting in the narrow confines of the tiny Northside Theater in Berkeley, summer of '73, where the film had been showing for months, I was overwhelmed. The sound was like a magic incantation, the rhythm, or *riddim* as the locals pronounced it, unlike anything I'd ever heard, loping, languid yet insistent, almost preternatural. Later I found out it was not mystical at all, but downright obvious—reggae's *riddim* is the beat of the healthy human heart at rest.

This is its deepest and most evident secret. Even if you don't understand the patois language of its heaviest adherents, you can't help but be moved by its beat. This film was the prow of the icebreaker of Jah Music, clearing the way for the more commercially malleable Bob Marley and others to rush through.

Q: The movie also incorporated some grainy footage, which somehow added to the impact.

A: Oh, yeah, absolutely. Grainy footage, jerky camera moves, and a hunch that much was improvised, all contributed to a cinema verité feel. Henzell says, "I wanted to make the smallest possible film with the most scope, to be experimental, because I felt that my contribution to film was that business of combining the spontaneous moment with the written moment so that you couldn't tell the difference. As I kept filming, I started to improvise more and more and I felt that I wanted to take it to the next stage in the next picture and build on [a film like] *The Battle of Algiers*. I figured that Pontecorvo, maybe Ken Loach, I figured that maybe two or three directors in the world were really on my wavelength."

Also, *The Harder They Come* was the first English-language film with subtitles. Indeed, patois can be well nigh impenetrable for the outsider—even for those who have been exposed to it for many years. So what does a novice listener make of something that sounds familiar but is jabberwocky, like Scotty urging, "forward and fiaca/menacle and den gosaca"? To this day I have yet to find anyone in Jamaica who can tell me what that means.

These were the first words on the soundtrack, metrical and maddening, and the few other words that one could decipher seemed to be about a girl leaving on a train, with little vocal asides to "express yourself brother," a combination of song and rap that had been filling the Jamaican airwaves for at least three years before the film was released. The style was called skanking or toasting by the wicked rudies on Beeston Street, a modern call and response that was the direct forerunner of rap and hip-hop in the States. This song could rightfully be called the first one to expose Americans to the form.

Q: So what was the film's story and how important was the role of music in it?

A: As Jimmy playing Ivan, a country boy come to the city to seek his fortune, visits his mother in shantytown to tell her that "grandma's dead," the mesmerizing "Rivers of Babylon" accompanies the scene of threadbare poverty and numb regret. Sung by the Melodians, it is a standard in the Rastafari hymnal, a plaint of dislocation and longing for return to Zion, heaven on earth. "If you know what life is worth, you will look for yours on earth . . . Almighty God is a living man," the prophet Bob Marley would sing not long after, in his anthem of human rights, "Get Up Stand Up."

It now begins to dawn on the viewer that the music is as much a part of the unfolding story as are the lines of dialogue. 'Cause here's Jimmy in an arcade, surrounded by the coolest of keen rudies, as Toots and the Maytals sing the haunting warning, "Pressure Drop," a throbbing pulsating prophecy: ". . . pressure drop/Oh yeh pressure will drop on you/I say when it drops you gonna feel it/Know that you were doing wrong."

A funereal organ opens "Many Rivers to Cross," which accompanies our hero on a fruitless search for work. He meekly approaches across a manicured lawn to the veranda of a wealthy woman, played by Beverly Anderson, wife of '70s Jamaican Prime Minister Michael Manley. She threatens him and shoos him off. Scenes follow of devastating impoverishment in the dungle's scrap heaps. "I've been licked, washed up for years/And I merely survive/Because of my pride," sings Jimmy in perfect synch.

In the choir of the church that eventually gives him shelter, he listens to discordant churchical chants, and catches the eyes of a young woman who is the preacher's pet, obviously being groomed for more than spiritual purposes by this lecherous wolf in clerical sheep's garments. Although "Johnny Too Bad" is heard briefly in a confrontational scene, this part of the movie has the sounds mainly of raucous revivalism, frenzied testifyin,' the glazed eyes of church merging into the opening eyes of passion, as Jimmy and his girl bicycle and romp naked in the sea.

Jimmy is still anxious to enter the music scene, and finds himself among the cool hipster hangers-on with their serious screwfacing, watching a Maytals recording session for "Sweet and Dandy." "It's a perfect pander," sings Toots, whatever that meant, "While they were dancing in that bar room last night." A sweaty, steamy tropical jam, continuing even after the tape went off.

And then comes Jimmy, working out the arrangement for "The Harder They Come" on a church organ, late at night, where he's caught by the preacher, who throws him and his girl out on the streets, but not before the law has been alerted, and Jimmy receives eight flesh-tearing wounds from a slave-master's whip. Eventually a producer named Mr. Hilton records the song, but tells the DJs he controls to play it just enough to make his money back, nothing more. Broke, with nowhere to turn, Jimmy is recruited for the ganja trade, obtains his first motorcycle, and "You Can Get It (If You Really Want)" is reprised, clouds gathering.

Q: The scene everyone seems to remember is the one with the ganja pipe.

A: (*laughs*) Oh, yeah, that's the scene that everyone waited for. Those in the know in the theater lit up prior to it, as the night turned black and the ganja-runners sat themselves in moonlit silhouette. Pshweeeeet!! The pull on the pipe was the signal for the whole audience to blaze away, "studio kinda cloudy," as dem a say. A massive herbiferous powwow, and we were all in the realm of what Michael Thomas called "Upper Niger Consciousness," just like the dreadies on the screen. A landmark moment in third world cinema, the one that indeed everyone remembers.

"Pressure Drop" appears again on the soundtrack as Jimmy chases a competing dealer through the concrete jungle and gully banks of Trench Town, shooting at his ankles and laughing madly as the crowds gather to cheer his bravado. The title track runs anew and we see graffiti on the walls taunting, "I was here but I disappear" and "I am everywhere."

He's now a folk hero, and an outlaw—after he kills three police. You must remember that the press release for the movie, and the album's liner notes, said that two of the main actors had died since the film was completed. This ain't Hollywood, and da ghetto ain't no set. The echoes of Orpheus abound.

Now the cops turn the screws and stop the ganja trade until the dealers turn Jimmy in. Hilton begins to push Jimmy's record aggressively, and it flies up the charts. In a show of fearlessness, the renegade singer steals a car in broad daylight in front of Kingston's biggest hotel, and drives it contemptuously, joyously across the adjacent parkland to a reprise of "You Can Get It (If You Really Want)."

When he poses for pictures as a flashy two-barreled gunman and they appear on the front page of the island's main newspaper, it becomes the final straw. Eventually, his woman tells the authorities that he is about to attempt an escape by sea to Cuba. In a final confrontation on tiny Lime Cay in Kingston Harbour, Jimmy, echoing the Clint Eastwood Italian spaghetti westerns in which "hero can't be dead till the last reel," is shot by a platoon of soldiers.

Q: It was based on real events, wasn't it?

A: The story is based on a real life anti-colonialist cop-killing folk hero of the late '40s named Ivanhoe Martin, called "Rhyging" or "raging" by the "thousands at the morgue" who paid tribute to him after he was shot and killed by the police. In an increasingly antiauthoritarian world, such a person could be seen as a standard-bearer for people everywhere around the globe who are in active rebellion against unjust and tyrannical "politrickal shitstems."

Q: The marketing was unique too.

A: Right. It took six years before the movie made its money back, through the Herculean efforts of Henzell himself who "four-walled" it in forty-two countries, subtitling it for local audiences as he made his way around the world renting theaters in some of the earth's remotest regions. Today, *The Harder They Come* is viewed as perhaps the most important Third World film ever made, and is a steady seller on DVD and videotape.

Q: It was rereleased in 2003, right?

A: Yes, in two different versions, one with a great accompanying track by Perry and Jimmy. The Island Records soundtrack album has never been out of print. I heard recently that the chief Tower buyer in their flagship store on Sunset Strip in Hollywood said he had never seen a soundtrack like that in his thirty some-odd years in the business. It has never stopped selling.

Chris Blackwell, Island's founder, visited my Reggae Archives a few weeks ago and told me that he was as proud of that record as anything he has ever done in his life. And he should be. It created an interest that led to a movement that was both political and spiritual, and that has become a universal vehicle for the downtrodden of the earth to gain a voice. It also led directly to Bob Marley's superstardom, although he declined to be in the picture. After the movie's release, Jimmy revealed himself to be a Muslim, not a Rasta, and put a more pop edge into his next couple of albums and lost the lead he had to others. Blackwell signed Marley and the Wailers, and the rest is history.

Q: *The Harder They Come* also set the stage for some other exciting and powerful reggae on film, like *Rockers*.

A: That's the natural successor to Henzell's film. It was released in 1980 by a Greek director who used to make commercials in Minneapolis, named Ted Bafaloukos. He shot some incredible scenes with some of the biggest names from the golden age of reggae for an often-humorous Robin Hood story.

It too has just been rereleased on a fine DVD. The very best Marley documentary came out a couple of years ago too, by an extraordinary music documentarian named Jeremy Marre. It's called *Soul Rebel* and it's the first film about Bob made outside the aegis of his family, so a lot of people who were never willing to speak publicly before about Bob finally came forward to tell their tales. Then there's *Stepping Razor: Red X*, about the music and murder of Bob's former partner in the Wailers, Peter Tosh, which incorporates Tosh's own recorded diary and recreated scenes of his final hour.

Marley's best concert film is *Live at the Rainbow, London, 1977*, which was chosen by the *New York Times* for inclusion in a time capsule they built to be opened in the year 3000, because it epitomizes the finest musical moments of the twentieth century. I think it's pretty incredible (if Bush hasn't killed us all off first) that people a thousand years from now will be dancing to the *riddims* of the humble dreadlock from Nine Mile, Jamaica.

※

Roger Steffens grooved to the early Alan Freed movies as a teenager growing up in the suburbs of New York City, before beginning his radio career on WVOX in Westchester County, New York, in 1961. He narrated documentary films for the South Vietnamese PolWar division during his twenty-six-month stint in the Army in Saigon, and continued that work in civilian life.

His credits include narrating the Academy Award-winning film, *The Flight of the Gossamer Condor*, and conarrating the Emmy winning film, *Dear America*. He is the voice of Haile Selassie, Marcus Garvey, and Peter Tosh in the classic reggae movie about the historic One Love Peace Concert in Kingston, Jamaica in 1978, *Heartland Reggae*. His voice-overs have been heard in *Wag the Dog, Forrest Gump, The American President*, and as the Loooove Jock in the teen fave *Can't Hardly Wait*.

Livicated a documentary about his life's work and Reggae Archives, is currently making the rounds of film festivals, as his archives are being prepared to become the founding collection of the National Museum of Jamaican Music. He continues to write for and edit the annual Bob Marley Collectors Edition of *The Beat* magazine, which he cofounded in 1982. In 2005 he presented his "Life of Bob Marley" video/lecture in Puerto Rico, Hawaii, Calgary, Australia, New Zealand, and Fiji.

JOHN FEINS

JOHN FEINS IS A poet and musician from New York City, Boston, Pittsburgh, Boulder, San Francisco, Santa Fe, and Los Angeles, where he was formerly Community Relations Coordinator producing music, film, and literary events for a leading entertainment retailer, and Director of Programs for the National Academy of Songwriters, now part of the Songwriters Guild of America.

I met John in a bookstore in the mid-'90s on the corner of Blackburn and La Cienega, down the block from where my grandparents used to live in Los Angeles.

Q: You discovered the music of Leonard Cohen from the big screen, when some of his tunes appeared in *McCabe & Mrs. Miller*?

A: Early on, I thought I would direct films. Growing up in the '70s, smack in the middle of the finest period of filmmaking the country would ever enjoy, I was mesmerized by the double features, like *Mean Streets/Clockwork Orange* and *Days of Heaven/Bound for Glory*, at the Harvard Square Theater in Cambridge, Massachusetts. I would eagerly cut class and take the Red Line right into the heart of the legendary streets that Corso portrayed and the great folksingers serenaded.

What else but cinema and rock 'n' roll for the turned-on visionaries stranded on the teenage wasteland at the corner of Bourgeoisie Street and Nixon Way?

Soon into my first films I realized that art by committee was not so much art as commerce. I jettisoned film and rocketed to writing: poetry—the most magical of arts. After discovering what an atrocity a writing program is at the university level—I was in a well-meaning program at Carnegie-Mellon—I started loading up on all the history courses I could, which were of far greater value than hearing my classmates prattle away about each other's lines in workshop.

The history department was practically populated with the likes of Freud, Engels, and especially Karl Marx. I am still astounded that while we worried about the Commies, people's parents paid kingly sums for educations that served good old Karl more than Jefferson, Adams, and Monroe combined.

My last year, I took dual classes from a very gifted professor named Eugene Levy, who turned out to be a cousin of Allen Ginsberg, with whom I later worked. The first half was a study of crime as depicted in American film, and the following semester there was a companion course for the American West. Crime was really great but the West—a revelation.

We traced the typical Hollywood sensationalism, racism, and revisionism from *She Wore a Yellow Ribbon* right up to the cynical realism of the '60s generation in *McCabe & Mrs. Miller*. I loved all the films, even *High Noon*, but *McCabe* floored me. I felt every scene deep in my sensorium and related heavily to the points of view and homesteading values, triumphs, and sorrows that permeated the raw, wintry, elemental landscape. The whiskey, the women, the songs, the road—things I loved most in life but happening somewhere I actually wanted to be and imagined being someday, with infinitely more honesty and poetry than any of the other films.

Perhaps the secret key to this effect was the soundtrack. I had always been into music and had heard of Leonard Cohen, but was not familiar with his stuff. As the gorgeous, opiated sequences of John McCabe's journey montaged into Cohen's first songs, tunes of astonishing lyric and beauty and as strong, fragile, haunting, and beguiling as the landscapes in the film itself, I knew I would watch the credits through, as usual, get the guy's name and race down to Panther Hollow to buy his recordings that night.

Q: Any other soundtracks that impressed you and made an impression?

A: I owned plenty of soundtracks and had often discovered a song or artist through movies: *Midnight Cowboy, Easy Rider, Pat Garrett and Billy the Kid, The Graduate, The Harder They Come, Deliverance, Apocalypse Now, Performance, Zabriskie Point, Koyaanisqatsi, Taxi Driver, Fool for Love, A Lie of the Mind, Trouble Man, Looking for Mr. Goodbar, Cabaret, All That Jazz, West Side Story, The Blues Brothers, Blue Collar, Fitzcarraldo, Paris, Texas, Diner, American Graffiti, American Hot Wax, American Pop, Repo Man,* the aforementioned *Clockwork Orange, Mean Streets, Days of Heaven,* and so forth.

There have been more since, like *Ghost Dog, Ghost World, Naked Lunch, Casino, Death Wish* 2*, Local Hero, Jackie Brown, Pulp Fiction, Kill Bill, Batman Forever, Until the End of the World, Dead Man, Dead Man Walking, Chelsea Walls, Smoke, Basketball Diaries, Summer of Sam, The Hot Spot, La Bamba, Divine Secrets of the Ya-Ya Sisterhood, Crumb, Fear and Loathing in Las Vegas, Leaving Las Vegas, Mulholland Drive, Lost Highway, Eyes Wide Shut, Masked and Anonymous, Genghis Blues.* Never before, though, had I seen a movie featuring an artist that I did not know, that was so well suited to the picture, and who bowled me over with such pure force.

I will never forget hearing "Winter Lady," "The Stranger Song," and "Sisters of Mercy" for the first time. I was awed to find that they weren't in fact written for the film. Lines like council fires in the cold falling snow. Olympian language that spoke heart-to-heart to the core soul of a young aspiring poet who had already known cold road nights with wind for money and darkness for a bed. A solemn, melancholic sincerity, miles beyond posture or attitude, that was an alchemic holy grail of voice for kids already being suicided by their own hopeless utopian lusts. After all, who needs a crucifix when you've got morning wood?

Q: You also were introduced to the songs of Elliott Smith from *Good Will Hunting.*

A: Flash forward a perfect dozen years, from the Year of the Tiger to the Year of the Ram. I run into a friend I recognize from Richard Schoenwald's masterful "Society and the Arts" course, from that same history department, at the Authentic Café on Beverly Boulevard in Los Angeles, California. He's an agent and some time later sets me up on a date with an alumna who also works in motion pictures. We choose to go see *Good Will Hunting,* partly as I grew up in Boston and mostly since the film was generating a good murmur, meaningless as that can be.

As we sat in the nondescript environs of the Beverly Six on 2 February 1998, I was enjoying the film well enough—though by now my scores of films a year was down to two or three—and then a moment I will never forget, as a song called "No Name No. 3" began to track, with an aching, whispering refrain: "everyone is gone/home to oblivion."

"Who in God's name is this?" I thought. How can *this* artist exist and I don't know him? Not possible. This is everything I believe in. He sounded like Nick Drake, but wasn't; like Leonard Cohen, but wasn't; and yet again, a pure and perfect aesthetic. I listened with all my might and as much as I felt I knew him, I knew I simply did not.

More songs came into that theater like exotic, intoxicating, familiar strangers: a devastatingly understated and incisive tune, ostensibly about the music business, with the prodigal title of "Angeles," a wonderfully optimistic love song, "Say Yes," and a song that has come to define the pathos of love affairs for an entire generation, much as "Suzanne" did for the one before: "Between the Bars," a song for beautiful losers now and forever. The song hits a perfect pitch and embodies the tone of the darkest yet redemptive night or thousand we have all somehow survived.

There was yet another unforgettable piece, "Miss Misery," an original for the film that was even nominated for an Oscar by the academy dweebs in the height of '90s pop diva idiocy. Such is the sheer grace of Elliott Smith, and his appearance is now the stuff of legend.

Next day I scored his available recordings and marveled at the greatest singer-songwriter-multi-instrumentalist of my generation. Someone who'd grown up on punk and indie records and yet wrote *actual melodies*, had the unmistakable pen of a poet, and sang with soft care, tenderness, intensity, and a huge range of genuine feelings: I had truly hated what had been happening in music and, even as I listened, could hardly believe this guy. He had obtained the ring.

As one looks back, you can see how the mighty have fallen in the generational span between the two films. An attempt to restore absolute truth and realism into western mythmaking and relationships contrasted to an entirely improbable storyline, feel-good flick complete with the protagonist heading west to get the girl back no problem.

The entire promise of the maverick *Easy Rider* generation ultimately collapsed under the rise of the agencies and packaging. *McCabe* would never get made today. Altman, after a slew of excellent pictures, has taken to satirizing Los Angeles and the movie business. While Leonard Cohen went on to enjoy a productive recording career at Columbia, continued to publish poetry, and evolved into spiritual enlightenment among the peaks of Mount Baldy, Elliott Smith fell into addiction and self-destruction, a problematic deal at DreamWorks, and a decadent industry and city that made him too uncomfortable.

He sort of went underground after releasing two brilliant, cathartic wonders, *XO* and *Figure 8*, finally cleaned up, and built a recording studio in the San Fernando Valley, but then apparently cut his life short despite a double CD breakthrough in the finishing stages.

A couple years after *McCabe*, journalists were tossing out a corrupt president—but a couple after *Good Will Hunting* they ushered in an illegitimate dictator and a disastrous war.

For a brief moment, and before the conspiracy to ruin democracy took root, we had a new troubadour in our midst, who possessed the same emotional candor and heart quality of that peak time in American culture so precociously displayed by Cohen in those *McCabe* songs. Elliott Smith was an absolutely uncompromising artist who played guitar beautifully, wrote melodies as nice as those of the Beatles, recorded like a champion, and who by all accounts was an uncommonly wonderful and generous guy.

He really reminded me that anything is possible—at least in art if not, for now, much else.

※

John Feins is a poet and musician. He has worked with numerous major film studios and music labels, promoting projects and talent, and also directed several programs that educate artists and provide opportunities in the entertainment business. He has been published in a diverse range of books including *American Magus Harry Smith: A Modern Alchemist* and *Scream While You Burn: A Caffeine Anthology*. He has served as editorial director of *The Songwriters Musepaper* and *Bombay Gin*; been a contributing editor to *Variety*'s "LA 411," "Producers and Directors," "Agents and Managers" and "High Def 411" guides; and is widely published in business, technology, and entertainment periodicals.

KIRSTEN SMITH

Kirsten Smith and Karen McCullah Lutz are the screenwriters of *Ella Enchanted*, *10 Things I Hate About You*, and *Legally Blonde*.

In 1995, a mutual friend of ours, Michael Hacker, suggested his pal Kirsten, newly graduated from Occidental College, would be good for the MET Theater Music and Literature series I was curating and coproducing in Hollywood.

I said, "Have her show up and I'll give her a slot, without audition or review, and I'll make sure she'll be in all the ads and promotion around the event."

Of course I got some stick for her booking. Anyway, I gave my own slot to Kirsten that night, partially because I was going to read on the closing evening, making my own stage debut at the Santa Monica Boulevard venue.

Naturally Kirsten, from San Pedro, California, delivered on the boards that '95 evening, offering a piece on Courtney Love, and afterward said to me, "I owe you a big one."

In March 2006, she cowrote the screenplay, along with Ewan Leslie and Karen McCullah Lutz, for the DreamWorks feature film *She's the Man*, starring Amanda Bynes.

Kirsten Smith. Photo by Jason Lust, courtesy of Kirsten Smith.

Q: Do you write to music playing? Radio, CDs, albums?

A: Yes, often I can't write until I've found the musical groove. I played Hole's "Heaven Tonight" over and over when writing two of the montages in *Legally Blonde*. With *10 Things*, I was listening to a lot of Bratmobile and Sleater-Kinney and Bikini Kill.

    I was listening to "Ray of Light" a lot when I was working on our (unproduced) surfing script, *Girl in the Curl*. Also, this Britpop band, Adorable, was on heavy rotation for that one.

Q: What have you been playing in 2002–2003?

A: 2002 was all about the Strokes, Sleater-Kinney, Hot Hot Heat, Spoon, Coldplay, White Stripes, French Kicks. 2003 has been about Interpol, Cat Power, Yeah Yeah Yeahs. I'm currently writing our new script, *Don't Ask*, to this New Pornographers record that came out a few years ago, and also No Doubt's *Rock Steady* when I need a party vibe.

Q: You might as well go to town and explain your fascination and fondness for Madonna and Courtney Love.

A: My office has an entire shrine to Courtney and Madonna. I even have a photo of Courtney topless that my writing partner gave me—how weird is that? Whenever I'm stuck, I glance around, see their faces—or their boobs—and I'm inspired. They epitomize powerful, edgy women who've done things their own way. What could be more inspiring than that? This year was a sad year for me because for the last twelve years, I've had the new Madonna calendar in front of my desk. This year Madonna didn't make a calendar, which to me signaled the end of an era. Madonna's too interested in being a mom and a Kabbalist and yoga expert to worry about doing a photo shoot for her calendar. It sucks! I had to go on a U.K. website and find some shitty knockoff calendar that contains photos of her in concert. It's just not as profound as her authorized calendar with photos you've never seen before of her in fabulous outfits and poses. Maybe that's why I'm having trouble writing recently!

Both Courtney and Madonna seem to lend equal focus to their music *and* to the manipulation and presentation of their image, in photo spreads and videos, personal appearances, and movie roles. They take the rock star thing to movie star proportions and vice versa. It seems like they both have created their own cinematic tableau in which they function as characters—complete with outrageous dialogue, fabulous costumes, makeup, and of course, musical accompaniment. They're both just very cinematic in their approach to their careers—fusing both image and music together as a soundscape with visuals, or as a visual landscape with music.

Q: Who can coexist in both worlds?

A: Rappers seem to be the only ones who can exist in both worlds. And Barbra Streisand and Bette Midler. So, Jewish girls and rappers. I think it might be over for Madonna. Until she's old and she can do some kind of ancient diva star turn. Courtney has what it takes—she got great reviews for her first movie, even though I thought she was just playing herself, but no one knew what "herself" was, so they were ecstatic—but she will continue to be plagued by her own drama and lack of focus.

Q: Does music even impact the way you and your partner write for the screen? I realize you don't formally do the music for the films where you've written the screenplay.

A: I don't know if a song we've written in the script has ever made it into the movie. However, I firmly believe in doing it, because in 10 Things, I wrote, "a happy indie power pop song plays," and all that was gleaned from that was the word "pop." The music supervisors didn't really know what "indie" or "power pop" meant to me.

Q: Can you define your relationship with your partner and how you two work in screenwriting? Is she a music junkie as well?

A: My writing partner likes classic rock and has much more mainstream taste. If we write in a song to be playing in a specific scene, it's usually me writing it, then her not knowing what it is, then me playing it for her before we agree to let it stand.

Q: Do you work with the music supervisor or director regarding potential music in your films? Any "comical" battles with these people? Also, do you work with the stars of your films in discussion about songs and music in the resulting film?

A: I gave Julia Stiles and Heath Ledger my own little "soundtrack" of about forty songs that I'd made for 10 Things. I also called Kathy Nelson, president of music for Disney, and introduced myself. She admitted that new indie rock was not her forte, so I volunteered to send her some songs I felt might work. She told me that one of the songs actually got very close, "Bitch Theme" by Bratmobile, which I thought could be a great opening song for Kat, but the lo-fi quality of the recording was an issue. At that point, it was too late in the process to contact the band and try and initiate them rerecording or finding a master, etc.

On *Legally Blonde*, I had a relationship with one of the soundtrack execs at MGM and I'd suggest things. One thing that broke my heart was that I heard that Liz Phair loved the movie and had sent them three songs, and they didn't put even one in. Sometimes Liz Phair can be a little bit of a soundtrack whore, but *still*! It's Liz Phair! They started putting on Mya and Hoku and the soundtrack to me is absolutely unlistenable. It is wall-to-wall cheese with the exception of Loball.

My sense is that music for film has become an increasingly political battleground. Studios usually allot a few million dollars specifically for the soundtrack, and because music is such a subjective art form, everybody involved (studio execs, producers, editors, director, writers, assistants) throws their hat into the ring. Suddenly, everyone's an expert. It's a very dangerous thing for the fate of good music in movies. Unless the director has a strong musical vision that is voiced almost immediately (in preproduction), then everyone starts pitching songs and it becomes decision by committee. It's also political in that the studio cuts a deal with a label and then it becomes about servicing the bands on that label.

Q: Do you take more of an active role in production of your movies, in regards to music and songs you would like to see in the films?

A: I took it upon myself to try and become as involved as I could. I worked with the director to choose a song for the "Bend and Snap" number in *Blonde*; I befriended some of the music execs at MGM—I was really pushing to get Phantom Planet into the movie—but ultimately none of my choices made it into the film. Until I have real power, it's unlikely that my voice will be heard, but I'll keep trying.

Q: What are your all-time favorite soundtrack albums, when the song met the screen, where the music and film relationship succeeds?

A: I loved Elliott Smith's soundtrack for *Good Will Hunting*. That is the kind of collaboration between songwriter and director that makes for a truly noteworthy soundtrack. Jon Brion's relationship with Paul Thomas Anderson seems to be very exciting. I also appreciated Mark Isham's collaboration with Alan Rudolph. Rudolph seemed to bring out the best in him, particularly with *Trouble in Mind* and *The Moderns*.

Sheltering Sky holds a dear and special place for me, mostly due to the time in my life when I saw the movie.

Q: Any films like *High Fidelity* or *Tank Girl*, for example, that really do it for you? Do you buy soundtrack albums?

A: What I find strange working in the teen genre is that when I was a teenager, some movies I loved, like *Sixteen Candles*, didn't even have a soundtrack! My friends and I would have to go buy the entire album in order to get the songs. But in a way, it was a great introduction to bands I'd normally never hear. Would I have purchased the Altered Images record for "Happy Birthday"? Probably not. Would Jaime have spent four years looking for a Rave-Ups album if the one song was on the soundtrack? No.

I distinctly remember the soundtrack for *Pretty in Pink* as being a major turning point for me. The music in that movie—Echo and the Bunnymen, the Smiths, Psychedelic Furs—was so cool and so far off the Top Forty dial that it made me change the kind of girl I was. I wanted to be like Molly Ringwald, driving a Karmann Ghia and listening to New Order and Suzanne Vega. John Hughes did a great job of bringing an off-beat, new wave vibe to his movies. *Some Kind of Wonderful* was one of my favorite soundtracks, with the Jesus and Mary Chain on it, and Stephen Duffy.

Jonathan Demme also did a great job of bringing a hip sensibility to his soundtracks. *Something Wild* had New Order and Fine Young Cannibals on it, and *Married to the Mob* had Sinead O'Connor, New Order, and Tom Tom Club.

Q: With the directors and writers I've talked to, divisions seem to be happening in regard to music in film. Do you like films packed wall-to-wall with tunes, or music in select situations?

A: A lot of times people are sticking songs in movies just to appease the label. Sometimes songs are just slapped onto the end credits as a favor to an artist or label. It seems disingenuous to have a song on a soundtrack that wasn't actually in the movie and didn't function as any kind of artistic corollary. Then again, if I were in charge, I'd probably end up honoring a band or song I liked with a place on the soundtrack via end credits, even if I couldn't find a place in the film. It just depends.

Q: Your opinions on this "trend," about "trailer" songs. Tunes used in commercials that aren't even in the movie, let alone the soundtrack album. Is that dishonest? Have you observed this? Is it just part of the business?

A: It seems really creepy to use score from other movies in trailers. I know a song from *The Mission* has been used in trailers for dozens and dozens of movies. People recognize it now and it's almost like a Pavlovian cue to the audience that the movie being advertised to them is "an epic with artistic merit."

Q: Any stories or feelings about the soundtrack albums issued from the movies you've written?

A: I never listen to the soundtrack beyond the first two weeks I have it—it's too depressing. I just don't like most of the choices. But I also never watch the movies again, either, beyond the initial theatrical release.

Q: Any dealings or observations about your language or text onscreen in conjunction with the sound editor?

A: I was watching an old movie recently, La Cava's *Fifth Avenue Girl*, and there was an emotional scene with no music, and I realized how much more valid the scene seemed without music to cue tears, and how music has become such a crutch to extract emotion from the audience. It really seems wrong to abuse score like that. In an action scene, yes, I can see it being useful. There was incredible, vibrant music playing in the freeway sequence in *Matrix Reloaded* and it really lent to the heart-stopping nature of what was going on onscreen, but in a scene that's about the actors acting, why slap score on top of them in that way? It seems like a refusal to trust performance.

Q: Do you like MTV? Do you like songs used in commercials?

A: I don't watch TV much, but tonight I heard a Morphine song from *Cure for Pain* coming out of the TV. I walked over to check it out and saw that it was playing over a Miller Light commercial. I said to my boyfriend, "That was a really important record in my life." I had listened to it constantly on a particular road trip, and it made me sad that he would never get to experience the song as an important song to me, but rather he would always experience it as "that Miller Light commercial" song. As with most people who've never heard the song on its own terms, it now can only conjure up subliminal images of a girl in a miniskirt strutting across the room toward a chiseled guy. Its purpose is to sell beer, not evoke any images of its own.

Ironically, Mark Sandman has a line in one of the songs on that record, "I'm free now to direct a movie, sing a song or write a book about yours truly," that makes me think he understands the cinematic nature of songwriting. Don't you think musicians are really directing movies of the mind with their songs? I always invent videos in my head when I'm listening to songs I love. It seems like a dream job— directing videos—so when a director misuses the emotional pull of the song, it seems like the most abusive kind of artistic error.

Q: Why do all actors want to be in a band, and why does everyone in a band want to act?

A: People in music think the movies are cooler and people in movies think music is cooler. There's always a battle about which business is the sleaziest.

For the performer, I think when success comes, the artist quickly realizes he or she is surrounded by corrupt businesspeople who are all about making money and making deals. The artist realizes it's not a playground—it's a *business*. So, in search of purity, he or she turns to the flip side of performing—be it music or acting. I think it's a natural self-preservationist instinct, an attempt by the artist to keep the joy of performing as uncorrupted as possible.

Q: What is the future of films, regarding the use of music in them?

A: Music will only become a bigger and more corporate part of filmmaking, unless directors take a strong musical stand early on, before the movie is even shooting. To me, directors who don't know music are like lead singers who can't play guitar. If they don't know, then they need to figure it out pronto.

Score and soundtrack in film will only become more and more dominant, until we reach the point where maybe there will be no dialogue. Watch a movie from the '40s today and you'll be shocked at how little score—and zero soundtrack—there is. The unfortunate thing is, soundtrack is becoming dominant for purely economic reasons, but it's distorting the shape of cinema in a major way.

⧯

Kirsten Smith: Select Filmography
WRITER:

She's the Man
Ella Enchanted
Legally Blonde
10 Things I Hate About You
Her first book, *The Geography of Girlhood*, a young adult novel-in-verse, will be published shortly by Little, Brown. ·

MICHAEL HACKER

Michael Hacker received an M.F.A. from the UCLA Film School, then worked as an assistant to Wim Wenders (*Hammett*) and Francis Ford Coppola (*One from the Heart*) at Zoetrope Studios.

In 1984 he completed *Downtown*, a forty-five minute dramatic film shot in 35mm. While alternating between writing screenplays-for-hire and scripts he hoped to direct, Hacker worked as a bartender, fishing guide, proofreader, legal deposition summarizer, and housepainter. In 1988, his play *Long Time Coming* had a sold-out run at the Powerhouse Theater and was named Critic's Choice by the *Los Angeles Times*.

In 1994, he directed *The Destiny of Marty Fine*, an independent feature film he cowrote with Mark Ruffalo that won the 2nd Jury Prize at Slamdance 1996. In 2000, Hacker wrote and directed *Guide Season*, an hour-long dramatic film for PBS television, and in 2001, he shot and edited the documentary, *Deconvention* about the 2000 Democratic Convention.

Hacker is currently working as a staff producer at E! Networks, turning out *True Hollywood Story* long-form specials on such figures as Courtney Love, Ellen DeGeneres, and Heather Locklear. He will be making another film in 2005.

I've known Hollywood High School product Michael Hacker a very long time. I met him on September 4, 1976 (Hacker's date), camped out in line at the Santa Monica Civic Auditorium waiting for tickets to a Bruce Springsteen concert. His uncle was the legendary "Shrink to the Stars," Dr. Frederick Hacker, who shunned big bucks to tell tales and sell out his clients, including Ray Charles, or his friends, like Herbert Marcuse.

This is a cat who never pulls his punches when discussing the music and film companionship onscreen and in the record stores.

I went to a recent Bob Dylan concert with him at the Wiltern Theater in Los Angeles and interviewed him for *Hollywood Shack Job* after Dylan's set. Hacker's brain had just recovered from helming an *E! True Hollywood Story* about MTV's *Real World* that he's just wrapped for fall 2003 broadcast and countless reruns on the channel.

Q: Do you listen to music when you write?

A: Sounds old school, but the usual music I prefer while writing is jazz. Jazz with a lot of space. Mingus's solo piano is my current fave. *Way Out West* by Sonny Rollins, *Steamin'* by Miles Davis, *Previn at Sunset*— Previn was sixteen when he recorded this, F.O.B. from France, playing like Tatum on Ecstasy—any 1940s Billie Holiday. Of course, I'm listening to Sly Stone right now and that feels just fine. Exception to the above is that my favorite script was written under the heavy influence of three songs, "Rodeo Girl" by Rickie Lee Jones, Tom Waits' "Who Are You," and "Asleep at the Wheel," a great song from the Wallflowers' first record. Then, of course, 1965 Dylan, especially the deep tracks: "Farewell, Angelina," "She's Your Lover Now," "Does She Need Me."

Q: You've never been a fan of music in movies, or songs and soundtrack albums?

A: Don't care about soundtrack albums. They're like a trivia item. Only time soundtracks (compilations of songs as opposed to recorded score) are worthwhile is when they've got a song that you can't otherwise get, like Van Morrison's "Wonderful Remark," which for a long time you could only find on the *King of Comedy* soundtrack. Exception to the above: *Pat Garrett and Billy the Kid*, a great, underrated standalone album, haunting and evocative as all get out. A few other good soundtracks: *Dead Presidents, Diner,* and *Breathless* (the remake that Jack Nitzsche produced).

There are times when one movie like *The Last Picture Show* has Bobby Vinton's "Blue Velvet," and over a decade later the same song becomes the title of another film.

I've put music in the movies I've made, mostly because there were things that I wanted to hear, but also as a cave-in to what people expect. I'd like to do a movie with no score, but you need serious chops to pull that off. I'm working on it.

Q: What about the current status of rock music in films?

A: We need a moratorium on music in movies. Ten years. No music at all—no pop songs, no score, nothing. Then we'd see who the real film-makers are. That's not to say there's no place for music in movies, there is—and in the hands of a great director, it can be fantastic. But it's become a crutch and a marketing tool.

Q: You don't dig the bedfellows that pair directors and music supervisors with music in their movies, do you?

A: Worst current offender: Martin Scorsese, because he put a U2 song (by the flag-wrapped hypocrite Bono) in *Gangs of New York*. This used to be a good director. How low can you sink? Especially since *Mean Streets* was probably the apotheosis for rock 'n' roll songs in a movie. The Spector-miked drumbeats from "Be My Baby" that kick open the movie were one hell of a wake-up call. Only problem is, they woke up a lot of weak directors and gutless studio executives.

Q: Has anybody delivered, fusing the two mediums, for you onscreen?

A: There've been a million great uses of music in the movies, but it's become a terrible crutch. I give Wes Anderson credit, but only for having fantastic taste in songs. When Luke Wilson puts on the record of "She Smiled Sweetly" by the Rolling Stones for Gwyneth Paltrow in *The Royal Tenenbaums*, forget about it. The sound coming off the turntable obliterates anything that's happening in the movie. People might think that the song is amplifying the moment. In fact, the power of the song overpowers not only that moment in the film, but the entire film itself.

A really interesting use of music in a movie is the score for Wim Wenders' *The American Friend* (by Juergen Kneiper). It works in almost complete opposition to what's happening on-screen, but creates a wonderful, lingering effect. Godard, of course. JLG still consistently pushes the effects of sound and image in a real way. His mix of image and music *allows* you—it doesn't force you—to feel something. But only about twelve people are paying attention to his movies now.

The experience of a great song is more direct and pure than any movie scene. Movies work in different ways. There's never going to be a film that has the same effect as, say, "Like a Rolling Stone." So the use of great songs is just a cheat, pure and simple. Think about this: a couple of years ago, Cadillac created an ad campaign to remake its image. They wanted to get away from "your daddy's Cadillac" and create identification with the whole eighteen to thirty-five demographic. Now that's a real interesting concept. So they redesigned their cars a little bit and shot a bunch of slick commercials. The commercials were absolutely "brilliant," brilliant in the sense that they accomplished everything they set out to do. What made those commercials "brilliant"? The Led Zeppelin song they used to hammer home every image. What Led Zeppelin song, you ask? "Rock and Roll," released on *Led Zeppelin IV* in 1971!!! A song *more than thirty years old* worked perfectly to bestow cutting-edge hipness onto one of the most familiar of all American brand names. If that doesn't illustrate the overpower of music in relation to an image, I don't know what would. One more thing: word is that Cadillac paid Zep *five million dollars* for the rights to use "Rock and Roll" in their ad campaign. Here's another way to look at this—imagine you're standing in front of a mediocre painting or piece of sculpture. Now imagine you're standing in front of the painting or sculpture while someone is blasting a great song. All of a sudden, the thing you're staring on isn't so bad to look at anymore. You start moving your feet and your heart lightens up a little bit—but it's not the painting or the sculpture—it's the goddamned song that's making you feel that way. I mean, *how hard is it* to pick a decent song and let it play underneath a scene in a movie? That's all these people are doing. Some, Quentin Tarantino, Wes Anderson, Bertolucci in *The Dreamers*, do it better than others, but it's still a *trick*.

Things probably started going downhill when director George Roy Hill put "Raindrops Keep Fallin' on My Head" in *Butch Cassidy and the Sundance Kid*. I worshipped the moment when I saw it in premiere release at the Grauman's Chinese, but I was ten years old.

I guess you knew it was gonna come around to Dylan. Dylan's influence on the movies has been pretty significant, but it's still a flea on the elephant's ass of his music. *Don't Look Back* is spectacular, and give D. A. Pennebaker a big share of the credit there. Pennebaker had the great gift of knowing not to explain, right in sync with Dylan. The combination was electric. In the eleventh grade I saw *Pat Garrett and Billy the Kid* at the Pacific Theater on Hollywood Boulevard in its first week of release and clapped like a fool whenever Dylan appeared on the screen. The soundtrack was considered filler around the "single,"

"Knockin' on Heaven's Door." It would be fifteen years before Guns N' Roses would reveal the song to be a true American anthem, a lot more fitting for this country than anything Francis Scott Key ever wrote. There were about forty people in the theater watching *Pat Garrett*. In case you've forgotten, almost no one cared about Peckinpah during the later part of his career, or Cassavetes for that matter. I saw the premiere of Cassavetes' *Killing of a Chinese Bookie* in Westwood (a friend of mine's dad cut John and Gena's hair), and the audience shifted uneasily back and forth, embarrassed by what they felt was an absolute disaster. But I'm digressing—back to Dylan.

Dylan's music has always been cinematic, thanks to his incredible use of *compression*, the medium by which time is manipulated in film. Even in some very early songs like "Ballad of Hollis Brown," Dylan could convey a story of epic proportion with very few (about 250) words. A little later, with "Desolation Row," Dylan wrote his first screenplay. In spite of a shifting point of view and fractured sense of time, every line in the song constructs a story that builds to a kind of climax and then release, just as in any good dramatic form. The magnitude and amplitude of Dylan's music in the '60s pretty much overwhelmed the specific and revolutionary technique that he'd stumbled upon. It was only later, with *Blood on the Tracks* that the technique started to make itself *seen*. Dylan even helped this discovery process along during interviews he gave in the late 1970s, where he guardedly discussed his painting teacher, Norman Raeben. According to Dylan, Raeben was the one who helped Dylan "do consciously what (he) used to do unconsciously." Talking about "Tangled Up in Blue," Dylan said, "I was just trying to make it like a painting, where you can see the different parts, but then you also see the whole of it . . . the concept of time, and the way the characters change from the first person to the third person, and you're never quite sure if the third person is talking or the first person is talking. But as you look at the whole thing, it really doesn't matter."

I make it an almost unbreakable rule to treat anything Dylan says in interviews as just more "songwriting," but in these comments he seems to be actually trying to elucidate for us simple folk, rather than paint on another mixed-up layer of confusion. And lo and behold, Dylan actually put his ideas into practice in the magnificent *Renaldo and Clara*. That's right, I said *magnificent*. Saw the untrimmed four-hour version twice at the old Fox Venice movie theater (my ass was a lot softer then). How fitting that it was Dylan himself who was the first to take his own revolutionary approach to songwriting and apply it to cinema. 2003's *Masked and Anonymous* movie is a continuation of *Renaldo and Clara*. Larry Charles is credited as the director, but it's a Bob Dylan movie. Charles was necessary because Dylan isn't able or willing to communicate to a film crew (not to mention financing executives) what he's after. Unlike the recording studio or the stage, where the language of musicians can usually accommodate Dylan's verbal legerdemain, a gaffer can't set a light if he's told, "Make it shine like a circus in the rain," or something like that. Charles did an admirable job of letting Dylan's vision through. Neither *Renaldo and Clara* nor *Masked and Anonymous* are entirely successful, because Dylan's art is music. Just like *Tarantula* is a great, underappreciated, experimental novel, but not entirely successful. One of these days, some brilliant filmmaker is going to realize two hours of images and sound that work just as well as the seven minutes of "Tangled Up in Blue." Now *that* is something to look forward to.

※

Michael Hacker holds an M.F.A. in Motion Picture and Television from UCLA. He was an assistant to Francis Coppola and Wim Wenders at Zoetrope Studios. He has written and directed critically acclaimed short films and theater work, and has taught screenwriting workshops in Los Angeles and Montana. He has penned numerous screenplays including *Ironmen*, which was sold to Walt Disney Pictures. He also wrote and directed *The Destiny of Marty Fine*, an independent feature film starring Alan Gelfant, Catherine Keener, and Mark Ruffalo, which won the 2nd Grand Jury Prize at Slamdance. In addition, Hacker also wrote and directed *Guide Season*, an hour-long drama filmed in Montana for public television, and directed *Deconvention*, a feature-length documentary (2001).

Michael Hacker is also coproducer on *Honey West*, a feature in development at Miramax Films. He was staff producer at E! Networks from 2003 to 2005, where he produced the two-hour documentary series, *E! True Hollywood Story*. He is currently developing *Flame of Darkness*, an independent feature film set in Butte, Montana.

JESSICA HUNDLEY

AFTER GRADUATING FROM Emerson College with a degree in creative writing, Jessica Hundley began her career in 1992 as an arts contributor for *The Boston Phoenix*.

That same year, she founded and edited her own magazine, a journal of alternative music, art, and independent film that gained worldwide distribution and critical accolades. Hundley, now based in Los Angeles, is a frequently published film and music journalist, working for publications such as the *Los Angeles Times*, *L.A. Weekly*, *Blender*, *SPIN*, *Salon.com*, and many others.

Over the last decade she has interviewed countless actors, directors, writers, and musicians, ranging from Kirk Douglas to David Lynch to Missy Elliott, and has written on a wide range of topics.

She currently serves as the entertainment editor for L.A.-based *Angeleno* magazine, as West Coast editor for the music magazine, *The Fader*, and as editor of the new magazine, *Helio*.

Q: You've been reporting and noticing the musician getting more in-volved in soundtrack work, films, and albums. Is this a trend, or are the new, younger music supervisors allowing some of this action to happen—beyond putting bands' songs in soundtracks?

Jessica Hundley at Joshua Tree, California. Photo by Jeaneen Lund.

A: I think it's logical that young musicians should be drawn to this sort
of work and I'm always surprised that it hasn't happened earlier.
Most of the musicians I've interviewed are also film buffs, and I think
now more than ever the genres tend to go hand in hand. We have
an entire generation raised on not just music, but music video, companion pieces that really integrate sound and image. I think not only
are some of the best soundtracks of recent years coming from rock
musicians rather than composers, but some of the best film directors,
people like Michel Gondry, Mike Mills, and Spike Jonze, are coming
from a music video background.

Q: What about some of the festivals you have attended, like Mods &
Rockers, Sundance, Slamdance? I just saw you at Monte Hellman's
Two-Lane Blacktop. Is there a reevaluation where at least these pioneers
of sound in cinema are being recognized?

A: I think the festivals, particularly Sundance, are very aware and ahead of the curve on this issue. Sundance has its Music Café events, which feature a lot of young soundtrack talent. This year Jon Brion played, an artist who is doing incredible work. He did the score for *Punch Drunk Love* and *Eternal Sunshine of a Spotless Mind*.

As far as Hellman, I think he's really one of the godfathers of music video (along with Dennis Hopper, of course). I mean, *Two-Lane Blacktop* stars two famous musicians and has basically no dialogue. It's just amazing imagery, matched with a killer soundtrack. I think all of his work is incredible, particularly *Cockfighter*, which is one of my favorite films, period. I think directors of his time and aesthetic naturally combined the music they were living with, along with the stories they were telling. That marriage is a large part of why cinema of that age is so emotionally resonant.

Q: What films have you enjoyed where music is very important to the moving picture?

A: Well, most recently I absolutely loved—as did everyone else apparently—the soundtrack for *Lost in Translation*. Brian Reitzell, who was the music supervisor and composer on that film, is really an incredible talent. He did Sofia Coppola's first film as well, *Virgin Suicides*, which I thought had an incredible soundtrack. He and Coppola work very closely together. He made several compilation CDs for her to listen to when she was writing *Translation*, which the producer, Ross Katz, told me they also listened to while location scouting. Reitzell comes from an indie rock background. He played with the L.A. band, Redd Kross for many years and now plays with the French band, Air. He worked with Air for the soundtrack to *Virgin Suicides* and again for *Lost in Translation*. The big news though, was that he managed to seduce My Bloody Valentine's Kevin Shields out of hiding to compose for *Translation* as well. No easy feat, if you know anything about that fantastic but doomed band. Also, I really loved the soundtrack to Roman Coppola's film *CQ* as well, which didn't get as much attention as it deserved. That soundtrack was written by another French band, Mellow, who are pals with Air. There's definitely something special happening in France right now musically.

Q: What about the use of musicians in films, and observations about musicians turned actors? This is not new. Ricky Nelson, Bob Dylan, or musicians like Kris Kristofferson in films.

A: Well, Kris is one of my all time faves. My hero. I think, in general, musicians have an innate knack for acting, because they already have a sense of timing and showmanship and beat. They have a lack of self-awareness too, that helps, a kind of childlike quality. I tend to enjoy musicians in films, because even if they're a bit awkward, they're usually interesting. I love John Lurie in all the Jarmusch films, for instance. Willie Nelson, when he's alongside Kris in a film, generally seems to be having a good time. Dolly Parton is a blast, Mick Jagger is perfect in *Performance*, and Bowie is always great. I think Mark Wahlberg, Snoop Dogg, and Will Smith have a certain charm too. In fact, hip-hop has produced some really strong actors.

Also, hands down the greatest performance by a musician in a film in recent years is Bjork's starring role in *Dancer in the Dark*. She deserved an Oscar for that, and any other accolades available. Her performance was truly stupendous. In general, if I like the music a person makes, I'm always intrigued when I see them working in a film. It's funny because the reverse isn't necessarily true. I think we tend to resent actors trying to be musicians, which certainly isn't fair. I can't think of too many, however, who do a good job of it.

Q: Who are the directors who you think really know how to mix music and rock 'n' roll in their movies, and who have done a good job merging music into their films?

A: I think Wes Anderson has impeccable taste in music. I'd like to sit down with him and explore his record collection. I bet it's amazing. I'm always delighted by the music in his films, the way he chooses these really lovely, touching songs that are the lesser known—and usually the best—tracks from hit artists.

I think Paul Thomas Anderson is adept at this as well, particularly with *Boogie Nights*. Spike Jonze has his finger on the pulse, and so do Sofia Coppola and Brian Reitzell. Tarantino would be another great person to have a music rant with. Rick Linklater has wonderful soundtracks. David O. Russell is amazing too, and I liked Ted Demme's work with *Blow*. Oliver Stone can be good when he wants to be. Todd Haynes did an amazing job with *Velvet Goldmine*, and of course Cameron Crowe and the Coen brothers. David Lynch is a genius with music. There's Wim Wenders too, who has always had really fantastic soundtracks to his films and obviously loves music.

And then there are all the classic folks, like Hopper and Hellman and Altman, and Nichols' *The Graduate* and Hal Ashby's *Harold and Maude*, which has one of the most heartbreaking, gorgeous soundtracks of all time. I know I'm forgetting people. There are just too many to count, really. In general I think great directors are naturally refined audiophiles. In my mind a director with bad music taste, or—worse—no music taste at all, is hard-pressed to make an emotionally nuanced film.

Q: We've talked about country music before. It always seems overlooked by many for movies, but is having a renaissance.

A: Recently, I think the Coen Brothers did a great job with *O Brother, Where Art Thou?* in bringing roots music alive again. I think in the late '70s and early '80s, country music really was part of the film scene, with a lot of country stars acting. Films like *Rhinestone Cowboy, Songwriter,* and *Best Little Whorehouse in Texas* aren't great cinema necessarily, but the soundtracks are fantastic. Then there are films like *Coal Miner's Daughter, Junior Bonner,* and *Tender Mercies,* that really get it right on both counts. *Badlands* has a sort of country-tinged soundtrack in parts, as does *Midnight Cowboy.* I think at the moment country has a bad rap. It's sad because many people are ignorant about all the great country and country-soul music that would really work beautifully with the right images.

Q: Warner Bros Records has just formed an alliance with Fox-TV for an ongoing series of soundtrack albums culled from their weekly program, *The O.C.* Selections have been made by the executive producer, McG, a well known music video director who previously helmed the *Charlie's Angels* feature film remakes, and by the show's creator, Josh Schwartz. I've heard Spoon, Belle and Sebastian, Finley Quaye paired with William Orbit, the 88, as well as singer-songwriter Alexi Murdoch, who also has had another tune in the *Dawson's Creek* TV series from his own independent CD. The *O.C.* show theme, "California," is performed by Phantom Planet, whose lead singer wrote it. The series also premiered a new Beastie Boys single, and later Beck introduced songs from his recent album, *Guero,* in an episode where five of his new songs were the only music featured.

A: There is a lot of really incredible music coming out at the moment and it never ceases to amaze me how little of it ends up in films. In truth, I think the music supervision industry is totally out of touch. There is so much fantastic music to be had on the cheap that beats anything that would cost you big cash. Why it's not being scooped up is beyond me. TV seems to be doing a better job in terms of using independent and newly released music. It's a sad state of affairs. If anyone is looking for a music supervisor, by the way, I'm available.

Q: What are your all-time favorite soundtrack albums, when the song met the screen?

A: I love the soundtrack to *Alice Doesn't Live Here Anymore*—goddamn that's good. And the "This Is the End" sequence in *Apocalypse Now*, and the beginning scene in *The Hunger*, where Bauhaus is playing "Bela Lugosi's Dead" in some sort of weird cage. Wow. Every moment of Leonard Cohen's soundtrack for Altman's *McCabe & Mrs. Miller* is stunning. *Dazed and Confused* has a fantastic soundtrack and one that has never gotten its proper due. I mean, no one has done a better classic rock movie, really. The film opens with this muscle car pulling into the high school parking lot in slow motion while "Sweet Emotion" plays. It's fucking beautiful. Also, let's not forget all the great John Hughes soundtracks, and what about *Fast Times at Ridgemont High*? That had some great music too. The sound of my youth. Also, recently *24 Hour Party People* had a great score. Badly Drawn Boy did a fantastic job with the score to *About a Boy*. "Tiny Dancer," when it was used in *Almost Famous*. *Easy Rider* still holds its own, of course, and *The Last Movie* is amazing. Hopper again. Another favorite is any Bob Dylan song in *The Big Lebowski*. They kick in at just the most perfect moments. Dylan under a Busby Berkeley bowling sequence? Brilliant.

I like soundtracks, but hardly ever buy them. I'm not sure why. I have a lot of the music anyway, if it's culled from classic back catalogues and, a lot of the time, there's something strange about listening to scores without the context of the image. Something forced.

Q: What about documentaries like *The Last Waltz*, *Truth or Dare*, or any other music documentary that has really impressed you?

A: If you love music, then films documenting the lives of musicians are always interesting. There was a great documentary at Sundance this year called *DIG!* that was fascinating, even if you didn't care about the bands (it was about The Dandy Warhols and Brian Jonestown Massacre). I think musicians are naturally compelling. I love the *Don't Look Back*, *Gimme Shelter* and *Isle of Wight* docs, and *Ziggy Stardust*, *Hate*, all of those.

Q: With the directors and writers I've talked to, divisions seem to be happening in regards to music in film. Do you like films packed wall-to-wall with tunes, or music in select context? How should music be utilized in films?

A: I think, as a director, you have to be very careful to balance the two. I think you can have a lot of music in a film and it can work, as long as you're not being lazy and attempting to manipulate the audience's emotion solely through the soundtrack. You can have great music and a shitty film, for sure. You also have to be careful what you choose to match with music, and realize, at times, that silence is more dramatically effective. Music and image together is pretty much the most powerful way we have of conveying and communicating emotion and, like anything powerful, it needs to be in the right hands. Like a loaded shotgun, you know?

Q: The DVD format. Do you like it? Do you like seeing some of your favorite films, and even music and rock films, being "deconstructed" and explained to you?

A: I love it. I have no time for magicians' secrets when it comes to film. I'm greedy. I want to know everything! Let there be cinematic revelations!

Q: The role of the composer and the underscore. There are some soundtrack albums where the composer has maybe a cue or one track, but the product is usually the songs from the movie.

A: I think it's a hugely important role in a film and one that deserves respect. Bad music can ruin a great film and great music can make a bad film better. I think both the songs *and* the score should be included on the final soundtrack (album), definitely.

Q: Your opinions on this "trend," about "trailer songs." Tunes used in commercials that aren't even in the movie, let alone the soundtrack album. Is that dishonest? Have you observed this? Is it just part of the business?

A: It's an easy trick, but what else is new? Tinseltown was built on flash and glitz and I like it that way. Although if I hear "Born to Be Wild" again, I'm going to shoot myself.

Q: Do you like music videos? I really didn't want to write about the music video directors in this book, but I realize it's the new cinema of music. Like Michel Gondry's camera technique, which inspired bullet time effects you see in movies like *The Matrix*. I know record labels are allowing these people to do their thing when interpreting a song for the screen.

A: They are the wave of the future, the place spawning by far the best directors of the moment. Chris Cunningham will blow us away someday soon with a terrifying sci-fi epic; Michel Gondry is an example of pure and untainted creativity; Spike Jonze is playful boyish energy; Mike Mills has delicacy and grace. Roman Coppola does great stuff, David LaChapelle. So many amazing people honing their chops with this form. I like videos that don't show the band, at least not in the traditional mock concert manner.

Q: What about the role of the festival in terms of music, rock 'n' roll, soundtrack albums, hustling, deals, meetings? Musicians and bands now performing at Sundance studio parties and receptions. Is it healthy?

A: I think any way a good musician can make money and get his music heard is a good way, short of selling the soul. There's nothing wrong with playing your music for people who can help your career, even if they're idiots. I think the best fest in this area has been South by Southwest in Austin. Great new bands and decent films too.

Q: Do you like MTV?

A: Nope, not for a long, long time. They are the enemy. Most of the great music videos being made never get played on MTV. An alternative is absolutely needed, but the monolith must release its stranglehold first.

Q: Do you like songs being used in commercials?

A: Nope. The more I like the song, the less I like it.

Q: What is the future of films, regarding the use of music in them?

A: The two are intrinsically linked and always have been. Even before films had spoken dialogue, there was the organ to set the tone. They need each other and that need is not going to diminish. Like I said, it's our most powerful method of conveying emotion, and when it's done right, there's really nothing better.

Q: Can soundtracks featuring various different areas of genres coexist together? Is the marketplace or age demographic a consideration?

A: I think you should match the best songs to the right cinematic moments and not worry much about anything else. If it works, it works. Fuck age demographics. I think that soundtracks are one of the most important ways that young people are introduced to old music and old people are introduced to new music.

Q: What about instrumental music? What about cues by Bernard Herrmann in *Taxi Driver*, or any older or current composers you enjoy?

A: Herrmann was incredible, Mancini in his heyday, '70s Randy Newman. Then there's Ennio Morricone, of course, and Nino Rota, who did such amazing things with Fellini's images. I think Rota and Fellini and Morricone and Leone are perfect examples of what the right composer and the right director can do together. I love Goblin's scores for the Dario Argento films, Badalamenti for Lynch, Neil Young's instrumental score for *Dead Man*. Danny Elfman and Tim Burton. All of these are incredible film musicians.

Q: What about the role of the musical in movies? *West Side Story* or *The Sound of Music* or *Chicago*?

A: I love, love, love musicals. In many ways, this is film at its finest. From all of the early Busby Berkeley to *Cabaret* and *Rocky Horror Picture Show*, to *Dancer in the Dark* and *Moulin Rouge*. *Singin' in the Rain* changes my life every time I watch it.

Q: Rock films that have blown you away?

A: The Monkees' *Head*, *The Trip* is mind-blowing psychedelic candy, Zappa's Claymation explorations, Mick Jagger in the tub in *Performance*. Again, too many to count.

Q: Why do all actors want to be in a band, and why does everyone in a band want to act?

A: Because actors are hams and musicians are greedy for attention and because each naïvely romanticizes the other's profession.

Q: Who can coexist in both worlds?

A: At one point, everyone did. Up until the '50s every actor had to be able to sing and dance and all that jazz. Over the past three decades? Bowie is good, although he hasn't done much impressive lately. Kris Kristofferson. Since the latter, not too many have proved themselves truly adept.

Q: What about the future? Trends for soundtracks? More people in current bands doing scores and getting tunes in films? The emergence of Cliff Martinez-type composers, who came out of punk rock and now do interstitial music and underscoring, and are vital to major budget films?

A: The best soundtracks will be made by the best musicians, people who know how to reach into their soul, how to translate feeling into sound, people who have a sense for cinema and movement and beat. I think those kinds of artists can emerge from any and every background and musical genre. If they love music and they love film, chances are they'll eventually take part in the continuing evolution of both.

※

Jessica Hundley is a filmmaker as well as a film and music journalist for publications such as the *Los Angeles Times*, *MOJO*, *Premiere*, and many others.

Over the last decade she has interviewed countless actors, directors, writers, and musicians and has written on a wide range of topics. She's also directed numerous short films and has written several feature-length screenplays. Her second book, *Grievous Angel: A Gram Parsons Biography*, published by Thunder's Mouth Press, hit the stands in November 2005.

HARRY E. NORTHUP

TEXAS BORN, NEBRASKA RAISED, New York mentored and living in Los Angeles since 1968—East Hollywood in California the last couple of decades—Northup is a working actor and poet. He lists thirty-seven feature films on his resume, including Martin Scorsese's first six films, among them *Taxi Driver* and *Mean Streets*. Northup portrayed Doughboy in *Taxi Driver*. Do I really need to say anything else? Harry also delivered in the Roger Corman cult classic, *Boxcar Bertha*.

Northup was later cast as Mr. Bimmel in the Academy Award-winning Best Picture, *The Silence of the Lambs*, for director Jonathan Demme, who gave him his first lead role in Corman's *Fighting Mad*. In 2004, he acted in Demme's remake of *The Manchurian Candidate*, with Meryl Streep and Denzel Washington. Harry is also top-billed in director Jonathan Kaplan's acclaimed *Over the Edge*. A DVD was released in September, 2005.

Northup has had nine books of poetry published and is also a co-founder of Cahuenga Press.

I've produced countless spoken word and poetry recording sessions with Northup over the last three decades. His relationship to music from his various acting stints is unique and informs his celluloid trek.

Q: Music has always been a part of your life?

Harry E. Northup, Laurel Canyon, Los Angeles, California, 1993.
Photo by Don Lewis, courtesy of Harry E. Northup.

A: I know that movies are an emotional thing and music goes deep, creates a mood, evokes memory. I remember when I was thirteen, living
in Sidney, Nebraska, and I took Nancy Voran, a thin, pretty, black-
haired girl, to the Fox Theater to see *The Glenn Miller Story*. I wanted
to hold her hand. I kept looking at the clock at the upper right of the

screen and I kept telling myself when the hands reach a certain time I would reach out and hold her hand. After resetting the time and execution three times, I finally did it. I reached out and held her hand. And looked into her eyes. Glenn Miller (James Stewart) was playing "String of Pearls." That tune and "Pennsylvania 6–5000" will always be in my mind. And hearing "String of Pearls" will always evoke that memory.

Q: What about in 2003?

A: *Kill Bill, Vol. I,* written and directed by Quentin Tarantino, opens with an Old Kingdom Proverb, "Revenge is a dish best served cold." Uma Thurman's character, her face partially covered with blood, moans. Bill, played by David Carradine, walks up to her. All you see of him are his boots and hands. He talks to her and cleans some of the blood off her face. She briefly speaks. He shoots her. Nancy Sinatra covers Sonny & Cher's "Bang Bang (My Baby Shot Me Down)" as the credits roll. A great opening with potent music.

Q: What is your favorite musical film?

A: *Carmen Jones,* directed by Otto Preminger. I love the music, and Dorothy Dandridge and Harry Belafonte. A sexual, sultry film. I also love *Show Boat,* directed by George Sidney, with Ava Gardner as Julie. "Can't Help Lovin' That Man," "Make Believe," and "Old Man River" are great songs.

Q: Are there any singers whose films you admire?

A: Elvis films. My favorite is *King Creole,* directed by Michael Curtiz, who is one of my favorite directors. I also love *Loving You,* in which Elvis sings "Teddy Bear" and "Loving You." Even "You gotta follow that dream wherever that dream may lead you" in *Follow that Dream* inspires me. *G.I. Blues* in 1960, directed by Norman Taurog, is one of Elvis's most enduring and enjoyable films. It is one Elvis film I watch parts of every time it's on TV. Elvis was young, handsome, sexy, and, boy, could he sing. When he sang "G.I. Blues" I empathized with his G.I. in West Germany, 'cause I was stationed in Hawaii in the Navy from 1959 to 1961, and I began to get island fever when I couldn't get leave and go stateside. The songs of *G.I. Blues* are fully integrated into the story: Army, travel, romance, with the lovely Juliet Prowse as a cabaret dancer.

As a matter of fact, I saw Elvis at the Pearl Harbor Auditorium in 1961 when I was a radioman stationed at Pearl Harbor. It was a thrill to hear him sing my favorite Elvis song, "Don't Be Cruel." It may have been his first appearance after his discharge. A fabulous show and each time he moved his little finger the audience went wild.

Q: What film has the best use of music?

A: To me, the best use of music in a movie, music as metaphor, is in Kenneth Anger's *Scorpio Rising.* "He's a rebel and he'll never ever be any good," as we see the Hell's Angels on their motorcycles roaring out—it all fits together: image and music. Film is sight and sound. I think, for me, he took these rebel figures and intercut them with religious imagery. I like that when everything adds up together.

In *Amass* magazine in November 2003, Kenneth Anger told writer Patricia Cunliffe that *Scorpio Rising* gave Martin Scorsese "the idea of using pop music as a soundtrack for *Mean Streets.*" In the same article, Anger mentioned he also had gotten a few references as the "godfather of music videos," and a few awards, like the Maya Deren Award at AFI.

The second best use of music in a movie is in *Mean Streets,* where Martin Scorsese uses rock 'n' roll, opera, and party music as a real part of these characters' lives. Scorsese works so close—no one works as close—he's right in the center of sight and sound. Jonathan Demme for *Philadelphia* and Jonathan Kaplan for *Over the Edge* are right up there.

Q: Scorsese has always had a relationship to music and rock songs in his movies. We were both on the set of his musical, *New York, New York.*

A: In his first feature film, *Who's That Knocking at My Door?* he opens with Little Richard singing "Jenny, Jenny, Jenny" as a street gang guy is kicking another street kid down the street. There's another beautiful, captivating scene when these Italian males are passing a gun around at a party in a slow, balletic movement to Ray Barretto's "El Watusi." Beautiful ballet with this force behind it.

I acted in Scorsese's first six films, and after I work with him and then see the finished film I am stunned by his use of image and music. There's almost an animal energy inside him. Blakean. You can feel it. In *Mean Streets,* the scene where Johnny Boy (Robert De Niro) enters the bar with a girl on either arm, Marty shoots it in a slow motion and has "Jumping Jack Flash," by the Rolling Stones, on the soundtrack. An indelible entrance.

In the party scene, Charlie (Harvey Keitel) dances around the bar to a party song, The Chips' "Rubber Biscuit."

Then there's opera on the car radio when Charlie, Theresa (Amy Robinson), and Johnny Boy are driving at the end and Charlie is singing along. The music comes out of real places and is a real part of the movie. Then, the Stones' song, "Tell Me."

I also knew he had worked on *Woodstock* and an Elvis Presley tour documentary.

Q: You've worked with other directors who have links to music and rock 'n' roll in their films, and even the casts. Jonathan Kaplan in *Over the Edge*, and Jonathan Demme on many movies.

A: Jonathan Demme was a music reviewer in his early adulthood, so he has an erudition and passion for music.

I played a juror in the film *Philadelphia*, directed by the compassionate Demme. I was given the video and soundtrack at the premiere, and each time I listened to the *Philadelphia* soundtrack, it evoked the emotional content of the film. The film can rightfully be called art. "The Streets of Philadelphia," by Bruce Springsteen, opens the film. A poignant, elegiac opening. There is also a song by Peter Gabriel. These songs are part of the heart and soul of the film. Pauletta Washington performs the Gabriel tune, "In Your Eyes," a lovely communion, and there is an elegant, pretty plea by Sade, covering Percy Mayfield's "Please Send Me Somebody to Love."

Q: What about the music in Jonathan Kaplan's *Over the Edge* movie?

A: In *Over the Edge*, written by Tim Hunter and Charlie Haas, in which I starred as Sgt. Doberman, the director, Jonathan Kaplan, used music that was important to the kids in the film. I remember once we were moving from one location to another in a van, and the actress, Pam Ludwig, who played the lead girl, gave me her earphones and I listened to Cheap Trick for the first time: "Surrender but don't give your self away . . ." "Your daddy's all right . . ." The music in that film was real and evocative of that time.

Kaplan's *Over the Edge*, which was the first picture from Orion, when Orion was based at Warner Bros., was shot in and around Denver in 1978. Cheap Trick was incredible. The film also used the Ramones and the new punk rock. Kaplan also has tremendous knowledge of music. A brilliant director, honest guy, he really did a great job with those young kids. I was once with him for a looping session and asked him what was his best film. Kaplan said, *Over the Edge*, "because it didn't need me as a director, it just had its own life." When Jodie Foster saw *Over the Edge*, she wanted to work with him, as she said, "*Over the Edge* was the only teen movie that made any sense." Then Jodie worked for him in *The Accused*, and won an Oscar.

Q: It never really got proper distribution.

A: What happened, it was the fourth gang picture in a row, after *The Warriors, Boulevard Knights,* and *Walk Proud,* so there was a lot of violence and Warner Bros. shelved the movie. Several years later, Joseph Papp at the Public Theater in New York had a Monday night screening called "Forgotten Films," and in 1981 he showed *Over the Edge.* *Time* and *Newsweek,* with my picture in the article, both ran superlative reviews. The *New York Times* called *Over the Edge* "one of the top twenty films in 1981." *L.A. Weekly* called *Over the Edge* "one of the best films made in the '70s."

Valerie Carter covering "Ooh Child" at the end is riveting. My character had been killed. The kids were on the bus and there was an image of fire from my death scene, music coming up, and the kids going off to jail. Imagistically, one of the most powerful scenes that there is. *Over the Edge* was about white kids, ages twelve to fourteen, using drugs and getting into drugs, too. Suburbs weren't depicted this way in big feature films and it was hard to get it distributed. The selected music underscored and amplified the performances. Frantic and exciting loud new bands were heard on the screen and in the soundtrack LP.

Q: The music video for Nirvana's "Smells Like Teen Spirit" was influenced by *Over the Edge* and filmed inside the gym at L.A.'s Fairfax High School.

Has there ever been a time when you were acting, or studying acting, when you went to a concert or a music event that was really monumental, even reinforcing your desire to continue to act and be in this business?

A: In 1968, when I was in New York one time, I was living between 77th and 78th on Columbus, and bought the *New York Times.* It was when I was studying with Frank Corsaro. He taught Method acting on 54th Street. In my class were Harvey Keitel, Billy Bush, Michelle Lee, Victor Argo, Ralph Waite, and Christopher Jones, who later starred in *Wild in the Streets.* That movie had a soundtrack with some Barry Mann and Cynthia Weil songs, including "Nothing Can Stop the Shape of Things to Come." Also in the class was Hector Elizondo, with whom I did my second scene from *Grapes of Wrath,* and everything just fell in place. As a matter of fact, Hector was the first guy who told me about the poet Rimbaud and he also taught me how to play guitar. He had a studio in downtown Manhattan.

I saw an ad in the *New York Times* that Bob Dylan was going to be at Carnegie Hall in a tribute to Woody Guthrie. So I went down there and got two tickets for my wife and me and we sat in the fourth row. I saw these guys playing with him who all looked older. Arlo Guthrie, Pete Seeger, Judy Collins, each would do a tune, but Dylan stood up at the end of the first half of the show and he did twelve minutes and really socked it home. Folk rock. The Band blew my mind. "Grand Coulee Dam."

Dylan was beautiful like Elizabeth Taylor. I loved the way Scorsese shot him in *The Last Waltz*. I always enjoy watching him on film.

Q: In 2005, Scorsese released his *Bob Dylan Anthology* project, a biography about the folk rock legend. Interestingly enough, the producer of *Mean Streets*, Jonathan Taplin, was The Band's road manager.

A: I think the way Scorsese came in on the opening title on *Mean Streets* with "Be My Baby" was incredible. It cuts to the rhythms.

Scorsese invited me to a screening of *Taxi Driver* on the Warner Bros. lot. The film was stunning. The Bernard Herrmann score was perfect. Scorsese's inner rhythms are all hooked up to the external rhythms.

I play a bartender in *Alice Doesn't Live Here Anymore* and there is great use of Mott the Hoople's "All the Way to Memphis." It introduced me to the band. I mean, in the movie, a little kid is on the floor listening to the song with his headphones on. The song jumps out of the screen.

I think Scorsese's music comes out of the characters of the situation. He doesn't use music as a bridge to take you from one scene to another. He takes you into the reality of the characters' lives.

I think everybody around Scorsese always knew he was a born filmmaker. When I acted in *Mean Streets*, it dislodged something in me psychically—the violence and the emotional aspect of it—and it really just put me on another plane. As a poet, too. *Mean Streets, Taxi Driver, Goodfellas, Raging Bull*, the one thing they have in common is there is a spiritual realism and an honesty to who these people are in real life, so the music that is hooked up with these guys is part of their lives. Even his *The Color of Money* has that real smoky sound, and Robbie Robertson was involved with that movie.

I was also in *Blue Collar* that Paul Schrader wrote and directed. We did it in Michigan. Jack Nitzsche's music in the opening scene with the men on the line really captures it. What a powerful opening.

Carmen Jones, The Buena Vista Social Club, and *Purple Rain* are some of the films that I will always watch and listen to for a while, whenever they come on TV, because I love their music.

Q: I recall from an old conversation that you were in an acting class decades ago, which reinforced music.

A: In Frank Corsaro's acting class in New York, we learned an exercise: sing a song at the beginning of a scene—"Girl From Ipanema," for example—and get caught up in it and the song will elicit an emotion to help you relax and believe in the scene. To bring the scene to life. To enter into the scene with your senses open.

So, music evokes emotion, songs are embedded in personal memories and emotions are deeply hooked up with memory.

Q: You've just worked with Jonathan Demme on a remake of *The Manchurian Candidate*, actually a movie property originally starring and produced by Frank Sinatra. I know Demme began as a rock music critic in Miami. His casts have included musicians Chris Isaak, and Steve Scales from the Talking Heads.

A: I worked a week in two scenes with Meryl Streep, Roger Corman, and Walter Mosley. I played Congressman Flores. Fab Five Freddy came on the set and I had a chat with him, during a break, about Grandmaster Flash's "The Message."

Q: You have always been an actor who has a relationship to music and rock 'n' roll, and you've always been impacted by music. Like you recorded for me a poem about seeing Savoy Brown at the Santa Monica Civic Auditorium. We later saw Bob Marley and the Wailers at the same hall.

A: I think the music and film mediums feed each other. Ezra Pound said the poem rests on the syllable. Basically, with each of these directors, their films are a reflection of who they are inside. So you have each person's energy and the music they grew up with that they love. I saw Traffic, I saw the Stones, I was at Altamont, seeing that show which the movie *Gimme Shelter* documents.

Q: What movie with music kicked your head in?

A: Dylan's "Knockin' on Heaven's Door" as Kris Kristofferson (Billy the Kid) rides on his horse around the lake and is reflected, in Sam Peckinpah's *Pat Garrett and Billy the Kid*; Scorsese's use of Elton John's song "Daniel" in *Alice Doesn't Live Here Anymore* as mother and son travel in a car; Scorsese's use of "Werewolves of London" in *The Color of Money* while Tom Cruise does karate movements around the pool table as he beats his opponent at pool; and in a real way, how much more real can it get than Neil Young singing "Helpless" or Muddy Waters singing "Mannish Boy" in Scorsese's immaculate *The Last Waltz*?

Q: You were in *The Rose* with Bette Midler. A film owing to the life and times of Janis Joplin.

A: I play a character that is a blind informer. I met the director Mark Rydell and got the part. Three days and made some good bread down in Long Beach. I'm sitting outside, and Bette had a scene in this bar. "Oh Harry!" and she sat on my lap. Quite a debut. An Oscar nomination for her. I knew Bette from the '60s. And she complimented me on my durability and really sticking it out. I met her in 1966 when I was working as a waiter at The Downtown, a discotheque. She was a dancer and would shake her tits, and was going with a guy, a young artist, Michael Pavao, who was my next-door neighbor on 25th and 10th.

I gave one party and invited some people from my acting class, including Harvey Keitel. He's from Brooklyn, and he brought two Jewish girls from Brooklyn, and I ended up falling in love with Rita Solomon, and ended up getting married to her. Bette sang while Michael played banjo on Dylan's "A Hard Rain's Gonna Fall." We used to go over to her apartment. She had just come to New York. Then I came to L.A. in 1968. I had an audition at 20th Century Fox last decade, and she was on the set and we talked. She was happy to see me. I wrote a poem about the encounter. Bette Midler said I was a sexy cowboy. She brought some deep, complex emotions to that character in *The Rose*. The music for the film was done by Paul A. Rothchild, who was the Doors' producer and worked with Janis Joplin.

Q: Do you ever sing any songs from movies?

A: I love Jimmy Cliff singing any song in *The Harder They Come*. I still play the movie and the soundtrack. I have sung one song, "Many Rivers to Cross," from *The Harder They Come*, many times, especially when I've been lost and lonely. It drew me to see Bob Marley and the Wailers play live at the Santa Monica Civic Auditorium. I think the film is like *Mean Streets*. It's raw, and you almost need subtitles to understand the patois from Jamaica. Outlaw thing, the guy wants to be a singer, with the one guy who controls the music. Just when he sings, the music goes so fast it almost burns the film it's so hot. "The Harder They Come," "Rivers of Babylon." Then it turns into a fantasy and just takes you away. It's a colorful, beautiful fantasy trip. The clothes, people on the island, rough times, drugs, gunrunning, they still learn to channel their emotions through music and dance.

Songs from *The Graduate* by Simon & Garfunkel touch my heart. I had a professor at Cal State Northridge, where I received my B.A. in English, and he stressed that Simon & Garfunkel were the poets of their generation. The harmony between the two. *The Graduate*. The boy falling in love. Director Mike Nichols is a genius. I liked *Quadrophenia*. Harry Nilsson singing Fred Neil's "Everybody's Talkin'" in *Midnight Cowboy* is exhilarating. Also loved hearing his "Dolphin" song on FM radio.

I loved *8 Mile* too. Curtis Hanson brought something to the game, and I liked his earlier *Wonder Boys*. I saw *8 Mile* at the Academy. Remember, I'm sixty-three years old, and in the Academy there are a lot of older guys and I'm one of the youngest guys there, but for *8 Mile* a lot of younger people came and that was promising. Hanson didn't shoot *8 Mile* like MTV, with all these fast cuts and off the wall. Very conventional movie, but the music was just incredible. Eminem's raps. He won the Academy Award for Best Song. It's great to see these new voices and images onscreen. I know some of the new directors have come out of the MTV or BET music video ranks and brought a lot of new energy into the movie genre.

I love *Superfly* and Curtis Mayfield's score to that movie. It blew my mind. See, I like to see a part of life I've never seen before, like his "Pusher Man" composition. I'm never going to cop dope in MacArthur Park, you know what I mean?

I met Quentin Tarantino when I read for *Reservoir Dogs*. He knew my credits. He had recently seen *Taxi Driver*, one of his three favorite films, on laser disc. He knew my lines and all my scenes. In one scene, I tried to sell De Niro a piece of Errol Flynn's bathtub, and on the Director's commentary, Tarantino quoted Scorsese as saying, "I love it; that was Harry's idea."

I told Quentin I really enjoyed his *Jackie Brown* film that had Bobby Womack and used his "Across 110th Street" as the opening and closing theme. People like him really think about the music they put in their movies. In *Pulp Fiction* I loved the way he put it together with the wrap-arounds. *Jackie Brown* was a lateral move. Brothers Johnson, the Delphonics in the soundtrack. The way he puts together the music. Like Scorsese, Kaplan, Demme and their sense of rhythms.

Sight and sound. Music has to do with the emotions of what is going on at the time.

I also love *Ghost World*. The blues record collector played by Steve Buscemi was fantastic.

I'm just as hooked up with the image as the emotion, because I listen to things with my emotions. Curtis Mayfield was a messenger. I loved *Sparkle* that I know your friends Rosemarie [Patronette] and Paul Body really enjoy. With *Sparkle* the music was beautiful. So many people in that movie "blew up," as the rappers say, after the movie was a hit. And the soundtrack was incredible. When I was doing *Blue Collar*, I told Richard Pryor, during filming, how much I loved *Sparkle*, and he gave me the thumbs-up. Lonette McKee was beautiful. The Staple Singers . . .

Q: You've also appeared in a music video.

A: I was directed by Jonathan Kaplan for a music video that played many times on MTV. John Cougar Mellencamp's version of Van Morrison's "Wild Night" with Me'Shell NdegéOcello. I was in a cab going down Hollywood Boulevard with another actor, Dick Miller, a Roger Corman regular, and model Cindy Crawford was driving. Lots of exposure—must have been on MTV sixteen times a day.

Q: I know you love documentaries. What music documentaries in recent times have you enjoyed?

A: The documentaries on Chet Baker (*Let's Get Lost*) and Artie Shaw (*Time Is All You've Got*) that we saw at the Academy's Samuel Goldwyn Theater. A great acoustical setting. I also loved *Thelonious Monk: Straight, No Chaser*. I like to watch documentaries as lessons in great acting, watching these geniuses and music people perform.

The best thing I heard is that the only place you can relax is at the movies. Chet Baker so soothing. Beautiful. Like James Dean. I liked the feature film, *Bird*. It was very dark. Forest Whitaker is one of my favorite actors. And I love the soundtrack to *Ghost Dog*. That music just blew my mind. Wu-Tang Clan.

My best memories are personal. A few years ago, near UCLA, I was invited to a Westwood movie festival. Actors from several films. The people voted on what they wanted to see. They sent a limo for my wife, Holly Prado, and me. I mean, this is after reading for the house at a poetry reading. We were taken to the Armand Hammer Museum for big food and then driven to a theater to watch the movie *Taxi Driver*, and I spoke. That was a thrill. It was included in the festival with *Saturday Night Fever* and *The Graduate*. And all three films had a lot of great music in them.

※

Harry E. Northup is that rare American actor who is also an accomplished poet. Northup has made a living as an actor for thirty years, acting in thirty-seven films, among them Scorsese's first six (including *Mean Streets* and *Taxi Driver*). Jonathan Demme has hired Harry for ten acting roles. Harry starred in *Fighting Mad*, directed by Demme, and *Over the Edge*, directed by Jonathan Kaplan. Harry Northup has acted in forty-three television shows, including *E.R.* (guest star), *The Court* (recurring role), *The Day the Bubble Burst* (Movie of the Week), *Knot's Landing* (recurring role), the film remake, *Reform School Girl*, and *In Cold Blood* (CBS miniseries), for Jonathan Kaplan.

Harry E. Northup's published poetry books are *Amarillo Born, The Jon Voight Poems, Eros Ash, Enough the Great Running Chapel, The Images We Possess Kill the Capturing, The Ragged Vertical, Reunions, Greatest Hits, 1966–2001,* and *Red Snow Fence.*

Harry received his B.A. in English from California State University, Northridge, where he studied verse with Ann Stanford.

EPILOGUE: FROM DOWNTOWN TO DOGTOWN

SOMETIMES I THINK there's too much music—particularly rock tunes—in movies and television today. Silence can be a narrative element in the story. But with so many vested interests and egos in the credit roll, everyone involved in the politics, business, nepotism, cronyism, ageism, racism, and machinations around music and sound insertion feels they can steer your imagination with contemporary songs, oldies, or record label catalogue items, capture your emotions, and trap your reactions anywhere you are seated these days. That said, I've been a willing audience member, consumer, viewer, listener, and product collector.

As I assembled *Hollywood Shack Job*, a lot of the contributors, as well as record and film executives, librarians, students, teachers, writers, musicians, friends, and fans constantly asked me, "What movie tunes, rock 'n' roll songs in film, soundtracks, DVDs, or televised music appearances did you really like, that made the most lasting impression?"

Well, I love the scene in *D.O.A.*, shot in 1949, of bar-walker James Von Streeter, who played later with Johnny Otis in the 1950s, wailing away on saxophone.

Blackboard Jungle pulled my coattails to the song "Rock Around the Clock" in the mid-'50s.

I profiled Motown Records founder Berry Gordy Jr. in my first book,

This Is Rebel Music and, to this day, I'll still sit home on a Saturday night if I know David Ruffin of the Temptations is going to get some face time on television.

Best use of a Motown song might be "The Love I Saw in You Was Just a Mirage" by Smokey Robinson and the Miracles as Richard Gere prepares for action in *American Gigolo*. Poet and TV personality Paul Body argues that another Motown label smacking soundscape is Junior Walker and the All Stars' "Shot Gun" in *Malcolm X*.

Body also works behind the counter at Video Journeys. He's always ahead of the curve in the frame game. Paul predicts the ongoing popularity of two hip things happening on cable TV in Los Angeles, *LaTv Live* and the Patricia Lopez-hosted *Mex 2 the Max*. "Two local shows which feature mostly Latin music with an odd mix of Morrissey and the Cure thrown in. It is a throwback to the old days of *9th Street West* and *Hollywood A Go Go*. Where else can you see Vicente Fernandez and the electro-trance group Kinky on the same TV channel? Nowhere but *LaTv Live* and *Mex 2 the Max*. Talk about a revolution."

I'm fond of an early '70s Traffic concert I went to, that was filmed at the Santa Monica Civic Auditorium, directed by Taylor Hackford and initially shown on KCET—a PBS station—and out last decade on home video. Traffic was touring with the Muscle Shoals Rhythm Section that cooked behind Stevie Winwood and company.

I like Jim Kerr of Simple Minds singing the title song "Don't You Forget about Me" from *The Breakfast Club*, a dreamy production by Keith Forsey.

I adore the David Bowie with Pat Metheney "This Is Not America" opener for *The Falcon and the Snowman*, especially the 12-inch mix version.

A forgotten gem is "When Joanna Loved Me," sung by Scott Walker as the theme to the movie *Joanna*. The song was cowritten by jazz-informed songwriter Jack Segal with Robert Wells. Little known, Segal wrote or cowrote many other good songs, including "Scarlet Ribbons," "When Sunny Gets Blue," "Laughing Boy," and "Where You At?"

My favorite dance scene in a movie is when Sidney Poitier and Judy Geeson cut a rug at the year-end school gathering to "It's Getting Harder All the Time" in front of the Mindbenders onstage in the 1966 film *To Sir, with Love*. Thanks to DJ Hal Lifson for playing both the entire movie and the soundtrack LP for me in February 2006.

Simon and Garfunkel's "Punky's Dilemma," originally written for *The Graduate* and produced by John Simon, wasn't heard in the movie, but later found its way into their *Bookends* album. During a May 2005 lecture

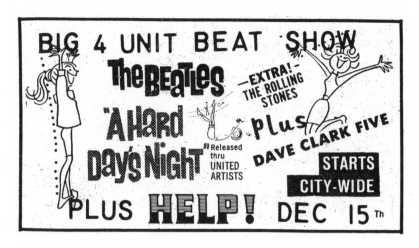

Four Star Movie Theater advertisement, Los Angeles, California, 1965.
From the Harvey Kubernik collection.

I attended in the Academy of Motion Picture Arts and Sciences' Samuel Goldwyn Theater in Beverly Hills, *Graduate* producer Lawrence Turman explained that the song had actually been utilized in a scene that was later edited out. Director Mike Nichols had heard the duo's previous LP and recruited them for the soundtrack.

In this millennium, Gabrielle Union for her moves in *Bring It On*. Last century, Wall of Voodoo had the fire in their "Mexican Radio" homespun video job.

I'm very impressed by the inclusion of Laura Nyro doing "Poverty Train" on the 2003 DVD of D. A. Pennebaker's film about the Monterey International Pop Festival. Sadly there is so little footage of her available. Music historian Kirk Silsbee saw her on *9th Street West* and I believe Laura was also a guest on the *Kraft Music Hall* TV series.

I've always kept copies of the major festival documentaries, *Monterey Pop*, *Woodstock*, and *Gimme Shelter*, for special occasions.

Hottest music video of this decade is Beyoncé's "Crazy in Love" with Jay-Z, for obvious reasons. Jay-Z's concert documentary version with her in *Fade to Black* also smokes.

The Commitments, the Alan Parker movie, exposed me to "Destination Anywhere," a fantastic copyright written by Nickolas Ashford and Valerie Simpson, sung by the actors in a bus sequence that pointed me to the Marvelettes' version.

As far as the Beatles on the silver screen, "Don't Bother Me," around the dance floor segment of *A Hard Day's Night*. The song and the film are still cosmic on the 2006 DVD.

I groove to Paul McCartney singing "A Taste of Honey," from the 1960 play and the 1961 Tony Richardson film of the same name.

ABC TELEVISION NETWORK / 4151 PROSPECT AVENUE / HOLLYWOOD 27, CALIF.

September 17, 1964

THE BEATLES MAKE THE "SHINDIG" SCENE OCT. 7

The Beatles head a stellar lineup that includes seven of Britain's other top music talents, on "Shindig" Wednesday, Oct. 7 (ABC-TV, 8:30-9 PM, PDT).

According to "Shindig" producer Jack Good, en route to London to tape show segments, the famous foursome -- John Lennon, Paul McCartney, George Hamilton and Ringo -- will probably do four numbers on the program and perform with the other entertainers.

Also appearing on the program will be Cilla Blacke, 21, Liverpool's "Queen of the Mods" (short for Moderns) in her American TV debut. A former coffeehouse waitress discovered by the Beatles' manager, Brian Epstein, Cilla's hit record is "U're My World."

Sounds, Inc., an instrumental group from the south of England that recorded the theme music for the film, "The Spartans," will also appear. The sextet, comprised of a drummer, two guitarists, a pianist on the electric piano and two saxophonists, one of whom alternates on the flute, recently recorded "Spanish Harlem."

Other talent for the "Shindig" show will be signed after Good's arrival in London, where he produced an hour-long special, "Around the Beatles," last May.

- abc-tv -

First page of ABC-TV *Shindig!* press release. Courtesy of Jim Roup.

On television, it's "Hey Jude" on *The David Frost Show*. Best Beatles TV audience would have to be the studio throng surrounding them and participating vocally during an explosive sing-along performance of "Shout," led by all four members, briefly glimpsed on the *Beatles Anthology* multipackage set. Steve Nice at Capitol Records gave me a copy. Own one yourself.

I still check out George Harrison and Friends' *The Concert for Bangladesh* every couple of years. In late 2005, an official, expanded, commercial DVD of the event was released, incorporating a loving and soulful forty-five minute documentary addition about the seminal 1971 Bangladesh event.

Musician and entrepreneur Dave Clark released three essential *Ready, Steady, Go!* compilations of the awesome British weekly music TV program from the '60s. Georgie Fame and the Blue Flames, Sandie Shaw, Otis Redding, the Rolling Stones, Marianne Faithfull, Dusty Springfield, the Fortunes, the Yardbirds, Ian Whitcomb, the Who, and the Beatles in glorious black-and-white documentation, merging the stage performers with the audience and dancers that somehow enhance the music delivered.

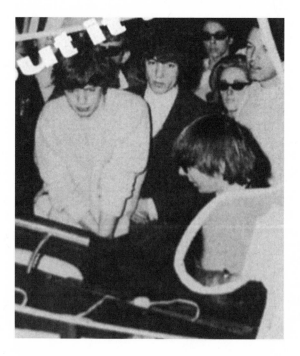

Left to right: Mick Jagger, Bill Wyman, Jack Nitzsche (foreground), Lesley Gore, Steve Binder, rehearsing for *The T.A.M.I. Show*, Santa Monica Civic Auditorium, California, 1964. Photo courtesy of Steve Binder.

Edited and repositioned tapes of *Shindig!* came out as well through Rhino Home Video. Songwriter Jeff Morrison left me his entire collection in May 2006. Host Jimmy O'Neil looked and sounded fabulous. The *Shindig! Presents Soul* lineup is indispensable: James Brown, Joe Tex, Major Lance, Aretha Franklin, Tina Turner, and Booker T & the MGs. Donovan, the Mamas and the Papas, the Byrds, the Beau Brummels, the Gentrys, and the Turtles are on another video.

MPI Home Video issued several volumes of *Hullabaloo*, the American music series. The 1965 and 1966 volumes feature great black-and-white and color clips of the Hollies, the Yardbirds, Chuck Berry, the Four Seasons, Herman's Hermits, the Animals, the Vogues, the Cyrkle, Paul Anka, Sonny & Cher, and the Lovin' Spoonful.

To be honest, I'm still recovering from the Beatles' February 1964 American debut concert in Washington, D.C. (with the Beach Boys and Lesley Gore) that I saw live in a closed-circuit broadcast at The Wilshire movie theater in Los Angeles just after their *Ed Sullivan Show* debut. A magnetic force. This Washington, D.C. gig is included in the Beatles' *First U.S. Visit* DVD on the Apple label that incorporates pivotal documentary film footage by the influential team of Albert and David Maysles.

Regarding the Rolling Stones, *Ladies and Gentlemen: The Rolling Stones*, shot during their 1972 U.S. tour, is my favorite concert film, maybe 'cause *Exile on Main Street* is my audio bible. On the same U.S. trek the more graphic companion documentary, *Cocksucker Blues*, that Robert Frank directed, with Stevie Wonder and Mick Jagger jamming and sharing the microphone on "Uptight," is a real keeper. And how subject-specific is the placement of the Stones' "Can't You Hear Me Knocking?" in the opening scene of *Blow*?

Even still in February 2006, "Lady Jane" on *Ed Sullivan* is my all-time favorite Stones color TV booking. I've also seen in this same year the totally wicked black-and-white *Ed Sullivan* rehearsal of the instrumental "2120 South Michigan Avenue" that never aired. Their "You Can't Always Get What You Want" incorporated in *The Big Chill* movie is delightful.

The T.A.M.I. Show is "right up there," as Clem Burke suggests. The Rolling Stones, Marvin Gaye, and James Brown testifying. In fact, in 2004, Capitol Records-EMI Music Marketing delivered a limited edition package of *The Very Best of the Beach Boys: Sights and Sounds of Summer*. What's important is that the newly compiled DVD features Beach Boys performance footage from the landmark *T.A.M.I. Show*, long sought after

Left to right: Steve Binder, Marvin Gaye, and Leon Russell at rehearsals for
The T.A.M.I. Show, Santa Monica Civic Auditorium, California, 1964. Photo courtesy
of Steve Binder.

by collectors and fans, which has never before been released commercially in its entirety.

Best holiday present for 2006 has to be the three-DVD package, *Muddy
Waters Classic Concerts*, which has Muddy's set at the Newport Jazz
Festival and a booklet with a foreword from Bill Wyman.

And don't forget the Rolling Stones on *The Red Skelton Show* in 1964.
Mick Jagger singing "Little Red Rooster," fondling a harmonica in a
haunted house, was mesmerizing.

The 2005 and 2006 Rolling Stones *Big Bang Tour* integrated several big
screens for arena and stadium venues that projected the band members
and their concert repertoire. Worked just fine for me. "The Stones were
on fire," mused paying customer Paul Body.

"Hey Little Girl," a Vee-Jay record Dee Clark sang, described it all
when I went on a date with Lesley Wilk to see the *Monterey International
Pop Festival* movie premiere in 1969 at the Fine Arts Theatre on Wilshire
Boulevard.

Watching "That'll Be the Day" with my close friends Ellen Berman and Nancy Rose Retchin at a Filmex premiere at the Wilshire Theater, with Ringo Starr sitting next to us. Hearing my soul sister home girl Rosemarie Patronette review and run down *Performance* over my telephone on a yearly basis.

Bob Sherman and I catching *2001: A Space Odyssey* at the Gilmore Drive-In on 3rd Street the first night it opened in 1970. Jack Nitzsche, Denny Bruce, and Gerry Goffin also caught it earlier when the film premiered in Hollywood. Eric Burdon and Jimi Hendrix had a real good time, sitting through it three times from the morning until dinnertime. Lovable Randy California of Spirit, sharing the experience on another showing, walked out from the audience and into the front of the screen.

Viewing *Boogie Nights*, when it acquired national distribution for the first time, at a movie house in Reseda, and coming to the stunning conclusion that all this action happened in my workplace neighborhood. I had to sit through the flick a second time the same evening, just to hear and groove again to the songs on the screen.

In 2003, Sir Paul McCartney's office invited me to an advance cast-and-crew screening of his *Back in the U.S.* tour and concert movie at the ArcLight Theater on Sunset Boulevard in Hollywood. I then went on a Wings kick for a full two weeks.

In 2004 I went back to the ArcLight for the Los Angeles Film Festival and a showing of *Z Channel: A Magnificent Obsession*, directed by Xan Cassavetes. A powerful examination of the tireless efforts of the late Jerry Harvey, programming head of Z, before HBO and Showtime were on your cable box. The musical score was provided by Steven Hufsteter, one time mastermind of the Quick.

Laurence Harvey as drummer Johnny Jackson in director Val Guest's *Expresso Bongo* is my all-time best actor as a musician in a music movie.

Rare sightings of Patti Drew and Tammi Terrell singing were always appreciated on the box in late '60s TV Land.

I enjoyed the Fortunes' 1966 performances of "You've Got Your Troubles" and "Here It Comes Again" on *Lloyd Thaxton* and *9th Street West*, *Shivaree*, and *Hollywood A Go Go*, as well as the Ventures playing their hits on KHJ-TV Channel 9's *Real Don Steele Show* in the early '70s.

Another seminal, local music TV program was *Shebang!* that DJ Casey Kasem hosted and Dick Clark produced. It was always required after-school viewing. In Spring 2006 I ran into Kasem at a local market and we reminisced about some of the exhilarating tapings, including memorable appearances by regional East L.A. live acts Thee Midniters, Cannibal & the Headhunters, and the Blendells, who had big records on KRLA and KFWB. Casey still sounds great. An early spot from the Doors, who hailed from the West L.A. region, was chilling. I pointed out to Casey that I was a dancer on Clark's *American Bandstand* when the Mamas and the Papas and Bob Lind were the on-camera talents.

In 2006 Roger Steffens played me the *Smothers Brothers Comedy Hour* Sunday night television series, which had Simon & Garfunkel, the Association, the Who, the Hollies, Cream, Donovan, Jennifer Warren, Glen Campbell, the Bee Gees, and Jefferson Airplane as musical guests. George Harrison even stopped by and introduced the Beatles' "Hey Jude" and "Revolution."

The 2005 Shout! Factory DVD release of *The Dick Cavett Show: Rock Icons* was very watchable—a devoted TV talk show host who gave a forum to George Harrison, David Bowie, Janis Joplin, Stevie Wonder, and Sly and the Family Stone.

The Hollywood Palace. Buffalo Springfield in color. I was also a fan of *The Jack Benny Show.* Besides the comedy, Jack, or his people, lined up a real

The Turtles performing on Della Reese's TV series *Della* in 1969.
Photo by Henry Diltz.

early appearance of the Beach Boys, and before that, the Mills Brothers, who did "(Up a) Lazy River."

Every episode of the ABC-TV series *The Johnny Cash Show* was memorable. I've just heard this year that finally, in 2007, a DVD of the series will be available.

The Mike Douglas Show always had the current bands of the day like the (Young) Rascals, the Hollies, Moby Grape, Sly and the Family Stone, and the Motown acts. Definite afternoon delights. John Lennon and Yoko Ono cohosted a whole week with Douglas once. Entertainer John Gary had a summer replacement TV show and booked the Electric Flag—the only time I saw them on the tube.

The Turtles on Della Reese's TV show, *Della*, in 1969. Sandy Baron was her cohost.

Tim Hardin's "Black Sheep Boy" in Charles Eastman's feature film, *The All-American Boy*, was lovely.

A groundbreaking combination television and music scene happened 1971–1973 on the PBS series, *An American Family*, about the Santa Barbara family, the Louds. One episode had son Lance playing Kinks and Procol Harum records in a room. That was the first reality TV for many of us watching.

Three other fantastic concert movies are the video of *Bob Marley and the Wailers Live*, a multiple camera shoot of Marley in England in 1977 now also out as DVD product in fall, 2005, and Peter Gabriel's *Growing Up Live* DVD, filmed on his 2002 world tour. I was absorbed in the mixture of Gabriel's stage theatrics and music combined with social concerns and spirituality. In the winter of 2005, a new concert and documentary two-disc DVD set, *Still Growing Up: Peter Gabriel Live & Unwrapped*, hit the Virgin megastores.

Wattstax, which Mel Stuart directed, was rereleased in 2003. The politics of truth revealed. Luther Ingram singing the entire "(If Lovin' You Is Wrong) I Don't Want to Be Right" is riveting. Thankfully there is some other L.A. Coliseum footage of guitarist-singer Albert King from that afternoon. King took the usual Gibson Flying V guitar and played it upside down. Huge hands. I'm glad it exists but wish Albert had a whole song.

Tom Dowd and the Language of Music, about recording engineer-producer Tom Dowd, is the most passionate music documentary I've seen in the last twenty-five years. The engrossing 2004 Palm Pictures DVD has eighty minutes of music and interviews not originally shown when it was first available in 2003. If you love the music of Atlantic Records, check out this innovative man of sound behind the dials for Ray Charles, John Coltrane, Dusty Springfield, Otis Redding, Aretha Franklin, Cream, the Allman Brothers, Rod Stewart, Lynyrd Skynyrd, and others.

I was really impressed by Norah Jones's Nashville concert, recently shown on PBS-TV as a fund-raiser and now available on DVD in stores as *Norah Jones and the Handsome Band: Live in 2004*, that includes a very believable version of The Band's "Life Is a Carnival."

For soundtrack albums, I'm currently spinning *The Thomas Crown Affair* to use as background for writing. I still stack *Performance*, *Last Tango in Paris*, *Boogie Nights*, *The Royal Tenenbaums*, *About a Boy*, *Superfly*, *The Hot Spot*, *The Best of James Bond*, and *Trainspotting*, where Iggy Pop's "Lust for Life" is a breathtaking addition.

In 2004 I discovered writer-director Robert Rodriguez's soundtrack to his *Once Upon a Time in Mexico*. "Flor de Mal" by Tito Larriva and Steven Hufsteter is beautiful.

Fahrenheit 9/11 filmmaker Michael Moore struck recording deals with two major record companies, Sony/BMG and Warner Music Group, in releasing two different albums of music based on his big screen movie. The Warner-released soundtrack contained the film's score and songs used in his production, while the Epic Records album showcased tracks that Moore mentioned provided inspiration to him and his crew while working on the project. Little Steven, Bruce Springsteen, Bob Dylan, the Clash, and System of a Down, among others, culled from previously available recordings, and a new song from the Nightwatchman, the alter ego of Audioslave's Tom Morello. The trailer music for *Fahrenheit 9/11* highlighted Ten Years After with "I'd Love to Change the World."

From 1999, *Boys Don't Cry* has some especially telling selections that underscore the story told on-screen, including "A New Shade of Blue" by the Bobby Fuller Four, "Who Do You Love?" from Quicksilver, and Timmy Thomas's "Why Can't We Live Together?"

I love all the disco music and Gamble-Huff production of the throbbing Thelma Houston tune "Don't Leave Me This Way" in the Richard Brooks-directed *Looking for Mr. Goodbar*, as well as the disco tunes and the period piece items on director Neil Jordan's *Breakfast on Pluto* soundtrack.

I'd insist you pick up the *Repo Man* soundtrack that has Burning Sensations doing the best version of Jonathan Richman's "Pablo Picasso" on it.

Days of Heaven with Leo Kottke's guitar score is really nice.

Director Monte Hellman (left) with actors Warren Oates and
James Taylor on the set of *Two-Lane Blacktop*. Courtesy of Monte Hellman.

I don't think a soundtrack LP is available from director Monte Hellman's
Two-Lane Blacktop, but Billy James did a great job placing the tunes in this
road movie that starred James Taylor, Beach Boy Dennis Wilson, and the
underrated Warren Oates.

Onstage at his Pantages Theater concert on May 3, 2005 in Hollywood,
Bruce Springsteen mentioned *Two-Lane Blacktop* in a song introduction
and then dedicated a piano-only version of "Racing in the Streets" to
director Hellman.

Director Floyd Mutrux's *Dusty and Sweets McGee*. I saw it again in summer of 2004 at the American Cinematheque's *Movies Not on Video* series.
Shot in a natural docudrama style, a 1971-era Los Angeles tale of real-life
junkies. Mutrux, who later helmed *American Hot Wax*, spoke at the special screening and said the film cost him $35,000 to make. He also pointed
out the influence of the *Cruisin'* radio soundtrack LP series at the time
on some of his music choices, which made him inject oldies like Gene
Chandler's "Duke of Earl." This was a year before *American Graffiti* was
even released. A soundtrack album for *Dusty* existed on Warner Brothers

Records, and the real stunner in the flick was the use of Harry Nilsson's "Don't Leave Me." Studio City never looked so inviting . . .

The evocative album of Sam Peckinpah's *Pat Garrett and Billy the Kid*, with Bob Dylan's movie music. "Knockin' on Heaven's Door" is a haunting vocal delivery. Jim Keltner, who played drums on the recording date in a Burbank studio, told me Dylan arrived for the session with a very bad cold and sore throat, but insisted on doing his live vocal on the track. Now listen closely to his singing on the record next time you hear it.

"Things Have Changed," Dylan's original contribution to director Curtis Hanson's *Wonder Boys*, is descriptive pop-rock form storytelling as well.

In 2005 I enjoyed Bob Dylan's "Boots of Spanish Leather" in *The Ballad of Jack and Rose*, a production that prominently features Dylan's music, from filmmaker Rebecca Miller and actor Daniel Day-Lewis.

The use of the Rolling Stones' "You Got the Silver," with Keith Richards on vocals, in *Zabriskie Point* is very cinematic. It's not included in the

Keith Richards, Studio City,
California, 1969.
Photo by Henry Diltz.

soundtrack LP, but there is an excerpt on the album from the Grateful Dead's "Dark Star," specifically geographical in setting and very potent in the film.

The movie *1969* had a time-sensitive soundtrack. Blind Faith's "Can't Find My Way Home" was very appropriate. Crosby, Stills & Nash's "Wooden Ships" was a joy to hear within the film's journey, as was the Zombies' "Time of the Season." But the real jolt was the Pretenders' offering of Bacharach and David's "Windows of the World." What a vocal performance by Chrissie Hynde! Produced by Nick Lowe; mixed by Bob Clearmountain.

A regular pleasure is listening to the hastily dubbed instrumental jazz and R&B tracks in director Robert Downey's *Putney Swope.*

The segment of the Rolling Stones' "Gimme Shelter" used on CBS at halftime in the NCAA basketball championship game between Illinois and North Carolina, with the Tarheels up by thirteen at the half. I never thought that in March 2005, I'd see a quick view of coach Roy Williams in front of thirty seconds of "Gimme Shelter." U2 was also played on the broadcast, but I was too busy talking to Chris Darrow on the telephone to recognize the song flash.

Then again, the following month on Channel 13, the golden voice of Vin Scully was calling a Los Angeles Dodgers vs. San Diego Padres baseball game in the April 2005 home stand, and in one inning the leadoff hitter entered the box to the sound of Jimi Hendrix's "Voodoo Child (Slight Return)." Long Beach's Milton Bradley, Dodgers outfielder and Jackie Robinson fan, has come to the plate with a Snoop Dogg track blaring over the stadium's loudspeakers and Bradley's face on the scoreboard.

I heard the Byrds' "Wasn't Born to Follow" again in the 2004 *Easy Rider* package and had forgotten how good it was. Every Byrds TV appearance from 1965 to 1967 was worthwhile. The Byrds' *There Is a Season* summer 2006 box set includes a DVD of ten vintage American and British TV clips from the 1960s.

The best use of rock 'n' roll songs, narration, politics, and film was nearly twenty years ago when Ben Edmonds supervised the music for the emotionally groundbreaking HBO program, *Dear America: Letters Home from Vietnam*, which was released theatrically in the United States in 1987 and also shown on PBS. The Rolling Stones, Bob Dylan, MC5, Sly and the Family Stone, the Doors, the Jimi Hendrix Experience, Bruce Springsteen, Love, Country Joe and the Fish, Buffalo Springfield, Smokey Robinson and the Miracles, and Tim Buckley all contributed their songs. Hearing

Love's "Signed D.C.," MC5's "Back in the U.S.A.," Tim Buckley's "Once I Was," the Rolling Stones' "Gimme Shelter" and "No Expectations," along with Sonny & Cher's "The Beat Goes On," propelled the graphic images of war onscreen.

On television I didn't miss an episode of *Playboy after Dark*, still airing on The Playboy Channel in the fall of 2006 and now available on DVD. I still play the program's jazz instrumental theme song by Cy Coleman. I caught the visits by Billy Eckstine, Sammy Davis Jr., Joe Williams, and George Kirby. There were some rock 'n' roll bands on *Playboy after Dark*, like Canned Heat, Deep Purple, Joe Cocker, Linda Ronstadt, the Grateful Dead, the Grass Roots, Steppenwolf, Three Dog Night, and the Sir Douglas Quintet. Entertainers Noel Harrison, the Clara Ward Singers, and Jackie DeShannon, with Barry White as a backup singer in a cool double-breasted suit, weren't treated as stepchildren. The musicians were always integrated into the whole show and they would be part of the couch conversation with the actors, athletes, and comedians, too.

"For Pete's Sake," the closing theme of the Monkees' TV series for the second season, will always be vibrant and alive!

The Monkees on the set of their TV series at the Columbia Pictures Lot, Burbank, California, 1967. Photo by Henry Diltz.

The November 1968 premiere of *Head* at the Vogue Theater on Hollywood Boulevard. Groovy trip is all I can say. The event was a true sense of community that used to exist in the town. As a teenager at the time, Dennis Hopper motioning to me in the lobby, "Hey kid . . . sit with us," was a real rock 'n' roll signal.

I dig some of the '70s blaxploitation movies. Joel Freeman for *Shaft*, Max Julien from *The Mack*, and Jack Hill and Antonio Fargas of *Foxy Brown* totally delivered. Tamara Dobson rules!

I still get a kick out of the cheesy R&B and jazz backing tracks that surround comedian-actor-producer Rudy Ray Moore's independent *Dolomite* movie endeavors and his albums. I went to a 1971 Wiltern Theater *Dolomite* premiere and had the worst wardrobe in the place. I helped Rudy on his 1988 Club Lingerie appearance, did a radio show with him on KPCC-FM, and I have a unique understanding and education of his original vinyl LP pressing, *This Pussy Belongs to Me*, from our car conversation.

Apocalypse Now, with "The End" by the Doors, is an immortal moment. What an opening! I first saw a preview of the Francis Ford Coppola movie—Michael Hacker got me in when he worked at Zoetrope Studios in 1978—without titles or credits on the screen, and it was compelling to say the least. This is what Ray Manzarek and Jim Morrison set out to do at the UCLA Film School with their songs. Manzarek once mentioned to me on campus that when Coppola made his student film, he used a crane when he shot his movie.

Jimi Hendrix's "Voodoo Chile" in *Withnail and I* is both cosmic and revolutionary.

Maverick indie filmmaker Hal Jepsen directed and edited the masterful mid-1970s surf movie *The Cosmic Children*. I saw it countless times with Hal and longboarder Peter Piper. The film contained an in-the-tube soundtrack housing the Paul Butterfield Blues Band, Crosby, Stills, Nash & Young, Jethro Tull, Cream, the Byrds, B. B. King, John Mayall's Bluesbreakers, the Chambers Brothers, the Rolling Stones, Jimi Hendrix, and the Dave Brubeck Quartet. A precise and sociological liquid documentation of Miki Dora on one of his last waves ever, in Malibu, simultaneously fronting the Pacific Ocean and "Sympathy for the Devil." Surfers don't ask permission.

And speaking of the beach, Stacy Peralta's 2004 *Riding Giants* movie and soundtrack—an epic surf and turf collection of many fun-tastic instrumentals—displays Dick Dale's "Misirlou," Link Wray's "Rumble," and

Santo and Johnny's "Sleepwalk" like you never heard these instrumentals before. The inclusion of David Bowie's "Stay," Alice In Chains performing "Them Bones," and the rendition of Mose Allison's "Parchman Farm" by John Mayall and the Bluesbreakers with Eric Clapton are eye opening in this big wave water world portrayal. The movie and the soundtrack forced me to listen to my life in a different way.

Seeing a preview of this epic surf movie with Peter Piper, a veteran surfer, and hearing his living DVD-like supplemental commentary track in the plush seat next to me, inside the screening room at Sony Studios in Culver City, was a whole other verbal bonus side trip. I was reminded of events from forty years ago when we saw *The Endless Summer* premiere at the Encore Theater in Hollywood and later at the Santa Monica Civic Auditorium.

Speaking of John Mayall again, kudos to the Trio cable channel. This new entry in the competitive pay station arena in June 2004 broadcast *The Turning Point*, a 1969 black-and-white U.K. documentary on Mayall about the making of his drummer-less classic album, *The Turning Point*. The same week, Trio aired *Pink Lady and Jeff* and *Tupac: Resurrection*. Fringe cinema for both the passionate music collector and the nerd-friendly pop culture film universe. Trio, along with premium cable TV stations like Sundance, Bravo, and IFC, is more active in scheduling pop culture documentaries and retrospectives that chronicle various music genres. However, in 2006 Trio became an Internet-only service.

The Ventures' "Walk, Don't Run" in the cable TV movie *61** about baseball players Mickey Mantle and Roger Maris and their season-long home run derby; the same band's recording of "Hawaii Five-0" in an AT&T commercial around the last turn of the century; and the 1966 Japanese documentary on the Ventures, *Beloved Invaders*.

One of my yearly pleasures is Robert De Niro's directorial debut, *A Bronx Tale*, that has a tasteful soundtrack full of early rock 'n' roll and some delicious R&B.

As much as I treasure the *Standing in the Shadows of Motown* documentary, having seen it five times, and interviewed the Funk Brothers twice, I get bummed knowing that bassist James Jamerson, who was on so many Motown Records hits, had to buy a ticket for the *Motown 25* TV show live taping, and sat in the balcony for the event at the Pasadena Civic Auditorium.

I watch the movie *In the Heat of the Night* once in a while just to hear Ray Charles' vocal on the title theme he did with Quincy Jones. In 2004 actor and pianist Jamie Foxx took it to the house in the Ray Charles biopic *Ray*. Oscar winner Kevin Spacey was also very believable in his own Bobby Darin vehicle, *Beyond the Sea*. The James Mangold-directed *Walk the Line*, the enjoyable Johnny and June Cash love story which features a marvelous performance by Joaquin Phoenix playing Johnny Cash, was released on DVD by Fox in spring 2006. There's a lot of pleasing extra features and short-form documentaries contained on the two-disc set.

Actor and fellow Pisces Terrence Howard in the rap flick *Hustle & Flow* was a rad, dad.

Also in 2004, Buddy Guy's emotional rendition of Jimi Hendrix's "Red House" in the concert film *Lightning in a Bottle*.

"Poptastic" vanilla soul examples include Dusty Springfield's measured vocal prowess on "Some of Your Lovin'" on *Hullabaloo* in the mid-'60s, which ranks right up there with the Carpenters performing "Superstar" from an early '70s A&M Records TV promotional film clip. Downey's Karen Carpenter was one of my all-time favorite singers. She sounded even better in concerts. Universal Music distributed a fine *Carpenters Gold* package of two CDs and one DVD for Christmas 2004 via the A&M Chronicles division. The same company also released *The*

Steppenwolf on *The Ed Sullivan Show*. Photo by Henry Diltz.

Marvin Gaye Collection on DVD. Go take a look at Tammi Terrell dueting with Marvin on "Ain't No Mountain High Enough" and talk to me about the heat you see onscreen.

The Turtles doing "You Baby" on *Hullabaloo*, and the same time-slot gave me the Lovin' Spoonful blasting away on "Do You Believe in Magic?" The Shangri-las held their ground on Lloyd Thaxton's L.A. show with "Give Him a Great Big Kiss," and made a permanent impression on my existence. I was even attracted to their New York accents—alongside the sonic dramas within the George "Shadow" Morton-produced songs—when I saw and heard them on other TV shows like *Shindig!* and *Hollywood A Go Go*.

James Brown's debut on *The Ed Sullivan Show* was like seeing a visitor from another planet in our living room. Ed's Sunday night bookings of Little Anthony and the Imperials, the Animals, the Temptations, Steppenwolf, the Supremes, the Dave Clark Five, and the Beatles, from Miami, carried me through school homeroom the following mornings.

The use of the Beach Boys' "Feel Flows" playing over the end credits of *Almost Famous*.

Another movie soundtrack album I relish is the *Collector's Edition: Music from the Motion Picture Pulp Fiction*. What's neat are some bonus tracks in this set, including "Out of Limits" by The Marketts and "Strawberry Letter #23" performed by Brothers Johnson, as well as "Since I First Met You" by the Robins. Another local surf instrumental and a couple of hot L.A. old school R&B tracks have been added into the original package, which has a second disc of Quentin Tarantino talking about his movie.

Other 2004 television action includes *Six Feet Under* and the music from that HBO original series. I think the compilation *Our Little Corner of the World—Music from "The Gilmore Girls"* that Gary Stewart helped produce, which has some songs by PJ Harvey, Ash, Elastica, and Joey Ramone, really delivers. I like the way the music is incorporated into that TV show.

I just picked up the soundtrack double album—on vinyl—of *The Strawberry Statement*. In the January 2004 issue of *MOJO* magazine, Rosanne Cash said that the very first record she ever bought was in a record store in Ventura, California, where she used her own money to purchase *The Strawberry Statement*, which she bought solely for that one Thunderclap Newman song, "Something in the Air." Good move.

In 2003, Fred Shuster, the music writer for the *Los Angeles Daily News*, introduced me to *24 Hour Party People*. An example where movie and music worked well together. The film does such a good job telling the story behind the songs.

Trumpeter Don Ellis laying out odd time signatures and unusual meters sparkled on a *Live at Tanglewood* PBS episode I remember from the early 1970s. Another Ellis sequence was originally from KQED-TV and then broadcast on KCET, a special on the 1967 Monterey Jazz Festival that featured his exhilarating "Electric Lady" number. Richie Havens, B. B. King, Carmen McRae, and Dizzy Gillespie were also on that great show.

Another Tanglewood tape document, circa 1971, courtesy of Bill Graham Presents, featured Jethro Tull. Ian Anderson and his early Jethro Tull members are showcased as well in Murray Lerner's *Isle of Wight* documentary, while Lerner's earlier *Festival!* is a musical education, which was issued in DVD format in summer 2005. Howlin' Wolf captured in black-and-white! In 2003 filmmaker Don McGlynn's *The Howlin' Wolf Story* came out on DVD and is highly recommended.

I also got a copy of the incredible BBC documentary that Elaine Shepherd put together in 2002, *Fame, Fashion and Photography: The Real Blow-Up*, an extensive examination of the Antonioni movie, *Blow-Up*. Besides all the interviews with models, photographers like David Bailey, magazine editors, Terrence Stamp, David Hemmings, Andrew Loog Oldham, Twiggy, Vidal Sassoon, and so many others, the music used in the documentary was so chronologically perfect and appropriate for the visuals put together. It should be required viewing for anyone who loves the marriage of music and movies. Just a stunning example of how to do it right.

Another celluloid import was perhaps the best viewing moment of 2004: *John Lennon's Jukebox*—originally a U.K. Channel 4 production, later broadcast on PBS in the United States—wove tales about his collection of 45 rpm singles, and the heat inside the aural culture rhythm track to their own lives that Johnny Beatle stocked for them. Commentary from Fontella Bass, Wilson Pickett, with sights and sounds from his *Hollywood A Go Go* appearance miming to "Midnight Hour," Steve Cropper, Donovan, Robert Parker, Richard Barrett, Sting, Jerry Leiber, and Mike Stoller. What an inspiring concept by Jon Midwinter.

And speaking of England, the BBC newsreel footage of Bruce Springsteen and the E Street Band's 1975 *Born to Run* tour that filtered over to the United States is powerful stuff. I was lucky enough to see the screening room "first cut" version of Peter Bogdanovich's *Mask* that was initially populated with Springsteen recordings, including "It's Hard to

Be a Saint in the City," that was mesmerizing in the context of the movie. Even the suits applauded. Then, apparently, there were some terse movie and music negotiations at Universal over Springsteen song use, and all his master recordings were subsequently wiped from that motion picture. Later on, the film *Baby It's You* eventually incorporated some Bruce sound copyrights, specifically "Adam Raised a Cain," and a cafeteria cruise scene linked to "It's Hard to Be a Saint in the City," that were really quite riveting.

Martin Scorsese's use of music in *Goodfellas*. Songs and productions from George Harrison, Muddy Waters, Harry Nilsson, the Rolling Stones, the Who, the Crystals, and Donovan move the storyline. Scorsese has big budgets for licensing, the money is on the screen, but so many performances in *Goodfellas* didn't get near the commercially released soundtrack.

Scorsese's appropriate use of Roxy Music's "Love Is the Drug" inside *Casino* is a pleasure to hear. I dig the 1970-ish B. B. King concert sequence in the *Medicine Ball Caravan* movie that Scorsese edited. Another memorable Scorsese movie music placement is Van Morrison's spooky "TB Sheets" in *Bringing Out the Dead*. I also love the 1965 live version of "Fly Me to the Moon" that Frank Sinatra sang with Count Basie, arranged by Quincy Jones, plucked by musical director Robbie Robertson for inclusion in his overlooked *The King of Comedy*.

Some other video picks are *Cracked Actor*, a documentary on David Bowie where the director Alan Yentob made the film in the '70s and then revisited Bowie over twenty years later; Elton John's *Tantrums and Tiaras*; and Patti Smith in 1979 on *Rockpalast*. I like Todd Rundgren. I suggest his *Live in Japan, Utopia: A Retrospective 1977–84* and *The Ever Popular Tortured Artist Effect* videos. There's also a 1977 edition of *Rockpalast* with Tom Petty and the Heartbreakers that is very, very good.

A cool rock 'n' roll television booking was Phil Spector's 1965 performance on the David Susskind show, *Open End*. Recording industry veteran Denny Bruce reminded me of another Spector TV event around the same time when he squared off against music managers and producers Brian Stone and Charlie Greene on *The Les Crane Show* in 1965 or 1966. Van Dyke Parks also did the same *Crane* slot with a stream of consciousness, informative ramble extolling the advent of technology in the music and recording world.

Leon Russell and Friends' *Sessions*, the 1970 (KCET) PBS program. Even if it was just for his piano playing.

In 1971, KCET also broadcast an episode on Cat Stevens, *Tea for the Tillerman*. Taylor Hackford directed. Hard folk and pop tales bridged me to Cat's songs, later dropped in mathematically in director Hal Ashby's *Harold and Maude* movie. Man, I'll even cop to watching VH1's *Behind the Music* on Stevens. This cat has been missing in action.

DJ Dave Diamond hosting TV's *Head Shop* for a full year in 1971 on UHF.

Steely Dan's early '70s television appearances, like *The Midnight Special*, were always interesting, partially because the band looked like a bunch of dudes who were picked off Beverly Boulevard to play on TV. And they were!

I'm a big fan of the way rocker Johnny Rivers interpreted songs from the movies. The Lou Adler-produced Rivers versions of "Days of Wine and Roses," "The Shadow of Your Smile" from *The Sandpiper*, and the

Left to right: Jeff Hanna, Lee Marvin, and Chris Darrow on location in Baker, Oregon, for the movie *Paint Your Wagon*, 1968. Courtesy of Chris Darrow.

Taste of Honey title number should be investigated. Exquisite West Coast pop-rock arrangements for Cocktail Nation digestion.

Director Eytan Fox's moving 2005 thriller film, *Walk on Water*, made effective use of Bruce Springsteen's "Tunnel of Love" and Buffalo Springfield's "For What It's Worth," a Stephen Stills song that was first performed at a 1966 KBLA concert at Santa Monica's Civic Auditorium. In 2005 the recording was placed appropriately in this tense mission drama.

Every once in a while the American Movie Channel airs director Josh Logan's *Paint Your Wagon*, and I always stay glued until my good friend, multi-instrumentalist Chris Darrow—a Nitty Gritty Dirt Band member at the time—sings, "Hand Me Down That Can'o Beans." There's something groovy about a hippie singing a Broadway tune . . .

Any TV footage of Spike Jones.

The opening prologue from the movie *West Side Story*. I was lucky enough a couple of years ago to attend the cast and crew forty-year reunion at the American Cinémathèque's Egyptian Theater tribute to director Robert Wise, and the house rocked the entire evening. The words and music of Stephen Sondheim and Leonard Bernstein never sounded better. If you don't own this movie, then at least hear it. In 2004 Sony/Classical Legacy Records issued the original soundtrack recording remixed. The Special Edition DVD Collector's Set restored and remixed in 5.1 audio includes a documentary, theatrical trailers, and original intermission music.

As far as James Bond is concerned, besides the George Martin-produced "Live and Let Die" by Paul McCartney and Wings, and John Barry's arrangement of Shirley Bassey belting out "Goldfinger," may I direct your attention to Lulu soaring away on another John Barry arrangement, "The Man with the Golden Gun," produced by Wes Farrell. Take a bow, Mr. John Barry.

"If I Can't Have You," the Bee Gees offering from their *Saturday Night Fever* compilation.

"God Give Me Strength," the Elvis Costello and Burt Bacharach collaboration for the *Grace of My Heart* movie, from director Allison Anders, was really special.

I sure missed it with Jeff Buckley until I heard his cover of Leonard Cohen's "Hallelujah." Then absorbing Buckley's version in various TV show positions, including *The O.C.*, *The West Wing*, *Without a Trace*, *Scrubs*, and *Crossing Jordan*, among other placements of the master, is graceful.

I first discovered "Summertime" from *Porgy and Bess* in 1959, and in

1969 singer Billy Stewart's energetic soul recording, with future Earth, Wind & Fire cofounder Maurice White pounding on the drums, jumped out of my transistor radio when I heard it. Find the long unedited album version.

Perennial long-form video favorites also have to be: *The Doors: A Tribute to Jim Morrison; 25 x 5: The Continuing Adventures of the Rolling Stones; The Jimi Hendrix Experience*, the concert movie that Peter Neal directed and Alexis Korner narrated; *Finally . . . Eric Burdon and the Animals; The Mamas and the Papas: Straight Shooter;* U2's *The Unforgettable Fire Collection; The Who: 30 Years of Maximum R&B Live;* and *This Is Elvis*.

One terrific DVD that ABKCO put on the shelves a few years back was Sam Cooke's *Legend*. Rare and never-before-seen Cooke performance clips, television footage, family photos, and interviews with Lou Rawls, Lloyd Price, Lou Adler, Bobby Womack, Aretha Franklin, L. C. Cook(e), and others. Jeffrey Wright narrates.

A handful of years ago, on the sad day I heard record producer Nik Venet had died, I was already scheduled to meet writer Nelson Gary. We were sitting in Sam Woo's Barbecue on Sepulveda in the San Fernando Valley, and in walked cool daddy songwriter and legendary musicmaker Bobby Womack, after parking his new Buick Deuce-and-a-Quarter ride. Over lunch with Nelson, I had just mentioned Nik Venet's catalogue, his album productions, the music he made or placed in movies and television, and wondered aloud if Nik's legacy would still make an impression in today's climate. As B. W. was waiting on some food to go, I said to him, "Any current action?" Bobby smiled, "I got the opening and closing track on this new film, *Jackie Brown*. Pam Grier is in front of my tune, 'Across 110th Street' we did years ago!" Nik Venet was the original soundtrack coproducer for the film *Across 110th Street*, when Bobby first released it on United Artists Records. So hearing Bobby got some new bucks and Nik smiling sweetly got me out of the bummer tent real quick that afternoon. I sometimes forget about the power of music to heal.

One recent explosive soundtrack from Shout! Factory is that culled from the Hughes Brothers documentary film *American Pimp*, which ran heavily on HBO. The CD features recordings by Curtis Mayfield, Marvin Gaye, the Ohio Players, an extended interview with Snoop Dogg, and dialogue from the movie.

2005 also saw the release of the awe-inspiring Al Green *Soul Revolution: Live in '72* DVD, culled from a New York TV program, *Soul*. Also available in the same series is a Stevie Wonder and Wonderlove show from

The Mamas and the Papas in San Diego, California, appearing on an episode of *Where The Action Is*. Photo by Henry Diltz.

the same era. Drummer Ollie Eugene Brown holds the beat flawlessly. Wonder and his band are also in DVD-land with a stellar 1975 *Musikladen* performance, portions of which have been broadcast on VH1.

My two favorite examples of Elvis Costello on film are his 1977 *Saturday Night Live* appearance, coupling "Less than Zero" and "Radio, Radio"; and his original promotional clip of "Pump It Up."

Al Kooper's "Brand New Day," sung by the Staple Singers, from the movie, *The Landlord*.

I still get chills from Santana's fiery performance in the *Woodstock* movie, and definitely worth seeking is a circa 1973 Japanese TV broadcast of the Santana band touring *Lotus* that vocalist Leon Thomas fronted.

The Mamas and the Papas at the Hollywood Palace in 1966. "Monday, Monday." I'm in the audience. Member Michelle Phillips, who went to nearby Marshall High School, got me into the taping. No one asked for ID or frisked us at the door, either. That choice performance, and many of their other audio and visual delights, were made available in March 2005 in *The Mamas and the Papas: California Dreamin'* (DVD) on Hip-O, distributed by Universal Music Enterprises.

Johnny Cash's *The Man, His World, His Music* arrived this decade and includes studio footage with Johnny and Bob Dylan on "One Too Many Mornings."

Coolness is the first Garbage authorized video compilation with "Only Happens When It Rains" and "Stupid Girl."

It's always interesting to see how some people stock their video and DVD shelves. I was over at photographer Heather Harris's to house-sit for a weekend recently. She has a real "Westlake Girl" mentality that even extends to the way she files her rock music videos and DVDs: There were two stacks, almost like mono and stereo albums. *Ladies and Gentlemen, The Fabulous Stains*, the 1981 Lou Adler-directed feature; *Gimme Some Truth*, the new John Lennon documentary; and then *Heavy Metal Parking Lot*, that's self-explanatory; and the concert film on Paul Westerberg, *Come Feel Me Tremble*. Between them was another pile with *This Is Spinal Tap*, *The Rutles, Festival Express, Prey for Rock & Roll, Still Crazy*, which people need to see—I discovered it from her—and *Sunset Strip*, based on the life of Hollywood rock photographer Ed Caraeff. What a score! Heather also had *Performance* in both the U.S. and U.K. video formats, as well as *O Lucky Man!*, plus the *London Calling* Clash video, which still sends chills whenever I watch it; and Bob Gruen and Nadya Beck's *All Dolled Up* DVD, containing an intimate series of short films examining the New York Dolls. Check this, she also has *Welcome to the Dollhouse*, taped on the same videocassette with *DIG!* and *I Am Trying to Break Your Heart*, the Wilco movie. Heather's stash also offered entertaining and educational items like *Swingers, Fritz the Cat* and *The SpongeBob SquarePants Movie*, as well as *The Beatles Anthology, Biggie & Tupac, The Clash: Westway to the World, Standing in the Shadows of Motown, Head* by the Monkees, DC5's *Having a Wild Weekend, Norah Jones: Live in New Orleans, Hairspray*, and *This Is Elvis*, the stirring documentary by Malcolm Leo and Andrew Solt, along with *Cisco Pike* and *Hype*.

I spent one long weekend at the tail end of 2004 thrilled and absorbed by DVDs of *The Grateful Dead Movie*, the 1974 concert film that also includes various Dolby mixes in the DVD extras; *Fly Jefferson Airplane*; The Beatles' *The First U.S. Visit*; and *The Brando Box Set*. Marlon Brando lived up the street from me.

A new visual and music discovery in 2005 was the *Old Grey Whistle Test* program collection on DVD. The Sensational Alex Harvey Band, Bill Withers, Alice Cooper, Captain Beefheart, Curtis Mayfield, and Bob Marley and the Wailers, from U.K. TV origins. The English two-disc set, not the abridged U.S. commercial version.

I also dug the TV music series, *Music Scene*, as well as *The Midnight Special*. I went to every *Midnight Special* taping in Burbank. The staff always treated me kindly. A spring 2006 infomercial touts the series now available on multidisc DVD.

Producer Robbie Rist's 2006 trailer for *Stump the Band* is the talk of the town. A former child actor and glitter critter band fan.

In the future, maybe this century's soundtracks will be akin to Neil LaBute's *The Shapes of Things*, an entire movie soundtrack scored by Elvis Costello recordings. The new arranged marriage made in Hollywood.

In June 2005 I viewed the 3-disc set, Elvis—*The '68 Comeback Special* (Deluxe Edition DVD), Presley's show for NBC that was first broadcast in December of 1968.

My friend Dan Kessel, a musician and producer, who is one of the sons of the late jazz great and session guitarist Barney Kessel, knew Elvis and was at the "If I Can Dream" recording session as well as the Presley TV

Ray Davies of the Kinks rehearsing for *The Midnight Special* TV show taping, Burbank, California, May 1974. Photo by Ellen Berman.

show taping in Burbank. Barney played on some Presley sessions, including "Return to Sender," and Dan's stepmom, background vocalist-contractor B. J. Baker, was a backup singer on some movie tunes Elvis cut, from "Flaming Star" through "Change of Habit." She is also heard on "If I Can Dream," and was in charge of hiring and directing the singers on that date at Western Studios in Hollywood.

Dan e-mailed me: "In the '50s and early '60s, before four-track and eight-track recorders became the norm, records were cut live and mixed live with all performances, EQs, echoes, reverb, all premixed simultaneously. With the later advent of multitracking, records became more fragmented, with performances stacked and layered. Singers would overdub their vocals, usually in an isolation booth, and often days after basic tracks were recorded—and then dub harmonies even later. The records were often mixed and edited over a further period of time.

"However, in these sessions, including 'If I Can Dream,' and 'Memories,' even though engineer Bones Howe was working with multitrack equipment, they went for more of an old school, live approach.

"Elvis was cutting vocals live, no isolation booth, on the floor with the musicians and singers. Elvis was pacing the floor, while singing into a hand microphone that was secured to his hand with lots of black electrical tape wrapped around his hand and wrist. Although Bones used 'limiting' to help control the inconsistent volume peaks on Elvis' vocal, he had to keep his eyes glued to the VU meter and constantly ride the lead vocal track fader to keep Elvis' vocal from dropping or peaking."

In November, 1970, I jumped on a bus by myself and went out to Inglewood and the L.A. Forum to see Presley do a concert.

Elvis, by the Presleys, a May 2005 CBS telecast, also on DVD, was a revealing portrait of Elvis by family members; the outtakes from the 1968 TV special, including "If I Can Dream," were very rewarding. Lisa Marie, Priscilla, and Jerry Schilling brought their "A" game to the two-hour program, but . . . no interview with the original *'68 Comeback Special* director, Steve Binder? My pal, Rodney Bingenheimer, who lives in a world of freebies, actually ordered the DVD of *Elvis, by the Presleys* over the phone from a TV advertisement he saw and even used his own plastic to pay for it!

From the '50s I think *Invaders from Mars* has the scariest atmosphere music. My bro' for over forty years, Bob Sherman, still gets freaked out when he hears those haunting voice cues mixed with the tension-driven anticipatory score that Raoul Kraushaar composed, especially the scenes near the sandpit, where the people disappear in that movie.

I once interviewed Barry White for *Melody Maker* at his home and we did a half hour just on *Invaders from Mars*, which he worshipped. He owned a copy on the original big reels for his screening room. A world before Betamax and VHS tape.

Every few years, if I saw Barry in a recording studio like Whitney Sound in Glendale, or a restaurant, at one of his rare concerts, or driving his Rolls Royce in the San Fernando Valley (his license plate read "Mo Love"), Barry would say something in passing to me. He had that incredible deep vocal delivery: "Don't get too close to the sand, young man." Or he'd joke: "You still in love with Hillary Brooke [the actress who played the mother in *Invaders from Mars*], even if she had one of those things implanted in her neck?" I miss him.

I'm so glad that White's "Love's Theme" for a time in the mid-'70s actually was used as the lead-in music for the afternoon *Million Dollar Movie* on Channel 9. It was a dream of Barry's as a kid growing up in L.A. He realized one of his ambitions of composing music for his favorite TV show when he went to the Jacob Riis School. Barry had an incredible sense of time. Hey, he was either the studio drummer or the road drummer on Jackie Lee's "Do the Duck," years before all his disco and dance chart hits. I even watched the VH1 *Behind the Music* episode on him, which was damn good.

In my record collection and video shelves, jazz sits next to rock 'n' roll, and in my memories jazz introduced me to rock 'n' roll. As a youth I never really knew that so many pop and rock hits in the '50s, '60s, and '70s had jazz musicians on the record dates, title themes, and soundtrack recordings. From Plas Johnson's saxophone solo on *The Pink Panther* to drummer Stan Levey bashing behind the soaring Gene Pitney vocal on *Town without Pity*.

My open secret, the black-and-white home video now out of Les McCann and Eddie Harris performing their "Swiss Movement" recital at the 1971 Montreux Jazz Festival. I saw a clip from it on BET a couple of years back. As sweet as carrot halvah.

2005 saw the long anticipated *Jazz on the West Coast: The Lighthouse* documentary put together by Ken Koenig, who managed to get everyone from Bill Holman and Buddy Collette to Howard Rumsey and Bud Shank—as well as bartenders and waitresses—to comment on this legendary jazz music venue.

I always watch anytime there's a TV rerun of *The Gene Krupa Story*, shot in 1959, released in 1960, directed by Don Weis, starring Sal Mineo, James

Darren, Susan Kohner, Susan Oliver (!), Red Nichols, Shelly Manne, Buddy Lester, and Gavin MacLeod.

I produced an audio biography on Buddy Collette. He'd recorded with Frank Sinatra, Percy Faith, Charles Mingus, Eric Dolphy, Jackie Kelso, and so many others, and told me that Marlon Brando was really influential, along with producer Stanley Kramer, demanding a jazz score for the movie *The Wild One*. Brando apparently liked an album Shorty Rogers and Milt Bernhardt were on. Marlon was being pressured to use Dimitri Tiomkin and the heavy composers for the film gig, and he wanted Shorty Rogers and some of the West Coast guys for the music. All the Stan Kenton men could really play, read music well, and were not junkies and juiceheads, which was the perception and vibe the big studios felt some of the time when they heard the word jazz musician in conjunction with potential movie work. Buddy was already well respected by both the classical and jazz community, plus he could double on a lot of instruments. In the very early 1950s Buddy was also instrumental in integrating the

Shelly Manne as his idol, Dave Tough, behind the drums on the set of *The Five Pennies*, Hollywood, California, 1959. Photo courtesy of Kirk Silsbee.

Musicians Union. So the local union, at the time filled with classical players, had to let the jazz cats further into studio work—record and especially movie dates—and an influx of jazz music started getting heard on camera and film. Then the soundtracks started really reflecting this as well. A lot of the Lighthouse Allstars started playing on soundtracks.

Jazz on television, as well as a 1960 art house showing of *Jazz on a Summer's Day*, the movie about the 1958 Newport Jazz Festival, guided me to seek the sounds of rock 'n' roll. Chuck Berry and Louis Armstrong in living color!

I'm improvising and doing a head chart, but I faintly remember a CBS TV special in 1957, *The Sound of Jazz*, that had Billie Holiday, Lester Young, Count Basie, and Thelonius Monk. Around 1960 to 1962, there were some jazz shows on local TV that were really hip. Steve Allen always had jazz guys on his TV talk shows, and Terry Gibbs was his bandleader in 1960. Jack Kerouac's 1959 TV reading on *The Steve Allen Show*, with Allen on piano, was inspirational. Then later on, Allen had the early national TV bookings for Frank Zappa, Jerry Lee Lewis, Jan & Dean, the Beach Boys, and Bob Dylan. Even earlier, in 1955, was *Rhythm and Bluesville* in Los Angeles on Channel 2 that DJ Hunter Hancock hosted before he was on the KGFJ radio station. One episode had Fats Domino, whose birthday I share. I came home from kindergarten and got exposed to this stuff. Might explain the reason you've made it all the way through my book.

Peggy Lee singing "Fever" in black-and-white on *The George Gobel Show* in 1958 was a real stunner, and her duet, in color, with Andy Williams on "St. Louis Blues" in 1963 on his variety show, with a swinging bongo-driven rhythm track, sent me to the record shop the next day.

The big one in my neighborhood was *Stars of Jazz*, a nationally telecast syndicated program on ABC that Bobby Troup hosted. Maybe that even ran from 1956 through 1958. Composer Don Specht, a friend of writer Kirk Silsbee, once told him, "Bobby introduced more great jazz players to middle America than anyone. The average claims adjuster tuned in to find out what was hip each week." You'd see stuff like Troup writing a song on the spot with a guest, then Johnny Mercer would show up weekly in the last segment, finishing the tune off. It was first a summer replacement show and then aired as the first public network show on an ABC affiliate, Channel 7. George Shearing, Chico Hamilton, and Julie London. It was produced by Jimmie Baker, who produced *Jazz Scene U.S.A.*, and Billie Holiday was on that show. Oscar Brown Jr. was the host. Thankfully, some of the episodes are out now on DVD. Bobby

Troup starred in an episode of *Perry Mason*, and his band on the show had Barney Kessel on guitar. Kessel and Shelly Manne appeared in an episode of *Johnny Staccato* shown on the Trio channel in 2005.

You can hear the influence of jazz a lot in TV shows, as well all through the late '50s and well into the '60s that impacted a generation of rock music and film buffs like the ones you've just read about in *Hollywood Shack Job*.

I know the movie *The Subterraneans*, based on the Jack Kerouac novel, is corny, but the soundtrack LP that André Previn assembled really moves; it includes Art Pepper and Gerry Mulligan, who appears in the flick and is still a cool West Coast jazz-informed breeze. In 2005, the label Film Score Monthly rereleased the album.

When they remade *The Twilight Zone* in 1985, the Grateful Dead along with Merl Saunders did a new version of the original show's main theme. That group also contributed much of the new program's incidental music. A soundtrack for that show was released as an album in 1998. Grateful Dead lyricist and poet Robert Hunter even wrote an episode for the new series.

I'm still watching the original black-and-white *Twilight Zone* on the Sci-Fi channel. Besides stock music, the *Twilight Zone* theme was by Marius Constant, and the series employed a variety of composers like Bernard Herrmann, Jerry Goldsmith, Fred Steiner, Nathan Scott, Van Cleave, Laurindo Almeida, and Tommy Morgan, who later added harmonica on *Pet Sounds*. These days I'm basically clicking on the repeats just to notice if jazz photographer William Claxton or actress Ida Lupino directed a show, and to hear the incidental music, since I've already memorized every goddamn episode from the last forty years. I even played the *TZ* theme sporadically through the summer of 1964 while drumming for the Rip Tides surf band.

I'm a big fan of other episodic black-and-white TV programs from 1958 through 1964 that featured jazz scores. I constantly dig Henry Mancini's *The Music from Peter Gunn*, the 1958 Grammy Album of the Year. In 1962 there was Nelson Riddle's "Route 66" TV instrumental that was heard on the show each week. I love the guitar tag at the end of the track. Bob Bain's lead guitar licks on "Route 66" are notes of freedom. I sure liked when the A&E channel in the mid-'80s ran *Route 66* episodes once a week.

I'm also very fond of the 1959 *Playboy's Penthouse* series. Lenny Bruce, Sammy Davis Jr., Dick Gregory, Ella Fitzgerald, and Nat Cole reminding me that my parents were "Born in Chicago."

The Miles Davis TV performance from 1959, *The Sound of Miles Davis*, with the band featuring John Coltrane, Paul Chambers, Wynton Kelly, Jimmy Cobb, and the Gil Evans Orchestra, is now available on DVD as *Miles Davis: The Cool Jazz Sound*.

Pete Rugolo composed the theme and interstitial music for *The Fugitive* from 1963 to 1967. I also dialed in for *Richard Diamond, Mr. Lucky, Naked City, 77 Sunset Strip, Checkmate, M Squad*. Even before that, there was a great TV drama with John Cassavetes as the piano-playing private eye lead character in *Johnny Staccato*, scored by Elmer Bernstein, who created the jolting title sequence to the film *Walk on the Wild Side*.

Whatever happened to television the last thirty-five years?

I admire *The Timex Show* from the 1950s that Frank Sinatra hosted. Elvis Presley was on it. Frank later had a bunch of excellent TV music specials: *A Man and His Music* was terrific. And a performance special with Antonio Carlos Jobim was marvelous. Then there was the documentary CBS did on Frank Sinatra, called *Sinatra: An American Original*, which aired in April of 1965. Frank allowed the camera into the session where he recorded "It Was a Very Good Year." What command! Frank even mentions to the session guys that he heard the song by the Kingston Trio on the car radio before he wanted to cut it. And his arranger Gordon Jenkins got a taste on-screen. The tracking angles, the control booth playback, all clearly showed how a record was created. And it was done in Hollywood at Capitol Studios. I've used that room and it looks exactly the same nearly forty years later.

Sinatra had a unique relationship with the screen and music because he respected partnerships and instinctive matchups. This even extends to movies like *The Manchurian Candidate* that he starred in and had a piece of. I talked to director John Frankenheimer and composer David Amram, who worked with him on the picture, and Frank, who had clout and participation on that film, had no problem with Amram doing the score. Amram had done the music for *Splendor in the Grass* and worked with Jack Kerouac.

Nat King Cole had his own TV show in the 1950s, and he always had great guests who worked for free to help him. But unfortunately, Nat King Cole couldn't get any sponsors for his efforts. Nat was smooth.

Sometimes there would also be jazz musicians, entertainers, and budding rock folk, like drummer Jim Keltner, on *Rocket to Stardom* in 1956. The norm on this Bob Yeakel-sponsored live telecast was amateurs— magicians, singers, balloon folders—and only occasionally someone

Drummer Jim Keltner and saxophonist Lloyd Keese performing on the Los Angeles television program *Rocket to Stardom*, 1956. Photo courtesy of Pat Keltner.

with real talent. Yeakel had a car dealership. Lenny Bruce, with Joe Maini or Jack Sheldon, sneaked on (ten different people will tell you ten different accounts) and disrupted the show with gross musical put-ons and antics. A teenage Phil Spector warbled "In the Still of the Night" on *Rocket to Stardom* that would air on both KHJ-TV (Channel 9) and KTTV-TV (Channel 11).

I went to a lot of tapings of *The Judy Garland Show* with my mother, including the duet that Judy sang with Barbra Streisand. Mel Tormé was one of the writers. My mom worked at Columbia Studios for the first half of the 1960s, briefly working with Marty Ehrlichman, who managed Barbra. I was a kid, but Streisand was around the office. I used to sit around and watch some of the advances of her TV specials and her soundstage musicals while they were being edited. I also saw a clip of Streisand singing a Harold Arlen tune, "Anywhere I Hang My Hat Is Home," that was monumental. What a vocal range. Some of the arrangers would come by Gower Gulch and carry sheet music with them for copyright filing. I would look at some of the scorebooks and notice writer names like

Harold Arlen. I'm glad they released all those Streisand TV specials a few years back as home video product. In addition, five Streisand TV specials on DVD were released as a box set in late 2005.

A film music highlight of 2005 was a visit to the Music Hall movie theater in Beverly Hills with Andrew Loog Oldham and his son Max to break celluloid and view *Ballets Russes*. The sound of the tympani over the documentary film's end credits was loud and proud. William Claxton in the lobby afterward was an added bonus to an already thrilling experience.

I support and suggest attending the yearly month-long *Mods and Rockers* film festival every summer in Hollywood at the Egyptian Theater, arranged in conjunction with the American Cinemathéque. It's been a fixture since 1999.

It's a series curated by Martin Lewis, Dennis Bartok, and Chris D. The scheduling sometimes illustrates the acute differences and styles between British directors and their American counterparts when it comes to documenting music in long form documentaries and features over the last fifty years.

You wish it, they show it. John Boorman's *Having a Wild Weekend*, Joe Massot's *Wonderwall*, Peter Watkins' *Privilege*. The calendar has included moderated tributes to Michael Lindsay-Hogg, discussions on Dirk Bogarde in *Modesty Blaise* and David Hemmings in *Blow-up*. Eleanor Bron was there in person to answer questions on *Help!* and *Bedazzled*. The Who's Roger Daltrey and Michelle Phillips from The Mamas and the Papas reflected on *The Monterey Pop Festival*. Spencer Davis and Judy Geeson reviewed *Here We Go Round the Mulberry Bush*. *Darling* is still Godhead! Thank you, director John Schlesinger, for Bogarde, Laurence Harvey, and Julie Christie in this lovely black-and-white swinging reality check.

In the spring of 2004, the UCLA Film and Television Archive at Melnitz Hall in Westwood held a month-long *Los Angeles: Site Unseen*. The program showcased films and musical literature "that presented itself not as a comprehensive panorama but as a truly kaleidoscopic experience."

Model Shop, directed by Jacques Demy, played at the festival. Spirit was in the movie, supplying some tasty 1968 music to the rich Los Angeles and Hollywood landscape. Open City is also lensed. So is Anouk Aimee.

There were also screenings of Columbia restorations: *Rock Around the Clock*, the fiftieth anniversary of the release, in an ongoing multipart series spotlighting Sony Pictures Entertainment's program to restore titles from the rich Columbia Pictures library. In Westwood new prints shone of *Don't Knock the Rock, Let's Rock!*, *Twist Around the Clock, Bye Bye Birdie*, and the producing team of Milton Subotsky and Max Rosenberg's *It's Trad, Dad!* (a.k.a. *Ring-A-Ding Rhythm*), directed by Richard Lester. Rosenberg with Subotsky made four music films, including *Jamboree* and *Rock, Rock, Rock!*, a 1957 drama starring Tuesday Weld and featuring the music of Chuck Berry, Frankie Lymon, the Moonglows, and Johnny Burnette. In 2000, Rosenberg told *The Hollywood Reporter*, "It took nine days to make. The exciting thing was collecting the music. As for the picture itself, there's not much to commend. It's just a bunch of songs connected to a stupid plot." When longtime horror film producer Rosenberg died in June 2004, Dennis Bartok, head of programming at the American Cinemathéque, praised his catalogue to *The Los Angeles Times*' Dennis McLellan, a staff writer, in the lead obituary. "What made him unique was a combination of commercial savvy—he was always able to tap into the zeitgeist, whether it was rock 'n' roll in the late '50s or the explosion of drive-in movies and supernatural and horror films."

Donovan and his songs translate well in several music videos. His slot with a jazz and rock combo backing him at the NME *Big Beat* show in England in 1965 is totally impressive. Other Donovan delights on the screen are his appearances at the *Newport Folk Festival '65* and in the 1966 *Sunshine Superman* promotional film.

The September 2005 *American Masters* PBS airing of *No Direction Home*, the Bob Dylan documentary directed by Martin Scorsese, was a pleasure to watch. Paramount Home Entertainment released a compelling and expanded DVD edition, and the companion *No Direction Home: The Soundtrack—The Bootleg Series, Vol. 7* double-album package on Columbia / Legacy Records is delightful to listen to and read. Even the liner notes from Andrew Loog Oldham, Al Kooper, and Eddie Gorodetsky, collectively describing the two discs of previously unreleased Dylan music from 1959–1966, are cinematic text.

In late November 2005, Columbia Records released a *Bruce Springsteen: Born To Run* 30th Anniversary Edition box set that contains a stunning DVD of the legendary 1975 Hammersmith Odeon concert in London and a new ninety-minute DVD documentary film of *Wings for Wheels: The Making of "Born to Run,"* with never-before-seen archival footage and brand new interviews with all the band members and many others. In addition, a CD of the remastered *Born to Run* was included. The Hammersmith Odeon gig, edited by Emmy Award winner Thom Zimny,

Bruce Springsteen onstage at The Bottom Line,
New York, 1975. Photo by Peter Cunningham.

is the only full-length concert film ever released of Bruce and the E Street Band's first twenty-five years.

In the category of long-form documentaries, director-writer Morgan Neville's PBS *American Masters* portraits on Muddy Waters in 2003 and Hank Williams in 2004 were thrilling. Neville's examination of the Jerry Leiber and Mike Stoller team and his feature-length piece about the legendary Brill Building songwriting factory in the two-hour A&E documentary, *Hitmakers: The Teens Who Stole Pop Music*, were exceptional.

Documentarian Nick Sahakian has done some exceptional work engineering and producing DVDs in assorted multi-genre music formats with countless recording artists, developing new catalogue items, from Alice Cooper, George Benson, and Foreigner to his stellar productions on Gwar DVDs and the illuminating Metalblade Records 20th Anniversary DVD.

I've always been glued to the educational, compassionate, and highly professional work of writer-director-producer David Leaf. His home video and DVD documentaries include *The Sinatra Duets*, *Vintage Sinatra*, and *When I Fall in Love: The One and Only Nat King Cole*. Leaf's production on the documentary *The Making of "A Hard Day's Night,"* about the Beatles' movie debut, broke new ground in assembling and reconstructing archive material for the home video market.

Leaf's original 2004 Showtime Networks world premiere, *Beautiful Dreamer: Brian Wilson and the Story of "SMiLE,"* a feature-length movie, was a priceless melodic tribute to the Beach Boy visionary and tunesmith. "Brian has always been an extremely visual writer, so musically, it was an amazing gift for us to be able to use the *SMiLE* music as the underscore for the film, essentially allowing us to subliminally introduce *SMiLE* to the viewer," Leaf suggested to me one night in Hollywood. "As to the story, it is such an honor that Brian entrusted us with this important chapter in his creative life, and we were privileged to help shine light on the legend, to be the vehicle through which Brian finally told the world what happened back in '66 and '67, and to show how he brought this legendary creation back to life in 2003–2004. It's a story unlike any other—it's music without comparison—and Brian is such a special person and artist that the combination of those elements and his willingness to tell his truth

Brian Wilson (right) and David Leaf, Studio City, California, April 2004.
Photo by Amy Rodrigue, ©2004 LSL Productions, Inc.

and let the truth be told made for a filmmaking experience unlike any I've ever had. It was truly a once-in-a-lifetime opportunity, and when Brian and Van Dyke Parks watched a rough cut in our edit bay and 'signed off' on the film, that was the best review we could ever get," he beamed.

Brian Wilson's *SMiLE*, on disc and on the concert stage, as well as a 2005 Rhino Home Video DVD product and, especially, Leaf's stirring psychological film portrait of the Wilson and Parks melodic and lyrical pairing, is a sight and sound team dream.

Leaf and his partner, John Scheinfeld, have two potent 2006 movies happening: the groovy feature-length documentary *Who is Harry Nilsson (And Why Is Everybody Talkin' About Him)?* had its World Premiere at the 2006 Santa Barbara International Film Festival; and the stunning saga, *The U.S. vs. John Lennon*, produced for Lionsgate Entertainment, had its theatrical release in 2006.

A high-water mark of 2005 was the moving and insightful debut documentary from director Josh Rubin and producer Jeremy Lubin, *Derailroaded* (Rhino Films), an examination of the life of manic-depressive, paranoid-schizophrenic cult music figure Wild Man Fischer.

In 2006 I was extremely jarred by the documentary film *The Refugee All Stars*, directed by Zach Niles and Banker White. It's an inspiring, life-affirming tale of six Sierra Leonean musicians, living as refugees in the West African nation of Guinea, who come together and form a band that gigs at camps while they try to record an album during Sierra Leone's civil war. A survival saga fueled by hope, courage, and songs, it was also shown at the South by Southwest Film Festival in 2006.

The Fuel Channel's *Chasing Dora* surf documentary that aired in March 2006. An expression session.

The 2006 BBC program on Mose Allison, *Ever Since I Stole the Blues*. Is there anyone around who gives better testimonial interviews on camera than Who man Peter Townshend? Mose knows.

In spring 2006 I was invited and then boldly walked into a *Prog Fest* film and video festival at a friend's home in San Pedro. This is a ritual I can deal with once every five years. I must have logged at least eight hours checking out the black-and-white and color footage, even 8mm and 16mm snippets of the Mahavishnu Orchestra, Frank Zappa, Gentle Giant, Genesis, Van Der Graaf Generator, Soft Machine, King Crimson, Roxy Music, Pink Floyd, and PFM. I truly appreciated the musicianship in the archives made available by assorted collectors and hardcore fans. My brother Ken is the resident prog music freak and jazzbo in our family.

In the summer of 2006, seeing a rough cut of director George Goad's breathtaking in-progress documentary on jazz vocalist Dwight Trible, *Joyous Noise: The Art of Dwight Trible.*

Rock bands and Hollywood have always had a cozy business relationship. Song samples in TV commercials and soundtracks are the by-product of alignments that increase the visibility of recording artists and their copyrights. Over the decades both the Yardbirds and U2 were introduced to the Hollywood music and acting community at private parties, which aided their future licensing activities and representation. In spring 2006 the Guillemots, in an exposure plan forged by their manager, developed a new road into Hollywood ears and coveted music supervisors by performing for an invited and hand-selected audience of filmmakers, local tastemakers, and influential friends at the Studio City home of their CAA agent.

The indelible image of my buddy, singer-songwriter, and comedian, Scott Goddard, on the big screen in the lobby of the FM Station venue in North Hollywood, performing his "Cow Punk" anytime in the 1980s and early 1990s. On February 26, 2006, watching the Johnny Cash music video of Trent Reznor's "Hurt."

※

I've been keeping notes and statistics for many decades, often conducting interviews filtered through my contacts and lenses, on filmmakers, writers, musicians, and friends, for magazines and newspapers, primarily focusing on learning the content, process, and motives of their cinematic endeavors. Initially some of the conversations were journalism assignments with movie directors, producers, songwriters, and a few industry folks, to discuss the soundtracks to their films and lives, and mine as well.

Hopefully, these now expanded dialogues, and many others, reveal time and sound invitational situations where eyes, ears, and souls operate and work in conjunction. Movies can be a life affirming or life altering set of emotions and responses. A location where entertainment, art, chords, and commerce collide and inspire collectively, where it's all about collaboration, not competition. It's my house in Hollywood and hometown court. An open door policy, a literary aural history and current riff scene where all are invited inside and everyone is "at the party."

In assembling the joint impulses, experiences, and printed oral results, I remembered and incorporated unforgettable specific musical and visual encounters where film framed the celluloid-bound melodic selections. Along with the contributors and original characters, I explored the introspective sonic and movie geography, developed around *Surf City*, *Naked City*, and *Suffragette City*. Appointments with destiny and tape, informing and acknowledging brain catalogue flashes of Genesis' "Supper Is Ready," U2's "Two Hearts Beat as One," the Surf Punks' "My Beach," *On the Waterfront*, *Chinatown*, *The O.C.*, and *The Twilight Zone*. My feelings and findings, along with the "Memory Motel" territory inspected, identify an audio neighborhood that integrates Evie Sands belting out "Take Me for a Little While" on a black-and-white television set, while later absorbing *Ziggy Stardust and the Spiders from Mars: The Motion Picture* in multiple viewing formats this century.

The merger of film and music can also be a cool zone of escape and appreciation following betrayal or joy, rediscovered after hearing Dave Grohl's drumming all over the *Backbeat* soundtrack, Nick Drake singing "One of These Things First" in *Garden State*, or the Traffic master recording of "Paper Sun" employed in *Stoned*. When I heard Zero 7's "In the Waiting Line" introducing the spin-the-bottle party scene in Zach Braff's *Garden State* movie, I wanted to join the fun.

A real, authentic native Angeleno, a child of Hollywood, actually had the opportunity to run it down from the page to center stage and deliver *Hollywood Shack Job: Rock Music in Film and on Your Screen*.

I'm thankful, stoked, grateful, and "Groovin'" that we dug the "Hot Stuff" together.

Mr. Slacks advertisement,
Los Angeles Free Press, 1968.
From the Harvey Kubernik collection.

ABOUT THE AUTHOR

HARVEY KUBERNIK is a Los Angeles, California native, a graduate of Fairfax High School, West Los Angeles College, and San Diego State University, and has been an active music journalist, writer, and interviewer since 1972. His work has been published nationally and internationally in *Melody Maker*, *The Los Angeles Free Press*, *Crawdaddy*, *Musician*, *Goldmine*, *MIX*, *The Los Angeles Times*, *MOJO*, *Music Life*, and *HITS*, among other periodicals.

Kubernik's writings have appeared in several book anthologies, including *The Rolling Stone Book of the Beats* and *Drinking with Bukowski*. He is the project coordinator of the recording set, *The Jack Kerouac Collection*.

Kubernik penned the liner notes for the Water Records April 2006 CD album reissue of poet Alan Ginsberg's *Kaddish* LP, recorded live on the campus of Brandeis University, originally produced by Jerry Wexler in 1965 for Atlantic Records.

Kubernik also wrote the liner notes on the expanded rerelease of the Ramones' *End of the Century* CD that was issued in 2002.

In the late 1970s, he produced and hosted the music and interview series *50/50* that was broadcast on Public Access, Manhattan Cable, and The Z Channel. More recently, he served as one of the creative consultants and wrote additional content on two *Hollywood Rocks the Movies* music-in-film documentaries that aired on the American Movie Classics (AMC) cable network in 2004. He has coordinated music for film and TV.

Kubernik was formerly a studio session percussionist with Phil Spector on several recordings, and subsequently produced over fifty spoken word and oral history music albums in the last twenty-five years. His studio credits include producing and editing audio biographies on Paul Kantner (Jefferson Airplane) and Ray Manzarek (The Doors), among others.

He is a former West Coast Director of A&R for MCA Records, a TV music and talk show host, and has produced and been involved in

Author Harvey Kubernik at the Jaxon House Gallery in Venice, California, June 2005. Photo by Brad Elterman. From the Harvey Kubernik collection.

various FM radio and webcast music and talk programs over the years. Kubernik is also a production consultant to the weekly syndicated radio show, *Little Steven's Underground Garage,* heard globally.

Music historian Kubernik is a feature interview subject in the seventy-five minute pop culture documentary film *Psychedelic Revolution '67,* commissioned by German public broadcaster ZDF for the Franco-German arts and culture TV network Arte and directed by Christoph Dreher, that will air in the summer of 2007.

His debut book, *This Is Rebel Music: The Harvey Kubernik InnerViews,* was published by the University of New Mexico Press in 2004.

ACKNOWLEDGMENTS AND SERVICE

Marshall and Hilda Kubernik, Ken Kubernik, Aunt Ray, Bob Sherman, Irving Sherman, Nancy Retchin, William Retchin, Jimmy Cliff, Rod Serling, Derek Fisher, Barney Kessel, Frank and Anthea Orlando, Mort Sahl, Kathe Schreyer, Velvert Turner, Rosemarie Renee Patronette and your father Sam, Denny Freeman, Jeff Morrison, Jeremy Gilien, Shelly Lazar, Steve Bing, Rachael Ray, Keith Richards, Ram Dass, Deepak Chopra, Howard Stern, Denny Bruce, Ellen Berman and your father Harvey, Dean Smith, Bennie Davenport, Rafer Johnson, Kobe Bryant, Roy Trakin, Jon O'Hara, Napster, Greg Loescher, Catherine Bernardy, Todd Whitesel, Wayne Youngblood, Kim Fowley, Raybert Productions, Hal Ashby, Eddie Izzard, Reni Santoni, Rachel Griffiths, Michael MacDonald and Linda Dixon, Stirling Silliphant, Paul Jarrico, Bernard Gordon, Frank Sinatra, Danny Weizmann, Rodney Bingenheimer, Vincent "Bing" Bingenheimer, Keith Sky, Stephanie Cornfield, Monique Raphel High, Susan Chin, Jim Capaldi, Mia Farrow, Hal Lifson, Mark London, The Association, The Monkees, Laura Nyro, Sammy Davis Jr., Timi Yuro, Bob Dylan, Mick Vranich, Sherry Hendrick, Toulouse and Sally Engelhardt and your "Twilight Zone" daughters, The Los Angeles Free Clinic, Pinky Lee, Wynn Stewart, Diane Baker, Mick Brown, Harold "Pee Wee" Reese, Chris Darrow, Caroline Dourley, Oscar Brown Jr., Willie Hutch, Lloyd Bochner, Ted Williams, Ian MacDonald, Sylvie Simmons, Marlon Brando, Jack Nicholson, Dennis Hopper, Robert Wise, Mama Cass, Eddi Fiegel, Cat Stevens, Courtney Kaplan, Hamburger Hamlet, Pita Kitchen, Jon O'Hara, The Luau, Ethan James, Phast Phreddie, Madman Muntz, Ray Bradbury, Doodles Weaver, Jimmy Rabbit, Richard Lester, Walter Shenson, Cosmo Topper, Morley Bartnoff, Donovan, Mickie Most, John Cameron, Pam Moore, Little Steven, Jack Nitzsche, Link Wray, Steve Binder, Russ Regan, Tom Dowd, Fred Walecki, Smush Parker, Phil Jackson, Ray Manzarek, Dave Diamond, Dino's Lodge, Woody's Hamburgers, Greg Noll,

Laird Hamilton, La Cabanita, Roscoe's Chicken 'n' Waffles, Barone's Italian Dinners, India Sweets & Spices, Marvin Gaye, David A. Barmack, Quinn Martin, Teddy Randazzo, Ann Francis, Marsha Hunt, Fred Shuster, Barney Hoskyns, Greg Dwinnell, Al "Jazzbo" Collins, Chuck Niles, Godfrey Kerr, Lee Joseph, Johnny Sample, Neil Kaposy, Kara Carpenter, Anthony Cantu, Pat Thomas, Art Kunkin, Gabrielle for her special ice tea, Courtney's iced green tea, Iris Keitel, Andy Street, David Raksin, China Kantner, TEA, Artie Lange, Robin Quivers, Lesley Gore, Aron's Records, Kevin Thomas, Larry McCormick, Lesley Ficks, Willie Crawford, David Myers, Richard Cromelin, Patrick Goldstein, Mike and Shannon, Marc Weingarten, Robbie Rist, Gary Pig Gold, Jac Zinder, John Payne, John Cody, K. J. Donnelly, Kenny Buttrey, Russ Meyer, John Peel, Barry Miles, Sir Paul McCartney, Terry Melcher, Johnny Green, Leonard Bernstein, Stephen Sondheim, Jerry Wexler, Arif Mardin, John Guerin, Donald Rawley, Walter T. Lacey, Nelson Gary, Denise Lento, Marilyn Laverty, Shore Fire Media, Nick Loss-Eaton, Leonard Freeman, Summer Sanders, Jerry Goldsmith, Steve Patterson, Chris Hillman, Nancy Sinatra, Lisa Freeman, Bella Lewitzky, Spring, Wyline, Peaches, Paul Mooney, Tom Shannon, The Kinks, The Supremes, Lesley Wilk, Ravi Shankar, Shay and Ferocious, Jen and Cheryl, Dave Roberts, Greg Shaw, Lonn Friend, Michael Franti, Tom Johnson, Pooch, Martin Banner, Bill Liebowitz, William "Bill" Sargent, Robert Koehler, Jim Brown, Ralph Wiley, Johnny Mandel, Lowell George, Peter Fonda, James Nicholson, Samuel Z. Arkoff, Roger Corman, Jimm Cushing, Harry E. Northup, Holly Prado, Michael Eric Dyson, Graham Nash, The Flying Saucer, Ben Edmonds, Elvis Costello, Sarah Elman, Robb Strandlund, John Frankenheimer, Cindy Hernandez, Tom Leykis, Blanca Gonzalez, Patricia Lopez, Lee Kroeger, Harry Dean Stanton, Dave Emory, Nick Bobetsky, David and Eva Leaf, Amy Rodrigue, Laurette, Tim Doherty, Good Earth, Dennis Dragon, Rick Klotz, Frank Zappa, Jello Biafra, Marisela Norte and your mother Eloisa, The Doors, Jewell Donohue, Gene Vincent, Dan Bourgoise, Kelley Ryan, Del Shannon, Percy Mayfield, Don Calfa, Mark Leviton, Tosh Berman, Robert Marchese, Richard Pryor, Al Ramirez, Bill King, Jerry West, Elgin Baylor, Larry Bird, John Feins, Doon Arbus, Adam Wolf, Elvin Jones, Les McCann, Gene McDaniels, David E. James, Shirley Clarke, Curtis Harrington, Miles Ciletti, David Gibson, Justin Pierce, Gail, Jack Kerouac, Dalton Trumbo, Toni Basil, *HITS, Goldmine, Melody Maker, MOJO,* XM Radio, Sirius Satellite Radio, Chris Blackwell, Gary Jackson, Jack Soo, Rufus Thomas, Fran, Leslie, Candy Dog, Yaphet Kotto, Dr. Goldenberg,

Curtis Mayfield, Smokey Robinson, Janis Zavala, Steve Nice, Dick Lane, Freddie Blassie, Randy Wood, John Wood, The Destroyer, Dr. Feldman, Lance Loud, Dimitri Tiomkin, Dustin Hoffman, Louie Lista, John Trubee, Will Thornbury, Kirk Silsbee, Mitch Meyers, Buffalo Springfield, Matt Greenwald, the Musso and Frank Grill, Love, Sandy Koufax, Wilt Chamberlain, Gene Autry, Aime Joseph, The Pantry, Twin Dragon, Handy Burgers, Johnny at Pink's, James Brown, Sam Cooke, Madam Currie, George Harrison, Sophie Auclair, Gene Clark, John Cassavetes, Carmen Dragon, Sam Fuller, Louis Lomax, Lloyd Thaxton, Hugh M. Hefner, Berry Gordy Jr., Burt Bacharach, Hal David, Richard Lester, Holly Cara Price, Peggy Lee, Jerry Lifson, Stan Levey, Charlie Watts, Johnny Mercer, Stanley Booth, Jimi Hendrix, John Mayall, Jack Webb, LeRoi Jones, Genmai Sushi, Jackie Robinson, Lanny and Diana Waggoner, Otis Chandler, Edward Nalbandian, Michael Rebibo, Sophie Evans, Don Paulsen, Henry Diltz, Jean Marie Périer, Brad Elterman, Heather Harris and her dogs, Mr. Twister, Kanary, Paul and Nancy Body, Lou Rawls, Nik Venet, Jan Berry, Pat and Lolly Vegas, El Cholo, Rupert Cross, Lincoln Kilpatrick, Rick the bass player, Gore Vidal, Cleavon Little, Dr. Stanley B. Baker, Buddy Collette, Barry White, Elliot Kendall, Poncie Ponce, Levi Stubbs, David Ruffin, Splat Winger, Samantha, Gena Rowlands, Frank Sontag, Tom Brennan, Craig B. Hulet, Alice, Waldo, Dan Swenson, Ralph Piper, Peter Piper and your mother Maggé, Mose Allison, Traffic, Dick Gregory, James Wong Howe, Martin Roberts, The Beatles, The Who, Margo from "Save The Tiger," John Bullard, Richard Bosworth, Seth Winston, Paul Buckmaster, Sheri Williams, Jonnie Zaentz, Jere Mendelsohn, Linda J. Albertano, Wanda Coleman, Norma Barzman, Richard Derrick, Lawrence Lipton, Richard Schuman, Dave Kephart, Bruce Springsteen, Dave Smith, Chick Hearn, Vin Scully, Lee Klein, Eric Gagne, Andrew Loog Oldham, The Rolling Stones, Stephen Woolley, Jo Laurie, Jim Keltner and Cynthia Keltner, Linda Arias, Olivia and Dhani Harrison, Quincy Jones, Waldo Salt, Roger and Mary Steffens, Geoff Gans, Bob Marley and the Wailers, Richard Williams, Marianne Faithfull, Peter Tosh, Drew Steele, Mark the Shark, Dr. Jamie Azdair, Charlie Sheen, Art Bell, Alex Jones, Bennie Cunningham, Ben Howland, Fiona Taylor, Jason Smith, Nick Sahakian, Chris and Paul Weitz, Damon Gough, Lydia Lennihan, Maya Allen-Gallegos, Robert Towne, Miki Dora, Mickey Munoz, Bill Lynch, Michael Kaplan, Gregory Mark Burgess, George Goad, Dwight Trible, Al Jarvis, Steve Allen, Ed Sullivan, Jimmy O'Neil, Mike Douglas, Dick Cavett, Gene Weed, Casey Kasem, Wink Martindale, Sam Riddle, Pinky Lee,

Soupy Sales, Walt Phillips, Stan Richards, the Premiers, Chris Montez, Herb Alpert, Jerry Moss, Hayley Mills, Dave Diamond, Pete Carroll, Coach John R. Wooden, Bill Walton, Jerry Garcia, David Dodd, Henry Mancini, Phil Bunch, Nelson Riddle, Phil Spector, B. J. Baker, Dan Kessel, David Kessel, Val Guest, Ian Copeland, Freddie Garrity, Tom Zotos, Harold Sherrick, Spike Jones, Roy of Hollywood, Gary Null, The Funk Brothers, Brian Wilson, André Previn, Gold Star Studio, Edward J. Yates, Billy Preston, Dean Dean the Taping Machine, Gary Stewart, Michael Hartman, Phil Yeend, NSI Sound & Video, Inc., Dick "Huggy Boy" Hugg, John Densmore, Bruce Gary, Joseph Stefano, Jimmy Robinson, Larry Yelen, Maria Sharapova, Martina Navratilova, Nomar Garciaparra, Russell Martin, Jim Freek, Tom Trocoli, Andy Krikun, David Arnson, John Alton, Anthony Mann, Tom Neal, Stephanie Bennett, Samantha Phillips, Norton Records, Jimmie Maddin, Richard Sinclair, Gene Norman, Neil Norman, Melissa Tandysh, Sonia Dickey, Amanda Sutton, Katherine MacGilvray, Dr. David B. Wolfe, David Carr, Beth L. Bailey, David Farber, David Holtby.

Touch the sound.

IN**D**EX